Ideas and Idealism in Philosophy

New Studies in the History and Historiography of Philosophy

Edited by
Sebastian Luft

Volume 11

Ideas and Idealism in Philosophy

Edited by
Jure Simoniti and Gregor Kroupa

DE GRUYTER

ISBN 978-3-11-162175-3
e-ISBN (PDF) 978-3-11-076076-7
e-ISBN (EPUB) 978-3-11-076120-7
ISSN 2364-3161

Library of Congress Control Number: 2022944048

Bibliographic information published by the Deutsche Nationalbibliothek
The Deutsche Nationalbibliothek lists this publication in the Deutsche Nationalbibliografie;
detailed bibliographic data are available on the internet at http://dnb.dnb.de.

© 2024 Walter de Gruyter GmbH, Berlin/Boston
This volume is text- and page-identical with the hardback published in 2023.

www.degruyter.com

Table of Contents

Abbreviations —— VII

Jure Simoniti and Gregor Kroupa
Introduction: Impulses for a New Idealism —— IX

Part I: **The Neglected Impulses of Idealism in the History of Philosophy**

James I. Porter
How Ideal Is the Ancient Self? —— 3

Jure Simoniti
**De-Symbolization of the World and the Emergence of the Self:
A Historically-Idealist Theory of the Subject** —— 27

Gregor Kroupa
Genesis, Structure, and Ideas: Genetic Epistemology in Early Modern Philosophy —— 69

Miran Božovič
Diluvian Philosophy: Utilitarian Motifs in *Moby-Dick* —— 93

Bojana Jovićević
Thinking Free Release in Hegel's System —— 111

Robert B. Pippin
Idealism and the Problem of Finitude: Heidegger and Hegel —— 127

Paul Redding
Hegel's Metaphysical Alternative to the Choice between an Unrealistic Platonic Realism and an Opposing Skeptical Anti-realism —— 151

Part II: Contemporary Impulses for a New Idealism

Slavoj Žižek
A Materialist Defense of an Idealist Subjectivity —— 173

Sebastian Rödl
Philosophy and Its History —— 193

Isabelle Thomas-Fogiel
Beyond Realism and Correlationism, the Idealist Path —— 209

Paul Guyer
A Typology of Idealism —— 231

Jela Krečič
Fiction: The Truth of Idealism and Realism —— 251

Mladen Dolar
Virus and Idea —— 269

Index —— 283

Abbreviations

Abbreviations for work titles

De An.   Aristotle, De anima
Gen.   Genesis
Metaph.   Aristotle, Metaphysics
Part. An.   Aristotle, Parts of Animals
PU   Wittgenstein, Ludwig: Philosophische Untersuchungen
Theaet.   Plato, Theaetetus

Abbreviations for specific editions

BP   Heidegger, Martin (1988): *The Basic Problems of Phenomenology*. Translated by Albert Hofstadter. Bloomington: Indiana University Press (GA, vol. 24).
BT   Heidegger, Martin (1962): *Being and Time*. Translated by John Macquarrie and Edward Robinson. Oxford: Blackwell (GA, vol. 2).
CPR   Kant, Immanuel (1998): *Critique of Pure Reason*. Translated by Paul Guyer and Allen W. Wood. Cambridge: Cambridge University Press. Cited by A and B, representing the original pagination of the 1st and 2nd editions, respectively.
CSM 1   Descartes, René (1985): *The Philosophical Writings of Descartes*. Vol 1. Translated by John Cottingham, Robert Stoothoff and Dugald Murdoch. Cambridge and New York: Cambridge University Press.
DC   Hobbes, Thomas (1839): "Elements of Philosophy. The First Section, Concerning Body" [=*De corpore*]. In: *The English Works of Thomas Hobbes*. Vol. 1. Edited by Sir William Molesworth. London: John Bohn.
EG   Heidegger, Martin (1998): "On the Essence of Ground". In: *Pathmarks*. Translated by William McNeill. Cambridge: Cambridge University Press, pp. 97–135 (GA, vol. 9).
EL   Hegel, Georg Wilhelm Friedrich (1991): *The Encyclopedia Logic*. Translated by T. F. Geraets, W. A. Suchting and H. S. Harris. Indianapolis: Hackett.
El.   Euclid (1908): *The Thirteen Books of Euclid's Elements*. 3 vols. Edited by T. L. Heath. Cambridge: Cambridge University Press.
FCM   Heidegger, Martin (1995): *The Fundamental Concepts of Metaphysics: World, Finitude, Solitude*. Translated by William McNeill and Nicholas Walker. Bloomington: Indiana University Press (GA, vol. 29–30).
GA   Heidegger, Martin (1978–): *Gesamtausgabe*. Frankfurt am Main: Klostermann.
ID   Heidegger, Martin (1969): *Identity and Difference*. Translated by Joan Stambough. Chicago: University of Chicago Press (GA, vol. 11).
IM   Heidegger, Martin (2000): *Introduction to Metaphysics*. Translated by Gregory Fried and Richard Polt. New Haven: Yale University Press (GA, vol. 40).
KPM   Heidegger, Martin (1997): *Kant and the Problem of Metaphysics*. Translated by Richard Taft. Bloomington: Indiana University Press (GA, vol. 3).

P   Heidegger, Martin (1998): *Pathmarks*. Translated by William McNeill. Cambridge: Cambridge University Press (GA, vol. 9).
SL   Hegel, Georg Wilhelm Friedrich (2010): *The Science of Logic*. Translated by George di Giovanni. Cambridge: Cambridge University Press. Page numbers to the German edition are cited in square brackets.

Other abbreviations

AMC   AMC Networks
DNA   Deoxyribonucleic acid
FX   FX Networks
HBO   Home Box Office
OOO   Object-oriented ontology
RNA   Ribonucleic acid
TMV   Tobacco mosaic virus

Jure Simoniti and Gregor Kroupa
Introduction: Impulses for a New Idealism

As arguably in every epoch before it, the philosophical legacy of the twentieth century is historically unique and poses a considerable challenge to the twenty-first. It might nonetheless be comparable to the aftermath of British empiricism toward the end of the eighteenth century. By way of subtracting primary qualities from perceptual things, Berkeley revealed a world devoid of any material substance and Hume a reality unsure of its causal necessity. It was Kant's version of idealism, one of performing a differential redefinition, hence, an "idealization", of the pure concepts of reason and shifting their origin into the spontaneity of the subject, that bestowed some order on the ontological chaos empiricism had left behind. This new "subjectively idealist" re-foundation of a lawful, to an extent firm, substantial, and reliable physical reality came famously at the price of assuming the stance of philosophical *antirealism*. However—and this finding represents the primary impulse of the volume at hand—the explicit Kantian antirealism also stands at the beginning of a more furtive and obscure, less tangible, sometimes unacknowledged and even silent tradition of *anti-idealism* of European thought.

It has become a sort of consensus to put the entire tradition of European continental philosophy from Kant to postmodernism on a level with antirealism (and implicitly idealism). This has been suggested particularly by the advocates of so-called speculative realism. However, the equation is one-sided and misleading since it neglects the fact that, alongside the repeatedly anti-realist self-interpretations of post-Kantian philosophy, simultaneously a contrary movement prevailed in the philosophical landscape. For what continental philosophy was faced with at the end of the era was a considerable disintegration of the normative and formal standards that traditionally guaranteed the possibility of constituting and achieving universal truths. It was left with nothing but the particularism and relativism of endless hermeneutic interpretations, the plurality of language games, infinite dialogues, and the deconstruction of the meaning of linguistic signs. Eventually, truth became partial, erratic, incomplete, contextual, metaphoric, or, at best, a result of the pragmatic consensus of a rational community. In short, after Hegel, a momentous but now largely overlooked downfall of idealism took place. For if "idealism" is not understood merely as an ontological doctrine (e.g., as Berkeley's immaterialism, Leibniz's monadology, or German idealism in its various iterations) but more broadly, as a right to postulate ideas that transcend the limits of particular contexts and at least lay claim to the universality of truth, then it seems that the decline of idealist stances unites the philosophy of the next nearly two hundred years (extending from Marx's critique of ideology until today) even more homogeneously than the alleged lack of realism. If one were to come up with just one tagline for the philosophy of the twentieth century, "anti-idealism" would perhaps be the most inclusive and accurate of all.

It is thus high time that we elaborated a more nuanced diagnosis of the fate of idealism. In the wake of Kant, we seem to have, on the one hand, lost *reality-in-itself*, i.e., the non-human facticity outside consciousness and language. Since reality is only a projection of multiple perspectives, interpretations, language games, etc., "occidental antirealism" is regarded as a variety of an implicit idealism. However, this loss did not motivate a triumph of idealism but, paradoxically, its demise. Because, on the other hand, we have also lost *truth-in-itself*, i.e., the truth that is not reducible to the circumstances of its particular reasons and uses. The truth harboring an ideal, trans-contextual, non-relative, and historically irreversible dignity has become a victim of the critical (Kant), anti-ideological (Marx), perspectival and genealogical (Nietzsche), existential and hermeneutic (Heidegger), therapeutic (Wittgenstein), archeological (Foucault), perhaps vitalist (Deleuze), deconstructive (Derrida), and dialogic and pragmatic (Habermas) claims of philosophy.[1] It could be argued that the devaluation of truth is correlative with the retreat of idealist tendencies. Perhaps a new idealism for the twenty-first century will refuse to return to straightforward ontological idealism, which insists on the existence of a mind-dependent reality; instead, it will address and reconsider the possibility of positing truths that can only be formed around a core of irreducible ideality.

In the general, if at times shrouded, anti-idealist atmosphere, this volume ventures to address the following questions: What can be saved of idealism in the twenty-first century? Can some sort of idealism offer an alternative to the now fashionable realism? If ontological idealisms in the Platonic fashion of ideas being embodied in some other world, or in the vein of Berkeley's immaterialism, are obsolete, why opt for the term "idealism" at all? Is, finally, the only

---

[1] Although some of these authors concurrently also cultivate the downright opposite semantics of "truth". Nietzsche first sentences "truth" to death, but then cannot help but evoke some better, nobler truth, which must be "dared" and requires "greatness of soul". Heidegger shifts focus to the eventful, albeit fateful and unpredictable *Wahrheitsgeschehen*. And most of the quoted philosophers are non-relativists anyway. However, what they all pursue and carry out, but probably fail to fully realize, is the ineluctable, necessitarian emergence of new cores of idealization in the processes of post-metaphysics. Post-Kantians were perhaps incapable of acknowledging the implicit idealism permeating and upholding their own conceptual moves; this is one of the underlying hypotheses and recurring motives of this volume.

variety to be salvaged an idealism which cannot but bring all the impulses of conceptual operations, semantic definitions, the universality of truth, and the autonomy of reason down to the core of "irreducible ideality"? Or is it necessary to conclude that every form of idealism and idealization is always already a distortion of truth, which itself can never find its mirror in ideas?

James I. Porter, for example, who opens Part I of this volume, suggests that our understanding of the notion of the self in ancient philosophy, but particularly in Heraclitus, has all too often been "idealized" in this way by the supposedly intuitive first-person perspectives of modern epistemology. It takes some effort—which Porter makes with the help of authors such as Hegel, Nietzsche or Snell—to recompose an idea of the self that is devoid of this rigid and irreducible privacy appropriating its surroundings and dominating it with its own rationality. Heraclitus' self is more a fragment of nature than nature depicted fragmentarily by the idealized self, Porter shows.

In his chapter, Jure Simoniti searches for new incentives and footholds of idealism in this, as he says, "hopelessly de-idealized world" of the twenty-first century. Proceeding from a novel reading of Augustine and Descartes, but also of German idealism, Nietzsche, Heidegger, and Lacanian psychoanalysis, he demonstrates how the idealist impulse might emerge historically, in instances where the process of the de-symbolization of the world triggers the formation of the philosophical subject. After the cosmos of early Christianity had renounced the pagan polarities of good and evil forces and assumed an entirely good valence, the famous Augustinian "inner self" contracted into herself by way of idealizing the expelled evil in the form of her innate, primordial sin. When the world of modern science dissolved the cosmic structure of two spheres, the sublunar and the supralunar, the Cartesian subject re-enacted the abrogated metaphysical values on her path of doubt and certainty; thus, the monism of Cartesian physics was strictly counterbalanced by the idealist dualism of Cartesian metaphysics. Etc. In short, instead of predestining all aspects of reality, the proffered kind of "emergent" or "historical" idealism, one still to be advocated in the twenty-first century, conceives of idealities as being created in the course of cultural and scientific advancement, in which the given world discards all semblances of possessing any ideal value.

Continuing the focus on Cartesianism and early modern philosophy, Gregor Kroupa discovers that many scientific and philosophical hypotheses of the seventeenth and eighteenth centuries have a common background in idealizing a series of supposed causes, in postulating a fictitious sequence of events, which operate as true causes even if they are contradicted by facts. Indeed, what makes disparate expressions, such as geometricians' definitions of figures by motion, Descartes' explanation of the mechanist principles of the universe, and Enlightenment speculations about the prehistorical origins of human institutions, "true" is precisely the maneuver of postulating ideal causal sequences, which every empirically or historically confirmed sequence of events, as if by a Platonist whim, only ever approximates and participates in. Since facts never reach the level of intelligibility of rational idealities, Kroupa concludes that it takes a "leap of reason" to abandon them in the name of truth.

Miran Božovič investigates the hidden balances between realist and idealist tendencies within a single set of beliefs. The essay proposes a reading of Melville's *Moby-Dick* as the prime literary expression of the utilitarian stance, and re-interprets the whaleship *Pequod* as an exemplary embodiment of a utilitarian universe, one in which every part of the whale is used for at least one, but often several functions. In an idealist turn, this secluded world of utter utility is shown to produce the light by which it showcases the ideality of its own frantic utilization of everything.

If Božovič's contribution indicates that even the most fundamentally non-idealist philosophy, utilitarianism, develops an inevitable idealist veneer, Bojana Jovićević shines a light on this balance from the other side. She demonstrates how the staunchest of all idealisms, the absolute idealism of Hegel, is ultimately compelled to hinge on the element of pure and irreducible externality to itself. At the crucial transition points of Hegel's system, the Hegelian "Idea", the metaphysical paragon of self-enclosure and all-embracing totality, resorts to the operation of *Entlassen*, or "free release", where pure thought thinking itself "releases itself" into nature. Even the Idea must therefore muddle itself with its external otherness in order to prove its true conceptual power.

According to Robert B. Pippin, idealism in Kant, Fichte, and Hegel does not entail the mind-dependence of the world, but rather endows human reason with a self-authorizing autonomy which alone determines the conditions of the knowable. Hegel's "absolute idealism" has predominantly been subjected to criticisms underscoring the finitude of human reason. This chapter thus explores the argumentative tensions between Hegel's infinite reason and Heidegger's essentially finite subjectivity.

Paul Redding concludes the section concentrating on Hegel by confronting the realist and anti-realist interpretations of Hegel's philosophy by Brandom and Rorty, only to find a middle ground in the interpretation Redding describes as weakened Platonic realism (or "realism *about ideas*"). His views are closely tied to debates in analytic philosophy about the modality of possible worlds (Lewis), particularly the "modal actualism" advocated by Arthur Prior and Robert Stalnaker. According to Redding, the verdict on Hegel's realism is thus dependent on how we align his views with the debate on modality. Redding advocates a "more modest realism", which rejects the hard "god's-eye view" of *possibilia* in favor of contextualized knowledge grounded in the actual world.

In his reading of Saroj Giri's formation of the Buddhist revolutionary subject and Todd Phillips's film *Joker*, Slavoj Žižek opens Part II of this collection with a defense of the strong concept of subjectivity, one emerging from its "materialist" causes but utterly transcending them in the process. What thereby comes forth is nevertheless a "minimalist subject of idealism". Žižek's theory designs the subject as an entity constantly and thoroughly undercutting, subverting, and casting off the conditions of its emergence, be it that of its ethnic, gender, cultural, historical background, or of its psycho-social genesis. Since the make-up of such a subject is conceived of as a stand-in for its own void or nothingness, it relies on an element that is not to be equated to its genetic causes, reasons, and circumstances, hence, an element of a certain "irreducible ideality" emerging in the midst of the contingent realities of the world.

Sebastian Rödl's article is an idealist attempt at reconciling and abolishing the tension between the historical, time-bound emergence of metaphysical truths and their timeless scope and validity. The paradox of metaphysics is that, on the one hand, it possesses a history, while, on the other hand, the only object of metaphysical knowledge is an internally apprehended thought which transcends the boundaries of space and time. Rödl's solution is that a judgment which apprehends itself through itself, hence, a judgment on being *qua* being, does not lie outside time but performs a perpetual annihilation of time and its difference between this and that temporal existence thinking it. Between the moment of Parmenides defending the identity between thought and being and myself, who comprehends this identity, time effectively implodes.

Isabelle Thomas-Fogiel revisits the dilemma introduced by Quentin Meillassoux and the speculative realists between realism and correlationism and questions the way in which idealism has been so casually associated with the latter. On the contrary, she proposes that both realism and correlationism (here represented by Meillassoux and Michel Bitbol, respectively) rely on a theory of truth that completely disregards what is valuable in idealism, namely, the appeal to the universality of ideas or idealities instead of the question whether something real corresponds to them. The process of idealization, of transcending the limits of a single perspective, is then found to open up spaces leading to the universality of Truth, which is exactly where, paradoxically perhaps, Thomas-Fogiel finds realists—with their appeal to mere "facts"—to be open to relativism.

Although unconcerned by this specific contemporary perplexity about what kind of idealism, if any, should be understood as a direct enemy of realism, Paul Guyer nevertheless brings some much needed clarity to the issue, clearly distinguishing in his typology the kind of idealism that metaphysically amounts to a monism, or, the straightforward claim that reality is ultimately mind-like, from the rich tradition of idealism that can be traced back to Plato and consists in an intricate dualism merely favoring mind (or ideas) over matter. Both versions, according to Guyer, can be shown to be supported either by metaphysical or epistemological arguments, while Kant's transcendental idealism adds practical reasons. Guyer does a great job at extracting the essential traits of different idealist currents in the history of philosophy, which opens up possibilities for new meanings of "idealism" traceable to these historical idealisms, albeit perhaps less literally faithful to them. And examples of these can certainly be found in this volume.

Jela Krečič, for instance, demonstrates that the "obsession with realism" in contemporary popular culture (reality shows, "authentic experiences" in quality television, ever more "direct" depictions of reality in Hollywood), paradoxically, misses and obfuscates the experience of truth. She rather advocates the return to more traditional modes of representation, as in classical Hollywood cinema, where an idealizing frame was always placed before reality in order to produce the effect of truth. In this chapter it is shown that the disavowal of the artistry of idealization in Hollywood can be traced to the currently widespread philosophical endorsement of realism. Inversely, Krečič argues that only genres which dare to deploy deliberately idealizing framings of the chosen topics (especially in classical Hollywood comedy) can provide both challenging political ideas and a new perspective on the dispute between realism and idealism.

Mladen Dolar finds an unexpected jewel, an especially topical passage in *The Phenomenology of Spirit*, where Hegel, citing Diderot, displays how "the silent weaving of the spirit" undermines the idols that superstition was holding on to. Hegel speaks of "the infection by the Enlightenment", implying that reason is a virus. In contrast to the virus being traditionally linked with the causality of matter, it is here the spirit, and its advancement, which spreads like a contagious disease. On this basis, Dolar intimates the possibility of developing a "viral ontology", for it is at this interstice between abiotic and biotic nature and, by extension, also between the physical and the metaphysical, that the idealist sway of the (in)human core is looming. As he says: "What we call humanity perhaps ultimately depends on this viral knot of spirit and body, on the virus as its intimate alien kernel, its extimate kernel ... If we are to fight the present massive viral danger affecting humanity at this moment, what better resources to rely on but our viral nature itself?"

Part I: **The Neglected Impulses of Idealism in the History of Philosophy**

James I. Porter
How Ideal Is the Ancient Self?

Abstract: Heraclitus is typically thought to have ushered in the concept of the individual self as a subject of experience that is endowed with the core attributes of singularity, integrity, mental and psychological coherence, and autonomous agency. A close look at his fragments along with some of the best nineteenth-century readings of him (Schleiermacher, Hegel, and Nietzsche, and then the early Bruno Snell in their wake) provides evidence that such a conception of the self was alien to Heraclitus, not because he was a primitive thinker, but because he had strong ontological and ethical commitments that led him in a different direction. Heraclitus did not pave the way for the modern liberal individual, which is how he is usually understood. Rather, he is best seen as a forerunner of the new posthumanism in contemporary ecology.

Philosophy has gone a long way towards renouncing the idea of the self, which has been variously condemned as an incoherent postulate, a myth, a loose concatenation of capacities and experiences, an intuition without reality, or a grammatical mistake.[1] To be sure, defenses of the viability of the self as an entity exist, but these are in a vanishing minority. I am interested less in the arguments for and against the coherence or existence of the self, which have always been inconclusive, than in the idea's persistence as an ideal. What most astonishes in the debates about the self is the uncanny ability of the idea to reassert itself, along with some if not all of its essential attributes, even after it has to all intents and purposes been dismissed.

Why is it so difficult to rid our minds of the idea of the self? Part of the reason seems to be rooted in our phenomenology and our habits of thought, the

---

Acknowledgement: This essay derives from a book in progress tentatively titled Being Beyond the Self: Heraclitus to the Roman Stoics. I wish to thank Miran Božovič and Gregor Kroupa for the opportunity to contribute to this volume. Further thanks go to Gábor Betegh, André Laks, Tony Long, Jure Simoniti, Mario Telò, Victoria Wohl, and audiences at the University of Illinois Chicago, University College London, and Harvard University for lively discussions around the paper and its themes. I am quite certain that I have not quelled every reservation that I encountered, but I remain deeply grateful for the feedback nonetheless.

[1] See Faruque 2021 for a well-informed survey.

James I. Porter, University of California, Berkeley.

https://doi.org/10.1515/9783110760767-003

feeling that we either have or are a self.² But it is one thing to acknowledge that a sense of self may be ineliminable from experience and quite another to endow the subject of that experience with attributes that are privileged in the modern traditions of liberal individualism, for example, singularity, mentality, psychological coherence, and autonomous agency. Galen Strawson's minimalist model of the "thin self", perceived by him as bitty, episodic, and discontinuous but unfailingly available at any given moment (Strawson 2009), comes as close to reducing the self to a primitive set of features as one might possibly wish to go before leaping into the abyss of the "neuronal" self (Malabou 2008 and 2013, building on Damasio 1995 and 2003). Thomas Nagel's attempt to imagine the world as it appears to itself, so to speak, by adopting the perspective of an "objective" or "true" self likewise drives the problem of the self to an extreme limit. "The objective self is the last stage of the detaching subject"—what is "essential about me" and my "mind"—"before it shrinks to an extensionless point"; it marks the "logical limit" of the subjective self (Nagel 1986, p. 62 with n. 3; p. 61). The point is not to challenge these reductions and others like them but to ask in what name they are undertaken. For when all is said and done, what survives these experiments with self-reduction remains an idealized notion of the self that is constituted as the subject and owner of its own internal experiences, whether this self is understood as "a free personality or singularity", as "a remarkably robust and almost tangible attractor of properties, the 'owner of record' of whatever features are lying about unclaimed", as "materialistically respectable [and] distinctly mental", or as a "proto-", "neuronal", "core", or "objective self" that is possessed of any number of other "anthropocentric remainders" (Malabou 2008, p. 70; Dennett 1991, p. 429; Strawson 2001, p. 150; Damasio 1999; Nagel 1986, ch. 4; cf. p. 7; Barad 2007, p. 135).³ What has been gained? Why do the idea and ideal of the self persist in these accounts, which elaborately set out traps for the self only to recuperate it at the end of the day? The real issue is not whether attending to the self credits it with too much reality but whether inquiries into the self credit it with too much significance.⁴ Sometimes the best policy for navigating through the world is simply to get out of our own way.

---

2 Strawson 2001.
3 See Turkle 2005, pp. 281–288 and Simoniti (this volume) on the recuperation of the idea of the self in the face of its repeated evacuations at epochal moments of paradigm shifts in history.
4 Nagel's project, for instance, originates in the "startling" and "remarkable" fact of his own existence, the "strange sense that I both am and am not the hub of the universe", which is for him an unending source of "amazement" (Nagel 1986, pp. 54–55, 60, 64).

Nowhere is the overattribution of meaning to the self more evident than in the efforts to trace the emergence of modern or contemporary ideas of the self in Greek and Roman antiquity. The search as it is undertaken today is in good part the legacy of an ideal of the self that was formed in the eighteenth century and was later cemented in polemical response to philosophical Idealism.[5] On a closer look, it can be shown that the ancient self in many of its most significant formulations was conceived not as a positive entity, be it subjective or objective, but only as an obstacle that had to be surpassed and ultimately left behind. In other words, what mattered in these cases was not the existence of the self but its relative insignificance to a set of larger ethical or philosophical projects.

To say this is not to deny that the ancients as early as Homer may have operated with an intuitive, first-personal sense of self probably not much different from our own, one that was equipped with a degree of autonomous agency, interiority, and personal identity (so Williams 1993 and Long 2015, both *contra* Snell 1946). But neither should we assume that a conception like this exhausts ancient views of what it is to be an individual or that it overlaps perfectly with our own notions of selfhood. But what are these? Claims about "us" and "them" can be deceptively simple, since there is in fact no consensus about what a self is today. (Psychoanalysis, so far unmentioned, adds a whole other dimension to the problem.) One way we can look for ourselves in the ancients, if that is the goal, is to acknowledge their puzzlement about what a self truly is, however that self may have been defined for them. Aristotle and Plato had no better idea of what to make of the self (typically anchored in the "soul") than contemporary philosophers and neurobiologists do, nor did they try to conceal this. As Aristotle notes, "To attain any conviction about the soul is one of the most difficult things in the world" (*De anima* 1.1, 402a10–11; trans. Smith, modified). But while some ancients made looking for a definition of the self the object of some of their inquiries and assigned it a preeminent value, this was not always the case. Others, at least those in the philosophical tradition that will be of concern in this essay, were not content to locate the self in some positive form, to define it as an isolate or a private possession, or to value it above all else, for example by recommending so-called "techniques of the self" (Foucault 2005). On the contrary, they had larger goals in mind—questions about nature, the ecosystem, ethical responsibility, justice, and social critique—that challenged narrow definitions of selfhood and that typically required a stripping away of the

---

5 The literature is vast. Beyond the influential work of Pierre Hadot and Michel Foucault, the latter beholden to the Enlightenment ideal of *Selbstbildung* (Porter 2005), see Gill 2006, Sorabji 2006, and Long 2015. See Pippin 1997 on the Idealist legacy in philosophy.

self and of selfhood. Whether scanning the world in its unfathomable dimensions or gazing on the life of the *polis* in its inextricable complexity, they found it more useful to dispense with the question of what a self is and to focus instead on whatever calls into question the very coherence of the self when the self is viewed in isolation from its environment and as an end in itself.

One way, then, to rephrase the problem with the self in antiquity is to say that it dwindles to insignificance precisely at that point where the most troubling philosophical and ethical questions emerge, which is to say, "at the [very] limits of our schemes of intelligibility" (Butler 2005, p. 21). Socrates, the Cynics, and the Stoics would have been in complete agreement with this assessment.[6] For them, to give an account of oneself was not to give an account of one's self. "What am I?" was not a Socratic question. "What am I in relation to others?" was. Ethical motives, then as now, were typically selfless ones. Similarly, calls to "unself" the self (Murdoch 2014, p. 82), reflecting something like a basic exasperation with the idea of the self,[7] were frequent in studies of cosmic nature. In those cases too, the self fades away into insignificance at the exact point where the universe becomes unintelligible. The latter disarticulates the former, rendering it opaque to itself, and for that reason takes precedence over it as well.[8]

Rather than tracking the gradual emergence of an idea of the self in antiquity that we can recognize as our own, and rather than seeking to identify positive features of selfhood that may or may not converge with those we believe we have, a different approach is needed, one that examines the ways in which ideas of the self were variously disarticulated and their coherence and importance were shown wanting. Given the complexity of the issues, I will focus on one case study, the Presocratic philosopher Heraclitus of Ephesus (*fl.* ca. 500 BCE), who is typically thought to have discovered the concept of the self that we

---

[6] See Porter 2020 on the Stoics. I discuss Socrates and the Cynics in the book in progress noted in the acknowledgments.

[7] Murdoch's study is a blanket rejection of the interiorized rational self or agent, and equivalent to what it wills at any given moment (hence, one that is as "thin as a needle" (Murdoch 2014, p. 52).

[8] The opacity of the self is a critical feature of Butler's notion of ethical accountability (Butler 2005, pp. 20–21, 40, etc.) just as it is for Arendt, for whom self-disclosure in the political sphere is not the unveiling of a self by an individual but a form of world-making that happens behind the backs of individuals (Arendt 1958). So viewed, the self looks like a "smaller and less interesting object" than it ordinarily appears to be (Murdoch 2014, p. 64). The same is true for the communitarian philosophies of Bataille, Blanchot, and Nancy. But in other traditions, notably those with an idealist inflection, the self returns on an even grander scale to fill in this constitutive lack (see Simoniti, this volume).

still operate with today. As we shall see, the picture is a bit more complicated than that.

1 The discovery of the self?

It is well known that there was no word for "self" in classical antiquity. In Greek and Latin, attention is inevitably drawn to the words for "soul", *psuchē* and *anima*, or to reflexive uses of pronouns, though neither equivalent exactly captures what is intuitively understood as a self today. Compounding matters is the assumption that self-awareness gradually dawns on Greek consciousness, with Heraclitus occupying a pivotal place in this story. Although consensus is rare in interpretations of this oracular writer, a majority opinion today is that with Heraclitus *psuchē* "emerges for the first time as an integrated center of motor, cognitive, and emotive functions" (Betegh 2013, p. 225) and as the locus of "the true or essential self" (Schofield 1991, p. 25).[9] Whether these functions describe, for Heraclitus, the core components of a human being who either has or is a self remains to be seen.

Three fragments in particular and one second-hand report attest to this new interest in the soul as a locus of the self. Each is dazzling.

§1. "I searched for myself" (B101 = D36).[10]
§2. "You would not find out the limits of *psuchē* even by travelling along every path, so deep a *logos* ["measure," "account," "logic"] does it have" (B45 = D98; my translation).
§3. "*Psuchē* has a *logos* that [continually] increases itself" (B115 = D98; my translation).
§4. "Everything is full of *psuchai* and *daimones* (divinities)" (Diogenes Laertius 9.7 = A1.7 = R46).

The case that Heraclitus marked the turning point in the ancient evolution of the idea of the self was most forcefully argued by Bruno Snell in his 1946 study, *Die*

---

[9] Betegh's language echoes that of Nussbaum 1972b, p. 169, Kahn 1979, p. 127, and Schofield 1991, pp. 13 and 24; Long 2015, p. 8 ("locus of mind and self") echoes Schofield 1991, 25 (quoted above). Cf. Kahn 1979, p. 116: "own (true) self"; Hussey 1982, p. 40: "own true self".
[10] Abbreviations and numberings used in this essay for Heraclitus's texts follow those of two editions: Diels and Kranz 1951–52 (cited as "A1," etc. for testimonia; "B1," etc. for fragments); and Laks and Most 2016, vol. 3 (cited as "P1," etc. = biographica; "D1," etc. = fragments; "R1," etc. = reports and testimonia).

Entdeckung des Geistes: Studien zur Entstehung des europäischen Denkens bei den Griechen. Though critiques of Snell's thesis exist and a richer historical picture has since been put forward, the fundamental premises of his account remain intact, and above all his conclusion: "The first writer to feature the new concept of the soul", conceived as an entity that endowed with "depth or profundity", distinct from the body, and defined by its mental and cognitive capacities, including capacities for self-expansion, "is Heraclitus", a development that signals a new era of self-awareness ushered in by the first-person lyric poets (Snell 1953, p. 17; cf. p. 19). Not every reading of Heraclitus takes this approach—some signal exceptions from an earlier era will be discussed below—but the vast majority do, and today this progressivist approach to Heraclitus is the academic orthodoxy.

In foregrounding the role of *psuchē* in Heraclitus, contemporary scholarship gives it a particularly human-oriented and humanistic spin that not even Snell gave it. With his "new talk of soul", Heraclitus is a "pioneer" in "human nature" (Schofield 1991, p. 24). "For the first time, apparently, in the history of Greek thought, man is seen, explicitly, as having a central 'self'" (Nussbaum 1972b, p. 169). "Speculation about the world has brought with it a new dimension of the self" (Long 1992, p. 265). Indeed, the actual *goal* of cosmic speculation in Heraclitus is to reveal "the meaning of human life" (Hussey 1982, p. 41).[11] He is "acutely aware of the specific character of psychic reality as such, with its characteristic dimension of 'inwardness'" (Kahn 1964, p. 201). In announcing a "general theory of the ['human'] soul" and a "psychology" of "human nature" (Schofield 1991, pp. 23–24), Heraclitus "made remarkable contributions to the idea and the ideal of rationality" (Long 2013, p. 201). Searching for himself, he found his self, or rather, the *idea* of the self. All of us are in his debt.

Heraclitus, it is true, invites us to search for something like an idea of the self in his writings. He tells us that he made the search himself (§1). But the rest of the inferences just mentioned go much further than his texts warrant. Humanism and individualism have no place in Heraclitus' philosophy. And exactly what is "the specific character of psychic reality as such"? There is very little agreement today. Heraclitus does give *psuchē* a prominence that is novel. But he also presents a novel theory of reality, call it nature, the cosmos, or the phys-

---

[11] "Self is a name for what we are in our individual identities, as distinct persons, minds or states of awareness", which is to say, as being "properly human" (Long 1992, pp. 260, 257). Heraclitus gives evidence of "the normative compulsion to realize one's humanity" and to "becom[e] fully human" (Moore 2018, p. 17). Similarly, Betegh 2013, p. 225: Heraclitus marks "a shift from an impersonal, objectivist description of the physical world" to "reflectio[n] on the human being who is striving to understand the nature of things". Dilcher 1995 is likewise strongly anthropocentric, despite acknowledging *psuchē*'s elemental nature (e.g., pp. 74–76).

ical world, that transforms the meaning of *psuchē*. Construing *psuchē* as the human soul and not as a cosmic life-force or cosmic substance that reaches beyond individual human beings risks underplaying the larger frameworks in which his thought moves. It is doubtful that "[Heraclitus'] real subject is not the physical world but the human condition, the condition of mortality" (Kahn 1979, p. 23). To see why, a brief look at his cosmic fragments will be needed. Then we can take a closer look at the ways in which Heraclitean *psuchē* fits into that larger context.

2 Cosmic questions

Diogenes Laertius offers a convenient thumbnail sketch of Heraclitus' theory of nature:

> His opinions, speaking generally, are the following. All things are constituted out of fire and are dissolved into it. ...[12] The things that exist are fitted together thanks to the contrariety of their character. And everything is full of *psuchai* and divinities. He also spoke about everything that happens in the world. (A1.7 = R46)

Diogenes gives us the original context of §4 above. From the surrounding testimony we can see how Heraclitus's philosophy took in the whole of nature, starting with the elemental masses (earth, water, and fire, as we learn elsewhere) and running up to the processes that govern them as they cycle incessantly through their transformations from one state to another. We also see how his theory gave extraordinary prominence to *psuchai* and divinities, seemingly attributing a kind of panpsychism and pantheism to every entity in nature, though exactly how remains to be determined. In each of these respects, Heraclitus has moved beyond his predecessors. But in one respect he has not. In Homer, the *psuchē* is a sign not of life *tout court* but of life's precarious condition. *Psuchē* is named "only in the contexts of life lost or threatened, never of life held or enjoyed" (Clarke 1999, p. 55).[13] *Psuchē* represents the fragility of existence. In distributing *psuchē* throughout the totality of nature, Heraclitus has distributed this same fragility throughout nature as well.

---

[12] I have omitted a reference to fate, which is a later Stoicizing touch. Heraclitus's thinking is fate-free.
[13] Cf. Nussbaum 1972a, p. 1: Homeric *psuchē* "is mentioned as present only insofar as it may depart".

The fragments bear this out. Heraclitean reality may be a living, changing thing, but it is at the same time *a dying thing* as it cycles through patterns of change. It is at once mortal and immortal, and the one because the other. "For *psuchai* [elsewhere associated with fire] it is death to become water, for water it is death to become earth; but out of earth, water comes to be, and out of water, *psuchē*" (B36 = D100). Or as he puts it in another fragment, "Immortals mortals, mortals immortals, living the death of these, dying the life of those", where the reference must be to cosmic masses (B62 = D70). *Psuchai* mark the unstable boundary between life and death in the cosmos. But although cosmic processes are mapped out as exchanges of life and death, it is a mistake to conceive of these processes as essentially cyclical, that is, as proceeding in a linear direction that circles back on itself without end. Heraclitus insists that we think every stage of this process as a simultaneity. Waters continuously lap the shores, leaving trace amounts that "become" their opposite, earth. Earth masses constantly dissolve into watery bodies. *Psuchai* are continually dying and being born—not again, but are simply being born as entities that are and are not mortal. In other words, life and death are not exclusive opposites, any more than *psuchē* and earth or water are. In Heraclitus' world, nothing is this.

The cosmos of Heraclitus is a matrix of relations among unstable and seemingly ephemeral identities that exhaust themselves not only in successive physical transformations of cosmic masses or stuffs but also in simultaneous oppositions, whereby each component, considered from another angle, is its opposite: thus, war is peace, up is down, life is death, and so on. In other words, the constituent entities of the universe exhibit relational rather than individual properties.[14] The result is a structure of immense complexity: a self-organizing and self-disorganizing fabric of converging and diverging strands, a harmony (*harmoniē*) that is simultaneously in and out of tune, fitting and not fitting together (this is the root sense of *harmoniē*), a unity that is a plurality, differing and agreeing with itself (B8, B10, B51). Neither whole nor not-whole, the cosmos is simultaneously whole *and* not-whole, an untotalizable sum that is forever alive and forever dying, exhausting and replenishing itself at every instant, in every entity, and with every transformation, not sequentially but simultaneously.

Heraclitus's theory of nature is often said to exhibit two principles, universal change and the identity or unity of opposites. But the coherence of identity and unity, whether applied to individual entities or to the cosmos as a whole, is precisely what his philosophy undermines. As in the famous river analogy (B12,

---

[14] See Arist., *De caelo* 298b29–32 = R36; Hussey 1982, pp. 44–45 on "the ambivalence of essence" in Heraclitus.

B49a), the world flows and is only nominally the same as itself at any given moment.[15] Nature is a plurality of contradictory instances. That is also why Heraclitus' language and thought flouts the law of noncontradiction at every turn, as if mimicking the very nature of reality itself. Heraclitean reality is counterintuitive by design. It is neither unified nor a plurality of unities, but is instead *both singular and plural*, which is to say, *simultaneously one and many* and *never identical to itself.*

Ancient and modern commentators wrestle with this refractory model of reality and work hard to reduce it to a rationally coherent singularity. What about any individual instance of *psuchē*, let alone of any individual human being as the presumed possessor of *psuchē*? *Prima facie*, it is unlikely that Heraclitus is operating with a stronger notion of singularity, identity, or selfhood when he sets about analyzing individual human beings than he is when he turns to the nature of reality and its component parts. As Karl Reinhard once observed, "The human is at once an *idion* [a singular private entity] and *xunon* [common, a portion of the whole]" (Reinhardt 1916, p. 216 n. 1). I think this is fundamentally correct, but its implications need to be drawn out.

3 What is an I?

The claim that "I searched for myself" tells us that Heraclitus went looking for himself, not that he found it,[16] and certainly not that he went searching for his *self*. However we construe the fragment, there is something quite strange about the conceit. Charles Kahn's comment on this fragment is apt: "Normally, one goes looking for *someone else*. How can I be the object of my own search? This will make sense only if my self is somehow absent, hidden, or difficult to find. ... [A subject like this] presents a problem for himself to resolve" (Kahn 1979, p. 116). The fragments suggest that Heraclitus succeeded in posing the problem of himself, or rather that he confronted himself in the form of a problem, but not that he ever resolved it, let alone that he framed the problem in such a way that it could in theory ever admit of solution.

If there are any doubts about the matter, these are quelled by the second fragment above: "You would not find out the limits of *psuchē* even by travelling along every path, so deep a measure (*logos*) does it have" (§2). *Psuchē* is apparently bounded, but we cannot reach its limits no matter what road we travel to

---

15 See n. 21 below.
16 Plotinus believed that Heraclitus did find himself (*Enneads* 4.8.1 = R88).

find them. Traveling looks to be a metaphor, but for what? Empirical inquiry can be ruled out: Heraclitus notoriously scorned polymathy (B40, B129). Some other kind of inquiry could be intended. Self-inquiry through introspection is typically suggested by scholars to whom the image of interior psychological depths is attractive. But we may have gotten off on the wrong foot. There is no mention of introspection in the fragment and no sense of depths within, only a search for the unreachable limits of *psuchē* and a *logos* (measure or account) that is itself illimitably deep. As Heraclitus says in B115 (§3), the *logos* of *psuchē* is infinitely expansive: it continues to "grow". But why assume that the *psuchē* mentioned in these fragments is that of an individual at all?

The only fragment that remotely suggests that the *psuchē* of B45 (§2) could refer to an individual *psuchē* is B101 (§1). But the link is weak. Heraclitus does not say there that he went searching for his *psuchē*. He went searching for "myself" (*emeōuton*). Neither is self-inquiry likely: the Greek does not permit this meaning.[17] What is possible is that Heraclitus was looking to find out who he was, not in the Delphic sense of "Know thyself", but in a different sense: he wanted to know *what* he was, what his material constitution was, how he could "be" while also "becoming" (like everything else in nature), and what his place in the greater scheme of things (the universe) was. Few readers would dispute that Heraclitus was keen to explore, if not unravel, the nature of the universe wherever he turned. What is objectionable is framing this inquiry as a search for "the meaning of human life" or claiming that "to interpret the cosmos it is necessary to study one's own self, and apply what one finds there to explain the world" (Hussey 1982, p. 41). The logic is backwards. The nature of the world is what illuminates the nature of the self. The starting point has to be nature, not some place located within ourselves. And to conduct that larger search is to divest oneself of one's intuitive self; it is to *unself* oneself. Only then can one learn not *who* one is but *what* one is. The self is a problem only if it blocks our view of reality, which it plainly does, as further fragments to be discussed below demonstrate. It is not an individual entity worth knowing *per se*. Quite the contrary. The idiosyncratic (private, individualized) self is anathema to Heraclitus' thought.

---

17 Diels translates: "*Ich durchforschte mich selbst*" (B45); cf. Curd/McKirahan 2010, p. 45: "I searched [or 'inquired into'] myself." LSJ gives the following meanings for the verb in question (*dizēmai*): "seek out", "look for", "seek for" (as also found in B22: "search for gold") and "seek out the meaning of" (the latter only in Herodotus). The verb is related to *dizō*, which means "to be in doubt" or "at a loss". For a critique of the introspection reading of fr. 45, see also Betegh 2009.

This is, in fact, how Bruno Snell understood the matter in 1926 before he changed his mind in 1946. With Heraclitus, "the self (*das Ich*) appears for the first time as a *problem*", and not as a newly minted entity that marks its own triumph (Snell 1926, p. 363; emphasis added). At a stroke, the conventional developmental view of the emergence of the self is here turned on its head. Quoting the two fragments we have been discussing (§§1–2), Snell adds, with astonishing frankness, "But when we now stand back from his statements and ask what Heraclitus found as he went in search for himself, what he discovered in the vast region of the soul, the answer is: *nothing at all*" (Snell 1926, p. 361; emphasis added). There is nothing to know and nothing that can be known, only an utterly dark spot, an opacity ("*Dunkel*", obscurity; the word glosses Heraclitus's famous moniker, *ho Skoteinos*, "the Obscure") that resists every illumination (Snell 1926, p. 363)—and not because the soul is a uniquely "difficult topic" and "hard to fathom" (Schofield 1991, p. 20), but because the very idea of a personal self is for Heraclitus inherently problematic.[18]

Heraclitus does not even *try* to make the self an object of his experience or knowledge, as Snell rightly sees: "the self (*das Ich*) is not the actual object of his reflection" (Snell 1926, p. 361). Rather, the self, or rather *psuchē* insofar as it belongs to cosmic nature, is registered as something external, "as something strange", as if it too came from without and not from within. So viewed, this strange self appears not as "mine" but "as the relation between things in the external world to one another" (Snell 1926, p. 361). The intuitive self of §1 is for this reason estranged, or rather displaced by a stranger, one that is not personal but is rather impersonal or suprapersonal (*überpersönlich*). This stranger, this not-self ("*Nicht-Ich*", Snell 1926, p. 367), is no longer recognizably human because it is in fact inhuman or extra-human (*etwas Außermenschliches*), and even daimonic (B119; see below). The experiences of both the self and its strange negation are not their own but are those of the cosmos to which it, as *psuchē* and not as the first-personal self (*das Ich*), belongs as a part (Snell 1926, pp. 357, 364). Nor is this characterization unique to *psuchē*. In Heraclitus's view, everything is in some deep sense interconnected, and so too estranged, from the human perspective. As tempting as it may be for us today, to personalize *psuchē* by translating it as "individual self" is the wrong way to understand Heraclitus's texts.

Readings of Heraclitus that relate the *psuchē* of texts §§2–3 to a first-personal self do not match the evidence, as text §4 alone suggests ("everything is full of *psuchai* and *daimones*"). Indeed, connecting the concept of an individual *psuchē*

---

18 I borrow the felicitous phrase "an utterly dark spot" from Božovič 2000, who borrowed it from Jeremy Bentham.

to a humanly individuated self in any of the four texts above is problematic. *Psuchē* is not obviously the "soul" of a human being. Rather, it picks out a feature of non-human entities in the universe that humans also share. Turning the tables on our intuitions, Heraclitus is impressing upon us the fact that human beings are a non-individualizable part of this world simply by belonging to the cosmic (material or physical) *psuchē*-stuff that runs through every inch of the universe in a never-ending cascade of transformations and in a permanent "war" of oppositions and contradictions (B8, B80). The exact role of *psuchē* in this larger scenario is hard to pin down, in part because Heraclitus refuses to paint in the details of cosmic processes (this is his way of lodging a protest against Ionian science and against science generally),[19] and in part because he is reluctant to individuate any of the components that make up the universe. These constituents tend to be masses of material stuff (not quite "elements" in the standard Ionian classifications),[20] while individual entities are in Heraclitus irreducible to self-identical things. Human beings are hardly exempt from this rule. They, too, are shot through with the enigmatic logic of contradiction and hence are not identical to themselves. They are at once self and not-self, I and not-I, human and not-human, mortal and immortal.[21]

Individuation is for Heraclitus a dubious concept, not least of all because it is methodologically sterile. There is no evidence that Heraclitus believed that a knowledge of the whole of reality could be arrived at by examining its constituents in isolation, no evidence, in other words, that any one of these constituents can open a privileged route of access to the structure of the universe that is not shared by all of its constituents, which stand on an equal footing in a kind of "democracy of objects" (Bryant 2011), or better yet, processes. Such knowledge is certainly not achievable through introspection, as if self-knowledge were the key to universal wisdom. And yet, this remains the most common way of making sense of Heraclitus today, for instance by linking inquiry into the self (as in §§1–2) to an ever-expanding knowledge of oneself and of nature (as in §3).[22]

---

19 It may be that "natural science (*die Naturwissenschaft*) owes nothing to [Heraclitus]" (Diels 1901, p. vii), but Heraclitus' philosophy of nature is no less significant for that.
20 Betegh 2013, p. 231 is probably right to maintain that the singular *psuchē* is a "mass noun" and not a "singular count-noun standing for a class of things, souls", and that the process described in B36 (quoted on p. 10 above) traces the birth, which is to say the transformative emergence, not of individual human beings but of *psuchē* stuff.
21 Cf. B49a = D65: "We step and we do not step into the same rivers, we are and we are not."
22 Bernays 1885, p. 105 is the modern ancestor of this view: "*in me ipsum descendi meaeque naturae leges perscrutando ad intellegendas universae rerum naturae leges pervenire conatus sum*". Cf. Snell 1953, p. 19; Nussbaum 1972a, p. 15: "there are no limits to man's power to develop

There is an undeniable self-satisfaction in such a view: it flatters the human ego and the inestimable powers of human nature. It idealizes the self. But everything in Heraclitus points to the exact opposite of this approach. It is only by *diminishing* the role of the human being, its claim to identity, reason, certain knowledge, and privilege, that a philosophical view of the universe is possible at all. To address the enigma of the self in Heraclitus, we need to look without, not within.

4 The extroversion of the human and the ecology of the self in Heraclitus

Heraclitus's gaze is turned outward for the bulk of his fragments and testimonia, not inward, and his most frequently used pronoun is the third person singular and plural, not the first. As I suggested, it is perfectly conceivable that *psuchē* in §2 does not refer to the first-personal self at all. If *psuchai* are everywhere (§4)—even in one's midden or hearth (A9; P15)—then there is no compelling reason to restrict the reference here to the human soul and not to assign it to the physical stuff from which all *psuchai* are made, which for Heraclitus is dry exhalation and fire itself,[23] or else to the general concept of what a *psuchē* is. The embarrassing fact that the human soul, endowed with the attributes of an interior self and a psychological richness within,[24] would have to be conceived of as made of fire or evaporation,[25] seems not register among exponents of this kind of reading. What is more, Heraclitus's universe is populated by a far richer range of objects than ourselves. It includes literally "everything", from rivers, tides, mist, and the course of the sun, to roads, barley drink, fish, pigs, monkeys, dogs, asses, corpses, dung, circles, carding wheels, children's toys, bows, and lyres. "Man" is decidedly not the measure of things; he is just one more object in the world.[26]

---

his understanding" through "self-seeking and self-knowledge"; Long 1992, p. 271: "the mind or the self is unlimited in its capacity for understanding."

23 B118, B64, B30, B31, B90; A15 (Aëtius). This physical makeup of *psuchē* is sometimes referred to as "soul stuff" (English 1913; Vlastos 1955, p. 363; Betegh 2013).

24 E.g., Kahn 1964, p. 201: "this new and rare sense for the human soul as an inner world, ... containing the secret of the universe within itself"; the soul's "characteristic dimension of 'inwardness'"; Hussey 1982, p. 40: "the inner realm of our selves"; Graham 2010, vol. 1, p. 188: "an inner world".

25 And potentially of earth or water (Kirk 1962, p. 348).

26 Cf. Rivier 1956, p. 154, n. 40; 157 with n. 45; 161 n. 50 (drawing heavily on Snell, *passim*); Marcovich 1967, p. 159; Emlyn-Jones 1976, p. 105 (citing Rivier).

Schleiermacher's early reading of Heraclitus, dating from 1807, is on a much better footing than current readings and a clear precursor to Snell:

> Heraclitus may well have said that he sought himself (*sich selbst gesucht*) in the eternal [cosmic] flux and did not find himself as a durable existent (*und auch sich nicht gefunden als seiend, beharrend*), and that precisely as a result [of this failure] the path to real knowledge opened up for him. ... Indeed, the catalyst for the whole of his wisdom can easily have been this very act of *losing and then finding himself again only in the logic of the universe* (*nur in der gemeinsamen Vernunft*). That is the most luminous and distinctive feature of his conception; everywhere it privileges what is universal (*dem Allgemeinen* [lit., "common to all"]), while completely subordinating the particular as derivative [of the universal] and as non-existent in itself (*in sich nicht bestehend*). (Schleiermacher 1808, p. 531; my translation)

Here we have, in a nutshell, the complete inverse of the contemporary approach to the Heraclitean self. For Schleiermacher, the self is a perishable entity that must be jettisoned only to be rediscovered in, or as, the greater commonality (rather than totality) of nature. The failure of the search for the self *produces* the successful reappraisal of what a singular self cannot be. The self is discovered at its own limits but is not positivized by them. Once "lost", it is not recuperated; it is "found" as *das Nicht-Ich*, the not-I into which it has dissolved. The key term in Schleiermacher's account is *"das Allgemeine"*, literally "the all-common", or "what is common to all". The term renders the foundational category in Heraclitus' thinking, *to xunon* (the Ionian equivalent of *to koinon* in later Greek), which means "that which is shared" and "in common". By the same token, "*der gemeinsame Vernunft*" renders Heraclitus' *xunos logos* (B2), which stands for the "logic" (rather than the "rationality") that is common to and exhibited by everything in nature. The *kosmos* represents this all-commonality, or as Schleiermacher puts it, this *"gemeinschaftliches"* quality of nature (Schleiermacher 1808, p. 475). What he is describing is not some abstract universality but rather an ecological "commons". By *to xunon*, "Heraclitus intends not only the entire external world (*Außenwelt*) but also one's own self (*Ich*), which is encompassed in this universal commonality (*diesem Allgemeinem*). ... The internal and external are as yet undifferentiated"—so Snell (1926, p. 376), building on Schleiermacher.[27]

In stressing the environmental meaning of *to xunon*, Schleiermacher and Snell bring us closer to a Heraclitean "ecology of the self" and further away from the humanistic readings of Heraclitus. The self on this alternative view is not a psychological entity teeming with a private inner life and depth, nor

---

[27] Snell 1926 engages with Schleiermacher twice (p. 355 n. 2; p. 371), but he has absorbed of Schleiermacher more than he lets on.

does it name an individual (*Individuum*): Heraclitus is anything but an "individualist" (Snell 1926, pp. 364, 367). On the contrary, the Heraclitean "self" exists in a purely extroverted form: it is turned outward, away from itself, and faces the cosmos, which is the only reality that it knows and the source of all its experiences—except for the fact that once this point is reached there is no subject left to experience anything at all, unless we were to say that it is the *cosmos* that experiences and thinks itself, not as a singular entity but as a process of diverging and converging opposites that cannot be rationally grasped by us and that cannot be encapsulated as a totality ("conjoinings" of opposites "are and are not wholes", B10 = D47; trans. mine). The Heraclitean world is a system of relational processes in which each individual entity has no essential and independent identity owing to their communally shared and relational features: they literally belong to one another in common. In Greek, they are *xuna*.

The *xunon* is the interobjective glue that binds every aspect of Heraclitean universe and colors every aspect of his philosophy, from his physics to his cosmology, his politics, and his ethics.[28] A taste of the power of this communal connection is found in a testimony by Sextus Empiricus: "The reason (*logos*) that [Heraclitus] proclaims to be judge of truth is ... the common (*koinos*) and divine one [and not our privately "owned" reason ([*tēn*] *idian phronēsin*)]", which is "drawn in ... through respiration" and thereby provides a "natural connection with what encompasses us", that is, our environmental surroundings (A16.127–129; 133 = R59; trans. Bett). For "the human being is not rational (*logikon*); only what encompasses us (*to periechon*) is rational and endowed with mind (*nous*)" (A16.134 = R60 = Sextus Empiricus, *Against the Logicians* 2.286, trans. Bett). What Heraclitus seems to be saying is not that the universe "thinks" but that it embodies the only *logos* there is, the logic of the commons or the whole. Its processes exhibit this *logos*, and hence are *logikoi* and "endowed with mind". Conversely, individuals, when they are cut off from the whole, only imagine that they are thinking, but in reality their thinking is a private—a false and empty—thinking. The irony is that once they relinquish their isolation and rejoin the whole in their minds, they cease to be individual beings in any significant sense. They merely partake of the commons.

---

28 The best treatment of Heraclitus's politics to date (Raaflaub 2017) takes its cue from this association.

5 Hegel with Nietzsche

In de-emphasizing the individual object or subject and in situating it within a greater totality but without idealizing that totality as a bounded whole, the modern German tradition of reading Heraclitus to which the early Snell is heir permits an objectivizing of the self but also a diminution of its privileged status. The self becomes an object—a *what* as opposed to a *who*, a *third-personal entity* as opposed to a first-personal one. In short, "the self (*Ich*) is not the actual object of [Heraclitus'] reflection" (Snell 1926, p. 361). It has "only a relative existence (*ein relatives Dasein*), one that obtains *only through and for another entity* (*nur durch und für ein Anderes*) that exists on equal terms with it". This last remark comes from Nietzsche's never-published essay, *Die Philosophie im tragischen Zeitalter der Griechen* (1873),[29] though it could as easily have come from Snell, but also, surprisingly, from Hegel in his own earlier lectures on Heraclitus, for instance where he writes,

> Every particular entity is different from an Other, but not abstractly, not from any Other whatsoever, but from *its* Other. ... Subjectivity is the other (*das Andere*) of objectivity ...—[that is,] *its* Other, and therein lies their identity: thus, every [Other] is the Other of the Other as its Other (*so ist jedes das Andere des Anderen als seines Anderen*). (Hegel 1971, p. 327; trans. mine)

Both Hegel and Nietzsche recognize that, because reality is for Heraclitus constructed out of relations that are revealed through a logic of contraries and oppositions, no single entity can provide evidence of this complexity on its own; everything in the world is not merely relationally interconnected but also relationally defined. Thus, grasping the universe requires that we see all things in common, not apart. *Psuchē* is no exception. That is why Nietzsche rejected the belief that Heraclitus discovered the self or soul as something distinct from the physical world. *Psuchē* is fiery warmth or warm breath, living material that, moreover, is in no way comparable to Anaxagoras's later notion of teleological and transcendental Mind, or *Nous* (Nietzsche 1995, pp. 274, 279–281).

Hegel, for his part, was equally insistent that individuated subjectivity had no place in Heraclitus's universe. Heraclitus, he held, rendered the processes of becoming, which obey a dialectical pattern of opposites, fully objective but also fully absolute. Being was brought into the realm of Becoming, the constitutive realm of true reality ("*Das Wahre ist das Werden, nicht das Sein*" [Hegel 1971,

---

[29] Nietzsche 1988, p. 824. Though Nietzsche is not explicitly addressing the self here, he implicitly is. His statement covers everything that exists in the flux of time and space.

p. 324; trans. mine]); the particularized subjective element was dissolved; and the Absolute was concretely realized in its own ongoing activity, in a "unity of the real and the ideal" and of the subjective and the objective (Hegel 1971, p. 326). In Heraclitus, Hegel reasons, dissonance lies at the root of every universal process. Unity as unicity is eschewed. The "One"—Heraclitus' *hen*—is not abstract, nor is it a form of simplicity (*das Einfache*); it is the activity of self-sundering, which is a "process of vitality (*Lebendigkeit*)", and so too of irreducible complexity (pp. 326–327), organized around the concrete unity of opposites (pp. 319, 324–325). The self is thereby made to cede to a universalized otherness, defined as the Other of its own Other, as with Nietzsche and later Snell. At issue, then, is "not becoming-Other (*nicht Anderswerden*), now this and then an Other (*ein Anderes*)", but a more fundamental (*wesentlich*) and insurmountable difference that is expressed in a concrete form in reality itself (p. 327)—not water as a discrete entity, for example, but water grasped as changing (*als sich verändernd*), which is to say as mere "process" (*Prozeß*) that lacks all permanence (p. 329): "absolute disturbance (*Unruhe*), absolute dissolution of all permanence" (p. 330, said of fire but applicable to all of nature). Negativity, understood as the presence of not-X in X, is thus made "immanent" to reality's very constitution (p. 327). So conceived, reality is guided by a negative dialectic, and individual identity is put into question.[30]

Proof is found, Hegel argues (pp. 339–341), in Heraclitus' theory of sleep, according to which "those who are awake have a world (*kosmon*) that is one and in common (*hena kai koinon*), but that each of those who is asleep turns aside into his own private world (*eis idion*)" (B89 = R56; trans. modified). For in sleep our mind is cut off from what encompasses it (*to periechon*, our "environment", with which the mind is "cognate"), which is to say that "the portion of what encompasses us, which dwells like a foreigner in our bodies, becomes virtually devoid of reason (*alogos*) in the case of separation [from the universe], whereas in the case of natural connection through the multiple passageways [to the universe] it becomes similar in kind to the whole" (A16.129 = R59 = Sextus Empiricus, *Against the Logicians* 1.129; trans. Bett, modified). Drawing in the divine *logos* of the cosmos in the air we breathe gives us the only intelligence we can ever have (cf. A16.127–129). In these two Greek texts and in Hegel's reading of them we can see one of the sources of Snell's interpretation of Heraclitus. The "private" self is a deprived self, whereas the waking, extroverted self is fully alive. Aliveness here is established by the self's connectivity to nature but also by its extroversion, the outward-facing posture of the self.

---

30 Cf. Hegel 1971, p. 331: "*Entzweiung als Realisierung ... – Diremtion und Setzen in Einheit*".

And yet, even to put things in this way is misleadingly self-centric. It is a mistake to say that *the self* faces outward towards the universe. It is the universe that faces itself and that is only ever in contact with itself. What is more, the property of being alive is not restricted to animate creatures. All parts of the universe, human and non-human, are equally alive and equally "ensouled". All of this has a direct bearing on the human conception of the self. Problems of terminology aside (*psuchē*, "us", "humans", and "self" are in no way clear equivalents), *it is only when we sleep that we become private selves*, endowed with an interiority that is all our own and an autonomy with respect to our surroundings and to all forms of what we consider "other". Indeed, it is only from the perspective of a self that otherness exists at all. From the perspective of nature, everything is other than it is, and selves (including "objective selves") do not exist.[31]

Heraclitus claims that when we are awake, we are entities that have been intruded upon by a "portion of what encompasses us that dwells like a foreigner in our bodies (*hē epixenōtheisa tois hēmeterois sōmasin apo tou periechontos moira*)", which is to say, that portion of the universe that, drawn "from the surrounding environment", has "taken up residence" in us and "is entertained by us as a guest", but also as a "stranger", a "*xenos*" ("*epixenōtheisa*" has both connotations) (A16.129–30). But this, too, is spoken from the perspective of the private individual self, albeit one that has suddenly become a stranger to itself.[32] The same point can be read out of the two fragments that reportedly opened Heraclitus's collection (B1–2) and that are corroborated by a further testimony (A16.133–134), all deriving from the same context in Sextus, who saw more of Heraclitus than has been transmitted to us. What they indicate is that humans are uncomprehending (*axunetoi*) of the *logos* that is in common (*xunos*): they are blind to the relationally shared features that constitute the reality of nature. In doing so, they go about their daily lives like somnambulists: nominally awake,

---

31 Nagel's "objective self" does not satisfy the laudable "impulse to get beyond a human-centered perspective" (Long 1992, pp. 266, 274). On the contrary, it problematically reinforces that perspective and remains a view from somewhere (that of a disguised subject). After all, why attach the perspective to a "self"? For one critique among many, see Metzinger 2003, pp. 581–586. Heraclitus, by contrast, does not try to give us a view from nowhere, nor does he find the fact of his own existence in any way "startling" (see n. 4 above). He merely offers us an account of the world that minimizes the significance of individual selves.
32 For a defense of the reliability of Sextus' testimony, which has recently come under fire, see Betegh 2013, pp. 245–248. For a contemporary ecological definition of the (non-)self, see Morton 2007, pp. 14–15: "Nature is thus not unlike 'the subject,' a being who searches through the entire universe for its reflection, only to find none."

they are in fact asleep.[33] Specifically, they view reality as though it were parceled out in individual packages disconnected from one another and from themselves. The experiences had by individuals are not inalienably their own but, unbeknownst to themselves, are experiences held by the cosmos to which they belong as a part. Made private, those experiences falsify the look of reality.[34] The upshot is clear: to recognize our true constitution is to become self-estranged, or better yet, to become estranged from the intuitive concept of "self". What was once interior is now exterior, like a sock that has been turned inside out. Our intuitively familiar individuality now appears to have been expropriated to the greater whole of which it is but a fragment.

But that is not all, for with this move not only does Heraclitus decenter the individual human being from nature but he also diminishes its presumptive powers. The privatized self, cut off from what is common, is *alogos*; deprived of intelligence, reason, and rationality (*logos*), it has no insight into the enigmatic rationality of the universe, which is the only intelligence there is. Reason as such belongs not to individuals but to the cosmos in the form of the externalized and exteriorized relations that comprise it. Thus, "fire is intelligent" (R51; cf. B118); "the human being is not rational (*logikon*); only what surrounds it (the *periechon*) is endowed with intelligence" (A16.134); "a gleam of light is the dry *psuchē*, wisest and best" (B118); "the thunderbolt steers all things" (B64). And yet, it would be a mistake to conceive of the reason and intelligence of the cosmos as a humanized intelligence.[35] On the contrary, to speak of the universe as intelligent is to speak of it as embodying the only measure of rationality that exists in nature, its inherent logic: "*logos* is in common (*xunos*)" (B2), i.e., shared, but only among all things insofar as they are *xunos*. The *logos* is *not* shared among individual selves or particulars when these are viewed in and of themselves and as autonomous entities. Individual entities that share in the universal "commons" do so at the price of forfeiting their individuality. Simply to share an insight into the workings of the cosmos is to surrender one's sense of particularity and selfhood—one's *humanity*—and to recognize one's partitive relationship to the whole. The point is not that human beings achieve cognition by virtue

---

33 Cf. Hegel 1971, p. 340: "*Somnambulismus*". This is the gist of B1 = D1: "But other men [i.e., those how fail to grasp Heraclitus' teachings] are unaware of all they do when they are awake, just as they forget all they do while they are asleep."
34 Hegel 1971, p. 341 grasps his argument clearly, as does Reinhardt 1916, p. 216 n. 1.
35 E.g., Hussey 1982, p. 50: "The cosmic intelligence [or "the cosmic self", p. 58] is in all essential respects *human*, just as human 'as you or me.' ... It is therefore a human being of an exceptional kind"—a somewhat bewildering remark.

of participating in cosmic *psuchē*-stuff, as Sextus Empiricus and recent scholars assert. It is rather that humans achieve cognition by becoming inhuman.

There are of course traces of anthropomorphism in Heraclitus' accounts of the universe, just as there are traces of the inhuman in his accounts of the human, as for instance in the well-known but widely misread fragment, *ēthos anthrōpōi daimōn* (B119), which can be loosely rendered thus: "At the core of a human being lies an inhuman entity that is extrinsic to it—a *daimōn*, or divinity".[36] I would suggest that these traces are not slips of the pen. Rather, they have a critical function: they betray and belittle the human perspective by juxtaposing human intelligence with the inhuman dimension, something that is akin to a distributed cognition and distributed agency. Instead of reflecting a naïve projection of the human dimension onto the inhuman cosmos,[37] anthropomorphic features at the cosmic level *deprive* the human of its most cherished qualities, as through a kind of expropriation. Human reason is shown to be insufficient for making the world intelligible, and most of all when it projects its anthropocentrism onto what fundamentally resists this kind of logic. Nietzsche grasped this point well:

> The human being, generally speaking, is an irrational [or "unreasonable"] creature. ... He does not occupy an especially privileged position in nature, the highest manifestation of which is fire, e.g., as a celestial body, but not the human being as such. To the extent that he receives a share of fire out of necessity, he is a bit more rational; but to the extent that he consists of water and earth [as he also does of necessity], his reason is in a bad way. (Nietzsche 1988, pp. 831–832; trans. mine)[38]

Humans insofar as they belong to the totality of the world are no longer individuals, first-person particulars, or even human. They are third-personal entities, an "it" or "them", composed of *psuchē*-stuff that is a cosmically dispersed material. As such they participate but do not occupy a privileged position in this democracy of things.

For these reasons, the self for Heraclitus has an ecological character that pulls it away from itself. It derives its identity not from within but from without, from what surrounds it and is in contact with it, the *periechon*, its environment.[39] Once expropriated to nature, the individual self dissolves and another view of

---

36 The usual understanding is given by Kahn 1979, p. 26: "it is a man's own character, *not some external power*, that assigns him the quality of his life" (emphasis added). Contrast B78 = D74.
37 Snell 1926, p. 361: "[das Ich] wird hinausprojiziert".
38 Along the same lines, Nietzsche 1995, pp. 267 and 281. Cf. Snell 1926, p. 364: "Ēthos [i.e., the human characteristic] has no knowledge."
39 For a quick survey of this concept understood broadly as *milieu* and *Umwelt*, see Spitzer 1942, with a mention of Heraclitus on p. 6.

reality opens up. The prospect is terrifying, which is surely one reason why Heraclitus could say of his audience that they "always fail to comprehend [are *axunetoi* towards] his account of nature, both before they hear it and once they have heard it" (B1 = D1; trans. modified). But that is no reason not to listen to Heraclitus today as we try to make sense of ourselves in the world that we have collectively created for ourselves, our very own Anthropocene. And there is very little that is ideal about that.

Bibliography

Arendt, Hannah (1958): *The Human Condition*. Chicago: The University of Chicago Press.
Aristotle (1984): "On the Soul". Trans. J. A. Smith. In: Jonathan Barnes (Ed.): *The Complete Works of Aristotle: The Revised Oxford Translation*. Princeton, NJ: Princeton University Press. Vol. 2, pp. 641–692.
Barad, Karen (2007): *Meeting the Universe Halfway: Quantum Physics and the Entanglement of Matter and Meaning*. Durham: Duke University Press.
Bernays, Jacob (1885): *Gesammelte Abhandlungen*. Edited by Hermann Usener. 2 vols. Berlin: W. Hertz.
Betegh, Gábor (2013): "On the Physical Aspect of Heraclitus' Psychology: With New Appendices". In: David Sider/Dirk Obbink (Eds.): *Doctrine and Doxography: Studies on Heraclitus and Pythagoras*. Berlin: De Gruyter, pp. 225–261.
Betegh, Gábor. 2009. "The Limits of the Soul. Heraclitus B 45 DK: Its Text and Interpretation." In: Enrique Hülsz Piccone (Ed.): *Nuevos ensayos sobre Heráclito: Actas del Secundo Symposium Heracliteum*. Mexico City: Universidad Nacional Autónoma de México, pp. 391–414.
Božovič, Miran (2000): *An Utterly Dark Spot: Gaze and Body in Early Modern Philosophy*. Ann Arbor: University of Michigan Press.
Bryant, Levi R. (2011): *The Democracy of Objects*. Ann Arbor: Open Humanities Press.
Butler, Judith (2005): *Giving an Account of Oneself*. New York: Fordham University Press.
Clarke, Michael (1999): *Flesh and Spirit in the Songs of Homer: A Study of Words and Myths*. Oxford: Clarendon Press.
Curd, Patricia/McKirahan, Richard D. (Eds.) (2010): *A Presocratics Reader: Selected Fragments and Testimonia*. 2nd edn. Indianapolis: Hackett.
Damasio, Antonio R. (1995): *Descartes' Error: Emotion, Reason, and the Human Brain*. New York: G. P. Putnam's Sons.
Damasio, Antonio R. (1999): *The Feeling of What Happens: Body and Emotion in the Making of Consciousness*. New York: Harcourt Brace.
Damasio, Antonio R. (2003): *Looking for Spinoza: Joy, Sorrow, and the Feeling Brain*. 1st edn. London: William Heinemann.
Dennett, Daniel C. (1991): *Consciousness Explained*. Boston: Little, Brown and Co.
Diels, Hermann (Ed.) (1901): *Herakleitos von Ephesos: Griechisch und Deutsch*. Berlin: Weidmann.
Diels, Hermann/Kranz, Walther (Eds.) (1951–52): *Die Fragmente der Vorsokratiker, griechisch und deutsch*. 3 vols. 6th edn. Berlin: Weidmann.

Dilcher, Roman (1995): *Studies in Heraclitus*. Hildesheim: Georg Olms.
Emlyn-Jones, C. J. (1976): "Heraclitus and the Identity of Opposites". In: *Phronesis* 21. No. 2, pp. 89–114.
English, Robert B. (1913): "Heraclitus and the Soul". In: *Transactions and Proceedings of the American Philological Association* 44, pp. 163–184.
Faruque, Muhammad U. (2021): *Sculpting the Self: Islam, Selfhood, and Human Flourishing*. Ann Arbor: University of Michigan Press.
Foucault, Michel (2005): *The Hermeneutics of the Subject: Lectures at the Collège de France, 1981–82*. Edited by Frédéric Gros. Translated by Graham Burchell. New York: Palgrave Macmillan.
Gill, Christopher (2006): *The Structured Self in Hellenistic and Roman Thought*. Oxford: Oxford University Press.
Graham, Daniel W. (Ed.) (2010): *The Texts of Early Greek Philosophy: The Complete Fragments and Selected Testimonies of the Major Presocratics*. 2 vols. Cambridge: Cambridge University Press.
Hegel, Georg Wilhelm Friedrich (1971): *Vorlesungen über die Geschichte der Philosophie I*. Edited by Eva Moldenhauer and Karl Markus Michel. Frankfurt am Main: Suhrkamp.
Hussey, Edward (1982): "Epistemology and Meaning in Heraclitus". In: Malcolm Schofield/Martha C. Nussbaum (Eds.): *Language and Logos: Studies in Ancient Greek Philosophy Presented to G. E. L. Owen*. Cambridge: Cambridge University Press, pp. 33–59.
Kahn, Charles H. (1964): "A New Look at Heraclitus". In: *American Philosophical Quarterly* 1. No. 3, pp. 189–203.
Kahn, Charles H. (1979): *The Art and Thought of Heraclitus: An Edition of the Fragments with Translation and Commentary*. Cambridge: Cambridge University Press.
Kirk, G. S. (1962): *Heraclitus: The Cosmic Fragments*. 2nd edn. Cambridge: Cambridge University Press.
Laks, André/Most, Glenn W. (Eds.) (2016): *Early Greek Philosophy*. With the assistance of Leopoldo Iribarren, Gérard Journée, and David Lévystone. 9 vols. Cambridge, MA: Harvard University Press.
Liddell, H. G., R. Scott and H. S. Jones. (Eds.) (1996): *A Greek-English Lexicon*. 9th edn. Oxford: Clarendon Press. (="LSJ")
Long, A. A. (1992): "Finding Oneself in Greek Philosophy". In: *Tijdschrift voor Filosofie* 54. No. 2, pp. 255–279.
Long, A. A. (2013): "Heraclitus on Measure and the Explicit Emergence of Rationality". In: David Sider/Dirk Obbink (Eds.): *Doctrine and Doxography: Studies on Heraclitus and Pythagoras*. Berlin: De Gruyter, pp. 201–223.
Long, A. A. (2015): *Greek Models of Mind and Self*. Cambridge, MA: Harvard University Press.
Malabou, Catherine (2008): *What Should We Do with Our Brain?* Trans. Sebastian Rand. New York: Fordham University Press.
Malabou, Catherine (2013): "Go Wonder: Subjectivity and Affects in Neurobiological Times". In: Adrian Johnston/Catherine Malabou: *Self and Emotional Life: Philosophy, Psychoanalysis, and Neuroscience*. New York: Columbia University Press, pp. 3–72.
Marcovich, Miroslav (Ed.) (1967): *Heraclitus: Greek Text with a Short Commentary. Editio Maior*. Mérida: Los Andes University Press.

Metzinger, Thomas (2003): *Being No One: The Self-Model Theory of Subjectivity*. Cambridge, MA: MIT Press.
Moore, Christopher (2018): "Heraclitus and 'Knowing Yourself' (116 DK)". In: *Ancient Philosophy* 38, pp. 1–21.
Morton, Timothy (2007): *Ecology without Nature: Rethinking Environmental Aesthetics*. Cambridge, MA: Harvard University Press.
Murdoch, Iris (2014): *The Sovereignty of Good*. London: Routledge.
Nagel, Thomas (1986): *The View from Nowhere*. New York and Oxford: Oxford University Press.
Nietzsche, Friedrich (1988): "Die Philosophie im tragischen Zeitalter der Griechen". In: *Sämtliche Werke: Kritische Studienausgabe in 15 Einzelbänden*. 2nd edn. Edited by Giorgio Colli and Mazzino Montinari. Berlin: De Gruyter. Vol. 1, pp. 801–872.
Nietzsche, Friedrich (1995): "Die vorplatonischen Philosophen". In: *Werke: Kritische Gesamtausgabe*. Edited by Fritz Bornmann and Mario Carpitella. Berlin: De Gruyter. Vol. 2.4, pp. 209–362.
Nussbaum, Martha C. (1972a): "ΨΥΧΗ in Heraclitus, I". In: *Phronesis* 17. No. 1, pp. 1–16.
Nussbaum, Martha C. (1972b): "ΨΥΧΗ in Heraclitus, II". In: *Phronesis* 17. No. 2, pp. 153–170.
Pippin, Robert B. (1997): *Idealism as Modernism: Hegelian Variations*. Cambridge: Cambridge University Press.
Porter, James I. (2005): "Foucault's Ascetic Ancients". In: *Phoenix* 59. No. 2 (Special issue: "Interrogating Theory—Critiquing Practice: The Subject of Interpretation". Edited by W. Batstone), pp. 121–132.
Porter, James I. (2020): "Living on the Edge: Self and World *in extremis* in Roman Philosophy". In: *Classical Antiquity* 39. No. 2, pp. 225–383.
Raaflaub, Kurt A. (2017): "Shared Responsibility for the Common Good: Heraclitus, Early Philosophy, and Political Thought". In: Enrica Fantino/Ulrike Muss/Charlotte Schubert/Kurt Sier (Ed.): *Heraklit im Kontext*. Berlin: De Gruyter, pp. 103–128.
Reinhardt, Karl (1916): *Parmenides und die Geschichte der griechischen Philosophie*. 1st edn. Frankfurt am Main: Vittorio Klostermann.
Rivier, André (1956): "L'homme et l'expérience humaine dans les fragments d'Héraclite". In: *Museum Helveticum* 13. No. 3, pp. 144–164.
Schleiermacher, Friedrich (1808): "Herakleitos der dunkle, von Ephesos, dargestellt aus den Trümmern seines Werkes und den Zeugnissen der Alten". In: *Museum der Alterthums-Wissenschaft* 1. No. 3, pp. 316–584.
Schofield, Malcolm (1991): "Heraclitus' Theory of the Soul". In: Stephen Everson (Ed.): *Psychology*. Cambridge: Cambridge University Press, pp. 12–34.
Sextus Empiricus (2005): *Against the Logicians*. Translated by Richard Bett. Cambridge: Cambridge University Press.
Snell, Bruno (1926): "Die Sprache Heraklits". In: *Hermes* 61. No. 4, pp. 353–381.
Snell, Bruno (1946): *Die Entdeckung des Geistes: Studien zur Entstehung des europäischen Denkens bei den Griechen*. Hamburg: Claaszen & Goverts.
Snell, Bruno (1953): *The Discovery of the Mind: The Greek Origins of European Thought*. Translated by Thomas G. Rosenmeyer. Oxford: Basil Blackwell.
Sorabji, Richard (2006): *Self: Ancient and Modern Insights about Individuality, Life, and Death*. Chicago: University of Chicago Press.

Spitzer, Leo (1942): "Milieu and Ambiance: An Essay in Historical Semantics". In: *Philosophy and Phenomenological Research* 3. No. 1, pp. 1–42.
Strawson, Galen (2001): "The Sense of the Self". In: M. James C. Crabbe (Ed.): *From Soul to Self*. London: Routledge, pp. 126–152.
Strawson, Galen (2009): *Selves: An Essay in Revisionary Metaphysics*. Oxford: Clarendon Press.
Turkle, Sherry (2005): *The Second Self: Computers and the Human Spirit*. 2nd edn. Cambridge, MA: MIT Press.
Vlastos, Gregory (1955): "On Heraclitus". In: *The American Journal of Philology* 76. No. 4, pp. 337–368.
Williams, Bernard (1993): *Shame and Necessity*. Berkeley: University of California Press.

Jure Simoniti
De-Symbolization of the World and the Emergence of the Self: A Historically-Idealist Theory of the Subject

Abstract: Idealism has commonly been regarded as a stance endorsing a timeless frame which precedes and preordains all the temporal, worldly phenomena. By contrast, this paper will indicate how the idealist impulse emerges historically, as a very specific juggling act which hangs suspended between two focal points, the process of the de-symbolization of the world on the one side and the formation of the philosophical subject on the other. The first case is provided by Augustine, the inventor of the "private inner space" of the contemplative self and simultaneously an advocate of an ontologically homonomous world, i.e., the Christian monism of good against the Gnostic and Manichean dualisms of good and evil. On grounds of this matrix, the Cartesian ego, the Kantian spontaneous, synthetic unity of apperception, Nietzsche's overman, Heidegger's Dasein, or the psychoanalytical subject of gender difference will also be construed as a reaction to the collapsing symbolic values of the world.

It is somewhat perplexing that the prevalence of what might be called the "antirealist self-understanding of post-Kantian philosophy" failed to give a substantial leg up to idealism, a stance which in European continental thought effectively died out with Hegel.[1] Why did this overarching success of antirealism[2] start to develop so adamantly anti-idealist tendencies, and that as early as with Marx

---

Funding note: The research included in this chapter was funded by the Slovenian Research Agency (ARRS) under the research project "The Possibility of Idealism for the Twenty-First Century" (J6–1811).

[1] Nietzsche already stated that *"every* sentence of my writings entails *contempt* for idealism" (Nietzsche 1888, translation mine).
[2] This diagnosis roughly constituted the foundational gesture of so-called "Speculative Realism". It was Meillassoux who realized that the antirealist "correlationist circle" represented an irreducible horizon and an unsurpassable limit to our thought, prohibiting any simple exit to the outside world (see Meillassoux 2008).

Jure Simoniti, University of Ljubljana.

and Nietzsche? Should antirealism not reinforce idealism and even be synonymous with it?

To put it most briefly,[3] the seldom observed, mysteriously little mentioned aspiration of the "continental antirealist" transition of the roots of conceptuality from outside reality to the autogenous circuits of subjectivity is, surprisingly enough, also to supply the means for revealing the sheer non-ideality of the world, its non-anthropomorphism. To be fair, Kant, Hegel, Nietzsche, Heidegger, and others routinely let the origin of their entire conceptual edifice hinge upon an "antirealist impulse"—one of the spontaneity of reason, the self-consciousness of the concept, the will to power, the meaning of being, etc.—but their attempts at inventing new sources of truth in a disenchanted world of modern science and the post-feudal, egalitarian society were always strictly counterbalanced by the willingness to come to terms with a universe indifferent to the existence of man. Post-Kantians were known to be veritable poets of human insignificance. Once Hume had intimated the possibility of a reality without substances, causes, and effects, the ambition of the philosophy to come was hardly to discern some hidden ideal order behind the veil of phenomena, but rather to make the "given" world be seen as bereaved of meaning, value, origin, or purpose. On the other hand, this anti-idealist sobering of outside reality was, albeit with some delay, reciprocated by a methodic disintegration and depreciation of human conceptual forms. Kant still imagined transcendental subjectivity as harboring an array of ideal, logically robust categories exempt from time. But Marx already submitted the central notions of human self-awareness to ideological critiques, and Nietzsche to genealogical analysis. Finally, what Hume did to reality in the late eighteenth century, Wittgenstein and possibly Derrida could be said to have inflicted upon language in the twentieth. Their endeavor was to break down the metaphysical pretension of any possible ideality, any firm identity inadvertently taking shape in language (say, in a sign being iterated or a concept being defined), by means of reducing the meaning of words either to their everyday use in the style of Wittgenstein, or to the contextual web of differences in relation to other signs in the style of Derrida. No part of language could remain organized into the systematic coherence of Kant's table of categories or Hegel's dialectical logic.

In a nutshell, by dint of Hume's agnostic interventions, reality never recovered in a way to allow a return to the metaphysics of substances in the vein of

---

[3] I have written extensively on the subject in *The Untruth of Reality: The Unacknowledged Realism of Modern Philosophy* (Simoniti 2016), where I argue that the "antirealist" whim of European philosophy must be placed on a par with its quite wittingly pursued "realist" leeway.

Leibniz, where every entity is a mere expression of its complete individual concept. But, after Wittgenstein's language therapy and Derrida's deconstruction, the inside of the mind, the logical structure of language, and the semantics of words could also no longer fall back on the net of perennial meanings. On balance, do these detriments not amount to an utter relativity of truth, one culminating in the postmodern end of grand narratives? Rather than answer in the affirmative, it will be argued that on grounds of the above-mentioned double loss, i.e., as a consequence of both reality and human conceptuality no longer being entitled to any kind of metaphysical backing, the possibility of a new idealism might flicker. My aim is to search for new incentives of idealism in a hopelessly de-idealized world.

The case for a new idealism could be presented in three steps:
- First, the world as it is does not manifest any ideal order.
- Second, the mind does not accommodate any *a priori* conceptual structure.
- And yet, third, if "truth" can still be said to exist, then, as I hope to demonstrate, it is a truth emerging in the historical events of positing ideas.

The question now poses itself, why idealism at all. On what grounds are we so fixated on this term particularly? And what gives us the right to still endorse some sort of idealist impetus in this supposedly disillusioned post-metaphysical era? The answer will draw from the intuition that there exist "truth events" so momentous that their impact can be deemed universal. They seem to consist in producing some sort of surplus, a discursive creation surpassing the common horizon of expectations, which potentially makes them non-relative with regard to facts, irreversible within time, and transcendent in relation to the context of use. It may be the audacity to posit an *irreducible ideality* that bestows upon them the status of "truth".

What will hence be put forward is an entirely different take on idealism. The objective is neither an ontological idealism in the Spinozist sense of *ordo rerum* coinciding with *ordo idearum* nor an epistemological idealism of the Kantian sort, where the mind is equipped with a perpetual set of pure concepts. On the contrary, my focus will be on those instances in which historically occurring collapses of mythical, traditional, dogmatic worldviews with their stark symbolic discriminants trigger the production of ideal surpluses, in the wake of which words acquire their semantic determinacy, thus becoming concepts and ideas, in exact proportion to the world being released from their conceptual grip. Perhaps language only takes on a systematic form in the throes of reality forfeiting it. This strategy is, of course, also diametrically opposed to the antirealist strand of Western philosophy which culminated in the (ultimately postmodernist) "languaging" of reality via a dissolution of all possible idealities. My own method of the discursive reconstruction of an idea will precisely *not* be performed for the anti-idealist, Nietzschean purpose of perspectival relativization and critical repudiation, but rather with the hope to grasp a certain logical surplus within idealization, which elevates it into a time-transcending truth. The stance to be elaborated could be named "reactive", "historical", "emergent idealism", one which weaves its idealist impulse into a fabric hanging suspended between three focal points. First, historically speaking, the reluctance of reality to embody the symbolic values projected upon it and to uphold traditional conceptuality sometimes culminates in an explicit process of the de-symbolization of the world.[4] Second, the very concept which is no longer carried by the corporeal world is usually not abolished and eliminated, but undergoes idealization; it resurges as an idea, a pure discursive product with no representative among the given things. And third, as the resulting dispossessed, "homeless" concept looks for a new home, the subject[5] emerges and offers her substitute "inner space" as a refuge for the terms that have lost ground in reality.

One of the recurring illusions of philosophical reason is that in times of ideological crisis, the soul, the ego, or the self will find in itself vestiges of something true, irrefutable, and imperishable: an ideal fundament of everything, a Platonic idea, a divine soul, an eternal concept, a future ideal, or at least an existentially binding meaning.[6] It is, however, possible to get a glimpse behind the curtain of

---

[4] The term "de-symbolization" is still underdeveloped. Alexandre Koyré, Jacques Lacan, and Jacques-Alain Miller have used it when referring to the shift performed in Galilean science. It is somewhat more systematically approached in Jean-Claude Milner's *L'Oeuvre Claire* (*A Search for Clarity*, Milner 2021). Here, however, "de-symbolization" will be used in a more definite sense, designating the process in which a seminal social, philosophical, or scientific event suddenly relieves the world of its traditional symbolically discriminated order. Neoplatonism and then Christianity, for instance, tend to distinguish themselves against the dualisms of two principles, good and evil; another example is modern physics, where the universe surrenders its polarity of two worlds, the celestial and the terrestrial.

[5] The term "subject" is not used in the ancient meanings of *hypokeimenon*, *subiectum*, or even *substantia*, but in the modern sense, developed in the period between Descartes and Leibniz and defined in German idealism as a self-reflexive, cognizant self.

[6] The implicit, perhaps subconscious narrative of the advent of the "subject" in her most remarkable forms, reaching from the early, still implicit ventures in ancient Greece to her full manifestation in the modern age and her subsequent variations, is usually the following. In the midst of an imperfect, untrue, treacherous, declining outside world, the "subjective interior" distinguishes itself as a place of constancy, certitude, meaning, and truth. Thus, as the political culture of the *polis* was deteriorating, Plato proposed the doctrine of *anamnesis* as a recollection of pure Forms, intuited in our previous lives. Against the backdrop of the Medieval cosmos falling apart, Descartes proposed a recourse to one's own ego, who in its inner relation to God hopes to achieve the certainty of knowledge. In view of nihilism, decadence, the rule of the weak,

these "inner eternities" and "intimate inevitabilities". What philosophy has deemed to be most *a priori*, primary, everlastingly given, fateful, a bare factum of some transcendent necessity or inborn destiny, can perhaps be exposed as a product at its purest, and hence as a discursive artefact to be genealogically reconstructed. While the finite things of this world may be shifted to and fro, thereby assuming a temporally unspecific, spatially blurred existence, it is the infinities whose fabrication is essentially geographically and historically situated. The emergence of an idea can always be pinned down to a specific moment in space and time, and the proper name of its author clings to it forever. Parmenides' positing of Being, Plato's invention of Ideas, Augustine's design of the private self, and Descartes' proof of the ego are all singular, chronologically documented events, whose respective truths are never entirely detachable from the place of their creation. My aim is therefore to expose the very entities which seemingly elude worldly time as created at the very moment in which they started to appear perennial. And it is this *creation behind the mask of aeons* that is, in my opinion, the true cradle of a new idealism, one still to be argued for in the twenty-first century.

I will build my case predominantly on Augustine, the reason being that there is a dimension in his procedures of self-examination which permits a certain amount of discursive schematization. My interpretation will draw on one correlation in this Church Father's teaching in particular, which might provide us with a clue for a new theory of subjectivity. Augustine is often called the inventor of the "private inner space" of a contemplative, soliloquizing self. And, given that he is also one of the most passionate defenders of the Christian monism of good against the Gnostic and Manichean dualisms of good and evil, he can also be considered an advocate, or perhaps even the architect of an ontologically homonomous world. It is on the basis of this rarely highlighted parallel that I will try to define some of the incentives which make the celebrated Augustinian "inner man" contract into himself.

Nietzsche designed his subject as a projective entity who pivots on the ideal reference point of the impending birth of the overman. And confronting the facticity of the cosmically infinitesimal existence of man, Heidegger devised *Dasein* as capable of answering the question of the meaning of being in the private realization of her own mortality. It would appear that the conditions for the infamous Western "turn inward" are satisfied when the subject, faced with the world's ground and firmament crumbling, finds in herself a firm, quasi Archimedean point, which is legitimated in the timeless horizons of previous lives, innate ideas, immutable forms, or the regulative ideas of an unactualized future.

The Augustinian self is famously unfathomable, motley, destitute, an abyss within itself, a problem to itself.[7] It is a hazy inner landscape lacking a center. And it is precisely in this intimate opacity that a specific kind of idealist agency may gain an unexpected foothold. If there is no given core within the subject, then there might exist a place where the "corelessness" reveals itself as such. It is perhaps this very revelation which provides a substitute kernel to subjectivity, keeps its inner world together, and delineates it from the outside. My thesis, however, is that in order to grasp this budding nucleus, a transition from the order of the real to the order of the ideal must be performed. What we are, Augustine seems to be intimating at times, as we will see below on the example of pear-theft, is not what we find within ourselves, but rather the "ideality" we must assume and maintain on account of falling short of any distinct "reality" of our own. It is exactly at the spot where there is no homunculus to be seized inside, where we are rather *not* anything than something, that we might earn the right to fashion ourselves *as subjects*, that is, as logical functions transcending our psychosocial geneses.

My goal is thus to reconstruct the procedure in which the centerless nihility of the self nonetheless evolves a kind of secondary center. Only one layer of the "inner self" will be touched upon. From this limited and biased perspective, Augustine will be shown to have let his inner self assume a certain logical consistency around the kernel of "sin" as the earthly representative of evil. I will try to demonstrate how the self "crystalizes" in order to interiorize the element that was excluded from the monovalent universe, thereby constructing a platform for the nowhere-to-be-embodied evil in the world of utter good. This transfer of evil from the outside to the inside then constitutes not the religious, psychological, anthropological, or sociological, but rather the structural, perhaps "logical" core of the subject. I do not claim that evil is the genuine, exclusive substance of the Augustinian self, and that this is everything that can be said about the richness of its inner life. My wager is rather that evil as manifested in human sin elevates the otherwise heterogeneous and bottomless self into a subject with a more definite, dissectible, resolvable inner logical morphology.

This reading might, to an extent, represent a case of the generally spurned teleological thinking. While it may not exhaust and encompass the complexities of Augustine's composition of the self, it will establish the matrix of a certain

---

[7] As Porter cautions, "Augustine does not discover or invent the self, let alone a hermeneutics of the self. On the contrary, what he discovers first is that the self is the name for an abyssal problem with no end or solution ... Destitution and extroversion of the self, not veridiction, and certainly not discovery, let alone fashioning of the self by the self, are the key characteristics of the Christian self" (Porter 2017, pp. 131–132).

"logicity" of the subject, which could well shed new light upon other embodiments of modern subjectivity from Descartes onward. It is on the strength of Augustine's intuition to conceive of the self as originally evil in a world of good that I will attempt to construe the emergence of the Cartesian *ego*. Finally, I will also intimate some still faint and speculative analogies to the Kantian spontaneous, synthetic unity of apperception, Nietzsche's overman, Heidegger's *Dasein*, and the psychoanalytical subject of gender difference as specific reactions to the collapsing symbolic values of their respective worlds. In short, my variety of idealism will make the subject be seen as arising not in parallel with her own world, but in that very opposition to it which ultimately enables a realist revelation of a no longer symbolically structured reality.

1 The clandestine topology of subjectivity

A guileless, fresh reader of the first few books of Augustine's *Confessions* may be under the impression that she is not witnessing an already established person recounting his life-story, but rather a slow construction of the self. Before her very eyes, a certain misalignment between the real and the ideal, between the given world and the value of words, seems to be playing out, and it is this semantic disjointedness at the heart of Christianity which unfolds a logical space for the filling of which a new entity will have to be devised: something different from the outside world, an irreducibly "inner" space, a subject.

The notion of the "ego" is a modern invention.[8] Despite that, some pre-modern thinkers have articulated a sense of selfness, self-realization, self-retreat, and even a self-referentiality of consciousness. Among them, none was as original and influential as Augustine. His works bore the titles of *Confessiones* and *Soliloquia* long before Descartes' *Meditationes*, and in a similar although not identical manner, he even anticipated the Cartesian proof of one's existence, the *cogito sum*. The road to personal intimacy, however, was paved with unchaste means. The *Confessions* are sometimes deemed the first Western autobiography ever written, and the author himself explained the title as *confessio laudis et peccati*, a praise of God interlaced with a confession of one's sins. At least within the

---

[8] "In Ancient and Medieval *philosophy*, the concept of I hardly exists; it becomes evident only indirectly from the concepts of soul, body, introspection, consciousness" (Herring 1976, p. 1, translation mine).

scope of his life's recollection, Augustine thereby authorized the negative element of sin to provide a spark strong enough to ignite the inception of the self.[9]

Already the opening of the *Confessions* deploys an imaginative, somewhat dazzling topology, which, on the face of it, strives toward being occupied by something singular and novel. The book begins with a prayer to God, repeating the words of the psalms. The introductory lines, however, also face a peculiar problem, one of God possessing too great a magnitude for us to be able to approach him at all. If God is everything, and everything is God, if we are forever in God, and God is in us, from what vantage point can we then address our praise to him? How can we refer to him as something nevertheless *other:*

> But what place is there in me where my God can enter into me? 'God made heaven and earth' (Gen. 1: 1). Where may he come to me? Lord my God, is there any room in me which can contain you? (Augustine, *Confessions* I, ii, 2)[10]

God is everywhere, in heaven and on earth, and in this *horror pleni* of a too divine universe the penitent searches for the last gripping surface which would allow him to place himself in opposition to God at least to the slightest degree. The intricacy of the following lines suggests that Augustine is genuinely rummaging for a blind spot within Creation, an excluded element into which God's gaze does not reach, so that it is from there that he, the penitent, might direct his gaze toward him:

> How can I call on you to come if I am already in you? Or where can you come from so as to be in me? Can I move outside heaven and earth so that my God may come to me from there? (Augustine, *Confessions* I, ii, 2)

The soul is evidently at pains to wring from God a different relation, one that would transcend the mere inclusion of created things in their Creator. In a sense, it desires to stand face to face with God beyond creatural participation in him. The entire narrative momentum of the *Confessions* seems to hinge on this invention of an emergent sphere, in which God can only become "whole" from the point of view of something which is not of him. In order to see God

---

[9] This coalition between sinning and developing an intimacy with oneself is not entirely new and is probably ingrained in the very semantic constraints of human discourse, whose scope might well be cross-cultural. In ancient Egypt, for instance, the heart, according to Assmann, "symbolizes the 'inner self' of the deceased, that is, his memory or conscience where the sins he committed during his life-time are stored" (Assmann 1999, p. 238).

[10] Augustine's works are hereinafter cited by title, book, chapter and/or paragraph. The sources are listed in the bibliography.

"at a single glance", so to speak, a new space must be opened within the otherwise complete, full, impermeable Creation, and an entirely different rationale must be introduced: here, the *turn inward* will slowly take shape.

The expressive drive, the instinctual accuracy behind this wary but persistent composition of a protruding, scandalous element in the initial books of the *Confessions* indicates that by orbiting around oneself, a blind spot is being pinpointed whose literary sublimation is so forceful that it appears as if it serves as a counterweight to the entire universal expanse. Of course, since God is everything, that which is not of him can only come into being by stealthy means, that is, as something originally negative. Already in the first book, Augustine sets out on a meticulous search for the smallest possible wound in the otherwise unblemished universe. This is how he finds it:

> Alas for the sins of humanity! (Isa. 1: 4) Man it is who says this, and you have pity on him, because you made him and did not make sin in him. (Augustine, *Confessions* I, vii, 11)[11]

It is here, on the inglorious inside of man, that the outside of God is finally reached. One could almost speak of two creations in the Augustinian universe. The first is God's conception of the world out of nothing, the second is man's concoction of an "auxiliary nothing" in the midst of the already created being. The price to pay for the human "logical spontaneity" is nevertheless considerable: man can only leap to his feet as a specific counterpoise to the cosmic tilt as long as he is not something initially good, but rather evil, bad.

What my interpretation of Augustine will ultimately amount to is the thesis that the reasons for the "original demonization" of the human being far outstrip the remit of individual salvation. For the time being, my argument rests on metaphorical evidence, on the feeling one gets reading the *Confessions*, where, in the second book, the discursive configuration of sin becomes so histrionic and implicitly rigorous, even formal, that it gives the impression of painstakingly trying to capture nothing less than a new, secondary *causa sui*, the absolute spontane-

---

[11] That Augustine is on the track of an entirely new topology of the "emergent inside" can be seen a few pages earlier, where he recounts his years as a baby. Although he could not have had any recollection of that period, he already portrays himself as an entity primordially separated from God, reduced to a pure form of sinning, a sort of monster of irreducible, impermeable inwardness: "Gradually I became aware of my surroundings, and wished to express my demands to those who could comply with them; but I could not, since the demands were inside me, and outside were their fulfillers, who had no faculty for entering my mind. ... Then, when I was frustrated—because I was not understood or was demanding something harmful—I threw a tantrum because adults did not obey a child, free people were not my slaves" (Augustine, *Confessions* I, vi, 8).

ity of something which will, at least "logically", rival and match God himself.¹² I refer, of course, to one of the dramatic climaxes of Augustine's autobiography, the depiction of his most notorious sin, the youthful stealing from the neighbor's pear tree.

This legendary scene reveals that there is much more at stake here than just private confessional concerns. Somewhat hyperbolically, Augustine starts to tie together a vast knot of tautologies, reflexivity, and endless repetition around a misdemeanor which in itself comes across as rather prosaic. He is quite adamant in emphasizing over and over again that he did not do it out of need or hunger, that the neighbor's pears did not look or taste good, and that he had enough of his own: "My desire was to enjoy not what I sought by stealing but merely the excitement of thieving and the doing of what was wrong" (Augustine, *Confessions* II, iv, 9). For if it is to serve as the *second fundament of the world*, it is crucial that the sin, just like God once, has nothing outside itself to provide it with a reason:

> Now let my heart tell you what it was seeking there in that I became evil for no reason. I had no motive for my wickedness except wickedness itself. It was foul, and I loved it. I loved the self-destruction, I loved my fall, not the object for which I had fallen but my fall itself. ... I was seeking not to gain anything by shameful means, but shame for its own sake. (Augustine, *Confessions* II, iv, 9)

Perhaps only this obsessive circumlocution around an almost void, trifling core, this wickedness seeking wickedness, this shame for the sake of shame, can yield enough energy to spark off some sort of surplus, a thing not to be included among worldly paraphernalia, making it an element that is ultimately unearthly. But what is the magical object that the young Augustine covets?

To the painful reminiscence of his youthful sin, an essential ingredient is finally added. Augustine is vexed by the question of why he had been tempted into this petty theft in the company of other boys. How come that peer pressure

---

12 It may seem that I have blown the role of sin, and the evil inside it, out of proportion, elevating it into a principle with an almost cosmic scope. However, Augustine himself always regarded sinning as a dimension of locking horns with God, thereby indicating the introduction of an additional factor, of something underivable, the spectral status of which perhaps plays a constitutive role in the entire ontological fabric. This is how he addresses God: "In their perverted way all humanity imitates you. Yet they put themselves at a distance from you and exalt themselves against you. But even by thus imitating you they acknowledge that you are the creator of all nature and so concede that there is no place where one can entirely escape from you" (Augustine, *Confessions* II, vi, 14). The hubris of being equal to God is the hallmark of sin already in the Bible, as the snake speaks to Eve, "and you shall be as Gods, knowing good and evil" (*Gen.* 3, 5).

was the decisive stimulus of the pointless act? The narrator finds himself trapped in an unusual compulsion to repeat one and the same excuse multiple pages long, declaring that he would not have done it on his own, that others made him do it. Note the duplication: "But alone I would not have done it, could not conceivably have done it by myself" (Augustine, *Confessions* II, ix, 17). It goes on and on in this vein, and this not original but nonetheless "inaugural" sin remains the great, inextricable puzzle of his life: "Who can untie this extremely twisted and tangled knot? It is a foul affair, I have no wish to give attention to it" (Augustine, *Confessions* II, x, 18). What is it, then, that Augustine discovers at this juncture, which consumes and repels him at the same time? Why does this self-reflexive creation of the "auxiliary nothing", as I have named it, require the presence of others, their gaze upon oneself?

One answer in particular seems to impose itself. What Augustine carries out here might be a furtive shift of the motive for stealing the pears *from the register of the real to the register of the ideal*. It lies in the nature of sin that its reason only exists in the relish of the act of sinning, for any outside impulse would reduce it to a creatural good, to the causes of the given world, thereby rendering it at least partially innocent. As baffling as it sounds, this is why the internal spontaneity of a sinful act must be performed for the external gaze. For only the intersubjective space of predicative attributions can establish the medium of the pure ideality of evil, detached from any of its real embodiments. The eyes of others, those participating in the act of sheer wantonness, ensure that the object the sinner grabs hold of in his vice is not a created thing, but something both more ephemeral and more definite: it is not this or that piece of fruit, but wickedness in the interest of wickedness, and hence a sort of emergent membrane, a thing beyond. It might be ideality itself. In the insipid guise of a pear, it could be argued, something immaterial, centering around the sublime *meaning* of evil, is endeavored to be grasped. This would imply that the entire episode has to do with words instead of things. But how come that words become objects of their own?

One might wonder: Why did Augustine place this minor incident at the strategic point of "initiation" into self-awareness? The narrative exigency with which the artificial, somewhat extorted space of evil is set up suggests that this self-sown sin, this sin for sin's sake, which represents a negative limit within an altogether positive universe, simultaneously serves to perform another task. What my interpretation will try to draw attention to is the fact that the new "logical space", which hollows out a loophole within God's jurisdiction, is as much in the interest of the penitent soul as it is in favor of God.[13] It is not only a case

---

13 Even the confession is devised as if triggered by God: "Augustine begins his confessions with

of the believer seeking his personal ascension to heaven, but also of God looking down for a firm ground on the earth to place his feet upon and finally finding it in the private, inner space of sin. The penitent, whose specific constitution allows him to be both inside and outside God, both created by him and by himself, will be interpreted as "ontologically" comprised within God but "logically" nevertheless his equal, his eccentric counterweight.[14] The almost epic momentum with which this sin is narrated indicates that its true purpose is to conceal and mend a certain deficiency of God's own, a deficiency which does not bear on the world as it is, but on how it is skewed with regard to the meaning of words. Would it not be better to define the sinner's function as inherently "idealist"? Could it be that what is at issue here is nothing less than the salvation of the word "evil", which has lost its right of domicile in a world of an exclusively good God? Not to mince words, Augustine's draft of the "inner self" will be reinterpreted as a playground for the "idealist" redefinition of good and evil, a stratagem to help a new cosmic arrangement get on its feet.

2 Sin as the neutralization of cosmic evil

Within the order of the real, the subject has the air of being an entirely spontaneous, groundless, gratuitous figure; almost a miracle. To Augustine, the self was an insurmountable enigma. It might, however, be worthwhile to look at

---

a prayer in which the movement of the human questions and the search for God is interpreted as if it is a movement ensuing from God himself" (Bernhart 2007, p. 427, translation mine).

14 That an "idealist impulse" is instilled here into Augustine's theory of the self is a matter of a discursive decision. It must be kept in mind that the said parity between man and God is exclusively "logical", that is, pertaining to the semantic symmetries that assign the parts in this cosmic drama, and does not mirror the explicit "ontological" arrangement. The logical equipoise rather represents the suppressed reverse side of the ontological disproportion. James I. Porter, for instance, upon reading this text, proposed an alternative, albeit not necessarily conflicting outlook: "The ontological being of the Augustinian subject is not fully what it (sinfully) desires to be—it is not so much an 'auxiliary nothing' as an '*almost* something', and it is in the 'almost' that its genuine sinfulness lies: it is *condemned to existence!* Evil (and fear of evil) gives it the cover it needs so that it can exist and persist, i.e., go on existing. Put differently, *its very existence is the cosmic disturbance itself.* To do so, to lay claim to a self, the subject has to make the assumption of a freedom and voluntarism for itself that is both deficient (constitutively doomed to incompleteness) and illegitimate—in other words, its presumption is not godlike, unless we allow that God's powers are as imperfect as the human self (self-creation is here the sign of an imperfect creation, not of sovereignty, autonomy, and power). This condemnation to the imperfect is the Augustinian subject's truth, and it is still our truth after Kant" (Porter, personal communication).

the subject's outlandish position from a different perspective, one which will hopefully allow for a more exact analytical deciphering. My undertaking regards the very gist of subjective self-recourse as an effect of the order of the ideal, hence, an entity arising when a gap opens up in the symmetries of meaning and longs to be filled. This reading will admittedly not span over the entire breadth of Augustine's introversion. It will rather strive to detect a specific stratum within the self where its vast and vague terrain exhibits a certain minimum of logically replicable operations. To this purpose, the emergence of subjectivity will be placed in the context of the tilted universe of early Christianity, which needed to be leveled by having the new source of evil put in the balance. Let us therefore first examine the historical transformations of the semantics of "sin" and "evil".

The meaning the word "sin" has today originated foremost in early Christian philosophy. In both the Greek translations of the Old Testament and, even more so, in the New Testament, by far the most commonly used word for "sin" is ἁμαρτία, followed by ἀδικία, ἀνομία, and ἀσέβεια. In the classical Greek, ἁμαρτία covered the whole range of meanings reaching from flaw, error, and missing the mark to the transgression of social or godly laws,[15] but in the Bible it underwent a semantic shift toward a personal, individual infraction. "Sin" is in fact one of the concepts used to distinguish the biblical from the non-biblical cosmogonies and theogonies of the time. In Greek philosophy, ἁμαρτία, error, ἀδικία, injustice, ἀνομία, lawlessness, and ἀσέβεια, ungodliness, usually refer to some cosmic disorder, while in the Christian setting the emphasis is placed on a specifically human disturbance of the divine order of things. Similarly, in Persian, Zoroastrian traditions, curses, maladies, and bad things in general were all based on a distinct autonomous principle, whereas already in the Old Testament the theory of evil is pronouncedly anti-dualist, and everything that is bad in the world, such as sufferance, birth pangs, or hard work, is considered to be the effect of human sins alone.[16] "'Malum' is not a sign of a substantial deficit, but rather of a violated personal relation" (Arndt 1980, p. 666, translation mine). Accordingly, "sin" draws its meaning from man's estrangement from God, and especially so in the New Testament, where, in its personification of the path of guilt, penitence, and God's mercy, it begins to signify an iniquity of man directed against

---

15 See Wrzecionko 1998, pp. 598–600.
16 According to Arndt, evil or bad (*Übel*, in Greek κακόν, πονηρόν) in the Old Testament is experienced as a "punishing answer of Yahweh to the primarily in idolatry performed departure of the people of Israel from the federal statues", while in the New Testament the "existence of 'malum' signalizes the separation from God by the sinners and the resulting wrath of God" (Arndt 1980, pp. 665–666, translation mine).

God as a person. In the Epistle to the Romans, for example, Paul uses ἁμαρτία mostly in the singular, thereby invoking an almost intimate power, which acts within and through man. To simplify these manifold linguistic displacements, one could be tempted to say that a certain "humanization" of a once predominantly cosmic category took place. But what might be the grounds for this semantic change?

Why did a stock of meanings once pertaining to the universal (dis-)order drift toward the intimate sin? The reasons for this development probably lie in the comprehensive metaphysical rearrangement that can be traced back to Greek philosophy. Arguably under the influence of the monist tendencies of the pre-Socratics and Parmenides, Plato superimposed the idea of the Good over other ideas, a move which not only elevated a practically-moral Socratic notion into an ontological cause, but also involved a certain symbolic homogenization of the Greek universe, notoriously fraught with a plethora of mythical forces inhabiting and acting in and through things. This slant of the world toward one valence alone had a major impact on the subsequent development of thought and provoked opposite reactions. Neoplatonists took up the implicitly monist predilection of Platonism and derived from it an entire ontology of the One, or the Good, and its emanations; even the lowest level, the material world, was thus comprised within God. But the religious teaching of Gnosticism, to an extent still displaying a link to Neoplatonism, opted for a moderately dualist resolution of the tension between the good and the bad share in the balance of things. A second principle was introduced, the Demiurge, who emerged spontaneously from his "fall" from God and created the material world of darkness and evil. The Gnostic dualist ontology was then radicalized in Manichaeism, where evil is equipollent with good, and hence a sovereign, separate operator incarnating in the material world. These two cosmogonic dualisms could not be reconciled with early Christianity, which, slowly differentiating itself from Gnosticism and only later denouncing it as heresy, regarded even the human body and the material substance as created by God and thus intrinsically good.[17] The Christian doctrine therefore, philosophically speaking, rather adopted the Platonist penchant for good and derived from it its own "bonification" of the world.

What is interesting is the field of antagonisms in which the Christian turn to the good embedded itself. It is as if this nascent religion needed a starkly dualist adversary outside itself so as to be able to elaborate its ontologically monist ac-

---

[17] Already the Book of Genesis shows God conceiving heaven and earth, the land and the seas, animals and plants, while every step of the way is accompanied by an exclamation, almost an incantation: "And God saw that it was good."

count of good and evil.[18] No act of monism, however, remains limited to one range of values alone, one conceptual binary, but involves many others with which it is semantically interwoven. As soon as one pair of opposites is unbalanced, the stability of the other pairs of notions is also threatened. The premise of an entirely good world thus also unsettles the cosmic symmetries of mind and matter, soul and body, day and night, heaven and earth, justice and injustice, or the Gnostic contraries of light and darkness, spirit and flesh. With this semantic tilt, the universe of meaning curves and unfolds a void within itself, which can only be filled with a supplementary creation. In the case of Christianity, it is not that difficult to notice a yawning gap at its heart, once occupied by "evil" mythical substances. The negative semantic space gaping within the poise of meanings is best exemplified by the somewhat ironic fact that precisely in this world of such exclusive and omnipresent goodness, the most critical issue, the question never to be silenced, becomes *unde malum*, whence evil. And it is this disparity, undoubtedly pressing for a re-equilibration of good and evil, which will then possibly prompt the formation of a new core, whose function will be to once again anchor and stabilize the shifting semantic values. In Christianity, the human being will have to enter the scene and assume a historically unprecedented role of being the origin of bad things:

> Already the apologists among the Greek Church Fathers (Melito of Sardis, Tatian, Theophilus of Antioch) emphasized that God, although he is the only origin of all things, is not the author of bad [*Übel*]; rather, man, abusing his originally good freedom, has with his moral evil [*Böse*] also caused the natural bad [*Übel*]. (Riesenhuber 1980, pp. 669–670, translation mine)

Other bishops, Church Fathers, and theologians, such as Clement of Alexandria, Origen, Gregory of Nyssa, Dionysius the Areopagite, or Tertullian, argued in the same style. In *The Legitimacy of the Modern Age*, Blumenberg mentions that the problem of the origin of evil was left unresolved in antiquity, leaving Christian philosophy from Augustine all the way to High Scholasticism to grapple with it. Needless to say, "the traditional means of solving it [were] cut off" (Blumenberg 1983, p. 132). Since the world in its entirety was created by the good God,

---

18 I am hinting at Augustine's clash with the Manicheans, which forms one of the dramatic arcs of his biography and resulted in a number of anti-Manichean writings. In the fourth and fifth centuries, the Manicheans were a fashionable and widespread religious branch in North Africa. Augustine was himself a Manichean in his early years and became Christian only at the age of 32, after having met Bishop Ambrose of Milan. What is more, it seems that had it not been for the opposition to this radical dualism, Augustine could never have defined "sin" and "evil" as pointedly, stringently, and conclusively as he did.

evil can no longer rely on its "natural" buttress, its many pagan deities, spirits, demons, or even its distinct principle, its Gnostic Demiurge, as it were. This is how Blumenberg sets the stage for the appearance of an exotic, unheard-of figure, who will be capable of taking the once cosmic detriment upon her shoulders:

> The answer that Augustine gave to this question [whence evil?] was to have the most important consequences of all the decisions that he made for the Middle Ages. With a gesture just as stirring as it was fateful, he took for man and upon man the responsibility for the burden oppressing the world. Now, in the aftermath of Gnosticism, the problem of the justification of God has become overwhelming, and that justification is accomplished at the expense of man, to whom a new concept of freedom is ascribed expressly in order to let the whole of an enormous responsibility and guilt be imputed to it. (Blumenberg 1983, p. 133)

Here, Blumenberg offers a half-baked version of the very correlation so painstakingly written out above. It concerns the new balance between rendering the world uniform under the sign of the good and the auxiliary hypothesis of human guilt for all that is bad in it. In this way, the scope of sin, once a merely personal deviation, is, to a degree, ontologically exalted. Its role seems to be to explain, compensate for, and thereby defuse the incidence of evil in worldly phenomena. Perhaps, by interiorizing the sources of evil, the sinner even begins to stand for its cosmic inexistence.[19]

Of course, the tidiest, most mature, even schematic readjustment between the cosmological ostracism of evil and its human repatriation was then delivered by Augustine. In the Neoplatonist manner, his ontological framework first assumes the conceptual constraint of assimilating the Creation into one value alone, the value of good.[20] In the short treatise *De natura boni (contra Manichaeos)*, good is identified with God, and then all things are derived from him:

---

[19] Blumenberg himself shifts the emphasis from the private moral concerns of a believer to the logical necessity of a certain cosmic operation. Mentioning Augustine's *De libero arbitrio*, he notes: "But the thematic question of his treatise is not the freedom of the will as an anthropological and moral quality but rather as the condition under which it was possible for the just God to punish man, on account of his failings, with the bad things in the world" (Blumenberg 1983, p. 133). And more poignantly: "Can man bear the burden of being responsible for the cosmos, that is, for seeing to it that God's design for His work does not miscarry?" (Blumenberg 1983, p. 134)

[20] Even matter, representing the lowest stratum of being, is only evil by way of the intermediary of human beings directing their attention to it rather than to the intelligible world.

> Every natural being, so far as it is such, is good. ... All are not supremely good, but they approximate to the supreme good. (Augustine, *The Nature of the Good*, i)

To be is to be good by tautology; if a being were not good, it would not be a being at all. The question now arises, what place can evil assume in this world? Augustine replies:

> If we ask whence comes evil, we should first ask what evil is. It is nothing but the corruption of natural measure, form or order. ... But even when it is corrupted, so far as it remains a natural thing, it is good. (Augustine, *The Nature of the Good*, iv)

The word "*malum*" denotes no discrete entity, but only a deficiency of something that is good simply because it is. Since Irenaeus, evil is a remnant of God's creation of the world from nothing. And it is on this ground that Augustine proposes his celebrated privation thesis: *malum est privatio boni*, evil is the absence/privation of good.[21] Following in the footsteps of the Neoplatonists on the one hand and opposing the Manicheans on the other, Augustine set out to abolish the mythical polarities of good and evil and to release the world into a state characterized by gradual "scales of good", thus warding off evil into a state of shadowy, privational subsistence. What raises him above both his Platonist and his Christian predecessors, however, and where his originality lies, is perhaps his almost artistic incapability of reconciling himself with the logically weak solution, which derives bad things from nothing, so he rather offset this tame and bland nothingness of evil by introducing the undreamt-of inner wealth of the introspective, confessional self as irreducible to anything created by God.

For even though the solution of undercutting the ontological independence of *malum* gives a neat systemic impression, something seems to be missing. One would expect for the privational neutralization of evil to be an act of universal appeasement, but what keeps knocking at the back door is the Christian preoccupation with sinning in general and Augustine's exposition of the opaque inside of man in particular. What we seem to be dealing with here is a massive repression and a vigorous reaction. Cosmologically, evil is debased into a mere privation, but "mythologically", as if in response, Christianity elevates sin as its fleeting representative into an object of unparalleled fascination.

My hypothesis is, of course, that in this filling of the still dispassionate space of privation with a richer, more colorful and definite negation, the original impulse of subjectivity looms.

---

[21] For instance in *Enchiridion*: "What, after all, is anything we call evil except the privation of good?" (Augustine, *Enchiridion*, iii, 11)

3 The immunity of semantic symmetries to ontological asymmetries

From this point on, I will start to recount the argument on my own terms, albeit at the risk of leaving the safe haven of Augustinian scholarship. What follows is an exercise in linguistic analysis, circumstantial reasoning, and a logical idealization of the conceptual moves that certainly imbue and uphold Augustine's opus but often remain implicit.

Going back to the drawing board of discursive logic, my reconstruction of Augustine's invention of the inner self will be based on differentiating three levels of good and evil. First, *ontologically*, there exist approximations to the first Good, with evil being merely a mark (perhaps a quantitative measure) of its privation. Second, *semantically*, there is an irresolvable parity of good and evil, i.e., a persistence of the meaning of "evil", necessary for the word "good" to mean anything at all. Third, *existentially*, the subject will be shown to take upon herself the drama of good and evil, thereby incorporating the inertia of symbolic binaries within the world becoming ontologically homonomous.

As previously mentioned, the Christian world is one of a certain axiomatic goodness. But the situation has its pitfalls. With Augustine's "privation thesis", both concepts, good as well as evil, forfeit some ground beneath their feet. When compared with the more immanently structured pagan or the more proportionate Gnostic or Manichaean cosmos, a further dissociation between the symbolic values and their real embodiments ensues. Good now encompasses the world itself, the Creation, the entirety of being. Yet, as a measure of all things, it can hardly be experienced fully in the here and now. It rather keeps infinitely withdrawing into an untouchable, unattainable Platonic idea of the *summum bonum*, while the things of Creation are tainted with the lack of good.[22] Evil, by contrast, is an ontological impossibility, but since it is defined as a privation of good, every concrete entity already bears witness to its indissoluble specter. Simply put, good is so total that it is nowhere to be grasped, and evil is so null that it pervades everything that is. Sometimes it seems that the entire Christian universe wavers in this discrepancy between the transcendental prohibition of evil and its empirical om-

---

[22] It is telling that in order to perceive the highest Good behind creatural things, their immediate givenness, their "thisness", must first be put in brackets: "This good and that good; take away this and that, and see good itself if you can; so you will see God who is good not by another good, but is the good of every good" (Augustine, *On the Trinity*, VIII, iii, 4).

nipresence.²³ To overstate the case, a world committed to being good *a priori* is doomed to become a vale of tears *a posteriori*.

We can easily imagine that with the advent of Christianity, the world remained just as good and as bad as it ever was, with the sole difference that the concepts of "evil" and "good" became increasingly less inclined to lend their names to earthly phenomena, thereby withholding from them the seal of a definite symbolic value. Thus, on the one hand, the semantic shift induces a disclosure of reality defying any candid symbolic discrimination into good and evil, while on the other hand, these two central metaphysical concepts suddenly lose their foothold and float in the air, craving a new ground.²⁴ In this hiatus, a vacuum opens up, possibly demanding a surrogate for the autonomous principle of the Manicheans and the Gnostics. Now, something "conceptually" strong enough must be introduced to take upon itself the defects of God's Creation, enshrine in itself the taboo of evil, and supply the framework in which good and evil can be stabilized.

My thesis is thus that a certain recondensation of meaning takes place in the transition from the ontologically marginalized, semantically homeless *privation-evil* to the subjectively repatriated *sinning-evil*; the first perhaps solicits and compels the second. It is the logical weakness of cosmic privation which makes room for the logical strength of subjective negation. Quite suggestively, even concerning the question of the existence of "natural evil", Augustine cannot but underhandedly shift responsibility to the self-reflexive circuits of the human being, as he lets slip in this logically revealing paragraph:

> If our fear is vain, it is certain that fear itself is evil, and that the heart is groundlessly disturbed and tortured. And this evil is the worse for the fact that it has no being to be afraid of. Yet we still fear. Thus either it is evil which we fear or our fear which is evil. (Augustine, *Confessions*, VII, v, 7)

---

23 This incongruity is often felt in Augustine. It is as if he cannot refrain from lingering at the delicate threshold where he does not allow himself to think about evil, yet is constantly haunted by it: "Then where and whence is evil? How did it creep in? ... Or does it not have any being? Why should we fear and avoid what has no being?" (Augustine, *Confessions*, VII, v, 7)

24 More figuratively speaking, the cosmos perhaps no longer provides a stage for the profuse Manichean and Gnostic dualist dramas between the World of Light and the Kingdom of Darkness, the spiritual God and the physical Demiurge. Given his love of theater, to which he pleaded guilty in the third book of the *Confessions*, Augustine surely missed the aesthetic superiority of Manichean writings after his conversion, much like he at first regretted giving up the refinement of Ciceronian prose for the crude language of the scripture.

Here it appears as if someone is not quite willing to accept the equation of evil and non-being, so he desperately circumscribes another linchpin for the concept, which is seemingly too vital to be propped up by mere nothingness. Almost unaware of what he is doing, he reverses the causation and makes it self-referential: there is no evil to fear except our fear, which produces evil. This means that the privational evil may be too smooth and inconsistent to be able to carry the ineradicable "voltage" stored in the opposite meanings of good and evil, so the new basis for the binary is now provided by human deficiencies, whose evil is, by contrast, a bit more negative and can thus put on a more or less positive face: that, for instance, of pear-theft. Thus, following the tenets of early Christianity, Augustine tends to reinterpret all the ache in the world as a specifically human suffering and locate its cause in human sin. An unevenness is thereby instituted in which natural evil is still mentioned in passing,[25] though it is mostly glossed over, while the human sin becomes the barycenter of fetishistic circumvolutions, restraints, denials, and literary exaltations. It is this stark inclination within a certain mental frame which allows us to speculate that Augustine is actually building a substitute shelter for the cosmic non-entity of evil, perhaps with a view to bestowing a new definitional closure to the concepts of good and evil.

In this regard, *De libero arbitrio* provides a beautiful rendering of the contraction of the inner space, which in the midst of a world of utter good things encircles the reason of evil and locks it away into a closed area of relative immunity to God. Augustine seems to be well aware of the logical constraints within which he is working. On the one hand, living in an imperfect world, man is haunted by the question of where bad things come from; on the other hand, his hands are tied by the stipulation that evil can never enter the world from the outside.[26] Thus, a new space must be instituted, and consequently an emergent "inside" contracts into itself around the element of sin, whose "moral" scandal is evidently pungent enough to be able to claim an excluded, spontaneous ontological status by comparison with the created world. On that account, Augustine still defines "sin" out of privation, but he imparts to it contours of greater concretion: he describes it as *defectus*, a defect originating from nothingness itself, *perversitas*, a perversion of a will that has *detortae*, turned away, as

---

[25] As in the seventh book of the *Confessions:* "But in the parts of the universe, there are certain elements which are thought evil because of a conflict of interest" (Augustine, *Confessions*, VII, xiii, 19).

[26] "For you [God] evil does not exist at all, and not only for you but for your created universe, because there is nothing outside it which could break in and destroy the order which you have imposed upon it" (Augustine, *Confessions*, VII, xiii, 19).

aversio a deo, the renunciation of God, and *conversio ad creaturam*, conversion to the creatural. From the leverage point of mere privation, an effectively "positive" space burgeons, the space of self:

> Thus it turns out that the good things desired by sinners are not in any way evil, and neither is free will itself, which we established should be numbered among the intermediate goods. Instead, evil is turning the will away from the unchangeable good and towards changeable goods. (Augustine, *On the Free Choice of the Will*, II, xix, 53)

Both the will and the things willed cannot but be good; evil is merely the transient moment of turning away from the highest to the creatural good, that is all. Then, skipping one sentence, this splendid passage continues:

> If this movement, namely turning the will away from the Lord God, is undoubtedly a sin, then surely can we not say that God is the author of sin? Therefore, this movement will not be from God. Then where does it come from?
>
> If I were to reply to your question that I do not know, perhaps you will then be the sadder, but I will at least have replied truthfully. What is nothing cannot be known. (Augustine, *On the Free Choice of the Will*, II, xx, 54)

We have apparently reached a blind spot, a "dead angle", upon which Augustine himself is reluctant to cast any light. It may be modestly surmised that these lines, hollowing out nooks and crannies in the otherwise gapless divine order of being, represent some of the most compelling early glimmers of subjectivity in Western thought.[27] The metaphors of lapsing, defecting, concealing, turning away, and turning to oneself serve to fixate a vanishing point on the sleek surface of a metaphysically monovalent and physically homogenous space. What is perhaps most modern about this endeavor is the design of a fundamentally

---

[27] In order to provide refuge to an impossible element, the subject must become furtive, allotting to her inner space a new kind of complexity; she is required to develop her own temporality, irreducible to the course of the outer world. This is why Augustine supplies the soul with the historical dimension of its previous sins and the sin of Adam. The only place within Creation lying outside divine jurisdiction seems to be the *temporal warp* of a personal history within the spatial relations of the created world. Rowan Williams points out that the source of evil cannot be treated "in a spatialized way": "if, in short, the relation between God and the mind is rightly spoken of in terms of time, rather than space, evil, as that which interrupts the relation of creator and creature, belongs in the same frame of reference. Its origins are to be sought in the interactions of the world history, not in a classification of substances within a single territory, a single medium of extension" (Williams 2000, p. 110). Perhaps it is only now that the inner life of man acquires the depth usually associated with the Western idea of subjectivity, that is, the implicit or explicit autobiographies in Descartes, Kierkegaard, Nietzsche.

negative self, who crops up from the obscure and ungodly movements of human resistance against God, from evil, defect, sin, and unhappiness.[28]

Augustine's entire universe thus barely keeps on its feet on the precipice of man standing face to face with God.[29] It is what distinguishes it from its Platonist predecessors, on whose ontology Augustine drew the most.[30] But what is the point of these almost compulsive struggles to outline the limits of a new topology of inwardness? As we have seen, the universally good world lives in a sort of ontological asymmetry, which nevertheless longs for a counterweight. There are parities of words that no cosmic rearrangement can permanently unbalance. The Christian worldview might have banned evil from the order of being, a move which made "good" and "evil" less comfortable in referring to given things, but it could never permanently withdraw "evil" from the order of words, from the vocabulary—if it had done so, "good" itself would have re-

---

28 The private inner space is originally negative; in Phillip Cary's words, "Augustine is different from most of his successors in the West in that for him this privacy is not natural or good but results from our estrangement from one eternal Truth and Wisdom that is common to all. The inner self is private only because it is sinful, fallen away from God" (Cary 2000, p. 5).

29 Occasionally, Augustine shows signs of trying to protect the soul from this self-referential primacy of evil. When he places love as an entirely positive relation to God into the *pondus* of the soul, its "weight", it is perhaps to protect it from the binary logic of good and evil. Nonetheless, even if the love of God is the highest of our feelings and sits deepest in our soul, it provokes, by the very nature of its willing, the possibility of self-willing and threatens to be corrupted into self-love as *perversa imitatio Dei*, a perverse imitation of God. Every impulse of subjectivity, however noble, Augustine seems to be conveying, already entails its own distortion. In *Civitate Dei*, the first sin, the fall of Adam and Eve, is derived from the ultimately "logical" bond between evil and the independence of the self, its spontaneity: *In occulto autem mali esse coeperunt*, "It was in secret that Adam and Eve began to be evil" (Augustine, *City of God*, XIV, 13). When Augustine is hailed as the true inventor of the inner self, it must be kept in mind that he regards subjective self-recourse quite unequivocally as evil at its most basic. Evil, in a way, is nothing but the pure form of man thinking about himself and thereby becoming a *causa sui:* "For it is a perverse kind of elevation indeed to forsake the foundation upon which the mind should rest, and to become and remain, as it were, one's own foundation" (Augustine, *City of God*, XIV, 13). "The first evil came, then, when man began to be pleased with himself, as if he were his own light" (Augustine, *City of God*, XIV, 13). It is therefore not some primal evil substance which makes man willful and obstinate; on the contrary, it is man's freedom which, by dint of willing itself, produces evil. Accordingly, freedom is the one to define evil and not vice versa.

30 The mark of Augustine's self-consciousness is to say, "I do not know myself" (Augustine, *Soliloquies*, I, iii, 8). As opposed to Plotinus, for instance, the soul is not a place of light, converging with God, but of opacity, and compared to Descartes, its self-reflexive recourse is not a point of clarity.

nounced its meaning.[31] One should expect that in the anti-Gnostic indiscrimination of the dualisms of good and evil, the need for the word "evil" would vanish, but in an uncanny return of the repressed, it has become one of the most obsessively recurring motives of Christianity. To put it pointedly, *unde malum* is the *idée fixe* of a world which has finally become altogether good. Something is at work in this quagmire, something that might be called the *immunity of semantic symmetries to ontological asymmetries*. In very plain terms, there is an inevitable, "primitive" advantage of good over evil, and so much so that good develops a tendency to occupy the world; its normative excess value spills over to being itself, so that it was not only Plato who derived other ideas from the idea of Good, but even the Gnostics strived toward the final victory of light over darkness. Still, the "ontological supremacy" of good in no way diminishes but rather makes explicit its "semantic dependency" on evil. No matter how well-made the world is, as a concept, "good" can only continue to have any content if, at least by way of definition, it stands against some kind of "evil". Due to the law of constancy of semantic equilibria, evil therefore becomes a sort of anti-matter, yearning to be accommodated in a realm where it can still symmetrically oppose its meaning to good. In Christianity, things outside man are only good and, as created from nothing, less good; in opposition to the pre-Christian cosmos of each thing bearing a symbolic value, the world started to exhibit its shortcomings with more ease. This description of the famous pears might strike us as quite non-pagan: "There was a pear tree near our vineyard laden with fruit, though attractive in neither color nor taste. ... But they were not for our feasts but merely to throw to the pigs" (Augustine, *Confessions*, II, iv, 9). Thus, hopes are placed on the inside of the soul to provide a stage for the spectacle of a distinct evil facing the equally patent good. The ultimate ground of *malum* is consequently shifted onto the human "sin without any reason".

From this point of view, the subject, being constructed around a kernel with no place in the cosmic exteriority, may well lack any sufficient reason for her contraction into herself in the order of the real. "What is nothing cannot be known", Augustine himself concedes, deeming the subject to be an arcane effect of the turn away from God, without any cause or purpose whatsoever. But precisely with this pathos of ignorance, he invites us to step behind his back. If the subject had reasons for her actions, she would be a mere human animal, an empirical being, a creature. But it is because her reason is not known that

---

31 This might touch upon God's own impotence. He created a world out of nothingness, and he may well be able to reduce it back to nothingness; as it would seem, however, it lies outside his power to erase a word from the balances of meanings.

she is a subject! I claim, accordingly, that the motive for her "turn inward" should instead be sought in the semantic order, in the order of the ideal. Since the good world can no longer cede any ground to the idea of "evil", which, however, keeps hovering vagrantly above, the truly effective impulse for the emergence of the subject might not lie in the *thing* of sin but in the *word* of evil, whose meaning will be backed up only secondarily by the worldly fact of sin.[32] This is what the pear incident might have betrayed; what tempted the boys were not the pieces of fruit but the incarnation of pure ideality in them, hence, the bare enjoyment of evil for the very reason that this evil is not allowed to be embodied in reality. In sum, the inertia of ideal meaning over real being, the semantic equivalence of evil beyond the ontological prevalence of good, is what, in my interpretation, actually provides a "logical" impulse for the turn inward, thereby providing the subject with a core and perhaps even bringing forth the introverted, ruminative self in the first place.

To repeat, this only shows that one can hardly purloin a word from the balances of meanings without triggering its even sharper redefinition in another sphere. The word "evil" is not finally disposed of, and the word "good" does not begin to pale for lack of an adversary. In fact, the opposite happens. By being relocated from the outside world of subtle shadings into the segregated area of starker polarities within the cosmically somewhat remote, perhaps inviolable inner space of the subject, the consistency of good and evil reaches a new level of determinacy in the theory of (original) sin and God's mercy. In this intensification of Augustine's theatrics of sinning, there perhaps lies the most elegant proof for my thesis that the provenance of the subject is in fact "idealist". Already Blumenberg detected the need for increasingly harsh accents:

> In order to deserve as punishment the world as it had been perceived and evaluated by the Manicheans, the sins of man, which take over the position of the wickedness of the Gnostic demiurge, had to be great, all too great. Even in the remorseful examination of his past life in the *Confessions*, Augustine found no sin that could have been measured on this scale. The balance between the condition of the world and the guilt of mankind, which he had drawn up in his early philosophy of freedom, caused him to become the theologian of

---

32 The ambition behind a discursive reconstruction of this sort is, naturally, to elevate the particular confessional self, say, that of Augustine of Hippo, into a "logical subject" with a universal claim. The private man may well be interested in the salvation of his soul, and the real-life Augustine may sincerely have felt remorse over this or that youthful vice. But he assumed his "systemic" role as the paradigmatic autobiographer of Christianity only as an agent of interiorizing the excluded element of evil and entrenching its floating, homeless ideality in the auxiliary hypothesis of the reality of his sin.

the uniquely great original guilt of mankind and of its mythical inheritance. (Blumenberg 1983, p. 184)

The *peccatum* of the *Confessions* becomes the *peccatum originale* of Augustine's later, anti-Pelagian writings. Why this crescendo? It could be presumed that Augustine was, for the immanent reasons of logic, forced to underpin the semantics of evil and good with two elements that are as unworldly as possible. He therefore converted sin into the original sin of Adam, from which all other sins ensue, and salvation into the sudden and absolute act of divine grace, which can never be earned by efforts in this lifetime. The transfer of the root of semantic determinacy from the cosmic dimensions of diluting values into the strengthened dramaturgy of oppositions on the path to salvation poses as another move away from the realism of incarnating the meaning of good and evil among the relative mediations of the created world toward the idealism of their conceptual redefinitions.[33]

Finally, the rough determinants of a new concept of subjectivity are now perhaps becoming apparent. As far as the "logicity" of the subject goes, its original function seems to be to provide a sanctuary for the concepts which have lost their ground in reality. It is, moreover, in this very ontological indiscrimination, followed in reaction by a subjective semantic recondensation, that I would like to recognize one of the fundamental operations of Western thought. On one side, an image of a de-symbolized universe of blurred boundaries appears, where it can never be conclusively decided what is good and what bad and where the dividing line between the two is to be drawn; it is a world of tasteless, colorless pears. On the other side, and against this background, the private arena of one's personal history could be said to reenact the drama that once played out in the cosmic exterior. From this perspective, the Augustinian overvaluation of a small private infirmity, the auxiliary hypothesis of human deficiency, might be viewed as an effect of the concepts losing ground in the world of things and striving to attain new equilibria in substitute worlds, where the cosmic slant toward good and away from evil can be compensated for and recalibrated. It is his

---

33 Given that Augustine's anti-Pelagian writings were so strident that even official Rome opposed them, it seems as if his intuition blindly insisted on the amplification of the contrast between the continuous gradualism of the outside world and the binary drama of the inside. Both sin and mercy become unmediated, fateful events, forbidding any negotiation or approximation between them. The descendants of Adam belong to the mass of the damned, *massa damnationis*, while God rewards with mercy only a few of them, arbitrarily and irrespective of their merit. Sin is not merited but innate, and mercy cannot be bought by good deeds, or else we would already be trading with the "relative goods" of the created world.

pronounced opposition to the Manicheans which allows us to foist on Augustine the logically idealized matrix of the transition from a bivalent cosmos of two substantial forces to a homogeneous universe of good, in the midst of which the inner world of man contracts into itself around the expelled kernel of evil. Or even more schematically, the universe used to be governed by two principles, possibly reflected in two souls inhabiting each man, and now we have an asymmetrical world of no evil and only gradually decreasing good on the outside, and a symmetrical opposition of sin and mercy inside man.[34] As the metaphysical binary loses meaning in reality, it thereby simultaneously regains meaning within the concentrated, logically more succinct sphere of the inner self invented precisely for this purpose.

To conclude, this reading of Augustine must come with the warning that his much richer theory of the soul possesses many positive dimensions, such as faith, hope, the love of God, a special temporality of reminiscence, and the capability of conversion and enlightenment. I have simplified it for one purpose only. My wager was that in this Church Father's account of good, evil, and sin, it is possible to detect and isolate a certain "zero-impulse" of subjectivity, whose universal features could be applied to the later forms of self-recourse found in the philosophical canon of the West. On that premise, I will now venture to examine the origins of the introspective, reclusive, to an extent lonesome Western subject as an emergent entity, whose function is to semantically re-invest the ontologically disrupted constant symmetries of meaning. Let us then try to define the subject as a reaction to the processes of the de-symbolization of the world.

4 Descartes' subject against the univalent cosmos of modern physics

When faced with the legendary subjects of Western philosophy, such as the Cartesian ego, the German idealist self-consciousness, the Nietzschean *Übermensch*,

---

[34] The alleged Manichean doctrine of two souls, the good and the evil, in one person is mocked by Augustine in *Contra Faustum*. In a reading similar to my own, Frederiksen argues how the two Manichean souls in one man became a single yet internally divided soul in Augustine: "Thus the single Augustinian soul, fractured through the sin of Adam, functions much as do the two Manichaean souls to explain the difficulty and struggle of man's moral existence. But whereas the two Manichaean souls correspond to a cosmic struggle and structure, the single Augustinian soul does not. Compulsive, labile, conflicted, this soul's divisions are historical and psychological, not cosmic, and therefore uniquely human" (Stroumsa/Frederiksen 1998, p. 214).

Heidegger's *Dasein*, or even the psychoanalytical subject of gender difference, one might wonder if they could be, not exactly brought under the common denominator of the general Augustinian formula, but nonetheless read in parallel with the motif of interiorizing and idealizing the element with no place in the incarnated world. It could possibly be observed that they tend to surface in parallel with a historically pivotal de-symbolizing event, one predominantly effected by modern science.

Descartes, the so-called "modern Augustine", certainly provides a worthy example. The tradition of disclosing deep similarities between the two is long and well-explored, reaching back to Descartes himself, who already faced and fought accusations of having copied Augustine's arguments. However, only one analogy is important here. In my view, the most striking, even explosive historical circumstance of Cartesian philosophy is the interdependence between Descartes having not only "invented" modern subjectivity in the most literal sense of the word, but also having been a part of the birth of modern science as arguably the greatest dissolution of universal symbolic values in history. It may be instructive to place this paragon of subjectivity, the *cogito*, and the most notorious act of de-symbolization, the Copernican revolution along with its impact on physics and the overall mindset, into a non-coincidental relation.

The "cosmological turn" of Copernican astronomy and Galilean physics consists in carrying out the downfall of the central symbolic discriminants of the Medieval universe, the most fundamental being that between heaven and earth. The boundary between the sublunar and the supralunar world dissolved, and with it all the semantically charged binaries of the physical and the metaphysical, the terrestrial and the celestial, the corporeal and the spiritual, the corruptible and the incorruptible, the fallible and the infallible. Descartes not only acknowledged this shift, but was one of its chief architects; he was nothing less than its philosophical founder. Against the Aristotelian hierarchy of animated, "ensouled" beings, against Scholastic forms qualitatively defining matter, against the Renaissance naturalism of living matter and occult powers, Descartes' claim was to establish a new physics that would exclude all psychic characteristics from nature, unconditionally separate mind from body, conceive of matter as an inert and passive extension, quantify and homogenize space in geometrical and arithmetical terms, and propose an entirely mechanical philosophy of nature.

Only in this respect can it be properly evaluated what Descartes' "dualism" really stands for. In a certain likeness with Augustine's anti-dualist, anti-Manichean asymmetric duality of body and soul, the origin of Descartes' divide between the spiritual and the corporeal does not lie in opposition to some monism of his time, but rather to the dominant "naturalist" dualisms of the Scholastics and the Renaissance. In fact, the Cartesian dualism of the soul being entirely exempt from matter must rather be regarded as a strict counterpart to the fundamental Cartesian monism of worldly reality. Metaphysical dualism thus merely represents the reverse side of physical monism. It is from this ontological constraint of material reality renouncing all traces of spiritual qualities that I would like to derive the actual genesis of the Cartesian incorporeal ego. From this angle, the soul in Descartes can be regarded as an originally negative entity whose genuine function is *subtractive:* it represents an element which no longer permeates the world with an additional substance, but rather, by means of its own exclusion, enables the autonomous causality of the material world.

Perhaps the greatest discursive paradox of Cartesian philosophy lies in the fact that at the exact time when the world *became one*, when metaphysics was absolved by physics and the space was finally all matter and no soul, Descartes built his entire system upon a metaphysical buttress which is well-nigh prevented from becoming a part of its own all-encompassing physical ontology. Whereas matter is now defined only by its extension, the *primum philosophicum* of the materially homogenized world is a non-extended *cogito ergo sum*, a point of great ontological impossibility, as all the difficulties of it being embodied and influencing outside reality show. Should it not strike us as rather curious that precisely in a "conception of nature startling in its bleakness" (Westfall 1977, p. 31), in a world-machine "indifferent to the existence of thinking beings" (Westfall 1977, p. 33), the entire knowledge of the world is concentrated in the soul, which transcends all corporeal limits and ultimately does not even require a body?

In a word, the unavowed equilibrium upon which this earliest modern philosophy seems to rest is that between the world free of all spiritual remnants on the one side and *res cogitans* monopolizing all metaphysical certainty on the other. Within the great uniformity of lifeless being, the ego should probably not even exist; and yet it is its prime necessity. In this light, Descartes' subject appears to be a construct emphatically opposed to the major trend of the physics of the time, which was, let us not forget, basically Cartesian.[35] The question,

---

[35] Even Descartes' philosophical biography seems to indirectly express this "productive suspense" at the center of his thought. Early in his career, he intended to first publish his physics, which was, of course, monist, corpuscular, geometric, and Copernican, and only later supplement it with metaphysics. Then, after the condemnation of Galileo, he withheld the publication of *Traité de monde et de la lumière* and altered his project, which from then on consisted not in overbuilding physics with metaphysics, but in reversing the sequence and postulating a metaphysical foundation of physics, i.e., first deriving all certainty from God and the soul. This

then, is, what motivates the subject's turn inward? Why must an "inner space" of a certain sophistication and self-reference be devised to authorize knowledge of a mechanical universe of mere matter?

Perhaps the step-by-step construction of the self in the *Meditations* can offer some clues. Let us consider the beginning phrases of the "First meditation":

> Some years ago I was struck by the large number of falsehoods that I had accepted as true in my childhood, and by the highly doubtful nature of the whole edifice that I had subsequently based on them. I realized that it was necessary, once in the course of my life, to demolish everything completely and start again right from the foundations if I wanted to establish anything at all in the sciences that was stable and likely to last. (Descartes 1996, p. 12)

It is, as it appears, a zealous *via negativa* which isolates the I and bestows upon him his ultimate solitude:

> I am here quite alone, and at last I will devote myself sincerely and without reservation to the general demolition of my opinions. (Descartes 1996, p. 12)

At the beginning, the soul is as if barred from having recourse to its ideal inner content, to an immediate intuition of eternal truths, or some kind of divine spark. Instead, it merely exemplifies the negative element of its own fallibility. The mark with which the Augustinian self flagged its existence in the world was, in my account, sin, and in Descartes it is the possibility of error.[36] The I is initially defined in physical terms, thrown into the material world, a being depending solely on its sense perception, but: "I have found that the senses deceive" (Descartes 1996, p. 12). Thus, within the gradual elaboration of this investiture of modern subjectivity, a deception, an entirely *inner privation* of clarity and distinctness of ideas, provides the first inkling of self-recourse, the first fulcrum of self-contraction. Illusions, blunders, confusion, mistrust, doubt are the levers for the non-extensional soul in the body of an animal to assume a distance to its natural embeddedness in the environment, to plunge the world of things into nothingness, and to turn toward itself. The thereby emerging self seems to be

---

turn of events can perhaps be said to have unfolded a "logical" loop, in which the birth of the subject would be inserted.

36 Menn argues that Descartes' origin of error is modeled on Augustine's origin of evil. Moreover, "Descartes needs a way to 'withdraw the mind from the senses' (AT VII, 12; AT VII, 131), and he finds a model in Augustine's discipline of contemplation: the mind must first 'withdraw [its] thought from its habit, removing itself from the contrary crowds of phantasms' (*Confessions* VII, xvii, 23)" (Menn 1998, p. 210).

so thoroughly "logically" dependent on severing all ties with the outside world that he even imagines everything he once held true to be false:

> I will suppose therefore that not God, who is supremely good and the source of truth, but rather some malicious demon of the utmost power and cunning has employed all his energies in order to deceive me. (Descartes 1996, p. 15)

Following the steps of the slow buildup of the argument, it is hence not God who makes me know myself but the supposed evil genius.[37] The ego thus convinces himself "that there is absolutely nothing in the world, no sky, no earth, no minds, no bodies" (Descartes 1996, p. 16), and in this total negation of everything outside himself, he realizes himself as a necessary being of *ego cogito*. Yet even his hard-won existence seems only to be stabilized around the condensation nucleus of an almost religiously, demonically exalted possibility of utter deception:

> But there is a deceiver of supreme power and cunning who is deliberately and constantly deceiving me. In that case I too undoubtedly exist, if he is deceiving me; and let him deceive me as much as he can, he will never bring it about that I am nothing so long as I think that I am something. (Descartes 1996, p. 17)

Here, Descartes refers to something which precedes any effort to prove its existence; it is a substance of self, an apparently timeless inner refuge immune to the tricks of the evil genius. Discursively, however, it is clear that the I would never have even known of his own self, had he not presumed that he was being deceived about everything else. And if we take self-consciousness to be not a stable thing but an act of thinking,[38] then the ego is—and in the profound ontological sense at that—an entirely *privational entity*, one emerging in the process of pitting itself against its outside. Fallibility as the initial discord with the world, the supposition of utter evil in deception, and the resulting self are, of course, reminiscent of Augustine.

---

[37] As with Augustine, the inner space of the self is originally one of stumbling in the dark, ignorance, and obliquity. Such might be the Western subject at her most unalloyed: "So serious are the doubts into which I have been thrown as a result of yesterday's meditation that I can neither put them out of my mind nor see any way of resolving them. It feels as if I have fallen unexpectedly into a deep whirlpool which tumbles me around so that I can neither stand on the bottom nor swim up to the top" (Descartes 1996, p. 16).

[38] The I is defined as a "processual" entity even by Descartes: "I am, I exist—that is certain. But for how long? For as long as I am thinking. For it could be that were I totally to cease from thinking, I should totally cease to exist" (Descartes 1996, p. 18).

If we are willing to read the early-modern invention of subjectivity with a sensibility for the discursive tensions behind it, then we might do well to place this "thinking being" in the context of the contemporary disclosure of the world, which elevates physics into the new overarching ontology. It comes across as somewhat ironic that the very philosopher who inaugurated the uniform cosmos of the scientific revolution, an essentially externalized landscape filled with the clear light of quantities and measures, then shifts the center of philosophical gravity to a being who first puts the entire corporeal reality in brackets,[39] feels the urge to turn away, resigns to the darkness of his private quarters, and discovers there his substitute inner world, a world that was induced by the threat of absolute deceit and that promises even greater clarity. What Descartes is doing is perhaps nothing but searching for a point of possible self-contraction in a world which, in its geometrical slipperiness, offers no grip, no blind spot, no shelter for the erstwhile matters of the soul. As in Augustine, where the sinner inhabiting the world of good was opaque to himself, the "unworldliness" of the modern spiritual subject at first fills her with unease,[40] the reason conceivably being that she asserts herself against the otherwise quite robust materialism of a new scientific ontology.

Similar to juxtaposing the evil Augustinian soul with the good world of Christianity, Descartes' subject can be placed against the broadest of all backgrounds, the universe of post-Copernican physics. But the question is, how far can these analogies go? Like the anti-Manichean collapse of two principles into one, the early-modern world renounces its two spheres and becomes univalent. It can, however, appear confusing that in Augustine the cosmically suppressed and subjectively rehabilitated element was the unmistakably negative evil, whereas in modernity the world at first sight surrenders its "positive" pole, i.e., the incorruptible, spherical, and homogenous heavens with their circular movements of the stars, so the entire universe becomes populated with telluric finitudes. Still, the rearrangement of symbolic values is more complex than that. Modern science is often said to have performed a sort of terrestrialization of the celestial, a one-sided universalization of the mundane, henceforth prolonged

---

39 "Yet now I know for certain both that I exist and at the same time that all such images and, in general, everything relating to the nature of body, could be mere dreams and chimeras" (Descartes 1996, p. 17).
40 The narrator himself seems perplexed by the unnaturalness of his own philosophical method: "But it still appears—and I cannot stop thinking this—that the corporeal things of which images are formed in my thought, and which the senses investigate, are known with much more distinctness than this puzzling 'I' which cannot be pictured in the imagination" (Descartes 1996, p. 16).

into the heavens. But the operations of Galilean physics cut both ways, so to speak, and simultaneously let celestial mechanics descend to the sublunar sphere.[41] The truth of perennial laws is thus also recognized as governing the motion of our own bodies. On the one hand, the heavens embrace changeability, on the other, earthly laws start to exhibit mathematical necessity.

It must therefore be defined with precision what exactly the "semantic value" which falls out of this universe so as to be repossessed by the subject is. Whereas the pre-modern cosmos was full of hidden meanings, mysterious qualities, and symbols encrypted in things, the modern universe is on the way to becoming expurgated, demystified, and, in a manner, ironed out; Cartesian space, in particular, has come close to this ideal long before Newton. There are two sets of values that are expelled from the new world of mathematized physics: first, the preconceived notions of innate forces, deep essences, and cryptic signs that once structured the corruptible earth; second, the metaphysical warranty of intuitive insight and transcendent truth, which no longer pervades the celestial sphere. Hence, it is in this quantifiable, measurable plane and the consequently monotonous and bland universe, one extending between exclusive secularism and the exactness of mathematization, that the erring Cartesian ego possesses an exceptional, almost poetic identity. In my reading, this subject, caught in the prejudices of her past and the chimeras of her present, enacts within the range of retreat into herself the drama which can no longer be acted out in the deflated outside world. The narrative of the "method", in a way, stretches out the subject between two opposing hinges, the fallacies of the senses and the distinctness of ideas, the illusions of customs and traditions and the necessity of proofs, the mortality of the body and the immortality of the soul, the imperfection of the human and the perfection of God, or, the ultimate dichotomy, absolute doubt and metaphysical certainty—all those motives and arguments which have no place in the modern universe of pure extension. Because the subject, in her very genesis, stands in for the possibility of utmost deception —including of there not being any world at all—she finally rejoices at a clarity of insight that surpasses all worldly certitudes, even those of geometry and arithmetic.[42] Not unlike Augustine's absolution of the aberrations of sin with a direct

---

[41] As Blumenberg said, Copernicus, by having made the earth into a "star among stars", not only "abolished the heavens but also elevated the earth into a heaven" (Blumenberg 1966, p. 28, translation mine).

[42] Inasmuch as I have tried to define the Western subject as a place of the metaphorical re-enactment of obsolete, in this case pre-modern cosmic equilibria and antagonisms within the bounds of one's private inner space, the "path of doubt" recounted in the *Meditations* could be seen as a fitting example of such a staging. The narrative begins with the still quite common

intervention of God's grace, which is greater than all the incarnated goods of the world, here the errancies of doubt are rewarded with the knowledge of God, which is, in the end, more reliable than any understanding of natural things or even mathematics. One way to picture the modern subject is thus to see her levitate between two unearthlinesses in a world becoming entirely earthly.

In a word, a possible perspective from which to cast a glance at Cartesian philosophy is to point out its immanent disparity between the universe involved in the dynamics of modern physicalist de-symbolization and the subject offering surrogate ground to the concepts of metaphysics. This is what Descartes' project of a metaphysical foundation of physics ultimately amounts to. In order to break the religiously consolidated barriers and constraints of Aristotelian physics, Descartes first needs to fixate an external, Archimedean point of a new, modern revelation of the world. This role is accorded to an element excluded from the world, a soul which is entirely dependent on God. This soul harbors the innate ideas of God, mind, and body, or even their union, which enables it, from its spiritual point of view, to first define the essence of matter as purely intellectual, that is, mathematical and extensional, and only then enrich it with a sensual knowledge of nature.[43] The Cartesian ego is therefore anything but an outdated remnant of the inertia of Scholastic ideas. She rather plays an emphatically modern role. Already Augustine's theory of good and evil might be viewed as an attempt to provide new supports and guidelines in the unsettling disclosure of a post-pagan, hazy, disoriented world, which could no longer lean on a cosmic order incarnating the binary structure of moral conceptuality. By demonstrating that both the normative distinguishability and the semantic co-dependence of good and evil would henceforth have to be produced in another, ideal, differential realm of the self, Augustine was perhaps developing an original, in its tendency modern ethics with which to get by in a more complex, less determinate reality lacking the socioreligious certitudes of previous times. But since the ultimate purpose of Cartesian philosophy was not the Augustinian return to God and the rewards of faith but the advancement of the empirical sciences of the material world, Descartes made the role of the subject as a correlate of the processes of de-symbolization even clearer. By means of internalizing metaphysical qual-

---

scruples about the unreliability of the senses, but then proceeds to starker contrapositions between madness and sanity, dreaming and waking, and reaches its dialectic climax in either being deceived by the evil genius, the *malin génie*, or being sure of the existence of the good God who created nature and instilled in us the innate ideas. By this escalation, Descartes perhaps sets out for the final metaphysical over-determination of the entire domain of physics.
43 In this sweeping overview, I rely on Michael Friedman's "Descartes and Galileo: Copernicanism and the Metaphysical Foundation of Physics" (Friedman 2007, see especially pp. 80–82).

ities within the ascent from private doubt to divine certainty, the subject, in her methodic vigor, can now be said to personify the perpetual effort to detach symbolic values from the outside world and to undercut any intermingling of symbols and things in the Aristotelian, Scholastic, or Renaissance fashion. She thereby facilitates a view upon the world finally freed from traditional conceptual discriminants.

5 De-symbolization and the formation of subjectivity

Perhaps the conditions for the "turn inward" will never let themselves be broken down as elegantly as in Augustine or, to an already lesser degree, in Descartes. Modern "subjects" are formed around much more labyrinthine ontological imbalances and semantic equilibria, and their discursive analysis is bound to be more intricate, sometimes to the point of unfeasibility. There are nonetheless felicitous coincidences to be pointed out. Although we are treading on uncharted territory, let us cursorily, without much justification, and only offering a couple of clues for future investigation, examine some further examples of the claimed reciprocity between the processes of de-symbolization taking place both inside and outside philosophy and the reactive emergence of the philosophical subject.

The term "idealist subjectivity" is usually connoted with German idealism, which invented one of the weightiest paradigms of self-recourse and world-making. It may come as a surprise that any type of idealism, much less its historic climax, could take shape in the aftermath of British empiricism and the ontological ashes it left behind. But in order to still advocate any kind of idealist tendency in the face of such devastation, a new logical space of accommodating ideal values had to be contrived; naturally, this was the subject reaching new heights of autonomy and, at times, self-indulgence. While the great rationalists, such as Spinoza or Leibniz, spared no effort to exhaustively superimpose, restrict, and circumscribe the *ordo rerum* with the *ordo idearum*, the merit of the empiricists was to realize the lack of any metaphysical guarantee behind the meaning of ideal concepts. The conceptual duality of two parallel, intertwining orders was thereby abolished, so that Berkeley's immaterialism flattened the world into a screen of sense perceptions and Hume's agnosticism into a fluid of disconnected impressions. This disentitlement of symbolic idealities to structure reality, amounting to the grand Humean vision of experience as a mere sequence of "loose and separate", "conjoined but never connected" events, found its formal expression in the eighteenth-century collapse of the difference between the primary and secondary qualities of perceptual objects. This very collapse is one of the main catalysts underlying the German variety of idealism. After Hume proclaimed the semantic emptiness of the concepts of substance, cause, and effect, Kant made the subject rise from the dead as a new root of "pure concepts", which indirectly stand for the "primary qualities" recently expelled from the inmost essence of things. Burdened with Hume's threat of the universe lapsing into sheer contingency, Kant tried to reestablish, as the famous quotation goes, a world without gaps, jumps, chance, and fate, and he accomplished this move by way of deriving the content of conceptual forms from the subjective "unity of apperception" as originally synthetic, self-determining, and productive. Once more, we witness the settling of a uniform, contiguous world resistant to being interrupted by symbolic forms on the one hand and the birth of a subject with her own internal symbolic structure on the other.[44] The discursive oxymoron is, of course, that only a spontaneous subjectivity can ensure the causal necessity of a world in which freedom should no longer intervene. The tense equilibrium of the impermeable chains of causes and effects on the outside, and the dialectic of the receptivity of the senses and the spontaneity of understanding on the inside of the subject, is then intensified within the moral subject, where the private inclinations abide by the "pathological (physical) laws", which, however, are internally set against the "absolute spontaneity" of freedom. This inner duality of Kant's practical subject laid the foundations for the subsequent evolution of subjectivity in German idealism. To lay this idealist subject on the Procrustean bed of Augustine's formula, she can be said to form around an element of fallenness and contingency, as per Fichte's *Anstoß*, Schelling's evil *Ungrund*, or Hegel's *Makel der Bestimmtheit*, while her aim is to achieve an increasingly absolute, godlike self-consciousness of freedom. Or a more modest advocacy of the irreducibly idealist kernel of subjectivity can be implied. Being one of the "outcast" notions of the empiricist, determinist, and materialist philosophies of the eighteenth century, "freedom" is precisely a concept with ideal content and no representative in reality. And the self-positing subject of German idealism is designed as an act of its interiorization, thereby elevating it into the ultimate reason of being. What therefore justifies the emergence of the idealist subject seems to be the fact that the cosmic prevalence of physical necessity does not imply the recession of freedom as its opposite but, on the contrary, triggers its philosophical apotheosis.

---

[44] This is a most brief summary of the "subtractive" function of Kant's pure concepts, that is, of how the subjective idealization of traditional concepts enabled Kant to disclose the "indiscriminate" world of Newtonian causality, all of which is elaborated on in my "Hegel and the Opaque Core of History" (Simoniti 2020, pp. 206–213).

To proceed, there is one coincidence worth highlighting in Nietzsche, one dimension in the way he imagined his version of subjectivity. While the Nietzschean subject possesses many layers and cores, an important impulse of his identity is the confrontation with his own animality after science has bereaved the concept of "man" of its substance. Arguably the greatest event of de-symbolization in the nineteenth century was the fall of the distinction between man and animal, as carried out by the evolutionary biology of the time. In the *Origin of Species*, Darwin insinuated the possibility of conceiving of man as a descendant from the ape; the idea had a broad public impact, and he expanded on it in *The Descent of Man*. Marx and Nietzsche were both very appreciative of this Darwinian turn and often referred to it. However, in a typical philosophical fashion, they responded to it by introducing new, projective, sometimes vulgarly self-made designs of humanity. Nietzsche's solution is perhaps the more pointed and exemplary one, seeing that he famously defined mankind as "a rope fastened between animal and overman—a rope over an abyss" (Nietzsche 2006, p. 7). But he also genealogically reconstructed the inception of the "inner life" as a particular mode of a "man of bad conscience", who in his interior extends between his suppressed animality and God.[45] Perhaps a new approach to the subject-function in Nietzsche would be to explicate it as an effect of a quintessential "philosophical" operation. When the existence of the referent of a concept is disproved, an irreducibly idealist thought, instead of simply withdrawing it from circulation, counters with its *subjective aggrandization*. Augustine located the source of evil things in the original sin, thereby opening the subject to the experience of the highest good of mercy; German idealism translated the semantics of free will into Kant's spontaneity, Fichte's self-positing, and Hegel's absolute; and in Nietzsche, the "refuted" man becomes the *Übermensch*. On the one hand, the overman is an idea of a future embodiment with no referent in the present world; on the other, his original determination, in contrast to the mere human being, is simply the capability of acknowledging and enduring his own

---

[45] Just consider this startling genesis of the Christian self-contraction: "[T]hat will to torment oneself, that suppressed cruelty of animal man who has been frightened back into himself and given an inner life, incarcerated in the 'state' to be tamed, and has discovered bad conscience so that he can hurt himself, after the more natural outlet of this wish to hurt had been blocked ... In 'God' he seizes upon the ultimate antithesis he can find to his real and irredeemable animal instincts ..., he pitches himself into the contradiction of 'God' and 'Devil', he emits every 'no' which he says to himself, nature, naturalness and the reality of his being as a 'yes'." But it is also followed by the positive version of the "*Greek gods*, these reflections of noble and proud men in whom the animal in man felt deified" (Nietzsche 1997, pp. 63–64). Here, the internal dialectics of man "pitching himself into the contradiction" arises quite literally and precisely from the collapse of an external dualism: man becomes aware of being an animal.

utter animality. By epitomizing the break between present animality and future super-humanity, the subject thus enacts the symbolically charged antagonism which the cosmos can no longer provide a stage for. And with this subjective restitution of a conceptual opposite, she simultaneously takes hold of the lever which opens up a view onto the no longer symbolically interlaced world. This is what Nietzsche's philosophy has always been about.

Another towering case of this operation is Heidegger's *Dasein*, whose inner composition, again, operates on so many levels that only one component can be touched upon here. It was a pronounced purpose of Heidegger's "fundamental ontology" to offer resistance to the processes of the scientific devaluation of the "qualitative" conceptuality of our life-worlds. To limit ourselves to the notions of temporality, some speak of a radical revolution in the human conception of time in the nineteenth century: the age of the universe and mankind expanded to an unimaginable degree. In physics, biology, and psychology—as well as in modernist art—definite temporal caesuras, beginnings and endings, began to lose their footing, thereby blurring the difference between finitude and infinity. It suffices to recall Einstein's time dilation, biological reproduction, the psychological compulsion to repeat, which culminated in Freud's concept of the death drive, etc.[46] The fact that Heidegger constructed the subject around his irreducible temporality, raising *Dasein* into a veritable personification of time,[47] could be seen in light of the historical circumstance of time losing its qualitative structure, its cosmic sovereignty, but most of all its habitability and conceivability. The central aim of *Being and Time* is precisely to restore the possibility of fixed and irreversible time frames in a universe reluctant to be constrained by temporal barriers. Many have observed that *Dasein*'s dramatic path leading from the *Verfallenheit ans Man* and the *Seinsvergessenheit* to the *Eigentlichkeit* of the meaning of being is modeled on the biblical narrative of sin and salvation. But what allows Heidegger to outline this biographically delimited inner space is to define the structurally absent element which will be interiorized by *Dasein*

---

46 Most notably, the physics of the twentieth century made time and space forfeit their absolute frameworks. In a peculiar accentuation, Einstein's theory of relativity rendered time relative to the spatial coordinates of its measurement and surrendered its independence, thereby forming a new, four-dimensional space-time continuum; a certain symbolic barrier to bid goodbye was that between space and time, although the impact of this move on the constitution of the philosophical subject is probably not crucial. Nonetheless, in his attempt to underpin the dimensions of "world-time" with *Dasein*'s own temporality, its "within-time-ness", *Innerzeitigkeit*, Heidegger expressly addresses the problem of measuring time in the theory of relativity (see Heidegger 1962, p. 499).

47 For *Dasein* "is time itself, not within time" (Heidegger 2004, p. 19, translation mine).

as her innermost core; this element is the merely anticipatory but inalienable absolute event of death (one that has, into the bargain, also lost any meaning in the relative measurements of physics, the reproductive success of biology, or the repetitive drives of psychology). And it is in this emergent space of "being-toward-death" that absolute values can still be bestowed upon time and space,[48] whose vast universal facticity of temporal and spatial boundlessness eludes any human form.

One last example, to be addressed only cursorily, is the psychoanalytical, Lacanian subject, expressly defined as the subject of gender difference. What my proposed matrix of subjectivity would highlight is the fact that this subject takes form as a reaction to the divergencies between the biological, the social, and the psychological sex; this has its origin in Freud's ideas of our original bisexuality and the fact that everyone is a synthesis of masculine and feminine features. One could observe the striking historical coincidence that gender difference became the condition of the formation of subjectivity in structuralism, predominantly in Lacan, precisely at the moment when it became apparent that the concepts of "masculinity" and "femininity" could no longer be supported by any strictly delimited biological essence. It is yet again the case of a disruptive equilibrium, one in which the subject "logically" emerges within gender difference, but this subjective restitution of ideal conceptuality simultaneously performs a de-symbolizing release of its outside: the social roles of gender can now be liberated from the alleged normativity of the biological sex. The uncircumventable limit of gender difference is therefore not a sign of any conservatism of psychoanalysis, but of its emancipatory potentials.

Let us conclude. With the aim to provide new incentives for gaining insight into the structure and genesis of the subject's inner space, a few historical events have been selected when the processes of de-symbolization were counterbalanced by the appearance of an unprecedented figure of subjectivity, the task of which was to re-ground the realm of ideal meanings no longer sustained by the outside world. The mechanisms of how the subject's interior architecture actually responds to, compensates for, and perchance influences these de-symbolizing operations still seem patchy and obscure. Nevertheless, an alternative model of the origins of subjectivity perhaps springs to mind.

---

48 In the analyses of space in the first part of *Being and Time*, Heidegger's claim is also to predetermine all spatial quanta, all relations, distances, and measurements, with qualitative distinctions, with what I, but not Heidegger, call "subjective", simple symmetric oppositions of the here and there, *Hier* and *Dort*, or closeness and remoteness, *Nähe* and *Entferntheit* (see Heidegger 1962, pp. 135–138).

I have outlined a certain matrix of the symbolic frames of the world dissolving, of words losing their cosmoplastic force, and then, reactively, of a subject emerging through an act of internalization of the very collapsing semantic values. I have stressed two consequences of the translocation of the semantic wealth of cosmic dualisms into the dialectical dramas of the self's inner space. First, this transfer seems to induce conceptual idealization. In the provided examples, good and evil, truth and falsity, freedom and necessity, man and animal, time and space, and man and woman have undergone an idealist redefinition, thereby gaining a certain amount of differential, logical, stringent determinacy. It appears, accordingly, that the world can only give up its human face concurrently with words stabilizing and sharpening their meanings within the circuits of the subject's own self-reference.[49] In this regard, the subject could be deemed a mere effect of semantic inertia, a necessary counterweight to the world caught in a process of symbolic disenchantment. My guess, however, is that the subject's role is active, positive, and essentially "modern". Thus, second, I propose to ascribe to the subject the function of interiorizing certain conceptual discriminants, hiding them in herself, so to speak, and redefining them as ideas averse to being embodied directly, all of it for the purpose of preventing symbolic meanings from being applied to the outside world.

With this move, a view upon subjectivity suggests itself which is entirely different from the conventional one. Traditionally, and especially in those accounts which equate Western philosophy with antirealism, the subject stood for an endogenous energy of projecting anthropogenic forms onto the world and dominating it. She was the Kantian condition of possibility of objectivity and, negatively, a source of illusions which form reality after the image of man. There is, however, a dimension of selfness which, as far as I am aware, remains neglected. Historically momentous instances of subjectivity tend to arise as integrations of the very conceptuality of which they absolve the world. As we have seen, it is possible to think the subject as emerging through the discursive contrast to the very world she is about to realize as objective. We therefore no longer seem to be dealing with monsters of anthropomorphism, *a priori* antirealists, "prosthetic gods", who will always only find their own mirror image in the outside world. What we have on our hands are *agents of de-projection*, who know how to undercut the referential claim of historically and culturally mediated symbolic values and

---

[49] The emerging self is in this sense a reflex of one of the most ancient philosophical instincts, the source of all idealisms from Plato onward, according to which the content of an idea achieves its relative definitional closure at the moment it sheds its referent among the embodied things.

then, in an idealist turn, fixate in them the Archimedean point of disclosing reality finally freed of any meaning. This is my case for a new idealism.

Bibliography

Arndt, Paul (1980): "Malum/III. Altes und Neues Testament". In: *Historisches Wörterbuch der Philosophie*. Vol. 5 (L–Mn). Edited by Joachim Ritter. Basel: Schwabe, pp. 665–666.

Assmann, Jan (1999): "Confession in Ancient Egypt". In: Jan Assmann/Guy G. Stroumsa (Eds.): *Transformations of the Inner Self in Ancient Religions*. Leiden, Boston and Cologne: Brill, pp. 231–244.

Augustine (1953): "The Soliloquies". In: *Earlier Writings*. Translated by J. H. S. Burleigh. Louisville: Westminster John Knox Press, pp. 17–63.

Augustine (1955): "Enchiridion". In: *Confessions and Enchiridion*. Translated by Albert Cook Outler. Louisville: Westminster John Knox Press, pp. 337–412.

Augustine (1998): *The City of God against the Pagans*. Edited and translated by R. W. Dyson. Cambridge: Cambridge University.

Augustine (2002): *On the Trinity: Books 8–15*. Translated by Stephen McKenna. Cambridge: Cambridge University Press.

Augustine (2006): "The Nature of the Good Against the Manichees". In: *Earlier Writings*. Translated by J. H. S. Burleigh. Louisville: Westminster John Knox Press, pp. 324–348.

Augustine (2009): *Confessions*. Translated by Henry Chadwick. Oxford: Oxford University Press.

Augustine (2010): "On the Free Choice of the Will". In: *On the Free Choice of the Will, On Grace and Free Choice, and Other Writings*. Translated by Peter King. Cambridge: Cambridge University Press, pp. 3–126.

Bernhart, Joseph (2007): "Kommentar". In: Augustinus: *Bekenntnisse*. Frankfurt am Main: Verlag der Weltreligionen, pp. 367–580.

Blumenberg, Hans (1966): "Das Fernrohr und die Ohnmacht der Wahrheit". In: Galileo Galilei: *Sidereus Nuncius: Nachricht von neuen Sternen*. Edited by Hans Blumenberg. Frankfurt am Main: Suhrkamp, pp. 5–73.

Blumenberg, Hans (1983): *The Legitimacy of the Modern Age*. Translated by Robert M. Wallace. Cambridge, MA: MIT Press.

Cary, Phillip (2000): *Augustine's Invention of the Inner Self: The Legacy of a Christian Platonist*. Oxford and New York: Oxford University Press.

Descartes, René (1996): *Meditations on First Philosophy: With Selections from the Objections and Replies*. Translated by John Cottingham. Cambridge: Cambridge University Press.

Friedman, Michael (2007): "Descartes and Galileo: Copernicanism and the Metaphysical Foundation of Physics". In: Janet Broughton/John Carriero (Eds.): *A Companion to Descartes*. Oxford: Blackwell, pp. 69–83.

Heidegger, Martin (1962): *Being and Time*. Translated by John Macquarrie and Edward Robinson. Oxford: Blackwell.

Heidegger, Martin (2004): *Der Begriff der Zeit: Vortrag vor der Marburger Theologenschaft, Juli 1924*. Frankfurt am Main: Vittorio Klostermann.

Herring, H. (1976): "Ich". In: *Historisches Wörterbuch der Philosophie*. Vol. 4 (I–K). Edited by Joachim Ritter. Basel: Schwabe, pp. 1–6.

Meillassoux, Quentin (2008): *After Finitude: An Essay on the Necessity of Contingency*. Translated by Ray Brassier. London: Continuum.
Menn, Stephen (1998): *Descartes and Augustine*. Cambridge: Cambridge University Press.
Milner, Jean-Claude (2021): *A Search for Clarity: Science and Philosophy in Lacan's Oeuvre*. Translated by Ed Pluth. Evanston, IL: Northwestern University Press.
Nietzsche, Friedrich (1888): Letter to Malwida von Meysenburg, 20. October 1888. http://www.nietzschesource.org/#eKGWB/BVN-1888,1135, visited on 1 November 2021.
Nietzsche, Friedrich (1997): *On the Genealogy of Morality*. Translated by Carol Diethe. Cambridge: Cambridge University Press.
Nietzsche, Friedrich (2006): *Thus Spoke Zarathustra*. Translated by Adrian del Caro. Cambridge: Cambridge University Press.
Porter, James I. (2017): "Time for Foucault? Reflections on the Roman Self from Seneca to Augustine". In: *Foucault Studies* 22, pp. 113–133.
Riesenhuber, Anton (1980): "Malum/V. Patristik und Mittelalter". In: *Historisches Wörterbuch der Philosophie*. Vol. 5 (L–Mn). Edited by Joachim Ritter. Basel: Schwabe, pp. 669–670.
Simoniti, Jure (2016): *The Untruth of Reality: The Unacknowledged Realism of Modern Philosophy*. Lanham, Boulder, New York and London: Lexington.
Simoniti, Jure (2020): "Hegel and the Opaque Core of History". In: *Problemi International* 4, pp. 201–230.
Stroumsa, Guy G./Frederiksen, Paula (1998): "The Two Souls and the Divided Will". In: H. G. Kippenberg/E. T. Lawson (Eds.): *Self, Soul, and Body in Religious Experience*. Leiden, Boston and Cologne: Brill, pp. 198–217.
Westfall, Richard S. (1977): *The Construction of Modern Science: Mechanisms and Mechanics*. Cambridge: Cambridge University Press.
Williams, Rowan (2000): "Insubstantial Evil". In: Robert Dodaro/George Lawless (Eds.): *Augustine and His Critics: Essays in Honour of Gerald Bonner*. London and New York: Routledge, pp. 105–123.
Wrzecionko, Paul (1998): "Sünde/I. Griechische und römische Antike; Altes und Neues Testament". In: *Historisches Wörterbuch der Philosophie*. Vol. 10 (St–T). Edited by Joachim Ritter. Basel: Schwabe, pp. 598–600.

Gregor Kroupa
Genesis, Structure, and Ideas: Genetic Epistemology in Early Modern Philosophy

Abstract: Although the idiom "genesis and structure" is usually associated with the rise of structuralism in the late 1950s and early 1960s, the two notions are arguably among the most persistent methods in the history of modern philosophy. This article outlines the emergence of "genetic epistemology" in the seventeenth century, when the seemingly antithetical character of the conceptual pair was reworked into a productive epistemological theory, especially in Descartes, Hobbes, Spinoza, and Leibniz, who increasingly used diachronic (genetic) narratives to explain the synchronic (structural) features in their theories. Against Cassirer, I argue that it was Descartes rather than Hobbes who first presented structural issues genetically. In Descartes' natural philosophy, his frequent claims that showing how a thing is produced reveals its true nature foreshadow precisely what Hobbes and Isaac Barrow later describe as causal definitions of geometric figures, in which the process of ideal generation by motion is what constitutes the very essence of a figure. I link this method to the historicizing discourse on origins in the Enlightenment and conclude by suggesting that there is a trace of Platonic idealism in genetic epistemology.

1 Genesis and structure

In the summer of 1959, a conference took place over the course of ten days in the château of Cerisy-la-Salle in Normandy. Prominent intellectuals of the time, such as Maurice de Gandillac, Lucien Goldmann, Jean Piaget (who also jointly organized this so-called *décade*), Jean-Paul Aron, and Ernst Bloch, delivered their papers, as did a few younger invited speakers, such as Jean-Paul Vernant and Jacques Derrida, for whom the conference also marked his first public lecture. The prescribed topic, "genesis and structure", would have probably appeared overly abstract if everybody involved hadn't already been acquainted with the phrase

---

Funding note: The research included in this chapter was funded by the Slovenian Research Agency (ARRS) under the research project "The Possibility of Idealism for the Twenty-First Century" (J6–1811).

Gregor Kroupa, University of Ljubljana.

thanks to Jean Hyppolite's famous *Genèse et structure de la Phénoménologie de l'esprit de Hegel* from 1946. Since then, this conceptual pair seems to have caught on as a cliché; indeed, the phrase "genesis and structure" (of a social institution, body of work or a philosophical concept) is still fairly commonly used today in titles of books and articles in philosophy and the social sciences in order to signal that a topic has been covered comprehensively, such as when the author combines the systematic and historical accounts of a subject.

However, during the mentioned *décade*, the conjunction of the terms "genesis" and "structure" also announced a special kind of methodological problem. The reason it was deemed to deserve such attention, even polemic, in post-war France was that what appeared as a simple conjunction in the title of Hyppolite's book later became a dilemma that ultimately invited a whole generation of theoreticians to choose between the *genetic* (i.e., dynamic, historical, diachronic or dialectical) principle of explanation as it had been advocated by Marxists, which were mostly close to Sartre, and the *structural* (i.e., static, systematic, atemporal or synchronic) analyses that were gaining popularity mainly following Lévi-Strauss's writings, inspired by the method of Saussure's linguistics.[1] The solution was not, however, in defending one and rejecting the other entirely, but in imagining how they could be reconciled by deciding which of them was superior. And indeed, reading the papers and conversations of the *décade*,[2] one finds that they often revolved around the question whether the genetic principle reigns over the structural one or vice versa; for instance, whether it would be fruitful to acknowledge that every structure, whatever it may be (a single concept, theoretical work, social phenomenon, scientific domain, etc.), has its past, and that the very genesis of structures is significant for understanding them *qua* structures, or, conversely, whether every genesis (emergence, event, historical milestone, change in time, etc.) merely fills some "always already" pre-structured scheme or format. Jean Piaget, for instance, emphasized that genesis and structure are inseparable, and tried to combine the two into the following general maxims: (1) *Every genesis begins with one structure and results in another*; and (2) *Every structure has its genesis* (Piaget 1965, pp. 40, 42). Similarly, the particular solution of Lucien Goldmann's "genetic structuralism", which was largely inspired by Piaget, was to frame the genesis *of* structures in a particular manner: he portrayed the structure of the structuralists as too partial and static, and as something the emergence of which must be questioned. Thus, the question of the genesis

---

[1] This division into two camps was suggested by Georges Lanteri-Laura (1967, pp. 805–811).
[2] The proceedings, including extracts from the discussions, were published six years later in Gandillac/Goldmann/Piaget 1965.

of every structure would have been answered only by showing how it was a part (and presumably an effect) of a larger structure that contained the conditions of its emergence, e.g., a particular socio-historical situation of the time. In Goldmann's view, to understand the genesis of, for instance, Pascal's *Pensées*, one cannot study only the written work preceding this work, but the larger structure determining and generating it, i.e., the whole social context of extremist Jansenism in the seventeenth century, etc. (Goldmann 1965, p. 10). In this way, Marx was forging alliances with Saussure in often unexpected ways.

These and numerous other examples[3] from the debate make it clear that structure and genesis are commonly taken to be external to one another. If one believes it necessary to establish between them a relationship of dominance and subordination, this naturally leads to the conclusion that one cannot simply be eliminated or even reduced to the other. However, their difference also cannot be explained away by pointing out that the two approaches simply follow separate goals and thus serve different purposes, as if a systematic account of anything had nothing to do with the causes that brought it about. The fact that any subject can be elucidated either from the temporal and diachronic perspective (the causes external to it, its historical conditions, the dynamics of its production) or atemporally and synchronically (by a comprehensive description of its parts and their relations, its features and functions as they operate in any given moment) would, by itself, be trivial if it were not for the fact that the goals of the two methods frequently overlap, and that historically they have often been competing rather than complementary methods. Saussure, for example, did not favor synchronic over diachronic linguistics because he was simply interested in different aspects of language than the historical (or, in his own words, "evolutionary") linguistics of the nineteenth century, but because he thought that the former alone was equipped to explain the essential features of language compared to the predominantly diachronic approach of the latter: "the linguist who wishes to understand a state must discard all knowledge of everything that produced it and ignore diachrony", he taught in his *Cours* (Saussure 2011, p. 81).

However, an epistemological shift in the opposite direction had already happened before Saussure. During the eighteenth century, philosophers believed that one cannot develop a satisfactory account of language relying merely on static abstract theories of signification and syntax, such as the one developed by the grammarians of Port-Royal. Since around the 1750s, modern theories of

---

[3] For an opposite view, which tries to defend the superiority of structures, see Kahn (1965) and especially the subsequent debate on pp. 193–195.

language instead tended to propose that to really get to the root of verbal communication one must uncover its *origins*—i.e., the historical and quasi-historical (more on that later) motivations and causes of its emergence. The almost obsessive quest for the origin of language, which was perhaps first set off by Condillac's *Essay on the Origin of Human Knowledge*, was taken up by Rousseau shortly after, followed by Adam Smith, Herder and the expanded debate in the Berlin Academy since the 1760s, then Fichte just before the end of the century, and many others in between. But this difference between the structural and the genetic approach can in no way be interpreted as if the "structural" linguistic thought of Port-Royal was addressing the *present* state of language or even language in general, after which came a "genetic" *historical* turn, which focused on its past evolution. Rather, as Hans Aarsleff once succinctly put it, "what one did atemporally in terms of structure alone, the other did on the scale of time" (Aarsleff 1985, p. 166), as both the genetic and the structural approach attempted to explain the causes and reasons that determine the purpose, substance, and form of language as such, but they did so from two distant starting points. Whatever the differences between the various accounts of the origins of language were (and they were considerable), they showed that to conjecture the possible beginnings of language in some prehistoric past has almost nothing to do with history but rather with causes and reasons operating in the present. For instance, Rousseau's placement of the origin of language in emotions rather than needs, even when presented (quasi)historically as a narrative about primitive men, completely determined his account of what language essentially *is* and *should be*.

But the Enlightenment genre of "discourse on the origins" of course wasn't limited to linguistic philosophy and theory. More generally, speculations about the emergence of human and social institutions included the Scottish tradition of "natural" or "conjectural" history (the term was coined by Dugald Stewart [Stewart 1982, p. 293], but it included thinkers such as Francis Hutcheson, David Hume, Adam Smith, Lord Kames, etc.), various theories by moral philosophers such as Bernard Mandeville, and the so-called *histoire philosophique* of everything from fables, sciences, and arts to religion, money, and law in the works of Fontenelle, Diderot, d'Alembert, Turgot, Condorcet, and many others. Similarly, many social contract theories (e.g., Locke's *Second Treatise* or Rousseau's *Discourse on Inequality*) also relied on quasi-historical narratives about the state of nature, which were, however, ultimately designed to legitimize the existence of the state. The general methodological aim of these genetic narratives was that they were elaborate attempts to give accounts of the present of these things, and not their past, their *structure* and not their *history*, insofar as the answer to the question "Genesis *or* structure?" was always: "Structure *through* genesis!" The grand "historical turn" of the eighteenth century therefore carries a good deal of ambivalence and complexity, since it is not simply the case that thinkers after Condillac focused on the temporal dimension of *where things came from* whereas the intent of Descartes, Arnauld, Hobbes or Leibniz was merely to describe and explain things *as they are*. On the contrary, there is a very strong connection between the above-mentioned theories of origins and the epistemology of the early modern giants; in fact—and this is perhaps the main point of this paper—it is here that the origin-seekers of the Enlightenment, perhaps even unwittingly, collected their methodological tools. By turning towards origins, they did not so much make a turn away from structure and systematicity in their investigations of social institutions as they provided a narrative answer to the atemporal question of structure; and this procedure, as we shall see, can be traced back to Descartes, Hobbes, and the tradition of ancient geometry.[4]

The issue of the interrelation between the two general epistemological strategies thus did not suddenly appear in the heyday of structuralism and Marxism in post-war France. Whereas "the origin issue" and the "genesis and structure issue" are rooted in two different and seemingly unconnected historical and intellectual contexts, they were nevertheless grappling with very similar methodological questions. However, the amalgam of genesis and structure that can be traced and uncovered in early modern and Enlightenment thought is methodologically perhaps more nuanced than the solutions of "genetic structuralists" ever were.

Whereas it is not difficult to find genetic narratives in the speculations of the eighteenth century, with its searches for the origins of ideas and social institutions, there are also very specific earlier examples of this approach. For this reason, in the rest of this paper, I shall try to: (1) briefly sketch out the tradition of causal (or genetic) definitions in geometry as an inspiration and predecessor of what I shall call "genetic epistemology";[5] (2) show that Descartes is the true

---

[4] Since the terms "genesis" and "structure" in this context were originally probably borrowed from eighteenth-century biology and the issue of preformation and epigenesis, many participants in the aforementioned debate in the late 1950s and early 1960s failed to connect the methodological principle to ancient mathematics. Maurice de Gandillac is a notable exception (cf. Gandillac 1965, p. 341).

[5] I shall use this label as an umbrella term for all kinds of genetically inspired explanations mentioned in the rest of this paper. I borrow the term from Catherine Labio (Labio 2004) but it should not be confused with *l'épistémologie génétique* of Jean Piaget, which (as is clear from what has been said above) falls under the same category in many respects but is not identical with the general method of genetic epistemology as I understand it here, mainly for the reason that the former is more specific.

modern originator of the latter; (3) point to the continuity between the genetic epistemology of Descartes and the quasi-historical conjectural speculations of the eighteenth century, such as the ones by Rousseau; (4) point out that genetic epistemology ultimately relies on idealizing a series of steps to uncover an immanent diachrony of a synchronic structure.

2 Genetic (or causal) definitions

It has been suggested that the origins-question was framed as a consequence of Locke's rejection of the Cartesian doctrine of innate ideas,[6] which lies at the center (or rather at the beginning) of the epistemological project of the *Essay concerning Human Understanding*. For the natural follow-up question to such a rejection is wherein lies "the original of our ideas" (Locke 1979, I.i.3, II.xxix.1), the sensualist answer to which was bound to become the cornerstone of empiricism and its extraordinary influence in eighteenth-century France. Locke's "historical, plain method" (Locke 1979, I.i.2), or, an inquiry into the genesis of one's own ideas, thus seemed to have influenced later investigations about the origins of ideas and the things dependent on these ideas and sensations. As I have mentioned, this is particularly true of language. But whereas in Locke's treatment of language in Book III of the *Essay* we do not yet find any historical speculations about the primitive stage of language which would become so characteristic of the Enlightenment, Locke's rejection of innatism in Book I nevertheless seems to have triggered the next generation of philosophers precisely in this direction: they sought to find out whether words originated in ideas or vice versa by postulating naturalist hypotheses about the primordial state of their relation.

However, despite compelling evidence of the lineage of genetic epistemology in British empiricism, I propose to complicate this picture significantly. In my view, the roots of this procedure go deeper and we may find them in potentially unexpected places, as similar tensions between the temporal and atemporal ways of grasping a particular subject have been appearing under various designations in different epochs since the ancients. At the beginning of *Parts of Animals*, for instance, Aristotle contemplates a methodological question similar to the one described above: whether the proper way of treating the subject of animals is "the way each thing is naturally generated, or rather the way it is"—and

---

[6] See, for instance, Aarsleff (1985, pp. 160–161) and also Lifschitz, according to whom the conjectural histories of the origin of language consist in "an application of Locke's genetic method [of ideas] to the Port Royal scheme" (Lifschitz 2010, p. 65).

he resolutely favors the latter (Aristotle 1991a [*Part. An.*], 640a). According to the Aristotelian view, an animal must be such and such to count as being of a particular species, and it is in virtue of this preconceived *telos* that an animal can *then* be found to be generated in a particular way: "For the generation [efficient cause by which something comes into being] is for the sake of the substance [defined by its telos or final cause] and not this for the sake of the generation" (Aristotle 1991a [*Part. An.*], 640a). The structural account not only takes precedence over the genetic account, the latter strictly speaking even adds nothing to the definition. In other words, what something *is* does not hinge on the explanation of how it *came to be*, which is why it is possible to know perfectly *what* something is, to have knowledge about its essence, and remain completely ignorant about its past or its constitutive causes. It is thus only natural for Aristotle to oppose the proto-evolutionist approaches to animal physiology by natural philosophers such as Empedocles, whose account of the spine was that it is a backbone that had been broken into vertebrae by the twisting of the fetus in the womb. Empedocles maintains that the essential features of animals are "the results of incidental occurrences during their development" (Aristotle 1991a [*Part. An.*], 640a), Aristotle complains, whereas for him the primary cause of any feature of the animal body cannot lie in the temporal, *efficient* cause that generated it; instead, it lies in the very fact that it was designed to perform a certain function, and therefore the development of this feature must have been determined atemporally, by its *final* cause.

This "essentialist" or "structural" view is consistent with the form of definitions by genus and difference and modern critics of Aristotle did not object to them merely because of the rigid ontology of the Porphyrian tree behind them. For the new philosophy that so vehemently emphasized explanation by causes, it was precisely the *static* essentialism of these definitions that was at issue, or the very fact that they produced abstract descriptions in which the essence of the defined thing was merely stated, as if isolated from the causal chain of which it was the result. It was this uneasiness with the fact that definitions, which became the very principles of every science, were completely devoid of the dynamic or causal element that was so central to the novelty of philosophy and science in the seventeenth century. Unfolding the chains of efficient causes became almost the whole story of the Baconian and Cartesian *scientia*, which is why the only proper account of what something truly *is* could be given by showing how it typically *is*, or *can be, produced*. And since there was a strong tendency in the period from Descartes to Darwin to expel final causality from science, it was efficient causality that took its place and completely monopolized scientific explanations. As calls for a new kind of logic of invention grew more and more powerful, the whole epistemological framework of logic shifted significantly from classifying and ordering the already known to researching and inventing the as-yet-unknown. It is only natural, then, that the new developments in logic and epistemology called for replacing the standard method of *genus proximum* and *differentia specifica* with a new kind of definition. Whereas Aristotelian essentialist definitions were descriptive and conveyed an essence that stood out as distinctive as a real common feature of all individuals of the same species, the new method of defining was determined to tell us what something is by giving us, so to speak, the blueprints for its creation.

In his *Logica vetus et nova*, the German logician Johannes Clauberg concludes his lengthy exposition of the technicalities of definitions by genus and difference with a seemingly unremarkable sentence: "Finally, sometimes the thing is described from its causes so that no genus is considered. Such definition is called causal and is distinguished from essential, which is based on genus and difference" (Clauberg 1658, p. 89, translation mine). That this sentence was only added in the second edition, which was published in 1658, four years after the first, is a telling detail. What most likely happened between the two publications was that Clauberg read Hobbes's *De corpore* (1655), where these so-called "causal" or "genetic" definitions[7] first appeared and were recognized explicitly as a key epistemic aid. Hobbes, too, thought that finding causes was the aim of science and knowledge and that philosophy was indeed *nothing but* knowledge of effects from the knowledge of their causes (DC I.i.2, I.vi.1). But if these causes were not already contained in definitions insofar as they were the principles of every science, he thought, they also could not suddenly emerge in the conclusions (DC I.vi.13). However obscure we may find such a justification of causal definitions, the geometrical example he had in mind is clear and stands as the model of causal definitions in philosophy: "[D]efinitions of things, which may be understood to have some cause, must consist of such names as express the cause or manner of their generation, as we define a circle to be a figure made by the circumduction of a straight line in a plane, etc." (DC I.vi.13) Of course, geometric figures had been defined by appealing to their generation by motion long before Hobbes, albeit neither exclusively nor systematically, by ancient geometers, and even by Aristotle, who described a line as the result of the rectilinear movement of a point, and a surface of a line (cf. Aristotle 1991b [*De An.*], 409a). Euclid, for instance, defined a sphere as a solid that gradually emerges when ro-

---

7 In primary literature (Hobbes, Clauberg, Leibniz, etc.) the term "causal" is used; Cassirer (1922, 1951) and Gueroult (1974), on the other hand, also use "genetic" in their seminal works on the topic. While in a more detailed discussion of the intricacies of the early modern theory of definition a distinction between the two could be made, I shall use the terms synonymously in this general exposition.

tating a semi-circle, whereas cones and cylinders are similarly produced by rotations of triangles and parallelograms, respectively (cf. *El.* XI, def. 14, 18, and 21). The procedure was particularly important in defining complex curves (conic sections, spirals, cycloids, etc.), which are better understood and imagined as resulting from more than one motion by their composite or concurring actions. Thus, Archimedes already gave such causal definition of a spiral by defining it as the product of a point moving with constant speed along a line and rotating with constant angular velocity.

In ancient geometry, genetic definitions were considered useful, but they were not the rule. It was not until the seventeenth century that they were elevated into a program, first by Hobbes and later by Newton's teacher Isaac Barrow, for whom definitions of figures using "local movements" were no longer merely heuristic tools appealing to imagination, as they seem to have been for the ancients, but became a fundamental concept of geometry.[8] Consider the following two ways of defining a circle, "static" and "genetic" (or "causal"):

1. *Static:* "a plane figure contained by a single line, [such that] all of the straight-lines radiating towards [the circumference] from one point amongst those lying inside the figure are equal to one another" (*El.* I, def. 15); or, as abridged by Spinoza: "a figure in which the lines drawn from the centre to the circumference are equal" (Spinoza 2002, p. 25).
2. *Genetic:* "a figure described by any line of which one end is fixed and the other movable" (Spinoza 2002, p. 26); or "a figure made by the circumduction of a straight line in a plane" (DC I.vi.13).

As in the case of historical and structural linguistics mentioned earlier, we see that the goals of the structural (or static) and the genetic (or causal) approach are exactly the same: to define a circle, that is, to express the essence of a circle and circle alone. But there are subtle differences: *Firstly*, the former only cites the condition that a figure must fulfill to pass for a circle, whereas the latter also gives instructions for its construction. This has very important ramifications. If we know how a certain geometric figure has been constructed or generated,

---

8 Although Euclid already did define most figures causally in his *Elements* (the circle being a notable exception), in *Examinatio et emendatio mathematicae hodiernae* (1660) Hobbes— whose reputation among mathematicians has never been good, to put it mildly—proposed to amend Euclidian geometry by transforming *all* of its definitions into causal ones. As Martial Gueroult noted, rather than inventing or revolutionizing the discipline, he thereby merely "retouched" it (Gueroult 1974, p. 483) and elevated what seemed to be its "accidental" feature into an "essential" one. For the views of Hobbes, Barrow, and Spinoza, see also Mancosu 1996, pp. 98–99.

then we also know what it is, whereas the opposite does not hold. As Hobbes notes, if we only see a circle already drawn, we may doubt whether it is a true circle. To have seen it being constructed, however, guarantees that it is indeed a circle (DC I.i.5), which also secures the correctness of all conclusions that can be deduced from it since the original assumption that it is a circle is confirmed before our eyes. Such generation or construction is therefore simply *a genetic expression of the figure's structure, a temporalization of its atemporal features*, achieved as if by projecting the figure's eternal essence onto a timeline. It is thus not surprising that Barrow considered time to be an essential ingredient of definitions in geometry and thought it was necessary to discuss it first (Barrow 1916, p. 35–39), before delving into the "Generation of magnitudes by 'local movements'" in the second of his *Geometrical Lectures*. The atemporal features of the *definiendum* are as if temporalized by the *definiens* in causal definitions.

Barrow also gave a nice summary of "the definitions of figures by motion", which are

> not only the most lawful, but the best: For they not only explain the Nature of the Magnitude defined, but, at the same time, shew its possible Existence, and evidently discover the Method of its Construction: They not only describe what it is, but prove by Experiment, that it is capable of being such; and do put beyond doubt how it becomes such. (Barrow 1734, p. 223)

Secondly, that by demonstrating the method of construction the *possibility* of the figure is proven is perhaps an obvious but philosophically significant consequence nonetheless. When a figure is defined by a kind of conceptual drawing in our imagination, the mind is not merely told what it is, but also understands that the definition can never turn out to be contradictory.[9] Moreover, as geometric figures are ideal objects, they are real as far as they are possible, and vice versa. Thus, if to secure the possibility of a figure by showing the means by

---

9 On a side note, Leibniz's criticism of Descartes' ontological proof consists in a similar argument: the proof would be valid only if Descartes had first demonstrated that his concept of God, or the essence he ascribes to him (a being possessing all perfections, including existence), is possible since "we cannot build a secure demonstration on any concept unless we know that this concept is possible, for from impossibles or concepts involving contradictions contradictory propositions can be demonstrated" (Leibniz 1975, p. 231). Descartes would thus have had to have reached his definition of God either by way of a complete analysis of the concept of God or by means of a genetic definition of the same. The latter establishes the possibility of the concept merely by considering hypothetical or possible ways of constructing the concept of God, for like in the case of geometric figures, "this is useful even though the thing in question often has not been generated in that way" (Leibniz 1975, p. 231). I return to this last characteristic of genetic definitions below.

which it can be generated means to confirm its existence as an idea, then the genetic definition of a circle amounts to nothing less than the *ontological proof of its existence*, since by proving the possibility of an ideal object, this ideal object is literally *thought into existence*. Because geometric figures only ever exist ideally, to define a circle causally is to performatively confirm its existence by the very act of showing how it may be generated.

Thirdly—and this is perhaps the most important feature of genetic definitions—as there may be more than one possible way of constructing such figures, there can be several alternative causal definitions of a single figure: "Mathematicians are not limited to the actual manner in which a magnitude has been produced; they assume any method of generation that may be best suited to their purpose" (Barrow 1916, p. 42). But since we are dealing with ideal figures, the methods of construction of course need not match the methods by which these figures actually appear in the physical world, or, as Hobbes put it, "by knowing first what figure is set before us, we may come by ratiocination to some generation of the same, though perhaps not that by which it was made, yet that by which it *might have been made*" (DC I.i.5, emphasis mine). Since a geometer is not in the business of investigating by what causes actual circles, triangles, spheres or curves appear, she is free to imagine a fictitious method of their generation that may even be physically impossible, but one that better conveys the logic of its intelligible essence. As the actual methods of constructing figures either cannot be observed or are too cumbersome to be epistemically valuable, for instance because they are bound by the laws of physics in addition to the laws of geometry, the process of their ideal genesis, which alone serves intelligibility, reverse-engineers the *fictional, ideal,* but no less *true* causes from the effects. Hence, to paraphrase Spinoza in the *Treatise on the Emendation of the Intellect*, even if no spherical objects have ever been created by the mechanical rotation of a semi-circle, the knowledge of a sphere, or rather, the *idea* of a sphere, has (cf. Spinoza 2002, p. 20).

Once we delve into the philosophical import of these characteristics, we see that geometry was influential for early modern philosophy in techniques that go beyond Descartes' method of analysis or the axiomatic presentation of Spinoza's *Ethics*. Moreover, to say that the early moderns merely emphasized the utmost importance of efficient causality in their definitions is to say too little, as causality was used in explanations in very specific ways. Objects of mathematics display an element of truth precisely when mathematicians ignore the real actual causes by which physical spheres are ordinarily made, and substitute them with ideal archetypal causes, or rather *reasons*, for the spheres' existence. The *causa sive ratio* principle that we find in Descartes, Spinoza or Leibniz thus also carries the following dimension: it seems to authorize translations between efficient causes and justificatory reasonings, it validates the rendering of logical reasons as if they were real causes.[10] What makes the concept "possible" and thus "true" in this case is not its factual correspondence with existing objects or beings, but rather the very "act of genetic construction" (Cassirer 1922, p. 127). All of the attributes of genetic definitions of figures described above—arriving at the superior intelligibility and certainty of the thing's essence by pointing out its immanent causality, the triumph of possibility over fact, and the ensuing fabrication of the causal scenario through the act of an idealized, imagined construction—had been characteristic of a significant part of epistemology since the seventeenth century, where genetic definitions were not to be used merely for finding *a priori* truths about ideal objects, but for all truths for which one may form hypotheses, that is, imagined ways of how something perhaps did not, but might have come about.

3 Descartes' fabulous genesis of the world

In his *Philosophy of the Enlightenment*, Ernst Cassirer was perhaps the first to have pointed out the far-reaching consequences of genetic definitions. The connection between the purely theoretical critique of Aristotelian definitions on the one hand and the growing need to grandiosely historicize every philosophical issue in the eighteenth century on the other has since been largely neglected. Cassirer shows that developments in the logic of definition and in social thought in early modern philosophy should be studied together (Cassirer 1951, p. 253). So, for instance, "Hobbes's political radicalism springs from [his] logical radicalism", but the connection between the two doctrines extends all the way to the origin-narratives of the Enlightenment (Cassirer 1951, p. 256). Hobbes understands the commonwealth as a political body which can be analyzed into its constituent parts, and is thus also composed and produced from them like any other body. Accordingly, Hobbes's social and political theory does not unfold from some abstract static description of the essence of the state, but from showing how the civil state is generated from interactions between individual wills, its primary constituent units, in the state of nature.[11]

---

[10] See for example Leibniz's *New Essays* (1996, p. 475): "A cause in the realm of things corresponds to a reason in the realm of truths ..."
[11] In Chapter XVII of *Leviathan*, entitled "Of the Causes, Generation, and Definition of a Common-Wealth", the definition runs like this: "*One Person, of whose Acts a great Multitude, by mutuall Covenants one with another, have made themselves every one the Author, to the end he may*

It is also widely accepted that Spinoza's views on definitions and knowledge in the *Treatise on the Emendation of the Intellect* were heavily influenced by Hobbes.[12] An additional problem Spinoza sees in traditional static definitions is that they mistake one of the thing's properties (which happens to be the *differentia specifica*) for its essence. For Spinoza, a genetic definition is not only the preferred way, but the *only* way in which the essence of the thing can be expressed, and this essence cannot be established without the proximate cause (Spinoza 2002, pp. 25–26). Martial Gueroult (1974, pp. 479–480) interpreted Spinoza's initial definition of God, on which the project of the *Ethics* hinges, as a veiled case of such genetic definition, in which Spinoza defines God like a geometer might define a circle or a sphere: God's essence (substance of infinite number of infinite attributes) is subsequently shown to constitute or stand for the cause from which all his properties—his perfection, omniscience, etc.—are *generated*.

Moreover, Hobbes's influence is clearly noticeable also in Leibniz's views. In *De synthesi et analysi universali*, a carefully composed piece on the key issues of his logic, where Leibniz makes use of the traditional distinction between nominal and real definitions, i.e., definitions explaining merely the meanings of words and those explaining the things themselves, he considers Hobbes's claim that all definitions are ultimately nominal outright scandalous since that essentially leads him to the conclusion that truth is arbitrary (Leibniz 1975, p. 231). Leibniz nonetheless adopts Hobbes's view on causal definitions and works it into his upgraded version of the distinction, so that it fits into the larger framework of his combinatorial logic of concepts. A real definition of a thing must produce knowledge of the thing by establishing the possibility or logical coherence of the defined concept. Ideally, this would be achieved by a complete analysis of the *definiendum* into "simple notions", the general categories from which complex notions such as "man", "circle" or "justice" are composed, but as this is rarely possible outside mathematics, there are alternative ways of showing that the defined concept is not contradictory. A particularly good method is precisely to show "the generation of a thing, or if this is impossible, at least its constitution, that is, a method by which the thing appears to be producible or at least possible" (Leibniz 1975, p. 230), which is "useful even though the thing in question often has not been generated in that way" (Leibniz 1975, p. 231). As we have seen above, possibility is what establishes the reality of

---

use the strength and means of them all, as he shall think expedient, for their Peace and Common Defence" (Hobbes 2005, p. 137).
12 For a detailed discussion, see Gueroult 1974, pp. 477–487.

ideal objects, such as geometric figures, but according to Leibniz this criterion should be extended to all *possibilia*, which is also the reason he has no patience for Hobbes's extreme version of nominalism.

Cassirer and Gueroult were among the few commentators who called attention to the far-reaching impact genetic definitions had on the central arguments of epistemology and metaphysics in the seventeenth century and beyond, and traced the views of Spinoza and Leibniz back to Hobbes. It is true that as far as the theory of genetic *definitions* is concerned, the line of influence is clear, since they both expressly discuss them, and Hobbes was the first to have spelled them out. However, I think that there is another step to be made because genetic *epistemology* as a general explanatory approach—though one that goes beyond merely involving efficient causal generation and very specifically mirrors the characteristics given above—predates Hobbes's *De corpore* by a couple of decades.

The fictionalized creation of the *nouveau monde* in Descartes' *The World* and its summary in the *Discourse on the Method*, but particularly the reworking of the same topic in some less dramatic passages of the *Principles of Philosophy*, are perhaps the true birthplace of modern genetic epistemology. Descartes' maneuver is well-known, although his motivations for it are less so. In *The World*, Descartes presents his physics reduced to the simple principles of extended homogeneous matter devoid of Aristotelian forms and the three laws of motion (laws of inertia, of rectilinear motion, and of the conservation of motion) by inviting the reader to imagine "another world—a wholly new one which I shall bring into being before your mind in imaginary spaces" (CSM 1, p. 90). The aim of this exercise is to prove to the reader that his system of physics is far more intelligible than the Aristotelian version ever could be. We are first invited to merely imagine that "God creates anew so much matter all around us that in whatever direction our imagination may extend, it no longer perceives any place which is empty" (CSM 1, p. 90), that this matter contains none of the forms and qualities associated with the theory of four elements, that it is also no "'prime matter' of the philosophers" but instead "a real, perfectly solid body which uniformly fills the entire length, breadth and depth of this huge space" (CSM 1, p. 91), and that God divides it into many particles of different shapes; and then

> he causes some to start moving in one direction and others in another, some faster and others slower (or even, if you wish, not at all); and he causes them to continue moving thereafter in accordance with the ordinary laws of nature. For God has established these laws in such a marvellous way that even if we suppose he creates nothing beyond what I have mentioned, and sets up no order or proportion within it but composes from it a chaos as confused and muddled as any the poets could describe, the laws of nature are sufficient to cause the parts of this chaos to disentangle themselves and arrange themselves in such

good order that they will have the form of a quite perfect world—a world in which we shall be able to see not only light but also all the other things, general as well as particular, which appear in the real world. (CSM 1, p. 91)

Descartes takes special care to emphasize that he is not describing how God *really created* our world but only how he *could have created* it, or rather *could create it anew* if he wished to do so (CSM 1, p. 92). The possibility of such creation is guaranteed by the intelligibility of everything Descartes is asking us to imagine, namely, the properties of Cartesian matter and its laws of motion. In Descartes' view, the problem with Aristotelian prime matter was that its extension was understood as one of its accidents and not as its essence, whereas in the mechanist Cartesian picture it is solely from extension and the laws of motion that all other sensible qualities and all natural phenomena, in short, all things "which appear in the real world", can be understood or "generated". Again, it is the process of generation or construction that establishes the intelligibility and thus the possibility of such a world, it is through the vision of genesis that the structure of anything can be understood, which is enabled by the fact that within the genetic discourse, the rational order of explanation matches the supposed chronological order of causes.[13] Similarly to what Hobbes, Barrow, Spinoza, and others said about geometric figures, in Descartes' view the nature (*structure*) of material things, too, "is much easier to conceive if we see them develop gradually [i.e., *genetically*] in this way than if we consider them only in their completed form" (CSM 1, pp. 133–134).

The motivation for this rhetorical fabulation in *The World* is not subversive per se; Descartes' agenda is not to plant an alternative cosmology in disguise and then cover his back by insisting that it is merely a fable. Rather, the role of fiction here is in every way the same as in genetic definitions: Descartes elevates possibility over reality like a geometer—truth is found in idealizations rather than facts. As Catherine Labio nicely summarizes the central point of these passages, "fiction creates its own truth and is therefore closer to geometry than to history" (Labio 2004, p. 15). Thus, Descartes has no reasons, at least no strictly *philosophical* reasons, for denying the first Book of Moses the status of true historical fact, it is rather that the structure of anything is better understood through development, and the Mosaic narrative unfortunately only gives us a creation of the universe in its "completed form". This passage from the *Principles of Philosophy* could not be any clearer:

---

13 Or, as Jacques Chouillet commented in a similar context, "the order supposed by history does not essentially differ from the order of reason" (Chouillet 1972, p. 49).

> Nevertheless, if we want to understand the nature of plants or of men, it is much better to consider how they can gradually grow from seeds than to consider how they were created by God at the very beginning of the world. Thus we may be able to think up certain very simple and easily known principles which can serve, as it were, as the seeds from which we can demonstrate that the stars, the earth and indeed everything we observe in this visible world *could have sprung*. For although we know for sure that they *never did arise in this way*, we shall be able to provide a much better explanation of their nature by this method than if we merely described them as they now are or as we believe them to have been created. (CSM 1, p. 256, emphases mine)

This is the Cartesian speculative and idealist (more on that later) moment: according to Descartes, we do know the "facts" about the beginning of the world because they are depicted in the Book of Genesis quite colorfully. The problem with these "facts" is not, as one might too hastily assume, their unscientific or dogmatic pedigree, but that they are just facts, events, and as such they might as well be random and thus useless to scientific explanation (cf. Labio 2004, p. 25). The problem with history, however detailed and accurate, is that a mere succession of indubitable facts does not add up to a genuine explanation of a phenomenon, and history therefore rarely gives us causes in the proper philosophical sense of the word, which is why Cartesian fiction is better positioned to satisfy our understanding. The fabricated narrative about the possible emergence of a new world, or the merely possible origin of our world, on the other hand, is an intelligible and idealized sequence which reveals truth beyond facts, it is a description of the structure of the material universe which coincides with the genetic unfolding of causes ruling it. Whereas according to Descartes our world was not in fact created in the way he proposes (God did not really let the planets and beings of the earth develop from such seeds but rather created them in their final shape during the six days), the truth his fiction conveys nevertheless *does explain our world* and not merely some alternative fictitious one. So, whereas the alternative narrative is fictitious, the truth it conveys is not; as Descartes insists, "[t]he falsity of these suppositions does not prevent the consequences deduced from them being true and certain" (CSM 1, p. 257). The *ex falso quodlibet* principle does not apply here for the reason that fiction in genetic epistemology is a kind of non-factual truth and not contradiction and the fabricated succession of causes is no less ideal then geometric figures are, which is precisely why Descartes' fictitious genesis belongs to "the order of geometry rather than history or literature" (Labio 2004, p. 24). And finally, just like there is more than one possible genetic definition of a single figure, so there can be more than one explanation of the genesis of the world and all natural phenomena even if none of these explanations are historical facts; for although this method may enable us to understand how all the things in nature could have arisen, it should not therefore be inferred that they were in fact made in this way. Just as the same craftsman could make two clocks which tell the time equally well and look completely alike from the outside but have completely different assemblies of wheels inside, so the supreme craftsman of the real world could have produced all that we see in several different ways. (CSM 1, p. 289)

Descartes orders the synchronically operating physical causes (which operate as *reasons* within an explanation) on a diachronic axis, which can be either fictitious, like the creation of the universe in *The World*, or merely a possibility of how "everything we observe in this visible world *could have sprung*", as we have seen in the quote from the *Principles*. In the latter case, he projects the present into the past, so to speak, in order to untangle the complexity of the universe into easily understood chains of causes and effects.

Catherine Labio made the point that insofar as Descartes rejected historical fact in favor of intelligible fable, he thereby brought the question of genesis from the past to the present, since Descartes' genesis of his *nouveau monde* brings a vision of its creation into the present, whereby he visually communicates its causes to the reader. And yet, since, as we have seen, the temporal dimension is a crucial component of genetic definitions (and Descartes' method in *The World* and the *Principles* is essentially an elaborated version of such "definition"), I cannot agree with her conclusion that Descartes' fable "collapses the past into the present and it attests to the superiority of the visual over the narrative" (Labio 2004, p. 18). Descartes' distrust in history and *verisimilitude* as its mode of knowledge in the *Discourse*, his alleged "ahistoricism", does not get rid of temporality or narrative, it merely abandons historical facticity as irrelevant. If there is an original feature of genetic epistemology, it is in the very fact that *it presents atemporal logical reasons and conditions as if they were causal events operating on a timeline*, albeit merely an ideal or imagined one. Is it thus not rather that in deciding to describe the structure of this world (its mechanical principles and laws of motion, etc.) by imagining an alternative set of events that had led to its present formation (passive homogeneous particles of matter to which laws of motion were prescribed by God, after which the universe, all by itself, gradually acquired its present form), Descartes in fact demonstrates the epistemological *superiority of the narrative over the visual?* It isn't that Descartes' geneticism (like any geneticism) "collapses" or translates the historical diachronic question into a synchronic question about the present state of the world; quite the opposite: to explain the structure of the universe operating now as it does at any other given moment, to make it more intelligible than the Mosaic narrative, he redistributes the synchronic causes onto a diachronic axis and thus *projects the present onto some alternative past*. It is precisely because in the case of describing the mechanical principles of the universe one has to account for the complexity of many simultaneous causes and effects, rendering the synchronic visual complexity less intelligible, that the narrative discourse, which segments the knot of concurrent conditions into a neatly spaced out chronology of causes and effects, is superior. But the real message of this ideal, quasi-historical narrative, this non-fact-based, fictitious, but entirely possible sequence of events, is to explain not how the world *could have come to be* but how it *really is here and now*. Instead of portraying the entanglement of essential properties of matter and the principles of its changes operating simultaneously, however conditioning one another, Descartes unties the knot of logical conditioning on a temporal axis in the form of a "first-then" narrative in order to separate the individual layers of his explanation. Again, it is the ambiguity of the *causa sive ratio* principle that enables this. The dichotomy is thus not between the past and the present, as Labio portrays it, but between diachrony and synchrony, and Descartes does not make historical issues present, but merely presents structural problems genetically, explains the intricacies of synchronic system diachronically. His frequent mentions that showing the producibility of a thing reveals its nature (which is precisely the business of genetic or causal definitions) confirms this: the thing's structure (nature) can be revealed by its genesis (its producibility), even if it is fictitious (how it *may be* or *may have been* produced, even if it *never is* nor *was* produced in this way), or rather, precisely *because* it is fictitious—since intelligibility is reached by idealizing.

4 Discourse on idealized origins

We cannot simply pit Descartes' "ahistoricism" against the eighteenth century's historically ornamented inquiries into origins because we cannot simply interpret their differences in the light of a move from essentialism to historicism, or from philosophy as a system-building endeavor to an obsession with our own past. In fact, if we compare Descartes with someone like Rousseau, we find that Rousseau's explanatory fiction of the state of nature repeats the method Descartes applies to his physics almost point by point. Let us recall Rousseau's brief reflections on his elaborate narrative about the state of nature from the preface to the *Discourse on Inequality:*

> [F]or it is no light undertaking to separate what is original from what is artificial in the present Nature of man, and to know correctly a state which no longer exists, which perhaps never existed, which probably never will exist, and about which it is nevertheless necessary

to have precise Notions [*des notions justes*] in order to judge our present state correctly. (Rousseau 1992, p. 13)

And a little later in the Exordium he adds:

Let us therefore begin by setting all the facts aside, for they do not affect the question. The Researches which can be undertaken concerning this Subject must be not taken for historical truths, but only for hypothetical and conditional reasonings better suited to clarify the Nature of things than to show their genuine origin, like those our Physicists make every day concerning the formation of the World. (Rousseau 1992, p. 19)

Rousseau leaves no doubt that conceptual truth of his *notions justes* regarding "the Nature of things" takes precedence over any historically accurate account of events. Regardless of the consistently used past tense, with which he goes on to describe the states and contingent events responsible for the progression of primitive men to the point of the emergence of private property and the formation of social bonds, he admits that the whole story has nothing to do with actual historical past. Not unlike Descartes and his *nouveau monde*, the aim of the better part of conjectural histories of the Enlightenment is not to describe a succession of states, but to disclose logical conditioning, or, the rational architectonic of explanation. Precise notions, correct concepts, and logical explanations are necessary for knowledge of the present structure of society, and an imagined but possible history of this kind merely happens to be the most convenient method of grasping them. What this means for Rousseau is that his conjectures about prehistory would lose nothing of their philosophical truth even if they were proven to be wrong, for history can only confirm these *notions justes*, never falsify them. The conjectural narrative of the "development" of civil society from the state of nature is supposed to show the internal structure of its present situation, to provide a systematic analysis of the struggles of men and the antagonisms of society.[14] As I have mentioned above, Cassirer was the first to make this bold connection between the logic of genetic definitions and the conjectural histories of the Enlightenment: "Rousseau offers us the picture of the development of

---

14 Similarly, Condillac's *Essay on the Origin of Human Knowledge* (Condillac 2001) employs a quasi-historical narrative about the gradually developing cognitive and linguistic abilities of men, but this story is also historical only in appearance. In fact, it is designed to unveil the structure of the human cognitive and linguistic apparatus. Rousseau's and Condillac's aim is to bring to light the relations of conditioning between human abilities and social institutions, to decide which are more primitive than others universally, regardless of whether they could actually be found anytime anywhere in their pure state, even if the rhetoric of their narratives suggests they could.

middle-class society not as an epical narrative, but as arising from that 'genetic definition' which is the fundamental method of the philosophy of law and of the state in the seventeenth and eighteenth centuries", and this "genetic" method is for Rousseau the only viable method of discovering the secrets of the "structure" of society and its "immanent forces" (Cassirer 1951, p. 270).

It is clear that the quasi-historical narratives about the origins of society in the *Discourse on Inequality*, or, for instance, of language in the *Essay on the Origin of Languages*, target the present state of society and language rather than their past, just as Descartes' fictional narrative of the genesis of his universe is bound to explain its mechanist principles at work "here and now", and not to compete with the Book of Genesis. What both Descartes and Rousseau essentially do is that they project the complex order of reasons and causes onto a temporal axis in order to present the logical relations of grounding to the imagination of the reader by means of a more accessible rhetorical vehicle—narrative. The differences between Descartes and Rousseau in this respect are essentially ones of degree, rhetoric, and subject matter, but not of method. Whereas Descartes leaves the status of fact to the Book of Genesis but proposes fiction as an alternative narrative because of its greater intelligibility, Rousseau does not know any specific facts about the life of savage men in prehistory but tells their story in the mode of "must-have-been" history. The sole reason why Descartes discarded history altogether whereas Rousseau skillfully, if selectively, weaved it into his narratives may well lie in the different kinds of subject matter their theories tried to cover—the basic principles of physics in the case of Descartes, and society in the case of Rousseau.

Genetic epistemology has been very persistent throughout the history of philosophy, and yet it seems that it still has not deserved to be mentioned in textbooks on philosophical methodology. Once its basic formula has been determined, it is not hard to find its traces everywhere, from Giambattista Vico's principle of *verum et factum convertuntur*, according to which we can know only what we ourselves create, to nineteenth-century theories of etymology and evolution. In philosophy, it seems to return on a regular basis, and the debate mentioned at the beginning of this paper was not its last occurrence. Mostly following Nietzsche, thinkers such as Foucault, Bernard Williams, and recently Matthieu Queloz recognized under the term *genealogy* a technique that is related, albeit more limited in its field of application: "A genealogy is a narrative that tries to explain a cultural phenomenon by describing a way in which it came about, or could have come about, or might be imagined to have come about"

(Williams 2002, p. 20).[15] Such narratives certainly *can* be historically accurate; however, they are truly epistemologically productive when they are not—when an imagined, fictitious, yet logical succession of steps or events is "truer" than the actual course of events ever was or could be. Moreover, "genealogical", "genetic", "diachronic" or "temporal"—terms I have been largely using synonymously as involving a succession of steps on a timeline—coincide with "historical" only sporadically also owing to the fact that the speculations of genetic epistemology are of such a nature that it is often in principle impossible to confirm them historically as facts. In this sense, despite their obvious and important differences, causal definitions of geometry and the ones advocated by Hobbes, Spinoza, and Leibniz, Descartes' cosmological fable, the origin-narratives of Rousseau, and other conjectural histories of the Enlightenment all align with the general definition of genealogy.

All these procedures are related to the concept of idealization, specifically "Galilean idealization", in philosophy of science, according to which the target that needs to be explained or described is replaced by a simplified and distorted model that is more "mathematically tractable" (Weisberg 2012, p. 99). Conjectural histories, causal definitions, and other genetic accounts, too, are idealized distorted models of a kind, more intelligible than overly accurate empirical descriptions because they are unspoiled by chance, individual idiosyncrasies, and other cognitive noise associated with minute historical or empirical facts, which is why they can be said to be "logically tractable". Through a kind of "leap of reason", fiction, one that relies on idealization, has turned out to be the superior path to truth. Genetic epistemology in this sense shows idealist contours, but in the following restricted, non-subjective Platonist sense: there is an archetypal explanation of every phenomenon that a careful description of observed facts only ever approximates and never completely matches, and which exalts possibility above fact, idea above its instantiation. When the "factual" events that have caused it remain forever unknown, its idealized, merely possible past is retroactively projected onto it as its "true" past, thereby uncovering an immanent diachrony of a synchronic structure.

Bibliography

Aarsleff, Hans (1985): *From Locke to Saussure: Essays on the Study of Language and Intellectual History.* Minneapolis: University of Minnesota Press.

---

15 See also Queloz 2021.

Aristotle (1991a): "Parts of Animals". Translated by W. Ogle. In: *The Complete Works of Aristotle*. The revised Oxford translation. Vol. 1. Edited by Jonathan Barnes. Princeton: Princeton University Press, pp. 994–1086.

Aristotle (1991b): "On the Soul". Translated by J. A. Smith. In: *The Complete Works of Aristotle*. The revised Oxford translation. Vol. 1. Edited by Jonathan Barnes. Princeton: Princeton University Press, pp. 641–692.

Barrow, Isaac (1734): *Mathematical Lectures*. Translated by John Kirkby. London.

Barrow, Isaac (1916): *Geometrical Lectures*. Translated by J. M. Child. Chicago and London: Open Court.

Cassirer, Ernst (1922): *Das Erkenntnisproblem in der Philosophie und Wissenschaft der neueren Zeit*. 3rd edn. Vol. 2. Berlin: Bruno Cassirer.

Cassirer, Ernst (1951): *The Philosophy of the Enlightenment*. Translated by Fritz C. A. Koelln and James P. Pettergrove. Princeton, NJ: Princeton University Press.

Chouillet, Jacques (1972): "Descartes et le problème de l'origine des langues au 18e siècle". In: *Dix-huitième siècle* 4. No. 1, pp. 39–60.

Clauberg, Johannes (1658): *Logica vetus et nova*. 2nd edn. Amsterdam: Elzevir.

Condillac, Etienne Bonnot de (2001): *Essay on the Origin of Human Knowledge*. Translated by Hans Aarsleff. Cambridge: Cambridge University Press.

Gandillac, Maurice de/Goldmann, Lucien/Piaget, Jean (Eds.) (1965): *Entretiens sur les notions de genèse et structure*. Paris: Mouton.

Gandillac, Maurice de (1965): "Jalons pour une conclusion". In: Maurice de Gandillac/Lucien Goldmann/Jean Piaget (Eds.): *Entretiens sur les notions de genèse et structure*. Paris: Mouton, pp. 337–353.

Goldmann, Lucien (1965): "Introduction Générale". In: Maurice de Gandillac/Lucien Goldmann/Jean Piaget (Eds.): *Entretiens sur les notions de genèse et structure*. Paris: Mouton, pp. 7–35.

Gueroult, Martial (1974): *Spinoza*. Vol. 2 (*L'âme*). Hildesheim: Olms.

Hobbes, Thomas (2005): *Leviathan*. Vol. 2. Edited by G. A. J. Rogers and Karl Schumann. London: Continuum.

Hyppolite, Jean (1946): *Genèse et structure de la Phénoménologie de l'esprit de Hegel*. Paris: Aubier.

Kahn, Gilbert (1965): "Genèse et structure dans les systèmes philosophiques". In: Maurice de Gandillac/Lucien Goldmann/Jean Piaget (Eds.): *Entretiens sur les notions de genèse et structure*. Paris: Mouton, pp. 181–199.

Labio, Catherine (2004): *Origins and the Enlightenment: Aesthetic Epistemology from Descartes to Kant*. Ithaca, NY: Cornell University Press.

Lanteri-Laura, Georges (1967): "Histoire et structure dans la connaissance de l'homme". In: *Annales* 22. No. 2, pp. 792–828.

Leibniz, Gottfried Wilhelm (1975): "On Universal Synthesis and Analysis, or the Art of Discovery and Judgment". In: *Philosophical Papers and Letters*. Translated and edited by Leroy E. Loemker. Dordrecht: Kluwer, pp. 229–234.

Leibniz, Gottfried Wilhelm (1996): *New Essays on Human Understanding*. Translated by Peter Remnant and Jonathan Bennett. Cambridge and New York: Cambridge University Press.

Lifschitz, Avi (2010): "The Enlightenment's 'Experimental Metaphysics': Inquiries into the Origins and History of Language". In: Tristan Coignard/Peggy Davis/Alicia C. Montoya

(Eds.): *Lumières et histoire/Enlightenment and History*. Paris: Honoré Champion, pp. 63–76.

Locke, John (1979): *An Essay concerning Human Understanding*. Edited by Peter H. Nidditch. Oxford: Clarendon Press.

Mancosu, Paolo (1996): *Philosophy of Mathematics and Mathematical Practice in the Seventeenth Century*. Oxford and New York: Oxford University Press.

Piaget, Jean (1965): "Genèse et structure en psychologie". In: Maurice de Gandillac/Lucien Goldmann/Jean Piaget (Eds.): *Entretiens sur les notions de genèse et structure*. Paris: Mouton, pp. 37–61.

Queloz, Mathieu (2021): *The Practical Origins of Ideas: Genealogy as Conceptual Reverse-Engineering*. Oxford: Oxford University Press.

Rousseau, Jean-Jacques (1992): "The Discourse on the Origins and Foundations of Inequality among Men". In: *The Collected Writings of Rousseau*. Vol. 3. Edited by Roger D. Masters and Christopher Kelly. Hanover and London: University Press of New England, pp. 1–95.

Saussure, Ferdinand de (2011): *Course in General Linguistics*. Translated by Wade Baskin. New York: Columbia University Press.

Spinoza (2002): "Treatise on the Emendation of the Intellect". In: *Complete Works*. Translated by Samuel Shirley. Indianapolis: Hackett, pp. 3–30.

Stewart, Dugald (1982): "An Account of the Life and Writings of Adam Smith, LL.D." In: *The Glasgow Edition of the Works and Correspondence of Adam Smith*. Vol. 3. Edited by I. S. Ross. Indianapolis: Liberty Fund, pp. 269–351.

Weisberg, Michael (2012): *Simulation and Similarity: Using Models to Understand the World*. Oxford: Oxford University Press.

Williams, Bernard (2002): *Truth & Truthfulness: An Essay in Genealogy*. Princeton and Oxford: Princeton University Press.

Miran Božovič
Diluvian Philosophy: Utilitarian Motifs in *Moby-Dick*

Abstract: Using utilitarianism as an example, the still obscure hidden balances between realist and idealist tendencies within a single either explicitly realist or explicitly idealist system of thought will be investigated. This essay considers the whaleship *Pequod* in Melville's *Moby-Dick* as a utilitarian universe and examines its narrator's notion of the utility of the skeletons of stranded whales. As the essay argues, this notion, alongside Ishmael's brief reference to Jeremy Bentham's skeleton, suggests that Melville may have had some familiarity with the highly unorthodox and radical ideas developed by the utilitarian sage in his last work *Auto-Icon; or Farther Uses of the Dead to the Living*, in which he set out the reasons for having his own skeleton preserved after his death and outlined its numerous possible uses. Both cases reveal that the utilitarian universe has a tendency to become self-referential, or even put itself on display; it not only engenders a world of utter and multifarious utility, but at the same time produces the light by which it showcases the ideality of this very doing.

Viewed from a sufficient distance, the history of philosophy may seem like a relentless oscillation between idealist and realist tendencies, a toing and froing never to be settled once and for all. Bearing in mind how Plato was succeeded by Aristotle, the rationalists by the empiricists, Kant and Hegel by Marx and Nietzsche, one might be tempted to surmise that an idealist "upswing" is commonly reciprocated by a more realist "earthing". What is, however, more interesting is the fact that even within a single either explicitly idealist or explicitly realist philosophical stance, there is always an implicit price to pay for the excluded, suppressed opposite. Just like the sum of bad habits is said to be constant, so the quantity of realism and idealism within one system seems to abide by the still obscure law of even balances and stable equilibria.

Funding note: The research included in this chapter was funded by the Slovenian Research Agency (ARRS) under the research project "The Possibility of Idealism for the Twenty-First Century" (J6–1811).

Miran Božovič, University of Ljubljana.

https://doi.org/10.1515/9783110760767-006

Typically, the idealists have a surprising propensity to reveal dimensions of reality perhaps unheard-of and uncanny even to the realists themselves. And vice versa, the realists tend to institute ideal frameworks that are superfluous in the philosophies of idealism. Plato, the originator of idealism, thus postulated the existence of *khôra*, the "third kind", a material substratum underlying and preceding any formation of forms; it is an indiscrete, pre-ideal spatial continuum. Similarly, the dualist Descartes unrolled his extension, a purely geometrical, inert, and passive three-dimensionality devoid of any psychic entities and spiritual qualities. And the transcendental idealist Kant advocated a variety of Newtonian space, i.e., a reality lacking any gaps, leaps, chance, and fate. On the other hand, the more empiristically and hence realistically inclined philosophers never seemed to be able to perform their anti-idealist descents and reductions without concomitantly setting up frames of unprecedented idealizations. Aristotle, for instance, imbues all matter (such as bronze) with "potentiality", which becomes "actuality" only by assuming a form (say, of a statue); as a consequence, his hylomorphism can only hold together the dynamics of matter and form by postulating the existence of teleological causes ingrained in nature itself: this "immanent teleology" is a frame of idealization absent in Platonist ontology. The empiricists perhaps make an even more striking case for the "return of the suppressed idealism", given that they soon discover that a world made entirely of sense perceptions can only be upheld by the constant presence of a mind possessing ideas. In its starkest form, Berkeley's elimination of primary substances boils down to the most outright idealism to date, i.e., an immaterialism in which the existence of things depends on their being perceived by a spirit. Here, paradoxically, the initial Lockean critique of the spiritual entities of innate ideas finally leads to the Berkeleyan ontology consisting of nothing but minds and ideas. On a totally different, otherwise incomparable plane, post-Hegelian philosophy prided itself on being categorically un-metaphysical, yet its program of anti-idealism was forced to adopt normative horizons of new ideals that are not to be found in traditional metaphysics. It is therefore quite telling that, while the "absolute idealist" Hegel ultimately declared the acceptance of the existing social order, it was the "historical realist" Marx who propagated the necessity of social change, burgeoning under the aegis of the idea of communism. Similarly, the entire Nietzschean devaluation of ideals could only be accomplished alongside their concurrent normative "transvaluation": the "realism" of Nietzsche's passive nihilism is strictly counterbalanced with the "idealism" of active nihilism, the eternal return with *amor fati*, the "twilight of the idols" with the future giving birth to the overman. In short, there seems to be no idealism without the remorse of realism and no realism without the final idealist touch.

In this vein, the paper will demonstrate one of the fundamentally non-idealist philosophies, utilitarianism, developing its unanticipated, peculiar, but nevertheless unavoidable, perhaps even sorely needed idealist "superstructure". Bentham, as will be seen, was so obsessed with the idea of an all-encompassing utility of everything in the world that he instructed for his body to be preserved after death as a skeleton for the use of future generations. Here, the founder of utilitarianism not only did something useful even with his own corpse—the benefits of preserving one's bones are of course debatable and arguably negligible—but he simultaneously erected a monument to his own idea of utility and, thereby, to himself: after his death, he became nothing less than an auto-icon. Perhaps the real crux of becoming an icon of oneself lies not so much in the compulsive conviction of the possibility of utilizing everything, even dead bodies, but rather in a single flesh-and-blood utilitarian, one by the name of Jeremy Bentham, finding himself incapable of merely perishing, leaving the world of things being useful without him. An accomplished utilitarian would presumably have to be ready to pass away without a trace; however, to leave behind something as futile and redundant as an auto-icon only shows that even the most consistent, consuming pragmatic system cannot do without succumbing to its own inherent idealism, one of creating ideas of itself, of immortalization and self-glorification.

Ensuing from a no less fascinating example, the paper will present the case of the happily, almost idyllically secluded world of the whaleship *Pequod* from Herman Melville's *Moby-Dick*. This vessel is conceived as a utilitarian universe in microcosm, a place where everything serves some purpose, every single thing expands its services to other, multiple uses, and nothing remains outside the remit of total utility. Nevertheless, even this seemingly benevolent whole of autarkic convenience cannot but produce an "idealist scaffolding", so to speak. In a number of ingenious literary scenes and inventions, Melville presents us with a utilitarian universe developing its own self-referential folds: a whale being cooked over the fire fueled by its own remains; its meat being eaten by whalers by the light of a lamp burning the whale's oil; the whaleship being cleaned of the remains of the dead whale by means of the same whale's other remains; books on whales being read through the magnifying lens made from whale skin; and finally, the skeleton of a whale being employed as an icon of itself. If one dares to read Melville in particular and utilitarianism in general metaphorically, one might detect a tendency to perpetually overvalue, overdraw, and almost idolize the inconspicuous elements of use into ideals of utility, thereby elevating this entire cosmos of mere practical functions into a glaring, flaunting, inevitably visible monument to itself. It may well be that a utilitarian universe is incapable of not praising and venerating itself; it not only engenders a world of utter and multifarious utility but also produces the light by which it showcases the ideality of this very doing.

Just like naïve realism could be deemed the "spontaneous ideology" of everyday life, so does some sort of automatic idealism often seem to pose as the most natural, primary philosophical outlook. According to Berkeley's "master argument", even while conceiving of things as existing without the mind, the mind still conceives of them as such, thus encapsulating everything within an idealist bubble. But perhaps a more persuasive case for idealism could be made from the other end, namely, by pointing out its obstinacy and fated inescapability. Even if one chooses to proceed from a perspective as contrary to idealism as possible—and utilitarianism is certainly such an attitude—some remnant of ideality, that of elevating the realist, materialist, empiricist, utilitarian, nihilist subject into an idea of herself, always creeps up on one from behind.

1

Of the several skeletons referred to by Melville in *Moby-Dick*, two can still be seen today. One is the skeleton of a sperm whale that washed ashore near Tunstall in East Yorkshire, England, in 1825, where it was dissected, its bones preserved, reassembled, and then exhibited at the Burton Constable estate nearby, where it remains to this day. The other is "Jeremy Bentham's skeleton" (p. 208),[1] perhaps better known today as the "auto-icon", as Bentham himself termed it. It was Bentham's last wish that after his death his body be dissected, and his skeleton preserved and exhibited, which, in fact, did happen after his death in 1832. Thus, Bentham's skeleton, like the skeleton of the Yorkshire whale, can still be seen today. Both dissections were accompanied by lectures given by the anatomists performing the dissection, which were both published soon afterwards.[2] Shortly before his death, Bentham wrote a pamphlet—a sort of philosophical companion piece to his preserved skeleton—entitled *Auto-Icon; or, Farther Uses of the Dead to the Living*,[3] in which he expounded his extraordinary last wish

---

[1] Whenever only the page number is given, the reference is to *Moby-Dick* (Melville 2018).

[2] See Alderson 1827 and Southwood Smith 1832. While Alderson gave his lecture about a fortnight after cutting up the dead whale, Southwood Smith presented his lecture over Bentham's dead body, which was lying on the dissecting table, that is, immediately before or during the anatomical dissection. For a view from the public and a vivid description of the atmosphere in the dissecting theater during the lecture and dissection, see Lewes 1898, pp. 46–47.

[3] There is no date of publication and no editor or publisher name given on the title page of this privately printed, 21-page volume. The copy I consulted in the Houghton Library at Harvard Uni-

as an example of the principle of utility. While the influence of the Yorkshire whale skeleton on *Moby-Dick* is incontrovertible and well studied,[4] that of Bentham's skeleton is perhaps less well explored and appreciated. It is uncertain whether Melville actually saw Bentham's skeleton when he visited London in 1849, or whether he read the *Auto-Icon*. In the fairly detailed journal he kept of the trip, there is no word of that. However, since he knew about Bentham's skeleton, it seems very likely that Melville had at least some knowledge of the highly unorthodox and radical ideas contained in the accompanying pamphlet. Melville's *Moby-Dick* is the earliest—and the only—direct reference to Bentham's preserved skeleton in nineteenth-century fiction that I am aware of.

Jacques-Alain Miller says somewhere of Bentham's Panopticon that it is "the model of the utilitarian world: in it, ... nothing is contingent, nothing exists for its own sake", and "no object is merely itself, no activity is an end in itself" (Miller 1987, p. 6). In the utilitarian universe, everything, including waste, must serve a purpose, often even several different purposes at a time. Utility, in short, should be maximized. As Ishmael discovers, the same also holds true, to a large extent, for the compact microcosm of the whaleship *Pequod*, in which the reason for the existence of most things lies in their utility.

The manifold utility of the objects making up the universe of the *Pequod*, that is, their polychrest nature, is perhaps best captured by the metaphor of the so-called "Sheffield contrivances" (p. 343), a concept used by Ishmael, in Chapter 107, to characterize the "singularly efficient" ship carpenter, who was "alike experienced in numerous trades and callings collateral to his own" (p. 341). Thus, on the ship's three- or four-year voyages, the carpenter takes care of everything, from woodwork and frequent carpentry repairs and piercing sailors' ears, to healing their injured joints and pulling out their teeth. As Ishmael says, the "Sheffield contrivance" is a *"multum in parvo"* (p. 343) device, that is, a pocket knife that contains not only blades, but also numerous other tools, such as screwdriver, corkscrew, tweezers, and so forth. Using the metaphor of the "Sheffield contrivance", Ishmael describes the all-purpose, do-it-all ship carpenter as an "omnitooled, open-and-shut carpenter" (p. 343).

On the outside, then, a "Sheffield contrivance" looks like "a common pocket knife" (343); but when we take it in hand and inspect it closely, we come to realize with surprise that it hides within itself numerous unexpected features and could therefore serve not only for cutting but also for several other purposes.

---

versity bears the following handwritten inscription: "Not Published & the few copies printed were suppressed."

4 See, for example, Credland 1989.

Similarly, throughout the voyage, Ishmael repeatedly discovers the polychrest nature of objects found aboard the *Pequod*. The objects he sees turn out to be not merely themselves. Thus, in Chapter 3, Queequeg's tomahawk turns out to be not only a hatchet but also a pipe; and, in Chapter 128, the coffin—after having already served as a sea chest in Chapter 110—turns out also to be a life buoy. These paradoxical, intermediary objects are, accordingly, termed by Ishmael "tomahawk pipe" (p. 58) and "coffin life-buoy" (p. 410). The polychrest nature of objects is closely worked into the very fabric of the novel itself. As is revealed in the "Epilogue", it is precisely because the coffin was not merely itself that we know of Ishmael's story of Ahab's quest for the white whale at all (p. 410).

2

Let us take a brief look at some examples of maximizing the utility of things found aboard the *Pequod* that seem to particularly attract Ishmael's attention.

Let us first consider the *Pequod* itself. Unlike most ships, which are loaded with "alien stuff", that is, with random cargo that they simply transport from one place to another, the *Pequod*, as we read in Chapter 87, carries "no cargo but herself and crew" (p. 285), together with their weapons and the items necessary for their survival at sea. The whaleship, in short, is its own—and only—cargo. Even the whaleship's ballast, that is, the heavy material used to stabilize it, is not an otherwise unusable substance, such as sand, lead, or iron, but, as Ishmael's keen eye notices, a three- or four-years' stock of drinking water that the whaleship carries all the way from Nantucket. The whaleship is "ballasted with utilities" (p. 285), Ishmael shrewdly observes. Here, Ishmael identifies a good example of the utility maximization: not only does the ballast benefit the whaleship through its sheer weight; it also helps ensure the crew's survival. Since it carries several years' worth of water, the whaleship does not have to stop at ports along the way in order to stock up on water. It can wholly dedicate itself to whaling, all the while replacing the weight of the water consumed with the whale oil produced along the way. Concurrently serving as both an essential good and ballast, the stock of drinking water thus makes it possible, to an important degree, for the *Pequod* to function as a self-sufficient, autonomous system, immune to disasters of even such epic proportions as the great biblical flood. What is more, the whalers, just as the whales themselves, would hardly take any note of a new Noah's flood descending on the world. Not only are they prepared for it in advance, but moreover, since they sail for three or four years in the open sea without calling at port or seeing dry land, they literally live all that time in conditions of a constant Noah's flood. Denis Diderot, in

"La philosophie antédiluvienne", one of the numerous philosophical articles he wrote for the *Encyclopédie*, examines the question of what philosophy must have been like in the pre-flood period (Diderot 1751, pp. 493a–495a). Diderot's answer is perhaps less interesting than the question itself. In the early modern period, there were other attempts at reconstructing antediluvian philosophy before Diderot. The most elaborate and perhaps the most convincing among them was made by Nicolas Malebranche, who argues that the metaphysical theory at work in paradise before the fall was nothing other than his own occasionalism (Malebranche 1980, pp. 564–565, 580–582). While antediluvian philosophy was clearly an established sub-genre of speculative philosophical historiography, Melville, with his *Moby-Dick*, can be said to have introduced a sub-genre of his own that could perhaps be termed "diluvian philosophy". In the novel, he tries to answer the question: What might philosophy have been like *during* the Flood itself? What sort of philosophical theory would have been likely to arise in the mind of someone sailing on Noah's ark? It is perhaps not unreasonable to expect that at least the practical branch of the diluvian philosophy—that is, the philosophy that helps the whalers survive in and make sense of the water world in which they live—would not be very different from Bentham's version of utilitarianism reflected in the organization and workings of his Panopticon, namely that the utility of everything should be maximized.

A further example of utility maximization can be found in Chapter 96 regarding the process of extracting oil from blubber. The fire under the pots in which the blubber is being boiled down into oil is first started with wood; not, however, with logs specifically intended for burning, but—again in the spirit of utility maximization—with wood shavings, that is, with the remnants left over from occasional woodwork repairs performed by the ship's carpenter along the way. However, once the fire is ablaze and the blubber begins to turn into oil, it is kept burning by so-called "scraps or fritters" (p. 312), that is, the remains of the tried-out blubber which end up floating atop the boiling oil and which are apparently still unctuous enough to burn. That is, the oil is obtained from the blubber by means of the remains created as a by-product in the process of obtaining the oil itself. The highly prized oil is obviously not the only good extracted from the blubber. The process of extracting the good from the whale yields not only that good itself, but also the key means of extracting it. Unable to hide his delight with this distinctively utilitarian touch, Ishmael remarks: "once ignited, the whale supplies his own fuel and burns by his own body" (p. 312). Feeding the fire under the pot in which it is being cooked, the whale is its own fuel.

An analogous example can be found in Chapter 65, where second mate Stubb is said to have eaten the whale "by his own light" (p. 230), that is, he dined on a whale steak by the light of a lamp burning the whale's oil. On the whaleship, then, the whale provides the light by which it itself is feasted on. Ishmael himself seems to be delighted by the idea of the whale being "his own light"; yet at the same time he notices that landsmen seem to find this sort of behavior—that is, the eating of whale by its own light—completely unacceptable. He considers this attitude on the part of the landsmen insincere and hypocritical. While the landsmen are repelled at the idea of seamen's eating "a newly murdered thing of the sea ... by its own light", they hardly seem to even notice that the handle of the knife they just used to cut the roast beef is itself made of beef, or, more precisely, of "the bones of the brother of the very ox [they] are eating" (p. 231); similarly, they do not seem to mind picking their teeth with a feather of the very same goose they just consumed, pieces of which having gotten stuck between their teeth. Here, Ishmael's reasoning seems to run along the following lines: While at sea, most often there is no other food than whale meat or meat of some other "newly murdered thing of the sea", and no other light than that provided by a whale—thus, at night, everything on a whaleship, including eating whale meat, must be done by the whale's own light. On land, by contrast, there are most probably plenty of other toothpicks, beside goose feathers, to pick one's teeth with after eating a goose, and plenty of other knives to cut roast beef with, not just those with handles made of ox bones. In other words, whereas on land maximizing utility may well be a matter of choice, on a whaleship at sea, by contrast, it is a matter of necessity.

Once the oil is decanted into barrels and the barrels are safely stowed below deck, the deck is covered with whale remains, blood, oil, and soot, due to the frenetic "post-mortemizing" of the whale and the processing of blubber into oil. Not for long, however. A mere day or two thereafter, as Ishmael is pleased to notice, the ship is spotlessly clean again. As we read in Chapter 98, the unprocessed sperm oil has "a singularly cleansing virtue"; as a result, "the decks never look so white" as they do after being soaked with sperm oil (p. 316). Furthermore, the whalers wash the ship clean of any remains of the whale there may be with "a potent ley" made, Ishmael explains, "from the ashes of the burned scraps of the whale" (p. 316). That is, the ley is made from the ashes of those remains of the tried-out blubber that were previously used to maintain the fire under the pots in which the blubber was melted down into oil, during which process these scraps themselves were formed as by-products. In the utilitarian universe of the whaleship, then, not even the remains of remains are left unused. Thus, the whale is not only its own fuel and its own light, but is also its own cleaner, as it is with the whale that the whalers wash the ship clean of the remains of the whale itself. In one of his essays, "Apology for Raymond Sebond", Michel de Montaigne says of rhubarb that, upon ingestion, it not only flushes the ill humors out of the body but also "carries itself off with them" (Montaigne 1965, p. 393). Just as the rhubarb purges the bowels of itself, so too does the whale clean the ship of itself.

In Chapter 68, Ishmael discusses the "infinitely thin, transparent substance" (p. 234) that covers the whale's body on the outside. Although it is the outermost layer enveloping the entire whale's body, this gelatinous substance is, strictly speaking, not yet the skin of the whale, but rather the "skin of the skin" (p. 235), as it is termed by Ishmael, ever the pedant. The skin of such a large animal as a sperm whale can only be the thick layer of its blubber. When the almost viscous, transparent "skin of the skin" dries up, it "contracts and thickens" and becomes "hard and brittle" (p. 234). Ishmael says that he is in possession of several pieces of such dried "skin of the [whale's] skin" that he uses for bookmarks —in the books on whales he is reading. Thus, whales themselves serve as bookmarks in books about themselves. Although the "skin of the skin" appears to be useless—it serves only to envelop on the outside that which is really useful about the whale, that is, the thick layer of blubber or the whale's real skin—Ishmael has nevertheless extracted a certain good from it. This, however, is not all. More accidentally than not, Ishmael has managed to increase the utility of the "skin of the [whale's] skin" even further. When marking the pages in books with the dried pieces of the "skin of the [whale's] skin", he noticed that they "exerted a magnifying influence" (p. 234) and could therefore be put to good use also in the process of reading. Seeing that he has managed, quite unexpectedly, to derive an additional collateral benefit from it, he adds: "it is pleasant to read about whales through their own spectacles" (pp. 234–235). Here, one can almost see Ishmael smiling contentedly at this clever turn of phrase. Whales, in short, serve not only as bookmarks in books about themselves, but also as the spectacles through which Ishmael reads these books.[5]

---

5 On a whaleship, even some human virtues, such as courage, are treated from a purely utilitarian point of view, that is, not in the light of their magnitude or their potential deficiency, but in the light of their usefulness or utility. As we learn in Chapter 26, in Starbuck's eyes, "courage was not a sentiment"; it was rather "a thing simply useful to him", that is, something that ought to be "always at hand upon all mortally practical occasions" (p. 97), which no doubt abound in whaling. Moreover, Starbuck, as Ishmael sees him, acts as though there were a fixed, depletable quantity of courage, which is therefore "not to be foolishly wasted" (p. 97) if it is to be available when really needed. According to Ishmael, then, Starbuck economizes on courage as if it were an essential good, a commodity such as "beef" or "bread", the quantities of which are necessarily limited on a ship.

3

The logic at work in Ishmael's examples of utility maximization, that is, the logic according to which a thing is its own object, may in this context perhaps seem somewhat contrived. But as Montaigne's example of the rhubarb shows—an example by which he illustrates the skeptical doubt that is itself an object of doubt, that is, its own object—it is nature itself that offers a good instance of this logic. In Chapter 66, Ishmael finds in nature a particularly vertiginous instance of this logic in the self-disembowelment of the sharks. In what is perhaps the most powerful scene in the novel, we see a wounded shark fiercely gnawing at itself and swallowing its own entrails oozing out from the gaping wound. The shark bites and swallows so violently and uncontrollably that its entrails—after having entered its body by way of its mouth and making a full circle through its body—come out again at the other end through the open wound. The shark is not devouring a random part of its own body, as for example the snake in the well-known *ourobóros* symbol devours its own tail, but its "entrails" (p. 232), i.e., its stomach and intestines, perhaps mostly the latter. That is to say, the shark takes into its body through its mouth that very part of its body to which its mouth leads. By entering into the body through the mouth, the intestines in fact enter into themselves. That is, the lower part of the alimentary canal enters into itself by way of the mouth, travels through itself, and exits the body again at the opposite end, within itself as its own content. In short, the shark's digestive system literally digests itself. Perhaps it is time for Melville's notion of the shark swallowing its own entrails "over and over again" (p. 232) to be given the place it deserves in the history of ideas, alongside the much older yet less complex motif of the snake devouring its own tail. While the *ouroboros*, as a symbol, has stood for many different things in its long history, a shark repeatedly swallowing its own entrails would not be a bad symbol of the utilitarian principle according to which, as Miller puts it, "everything must be usable *several times*" (Miller 1987, p. 8).

What Ishmael's examples of the manifold utility of things have in common is clearly the utility maximization of things by applying them to themselves. Thus, as we have seen, the whaleship is its own cargo, while the whale is its own fuel, its own light, and its own cleaner, and the shark's intestines are their own content, and so forth. Judging by the unmistakable passion Ishmael displays in discovering and describing these examples of utility, it seems as if, in his eyes, the ultimate good can be extracted from a thing—for obvious reasons, most often a whale—only by applying it to itself, that is, by making it its own object. The majority of these examples—such as the whale as its own fuel, its own light, and its own cleaner—come from Ishmael's attentive observation of the structure and workings of the utilitarian microcosm of the whaleship, whereas the notion of whales as spectacles, through which Ishmael reads his whale books, appears to be his own invention. With this example, Ishmael perhaps overstretches the principle of utility. It seems as if he wanted, at any cost, to enrich the series of examples mainly derived from observation of the utilitarian universe around him with an analogously structured example of his own, and, in so doing, to show off what he has learned at "[his] Yale College and [his] Harvard" (p. 95) —among other things, the central premise of the utilitarian philosophy that utility should be maximized.

4

Which brings us to Bentham and his own skeleton, which, Ishmael says, is kept "in the library of one of his executors", where it "hangs for candelabra" (p. 208). While Bentham would most probably enthusiastically approve of the "farther uses" of the dead whale identified by Ishmael, that is, his notions of the whale as its own fuel, its own light, its own cleaner, and so forth, he would, no doubt, add at least one further notion—that of the dead whale as "[its] own image". In support of this view, he could cite his last work, *Auto-Icon; or, Farther Uses of the Dead to the Living*. This essay on his own death and the subsequent fate of his body—the genre of which he aptly labeled "auto-thanatography" (Bentham [1842?], p. 2)—could perhaps best be described as a sort of philosophical funerary object that accompanies Bentham's skeleton in its afterlife and describes in detail various aspects of its utility for the living.

According to Bentham, the burial of the dead deprives the living of a certain benefit they might otherwise have reaped from their bodies. Of what use might the dead be to the living? The utility of the dead as material for teaching anatomy is obvious: dissecting and studying the bodies of "the insensible dead" brings "alleviation and healing ... to the susceptible living" (Bentham [1842?], p. 1). But that is not all. In *Auto-Icon*, Bentham further augments the utility of the dead by introducing the so-called "conservative, or statuary" purpose of their bodies, in addition to their "anatomical, or dissectional" (Bentham [1842?], p. 2) purpose. He argues for this "farther use" of the dead as follows: Since nothing can resemble a thing more than that thing resembles itself, each particular thing is its own best image. In order for people not to be represented after death by paintings or statues—which inevitably fall short in resemblance of the things they represent—their bodies need to be preserved as their own most perfect representations. Or in Bentham's inimitable prose: "What resemblance, what painting, what statue of a human being can be so like him, as, in the character of an Auto-Icon, he or she will be to himself or herself? Is not identity preferable to similitude?" (Bentham [1842?], p. 3) Preserving the bodies of the dead, or their skeletons, would make it possible for anyone to go on being, even after death, "his own image" or "his own statue" (Bentham [1842?], p. 2). Thus, putting the dead bodies to their "conservative, or statuary" use would ultimately render obsolete any further need for painting and sculpture in portraying the dead.

Not only did Bentham leave his body for dissection and anatomical demonstrations; in his will, he also instructed the anatomist Dr. Thomas Southwood Smith—the "executor" who is said by Ishmael to have kept Bentham's skeleton in his library where it served as a candle holder—to preserve his bones and reassemble them into a skeleton, to put thereon his preserved head and clad it in his clothes and seat it in his chair. The executor was further instructed to equip the skeleton with "the staff in my later years borne by me" and place it in "an appropriate box or case" (quoted in Marmoy 1958, p. 80). And, in fact, Bentham's skeleton can still be seen today sitting in a wooden cabinet in the main building of University College London and embodying—both literally and figuratively—the ultimate utility maximization of the dead.

5

While, according to Ishmael, Bentham's skeleton "correctly conveys the idea of a burly-browed utilitarian old gentleman" as well as even "all Jeremy's other leading personal characteristics"—as Ishmael perhaps slightly overestimates the virtues of Bentham's auto-icon—the whale's skeleton, on the other hand, "gives very little idea of [its] general shape" (p. 208). In Ishmael's eyes, the gap between the whale's "naked skeleton" and its "true form" (p. 208) is apparently unbridgeable. Accordingly, the skeletons of the stranded sperm whales discussed by Ishmael in the novel will be put to some other Benthamite "farther uses". Furthermore, Bentham's skeleton, which, arguably, adequately represents the utilitarian sage, will be put by Ishmael to an additional original and innovative use—a use that perhaps only someone self-schooled in utilitarianism on a whaleship could have come up with.

Auto-Icon and *Moby-Dick* have at least two thematic motifs in common that suggest that Melville may have been familiar with the radical ideas behind Bentham's last wish to have his own skeleton preserved and displayed: first, embalmed human heads, processed in the style of the New Zealanders; and second, a preserved skeleton as an object of worship.

First, in *Moby-Dick*, the "'balmed New Zealand heads" (p. 29) are one of the numerous minor side motifs. In the novel, Queequeg is said to be in possession of several such heads, which he has brought along from the South Seas and is now selling around town. In New Bedford, there is obviously a market for mummified human heads, which, as the landlord at the Spouter-Inn says, is currently "overstocked" (p. 28). At first, Ishmael is horrified by Queequeg's "cannibal business" of "selling the heads of dead idolators" (p. 29). But when he is given the last of Queequeg's embalmed heads as a present, Ishmael, without any scruples whatsoever, passes it on to the town barber, who intends to utilize it as "a block" (p. 56), that is, a wig stand. In *Auto-Icon*, on the other hand, such heads—and especially the method of their preservation used by the Maori—are of absolutely key importance. That is because the head is considered to be the primary bearer of identity. Bentham writes: "The head of each individual is peculiar to him and, when properly preserved, is better than a statue" (Bentham [1842?], p. 2). He therefore advised that, in the process of auto-iconization, the heads of the dead be treated like the heads of New Zealanders, who "have preceded the most cultivated nations in the Auto-Icon art" (Bentham [1842?], p. 2). At one point, Bentham himself seems to have contemplated trying his hand at mummifying a human head (Marmoy 1958, p. 78). As is well known, the auto-iconization of Bentham's own head failed: the preserved head was quite unlike the head of the living Bentham and had to be replaced by a wax replica, which adorns Bentham's skeleton to this day.

The use to which the New Bedford barber intends to put the last of Queequeg's embalmed heads would make Bentham's hair stand on end. Admittedly, by putting a wig on it, the barber has found a seemingly good use for the embalmed head for which Ishmael apparently had no use. According to Bentham, it is first and foremost each individual's auto-iconized head that makes his preserved body "his own image" after death. In its role as the anchor point of each individual's auto-iconicity, the head is absolutely irreplaceable. In direct opposition to this, and as if he was deliberately mocking Bentham, the barber assigns the embalmed head the role of a wig stand. That is, he assigns it a role that could equally well be, and normally is, played by a generic head replica or a dummy head made of wood or Styrofoam, which not only has no expression on its face but most often has no face at all. In short, instead of the role for which the embalmed head is absolutely irreplaceable, the barber, by putting a wig on it, assigns it the role of a replacement, a mere substitute. There is hardly any other use of an embalmed head that would be in more direct violation of Bentham's principles of auto-iconism. Indeed, using the embalmed head as a wig stand is in such a direct violation of the principles of auto-iconism that one is almost led to wonder if it is really purely accidental.

Second, in perhaps the most Benthamite-inspired chapter of the novel, "A Bower in the Arsacides", Ishmael describes a stranded sperm whale's skeleton preserved on one of the Arsacides islands, where it serves as a shrine and its skull as an altar upon which "the priests" maintain an eternal flame. Its massive lower jawbone, hanging from a branch, sways ominously above the heads of the "devotees" worshipping what is apparently some kind of cetacean deity. The other preserved skeleton mentioned by Ishmael in the same chapter, the Yorkshire whale skeleton, has also been put to Bentham's "farther uses of the dead to the living". As if he wanted to emphasize specifically the latter skeleton's manifold usefulness, Ishmael gives a detailed, although not entirely serious, account of its functionality: the skeleton can be opened and shut "like a great chest of drawers" and its ribs can be spread out "like a gigantic fan", while its lower jawbone can even serve as a swing (p. 332). Bentham's skeleton is assembled in a similar way; it, too, is flexible at the joints and, if necessary, can even be dismantled (Richardson/Hurwitz 1987). As Bentham directed in his will, his skeleton holds his walking stick in hand, whereas according to Ishmael, it is used as a "candelabr[um]", which most probably means that it has a candle or a lamp in its hands. At the time of Melville's visit to London at the end of 1849, Bentham's skeleton was not as much in the public eye as it is today. At that time, the case containing the skeleton was indeed in the possession of "one of [Bentham's] executors", as Ishmael says, that is, Southwood Smith, who kept it in his house in Finsbury Square until the beginning of 1850, when he donated it to University College London (Marmoy 1958, pp. 83–84). The notion of Bentham's skeleton serving as a candle holder or lamp holder is most probably just a product of Ishmael's imagination. The image of Southwood Smith suggested by Ishmael's fantasy scenario is not very far from the one Ishmael paints of himself in Chapter 68, where he considers the "skin of the [whale's] skin" and its possible uses. In the latter case, Ishmael is reading about whales "through their own spectacles", although he neglects to specify whether it is by whales' own light that he does so—but if he is reading at night on a whaleship that, perhaps, goes without saying. In the former case, Southwood Smith is sitting in his library and, to develop Ishmael's fantasy scenario a little further, reading—perhaps even Bentham's writings—if not exactly by Bentham's own light, then at least by the light of a candle or lamp placed in the hands of his skeleton. One is almost tempted to speculate as to whether the candle held by Bentham's auto-icon is made from spermaceti or whether the lamp in its hands burns sperm oil. Furthermore, Ishmael's idea of Bentham's skeleton, kept in the library of one of his most faithful disciples and a fellow utilitarian, encircled by books, some of them very probably written by Bentham himself, roughly corresponds to the post-mortem fate the utilitarian sage anticipated for himself in *Auto-Icon:* in a passage in which he gives free rein to his imagination, Bentham pictures his preserved skeleton safely stored in a depository and surrounded by "his unedited and unfinished manuscripts, lodged in an appropriate case of shelves" (Bentham [1842?], p. 15).

Ishmael, who on his visit to the island made a pilgrimage to the whale skeleton, says that the islanders had carved the "Arsacidean annals" into its vertebrae (p. 330). As yearly records of the most important events, these annals, written in "strange hieroglyphics" (p. 330), are most probably nothing other than the history of the island. The moment when the big dead sperm whale whom they would consider a deity washed up on their shores must have surely been a major event in the island's history. Therefore, one can reasonably assume that in the annals for the year when this occurred, there must be some record describing the whale carcass dissection, the reassembling of its preserved bones into a skeleton, its transformation into an object of worship, and so on. In short, the "Arsacidean annals" for that year, or at least a portion thereof, must have read like Bentham's *Auto-Icon*. But unlike Bentham's "auto-thanatography", the whale's thanatography is not a funerary object distinct from the skeleton, but a part thereof. With the account of its death carved into its skeleton, the Arsacidean whale is its own thanatography. While recounting his pilgrimage to the Arsacidean skeleton, Ishmael says that he had its dimensions tattooed on his right arm, giving only the feet while intentionally leaving out the inches in order to keep blank as much of his skin as possible, which he will soon need for the poem he was composing at the time (p. 332). Here, Ishmael clearly imitates the islanders' practice: while the latter carved their annals into the whale's skeleton, he carves the dimensions of that skeleton into his own body. Having to his satisfaction maximized the usefulness of the "skin of [the whale's] skin" for reading, Ishmael then goes one step farther and demonstrates and maximizes the usefulness of his own skin for writing. Ishmael, who has his body tattooed not with a random inscription but with "valuable statistics" (p. 332)—as he himself terms the dimensions of the Arsacidean whale deity—all the while taking great care not to use any more precious space than necessary, apparently views even his tattooing through the prism of utilitarianism.

In the afterlife as conceived by the utilitarian eschatology, the preserved skeletons would by no means sit about in idleness. In *Auto-Icon*, Bentham identifies no fewer than 11 different uses—such as, "economical, or money-saving", "lucrative, or money-getting", "genealogical", "architectural", "theatrical, or dramatic", and "phrenological" (Bentham [1842?], p. 3)—that the auto-iconized dead could be put to in order to benefit the living and contribute to their happiness. It is almost as if—in accordance with the utilitarian belief that gave rise to them—the auto-iconized dead would have to earn their post-mortem living themselves. The owner of the Yorkshire whale skeleton is planning on primarily putting it to the "lucrative, or money-getting" use. He is thinking, says Ishmael jocularly, of collecting an admission fee for viewing it, with "the unrivalled view from his forehead" (p. 332), priced at "sixpence", being the most expensive attraction. Here, Melville does indeed parody "guidebook language", as observed by Howard P. Vincent (1980, p. 361); yet, the utilitarian undertone is unmistakable. Compared to the Yorkshire skeleton, which, besides serving as a swing, will also generate revenue from admission fees, the "worshipped skeleton" of the Arsacidean whale may indeed seem to be a "gigantic idler" (p. 331), as Ishmael puts it, as if he wanted to imply that by serving as a shrine the sperm whale skeleton may well benefit the living and contribute to their happiness, yet not all the good has been extracted from it. Ishmael may have considered Bentham's skeleton to be an idler, too; and perhaps that is why, in his fantasy, he replaces the walking stick in its hands with a candle or a lamp. If Bentham's skeleton is truly to benefit the living, it should not just merely represent Bentham, but also provide adequate light for the one sitting in the library and reading (among other things, also Bentham's own writings on the philosophy of utilitarianism). Here, Ishmael appears to be more Benthamite than Bentham himself. Nowadays, Ishmael perhaps might not have found Bentham's skeleton to be an idler anymore. Not only is Bentham's skeleton occasionally moved around the world and displayed at various expositions, presumably as "his own image", but even in its glass and mahogany case at University College London, it does not sit entirely idle: in 2015 and 2016, for example, the auto-icon was a vital part of a research project in which an online camera—most accurately termed "PanoptiCam" ("Watching you watching Bentham")—was placed on top of the case containing the skeleton, streaming live images of visibly puzzled visitors observing the utilitarian sage representing himself after death. As the camera was placed directly above the auto-icon's head, in this case everyone was afforded that which Ishmael called, in the case of the Yorkshire sperm whale skeleton, an "unrivalled view from his forehead".

Just as the "devotees" of the apparently fictional cult in the Arsacides worship the whale's skeleton as a deity, so too did Bentham predict the "*quasi* sacred" (Bentham [1842?], p. 15) status of his own skeleton and foresaw the "pilgrimages" made thereto by the "votaries of the greatest-happiness principle", or the utilitarians. If there are pilgrimages made to Mahomet's tomb, why not also to "the old philosopher preserved in some safe repository", Bentham wonders in a passage in his *Auto-Icon*, and then goes on to ask: "Is not Bentham as good as Mahomet was? In this or that, however distant, age, will he not have done as much good as Mahomet will have done evil to mankind?" (Bentham [1842?], p. 15) Bentham believed that "the Auto-Icons of the virtuous in their silence would be eloquent preachers"; and the lesson they would preach to the pilgrims would be: "Go thou and do likewise" (Bentham [1842?], p. 7), that is, like the virtuous individual to whose auto-icon or skeleton they came on pilgrimage had acted in his or her own lifetime. Thus, the lesson the preserved skeleton of the founder of the principle of utility would preach to the pilgrims would be: Go thou and act in accordance with the principle of utility, or the greatest-happiness principle. Therefore, what would be propagated by Bentham's auto-icon in this way would be nothing other than the utilitarian belief itself. It seems that Melville—or his narrator Ishmael—learned, at least to some degree, the lesson taught by Bentham's auto-icon—regardless of whether or not the pilgrimage to "Jeremy Bentham's skeleton" actually took place.

Bibliography

Alderson, James (1827): "An Account of a Whale of the Spermaceti Tribe, Cast on Shore on the Yorkshire Coast, on the 28th of April, 1825". In: *Transactions of the Cambridge Philosophical Society* 2, pp. 253–266.

Bentham, Jeremy (n.d., [1842?]): *Auto-Icon; or, Farther Uses of the Dead to the Living*. N.p., n.d.

Credland, Arthur G. (1989): "Moby Dick, Hull and East Yorkshire". In: *The Great Circle* 11(1), pp. 44–54.

Diderot, Denis (1751): "La philosophie antédiluvienne". In: *Encyclopédie, ou Dictionnaire raisonné des sciences, des arts et des métiers*. Edited by Denis Diderot and Jean Le Rond d'Alembert. Vol. 1. Paris: Briasson, pp. 493a–495a.

Lewes, Gertrude (1898): *Dr Southwood Smith: A Retrospect*. Edinburgh and London: William Blackwood.

Malebranche, Nicolas (1980): *The Search after Truth*. Translated by Thomas M. Lennon and Paul J. Olscamp. Columbus: Ohio State University Press.

Marmoy, C. F. A. (1958): "The 'Auto-Icon' of Jeremy Bentham at University College, London". In: *Medical History* 2, pp. 77–86.

Melville, Herman (2018): *Moby-Dick; or, The Whale*. 3rd edn. Edited by Hershel Parker. New York: W. W. Norton.

Miller, Jacques-Alain (1987): "Jeremy Bentham's Panoptic Device". Translated by Richard Miller. *October* 41 (Summer), pp. 3–29.

Montaigne, Michel de (1965): "Apology for Raymond Sebond". In: *The Complete Essays of Montaigne*. Translated by Donald M. Frame. Stanford, CA: Stanford University Press, pp. 318–457.

Richardson, Ruth/Hurwitz, Brian (1987): "Jeremy Bentham's Self Image: An Exemplary Bequest for Dissection". In: *British Medical Journal* 295 (July), pp. 195–198.

Southwood Smith, Thomas (1832): *A Lecture Delivered over the Remains of Jeremy Bentham*. London: Effingham Wilson.

Vincent, Howard P. (1980): *The Trying-Out of* Moby-Dick. Kent, OH: Kent State University Press.

"Watching You Watching Bentham: The PanoptiCam". *UCL News*. University College London, 17 March 2015. https://www.ucl.ac.uk/news/2015/mar/watching-you-watching-bentham-panopticam, visited on 31 January 2017.

Bojana Jovićević
Thinking Free Release in Hegel's System

Abstract: This chapter attempts to think Hegel's term "free release" as a concept and to delineate its meaning with reference to the paradox between the idea and nature in Hegel's philosophical system. The idea, according to Hegel, is only the idea in the proper sense: if it realizes itself as something concrete in the world of empirical objects, nature. However, since all there is is the idea, the only externality that the idea attains is—itself. So, in the end, the externality of the idea amounts to the idea realizing its own logical determinations in nature. On the one hand, the idea and nature are in a relation of genuine incongruence. On the other hand, nature itself is the result of the self-determining process of the idea—and thus entirely dependent on it. To resolve this paradox, I will introduce Hegel's concept of "free release."

1 Introduction

It is a commonplace among philosophers that Hegel's philosophical system,[1] both in terms of its principle and its method, is a variety of idealism, famously referred to as absolute idealism. It is a stance according to which the external world of objects, facticity as such, is subjugated to the absolute immanence of thought, and hence entirely dependent on thought determinations. As I will demonstrate, however, even such a self-enclosed system, in its all-embracing totality and necessity, cannot but ultimately rely on the contingent, non-conceptual externality in order to positively verify its own logical character. In short, I will try to follow the path of pure thought thinking itself, or simply: the regime of the idea that has to "freely release" itself into nature, to muddle itself with an irreducible otherness, in order to prove its true conceptual power. The idea[2] is de-

---

[1] Under the term "system", I refer to the regime of pure thought thinking itself as it is exposed in the *Encyclopedia of the Philosophical Sciences*. *The Science of Logic* constitutes the fundamental part of this system and functions as a unifying conceptual foundation for the three sciences of logic, nature, and spirit.
[2] All of Hegel's categories will be consistently written in lowercase and used in the same way as in the English translations, where capitalization is preserved. This is to make the text more approachable to the readers. In addition, this practice varies among Hegel's interpreters and translators (compare Illetterati 2020 with Di Giovanni in Hegel 2010).

Bojana Jovićević, University of Ljubljana.

fined as the self-determining movement of thought that actively produces all its determinations and contains a positive ground of its existence within itself. In other words, the idea is an all-encompassing subjective principle denying anything external to it to be its ultimate foundation, ground. "But the Idea shows itself as the thinking that is strictly identical with itself, and this at once shows itself to be the activity of positing itself over against itself, in order to be for-itself, and to be, in this other, only at home with itself" (Hegel 1991a, p. 42). Being subject only to its own *"universal absolute activity"* (Hegel 2010, p. 737), with no object that could offer resistance and suspend it, the idea has no externality in any strict sense of the word. Consequently, nature exists only negatively, as a necessary mode of the idea's own existence. In fact, nature is, as Hegel would put it, "the Idea self-externalized" (Hegel 2004, p. xiii). But if the idea contains *"all* determinateness within itself" (Hegel 2010, p. 514), in regard to which therefore nothing can be external, why does it decide "to determine itself as external idea" (Hegel 2010, p. 753) in the first place? Furthermore, if the act of self-externalization of the idea is truly logically necessary, what does this have to do with a decision?

Since the idea is a self-determining principle, any relation to externality is the idea's own relation to itself, to its own determinations. Nature, in this sense, is nothing but a representation of the idea's own form of self-reflectivity, or simply: "the negative of the Idea" (Hegel 2004, p. 19). But at the same time, the idea has to determine itself as nature, that is, in the form of concrete existence, otherwise it becomes an empty abstraction devoid of truth, a sheer nothingness.

On the one hand, nature is a manifestation of the idea and therefore entirely determined by it. "The Idea is present in each grade or level of Nature itself" (Hegel 2004, p. 14). On the other hand, however, Hegel insists that the existence of nature cannot be reduced to the idea's own activity and is, in some sense, thoroughly independent of it.

> Nature has presented itself as the Idea in the form of *otherness*. Since therefore the Idea is the negative of itself, or is *external to itself,* Nature is not merely external in relation to this Idea (and to its subjective existence Spirit); the truth is rather that *externality* constitutes the specific character in which Nature, as Nature, exists. (Hegel 2004, p. 14)

Therefore, it follows that the idea and nature are mutually dependent and independent of each other at the same time. To explain this paradox between the idea and nature, let me introduce the logical operation of "free release" *(frei entlassen)*. Although it is used only sparingly in Hegel's texts and lacks an elaborate and explicit treatment by Hegel himself, it is also plainly used deliberately, occurring at architectonically key places and with a similar conceptual emphasis.³ Paradigmatically, "free release" appears in the very last passage of *The Science of Logic*, marking the transition of the idea into nature. It conceptualizes the moment of the sheer positivity and externality of the idea, whose existence is neither ontologically prior to the idea's own determinations nor completely deducible from them.

On the side of nature, "free release" implies the affirmation of external existence in its irreducible independence from the idea, hence as something "absolutely existing for itself without subjectivity" (Hegel 2010, p. 753). It signifies a limit to the idea's own form of subjectivity, a moment of incongruence, of structural disparity of the idea with itself. In order to gain identity, the idea liberates itself from its pure form of self-reflectivity and incorporates "the opaque being of nature" (Hyppolite 1997, p. 102) within itself. Nature, in this sense, functions as a manifestation and self-degradation of the idea at the same time.⁴

Before I try to resolve this paradox, however, I need to understand some of the structural tensions within Hegel's system and the rationale behind the idea of "free release". Let me therefore take a step back and examine the conceptual genesis of "free release" and its wider philosophical context.

---

3 The last passage of the *Encyclopedia Logic* ends with, "The absolute freedom of the Idea is that ... it *resolves to release out* of itself into freedom ... *the immediate Idea* as its reflection, or itself as *Nature* (Hegel 1991a, p. 307). In the original: "Die absolute Freiheit der Idee aber ist ... die unmittelbare Idee als ihren Wiederschein, sich als Natur frei aus sich zu entlassen" (Hegel 1830, p. 231). By releasing itself into nature, the idea realizes itself into externality, which, through this very act, becomes independent of its reflective determinations. And it does so freely, by means of decision (resolve). It is not so, as it is suggested in the English translation, that the idea releases itself into nature, which is itself the realm of freedom. The emphasis lies elsewhere. By releasing itself into nature, the idea freely decides to suspend its own reflective activity and treat nature as independent of it. Similarly, in the *Elements of the Philosophy of Right*, individuals who are attached to the unity of natural substance (family), and thus completely dependent on it, "must be released from the concept to [attain] self-sufficient reality" (Hegel 1991b, p. 219), that is, as free independent citizens. Structurally speaking, "free release" always appears in those places in Hegel's system where the idea is confronted with the moment of an irreducible otherness that it cannot totally absorb into its conceptual regime.

4 Illetterati developed a reading of what he characterizes as Hegel's Non-Naturalistic Naturalism, which comes very close to our own, according to which nature is simultaneously independent of the causal impact of the idea and completely subjugated to it. "The extraordinary ambiguity of Hegel's concept of nature finds, in this way, its ground in the fact that nature is simultaneously a manifestation of the Idea and a destruction and a fragmentation of it. This ambiguity makes nature—in Hegel's words—'the unresolved contradiction'" (Illetterati 2020, p. 63).

2 The genealogy of free release

The first conceptual impulses for the introduction of "free release" into Hegel's system can be historically traced back to Jacobi, more specifically, to an answer to Jacobi's criticism of the principle of self-determining thought. In Jacobi's framework, which in this aspect very much corresponds to Hegel's, thought becomes "self-determining intelligence" by virtue of its power "to think to the end" all there is (Jacobi 1994, p. 502). By conceiving the existence of any self-subsisting object through its self-reflective activity, thought abolishes the object in its immediacy, representing it in the form of its own determinations.[5]

> So if a being is to become for us a *fully* comprehended object, we must cancel it in thought as something *objective, as standing on its own*; we must annihilate it in order to let it become something thoroughly *subjective*, our own creation, *a mere schema*. ... Abstraction lies at the basis of all reflection, in such a way that reflection becomes possible only through abstraction. The same applies the other way around; the two are inseparable and fundamentally one, an action of dissolving *all being into knowledge*, a progressive annihilation through ever more universal concepts leading up to science. (Jacobi 1994, pp. 508–509)

Self-determining intelligence or reflection, as Jacobi would put it, actively produces its own determinations by way of negation of anything existing as external to it. However, by abolishing any form of existence, thought "must annihilate itself according to its *being*" (Jacobi 1994, p. 508). Since thought exists only as a negative principle of the mediation of all that is given, immediate determinacy, it cannot determine anything, not even its own existence. By thinking to the end all there is, thought thinks its own nothingness.

It follows from the above that Jacobi does not ascribe any positive determination to the activity of thought. It has no genealogy and emerges as a "pure absolute exodus and return (*from* nothing, *to* nothing, *for* nothing, *into* nothing)" (Jacobi 1994, p. 508). The only way that thought can combat nihilism, towards which it immanently strives, is to "establish limitations for itself" (Jacobi 1994, p. 508). But how can a thought that abolishes any form of fixed determinacy delimit itself: is this not self-contradictory? And what kind of limitation does Jacobi have in mind? To describe the character of such limitation, Jacobi uses an analogy between the movement of thought and that of a pendulum. An oscillating

---

[5] Hegel, in a similar way to Jacobi, understands the moment of negation of any form of positivity as a necessary condition for thinking. "In fact, thinking is essentially the negation of something immediately present. Thinking deprives positivity of its power" (Hegel 1995, p. 71, my translation modified).

pendulum, when oscillating in a vacuum with no force of resistance, can go on indefinitely. In real life, however, the pendulum will always eventually stop because of friction.

So, although friction can be neglected within the theoretical outlook, it nonetheless, from the practical viewpoint, represents "an incomprehensible limitation" (Jacobi 1994, p. 508) to the movement of the pendulum. In a similar manner, the self-determining activity of thought enclosed in the realm of pure logic may run off into infinity. But there is an "empirical intervention" (Jacobi 1994, p. 510) that stabilizes thought in its infinite self-reflective activity: the true.

> I understand by "the true" something which is *prior to* and *outside* knowledge; that which first gives a value to knowledge and to the *faculty* of knowledge, *to reason* ... To empty out the infinite, I cannot help wanting to *fill* it, as an infinite nothing, a pure-and-total-in-and-for-itself (were it not simply impossible!): since, I say, this is the way it is with me and the *science* of the true, or more precisely, the *true* science, I therefore do not see why I, as a matter of taste, should not be allowed to prefer my philosophy of non-knowledge to the *philosophical knowledge of the nothing*, at least *in fugam vacui*. (Jacobi 1994, p. 519)

The only way to prevent thought from turning into a frictionless spinning in the void[6] is to recognize its true limit, a self-subsisting externality whose existence is entirely independent of it. The status of this externality must be preconceptual, pertaining to the realm of "non-knowledge" (Jacobi 1994, p. 503). If the opposite were the case, if such an externality did not exist ontologically prior to thought, I would be caught in a self-reflective loop of endless thought determinations leading me into indeterminacy. Therefore, Jacobi concludes, self-determining thought is not completely self-determining, but is always already determined from the outside.

But the solution that Jacobi offered, in Hegel's view, perpetuated, structurally speaking, a series of contradictions that he sought to refute. If thought determines itself by an externality that cannot be reduced to its own activity, but is, on the contrary, a positive condition of its very existence, what are the criteria by which Jacobi separates the true externality from the false one? In other words, how does Jacobi know that the notion of externality that he clings to is "the true itself" (Jacobi 1994, p. 506), an absolute limit to all thinking and not another empty thought determination? What is more, if the inner inconsistences of self-determining thought are solvable only in the realm of non-knowledge, beyond discursivity of thought of any kind, what grants Jacobi the validity of his own

---

6 I borrowed the phrase from McDowell's *Mind and World*, where he uses it to characterize the self-contained activity of thinking, its spontaneity.

claims? Simply put, by rejecting the standpoint of thought and simultaneously asserting the truthfulness of his claims, which are themselves merely thoughts, Jacobi is contradicting himself. So, the only way to break this vicious circle of reflection at all levels of thought is, paradoxically, by thinking it to the point where the very impossibility of its resolution opens up a new regime of thinking.

3 The logic of being, the logic of essence

The project of *The Science of Logic* can be described as an all-encompassing regime of thought, in which thought itself becomes the object of its own inquiry. It signifies a system of thought within which it is possible to reflect and transform the conditions of thought's own activity. Consequently, what from the standpoint of traditional logic[7] seemed to oppose the activity of thought and be outside its conceptual domain (freedom, individual existence, being as such) appears as a moment within the unified processual movement of thinking itself. In a word: *The Science of Logic* is the science of pure thought in its immanent genesis, where there can be no *a priori* division between subject and object, reflection and immediacy, thought and the world of empirical objects as such.

> Accordingly, logic was defined as the science of pure thought—the science that has *pure knowledge* for its principle and is a unity which is not abstract but living and concrete, so that the opposition of consciousness between *a being subjectively existing for itself*, and another but objectively *existing such being*, has been overcome in it, and being is known to be in itself a pure concept and the pure concept to be true being. These, then, are the two *moments* contained in logic. (Hegel 2010, p. 39)

The positive task of *Logic* consists in thinking what there truly is, before the opposition posed by our finite consciousness takes hold.[8] To paraphrase Hegel: the

---

[7] Unlike traditional conceptions of logic, according to which the act of thinking is conceived of as independent of the content of the objects that are thought, in *The Science of Logic* thinking is not merely a formal activity with no causal impact on the empirical world of objects, but actively transforms this world. Conversely, objects themselves do not exist as self-subsisting wholes, independent of thought determinations. On the contrary, it is only through thinking itself that they become what they truly are. "Logic has nothing to do with a thought *about* something which stands outside by itself as the base of thought; nor does it have to do with forms meant to provide mere *markings* of the truth; rather, the necessary forms of thinking, and its specific determinations, are the content and the ultimate truth itself" (Hegel 2010, p. 29).

[8] As thought determinations are simultaneously real determinations of the objects themselves, it follows that *Logic* is, by its very principle, metaphysics. On the same line of argumentation, asserting that thought in its self-conscious character determines the world in its facticity, stands

standpoint of *The Science of Logic* unfolds entirely within the divine purview, representing "*the exposition of God as he is in his eternal essence before the creation of nature and of a finite spirit*" (Hegel 2010, p. 29).

Let me begin by reading *The Science of Logic* so as to demonstrate that by means of pure thinking itself, thought indeed produces the stance of immediacy, and that conversely the world of empirical objects, nature as such, is immanently structured as thought. Hegel's *Logic* opens with *The Logic of Being*, with the most minimal category of pure being, completely indeterminate in itself, with no relation to itself and to the other. "*Being, pure being*—without further determination. In its indeterminate immediacy it is equal only to itself and also not unequal with respect to another; it has no difference within it, nor any outwardly" (Hegel 2010, p. 59). This category of being famously generates the categories of nothing and becoming. Since in its immediate self-equality no relation of otherness, no mediation can be ascribed to it, being turns into an empty category devoid of any content and hence into pure nothingness. The category of being, structurally speaking, coincides with the category of nothing. This transition of the category of being into nothing, the act of "passing over into the other" (Hegel 2010, p. 454), is immanently resolved, sublated (*aufgehoben*) into the category of becoming. "*Becoming* is this immanent synthesis of being and nothing" (Hegel 2010, p. 186). The becoming itself results in determinate being, which in its conceptual implications produces the entire sequence of all three categories.

At the end of *The Logic of Being*, this triad culminates in the category of absolute indifference. "This unity with itself of determinacy and indifference to it is the truth of being. ... In not being what it is, and being what it is not—as this simple negativity of itself, being is essence" (Hegel 1812, p. 275, my translation).[9]

Absolute indifference is an immediate self-equality and its own negation at the same time, and is therefore self-contradictory by its own principle: it is the explication of the category of being in its purest form! By thinking what there truly is, immanently, and to the end, with the means of pure thought itself, Hegel is either in contradiction with himself, or produces completely indeterminate thought determinations.

How is this possible? How can it be that, by way of the positive demonstration of the absolute power of thought, and even from God's own perspective, Hegel has reached the same result as Jacobi in his critique of the self-determin-

---

Rödl: "Logic is Metaphysics. Thought thinking itself is the knowledge of what it is, as it is" (Rödl 2018, p. 401, my translation).
9 In the original: "Diese Einheit mit sich der Bestimmtheit und der Gleichgültigkeit gegen sie ist die Wahrheit des Seins. ... Das Sein, indem es ist, das nicht zu sein, was es ist, und das zu sein, was es nicht ist—als diese einfache Negativität seiner selbst, ist das Wesen" (Hegel 1812, p. 275).

ing character of thought? The category of absolute indifference is, in this sense, the ultimate proof of the failure of *the Logic of Being* as such, of its inherent circularity and emptiness.

The legacy of *The Logic of Being*, grasped in its positive result, implies that in order to conceptually reconcile pure thinking with pure being, mediation and immediacy, new categories of thought need to be developed, ones that will be able to "endure contradiction" (Hegel 2010, p. 382). *The Logic of Being* can therefore be read as Hegel's immanent demonstration of Jacobi's critique and its annihilation at the same time; as a task that has yet to be resolved in *The Logic of Essence*.

Hegel defines the determinations of essence in direct opposition to those of being. "This determining is thus of another nature than the determining in the sphere of being, and the determinations of essence have another character than the determinations of being" (Hegel 2010, p. 338). The determinations of being are something immediate, given. In their simple self-equality, they pose any relation to mediation, otherness, as necessarily external and opposite to them. Conversely, the determinations of essence are nothing predetermined and fixed, but rather an expression of an inherent processuality that "starts off from another, from being, and has a prior way to make, the way that leads over and beyond being or that rather penetrates into it" (Hegel 2010, p. 337). In the regime of essence, thought therefore constitutes itself by going beyond itself, towards that which is other than itself. It is a thought that is able to conceptually integrate the resistance of what is alien to it, that is, of merely given determinations, and thereby sustain itself. To paraphrase Hegel: essence is the unity of mediation and immediacy, containing the categories of being itself.

> Essence is sublated being. It is simple equality with itself but is such as the negation of the sphere of being in general. And so, it has immediacy over against it, as something from which it has come to be but which has preserved and maintained itself in this sublating. (Hegel 2010, p. 341)

Essence is the negative thought principle that supersedes all given, immediate determinacy, even its own. In this negative relation to all immediacy and to itself, essence is, in terms of its method and its structure: reflection. The movement of reflection is, hence, an immanent explication of the category of essence in its purest conceptual form.

> For essence is an infinite self-contained movement which determines its immediacy as negativity and its negativity as immediacy. It determines its immediacy as negativity and its negativity as immediacy, and is thus the shining of itself within itself. In this, in its self-movement, essence is *reflection*. (Hegel 2010, p. 345)

4 The self-determination of reflection

Hegel defines reflection as the movement of thought "*from nothing to nothing and thereby back to itself*" (Hegel 2010, p. 346). Through this movement of absolute negativity reflection produces its own determinations as something immediate, merely given. How can I think this unity of mediation and immediacy? Marx, in his reference to Hegel's *Logic*, draws an analogy between the determinations of reflection and those of sovereignty. A man is a king not by virtue of his royal nature, that is, by being born as a sovereign, but only because other men stand in the negative relation of subjects to him. Conversely, other men perceive themselves as subjects only through the negative relation to him as the king. But this does not mean that he is not a king. He is. It is only that his kinghood cannot be thought independently of the way others relate to him as the king.[10] In a similar manner, within the movement of reflection, what is known are not objects taken independently but their negative relations of mutual determination. Since they are posited only in relation to one another, it follows that objects in their immediacy are merely products of reflection's own circuit of presuppositions.

To understand what exactly Hegel means by the reciprocal relation of positing (*Gesetztsein*) and presupposing (*Voraussetzung*), let me make a brief excursion to Fichte, since both logical terms are originally imported from Fichte's theory of subjectivity.

In Fichte's framework, positing refers to anything that from the standpoint of absolute I-hood (*Ichheit*), of the pure subject, appears to be immediate or merely given. The fact that something is posited signifies that the realm of immediacy, the world of empirical objects as such, is not something external to the thinking subject, in relation to which it is merely receptive, but, on the contrary, that it is the I's own product, an expression of its spontaneity. Everything contained within the absolute I is posited by the I itself. In a word: to be determinate is to be posited, or, to paraphrase Fichte, being is positedness. If, however, all immediate, given determinacy is the product of the I's own positing, how and why is it that something appears to it as something merely given in the first place? Since there is nothing to delimit its activity from the outside, no object in relation to which it can express its own spontaneity, the absolute I itself turns into something empty and indeterminate. Hence, in order to posit itself as a pure subject and the world of empirical objects, the absolute I, paradoxically, has to presuppose the realm of non-positedness, immediacy as such, within its own self-reflec-

---

10 The summary of the analogy is taken from Marx's chapter "Commodities and Money" in *Capital*, vol. 1 (Marx 1990, p. 149).

tive activity so as to acquire positivity. In this way, I gain Fichte's famous reflective circle, within which the notion of a pure, self-positing subject is always already mutually determined in relation to an element of pure facticity (*Anstoss*), which cannot be entirely reduced to reflection's own activity, and yet it is a necessary moment for its positive self-realization.

Unlike Fichte, who considered this inherent circularity of reflection to be the positive condition of all thinking and, even more, saw the highest task of all philosophy in its explication, Hegel insisted upon its insufficiency and the need for its conceptual resolution.

According to Hegel, reflection is positing in that it supersedes immediacy in order to make posited being out of it. That is, reflection makes being into something that is determined by thought and is insofar reflected immediacy as such. By negation, abstraction of all immediacy, reflection hence returns to its own determinations. However, this immediacy is none other than its own presupposition. In its return to itself, reflection hence retroactively posits itself, its own being. In Hegel's words:

> The movement [of reflection], as forward movement, turns immediately around into itself and so is only self-movement—a movement which comes from itself in so far as *positing* reflection is *presupposing* reflection, yet, as *presupposing* reflection, is simply *positing* reflection. Thus, is reflection itself and its non-being, and only is itself by being the negative of itself, for only in this way is the sublating of the negative at the same time a coinciding with itself. (Hegel 2010, p. 348)

The problem is, however, that these two operations occur simultaneously and function as two moments within one and the same congruence of reflection with itself, eliminating each other reciprocally. So, in order for reflection to posit something, it has to first presuppose some kind of immediacy that needs to be posited. However, this posited immediacy is itself, retroactively, the product of its own presupposition; in fact, it exists only through this act of presupposing as such! In Hegel's formulation: "Reflection thus *finds* an immediate *before it* which it transcends and from which it is the turning back. But this turning back is only the presupposing of what was antecedently found" (Hegel 2010, p. 348).

Hence, positing reflection is, Hegel concludes, structured as an empty, self-enclosed circle that, paradoxically, cannot posit anything. By an incessant self-transition of its own negativity, it annihilates itself by its own logical means.

To break this circularity, there needs to be, structurally speaking, some kind of a split, a demarcation line between positing and presupposing. How is this to be achieved? In their absolute self-mediation of its own negativity, all determinations of reflection appear to it as something immediately self-evident and true. Therefore, the only way to cut into the continuity of reflection's own being is through a moment that remains ultimately opaque to it and resistant to its self-negativity: that moment is external reflection.

> The immediacy which reflection, as a process of sublating, presupposes for itself is simply and solely a *positedness*, something *in itself* sublated which is not diverse from reflection's turning back into itself but is itself only this turning back. But it is at the same time determined as a *negative*, as immediately in opposition to something, and hence to an other. And so is reflection determined. According to this determinateness, because reflection *has* a presupposition and takes its start from the immediate as its other, it is external reflection. (Hegel 2010, p. 348)

External reflection therefore functions as an inner "opacity of brute existents" (Hyppolite 1997, p. 102) within the movement of the pure self-transparency of thought, by which reflection, paradoxically, gains positivity. It is a moment that brings the "externality of space and time" (Hegel 2010, p. 753) into the process of the negative reciprocity of positing and presupposing and provides thought with a stable relation to immediacy. External reflection can be conceptually understood as Fichte's notion of *Anstoss*, as some kind of stumbling block, *a priori a posteriori*, a sheer positivity that cannot be deduced from the pure relational movement of reflection and is, at the same time, a necessary condition for the realization of reflection's own determinacy.[11]

By recognizing a structural disparity, an irreducible otherness, as a moment essential for the positive realization of its own identity, reflection finally determines itself. Instead of positing being as the product of its own presupposition, reflection posits essential determinations. "In its determining, external reflection posits an other in the place of the sublated being, but this other is essence; the positing does not posit its determination in the place of an other; it has no presupposition" (Hegel 2010, p. 351). In other words, in determining reflection, positedness itself becomes a determination of reflection. Posited being ceases to be a "disappearing semblance" (Longuenesse 2010, p. 53) within which reflection shines through. It is itself reflection, for reflection has found its own determinations in it. If the object is none other than reflection itself, the determinations of the movement of reflection are now determinations of the object itself: *"thought*

---

11 Longuenesse, in her remarkable book *Hegel's Critique of Metaphysics*, emphasizes a similar point, that the form of immediacy is, in the conceptual sense, essential for understanding the way reflection is determined. "In other words, reflection reveals what seemed to be immediate as being, in fact, thought, mediated, 'posited'; but it had to be the case that there was something presenting itself as immediate for reflection to reveal it as identical to itself" (Longuenesse 2007, p. 52).

is equally the fact as it is in itself; or *the fact in itself* in so far as this *is equally pure thought*" (Hegel 2010, p. 29).

The goal of *The Science of Logic* has been successfully accomplished. The realm of externality, or nature, has produced thought determinations, subjectivity as such, and thought itself has gained positivity. In thinking pure thought in its immanence, I think what there truly is in the world. However, if thought is "within it the *determinate side* and the *reference* of this determinate side as determinate" (Hegel 2010, p. 353), how can I positively validate its determinacy? How can I know that these thought determinations are not arbitrary, a mere frictionless spinning in the void?

Hegel resolves this new problem through the logical operation of "free release", a conceptual approach that allows me to think the relationship between the reflective structure of thought and its relation to pure externality, hence, to the "blind manifoldness of nature" (Hegel 2010, p. 536), in a positive, non-trivial manner.

5 Reflection desubjectivized: The notion of free release

Through the movement of determining reflection, thought has constituted itself as a recursive and self-determining activity, containing the world of empirical objects and itself as the object of its own determination. In determining its reflective content and the realm of externality as two aspects of its own self-determining character, thought becomes the idea. The idea is, as Hegel would put it, the subject-object, the unity of itself and objectivity. "The idea, namely, in positing itself as the absolute unity of the pure concept and its reality and thus collecting itself in the immediacy of being, is in this form as totality-nature" (Hegel 2010, p. 752).

In referring to its own determinations, the idea therefore refers to nature; or, conversely, nature, in its self-subsistence, is the truth in which the idea reveals itself. This mutual determination of the idea and nature results in a completely unified system of thought, by which any possibility of failure or distortion is always already incorporated within the system itself. Even the laws of nature, in the empirical sense of the word, become thoroughly intelligible, entirely subsumed under the logical category of mechanism in Hegel's *Logic!*

In other words, I gain a system of thought without holes (*ein lückenloses System*), which is absolutely consistent in itself, that is, a system where everything happens by its own logical necessity. However, in its apparent strength also lies its weakness. Since it cannot be positively falsified, I cannot know if such a system ultimately refers to any positivity at all. How can I know, to turn Hegel's criticism of Jacobi against himself, that it is "the true itself" (Hegel 2010, p. 206) and not yet another empty phantasmatic construct (Hirngespinst) produced by my own reflective reasoning? In what way can I therefore externally verify a system of thought that has no externality in any strict sense of the word and is immune to any critique outside its own conceptual means?

The notion of "free release" signifies a logical operation in Hegel's system by which thought verifies its own truth in "the externality of space and time absolutely existing for itself without subjectivity" (Hegel 2010, p. 176). Or simply: thought desubjectivizes itself.[12] Specifically, this implies a free decision of thought to release externality from its jurisdiction, by way of retracting its own determinations from nature. Since this decision is free, I cannot provide any sufficient reason for its logical genesis and consequently subsume it under the "mediation of reflection" (Hegel 2010, p. 603). And yet, it is logically necessary if the reflective circle of thought is to be externally verified. With respect to nature, "free release" entails that nature, in its specific mode of externality, becomes independent of any conceptual restraints of thought, thus becoming the realm of sheer positivity, "bare of references" (Hegel 2010, p. 92). Thus, a successful verification of thought implies that nature, in accordance with its own mechanism, and out of its "blind manifoldness" (Hegel 2010, p. 536), should produce the regime of subjectivity of the idea within itself.

Nature, the realm of chaos and contingency or, to paraphrase Hegel, the realm of impotence, one no longer governed by the laws of thought, can, of course, fail in fulfilling this task. However, the very possibility that it may not succeed is the ultimate proof that the idea is finally externally verified. If nature fails, so much the better for the idea! Paradoxically, it is through nature's own failure to produce the idea in the world that I prove the non-totalizing character of the conceptual regime of the idea and open up the possibility of its verification. To illustrate: in Hegel's *Elements of the Philosophy of Right*, the subjects that are integrated into the natural unity of the family as family members are completely immune to the unpredictability and chaos of the civil state. Once freely

---

12 Hegel makes a conceptual distinction between truth (*Wahrheit*) and accuracy, correctness (*Richtigkeit*). The former refers to the agreement between the object and its being thought, within the regime of the idea, while the latter refers to the agreement between the object and its subjective (thought) representation. In this context, our question can be formulated as follows: How does a system that is a self-enclosed totality and is, by its principle, true acquire correctness? How does it verify its positivity?

released into the civil state,[13] they have to renounce their unifying bond with the family and constitute themselves as individuals in accordance with the system of needs of the civil state. Nobody knows if they are up to the task, but the very possibility that they can fail is a positive condition for them becoming individuals in the first place!

6 Conclusion

In the present chapter, I sought to resolve an unsettled paradox between the idea and nature in Hegel's system, according to which the idea, as an absolutely self-enclosed principle of subjectivity, has to externalize itself into nature. Nature is, in this sense, simultaneously a logical manifestation of the idea and an annihilation of its principle. To resolve this paradox, Hegel introduced the notion of "free release".

"Free release" signifies a logical operation by which the idea, in order to externally verify its self-determining activity, liberates nature under the domain of its own jurisdiction. Only by renouncing the omnipotence and infallibility of its own principle, by recognizing that not everything can be subsumed under the order of reason and therefore transparent to it, the idea positively validates its own truth. This raises some serious conceptual issues both for Hegel's system in general and in reference to the specific paradox between the idea and nature.

If Hegel's system not only tolerates nature in the form of irreducible otherness but nature is, in fact, a positive condition of the system's own self-verification and even "sets limits to all philosophy" (Hegel 2004, p. 23), then it follows that there is no ultimate irreconcilability between absolute idealism and realism. In other words, absolute idealism does not necessarily deny the validity of empirical facts, but can actually provide a most sophisticated theoretical justification of their necessity.

The idea—in its absolute self-determining activity—is always already externalized in space and time. If this is so, then there is no linear time sequence of conditioning between the idea and nature. Specifically, there is no temporal transition from one regime to the other; there has never been a cosmogonic event of passing over from the eternal essence of God to the creation of the finite spirit and nature. The idea does not pass over into nature historically, and nature does not pass into the idea. On the contrary, the very form of transition is inad-

---

[13] The summary is taken from Hegel's chapter "Transition from Family to Civil Society" in the *Elements of the Philosophy of Right* (Hegel 1991b, p. 219).

equate to conceptualize the relation between the idea and nature, which is rather "to be grasped as free release" (Hegel 2010, p. 576). In this sense, it turns out retroactively that there was no paradox to be resolved in the first place.

Bibliography

Fichte, Johann Gottlieb (1982): *The Science of Knowledge*. Edited and translated by Peter Heath and John Lachs. Cambridge: Cambridge University Press.

Hegel, Georg Wilhelm Friedrich (1812): *Wissenschaft der Logik: Das Sein*. Hamburg: Meiner.

Hegel, Georg Wilhelm Friedrich (1991a): *The Encyclopedia Logic*. Edited and translated by T. S. Geraets, W. A. Suchting and H. S. Harris. Indianapolis: Hackett.

Hegel, Georg Wilhelm Friedrich (1991b): *Elements of the Philosophy of Right*. Edited by Allen Wood. Translated by H. B. Nisbet. Cambridge: Cambridge University Press.

Hegel, Georg Wilhelm Friedrich (1995): *Lectures on the Philosophy of Religion*. Vol. 2. Translated by R. F. Brown, P. C. Hodgson, and J. M. Stewart with assistance of H. S. Harris. Berkley: University California Press.

Hegel, Georg Wilhelm Friedrich (2004): *Philosophy of Nature*. Edited and translated by A. V. Miller. Oxford: Oxford University Press.

Hegel, Georg Wilhelm Friedrich (2010): *The Science of Logic*. Edited and translated by George di Giovanni. New York: Cambridge University Press.

Hegel, Georg Wilhem Friedrich (2018): "Enzyklopädie der philosophischen Wissenschaften (1st edition 1830)". In: *Hegels Werke*. Vol 6. Hamburg: Meiner, pp. 1–681.

Hyppolite, Jean (1997): *Logic and Existence*. Translated by Leonard Lawlor and Amit Sen. New York: SUNY Press.

Illetteratti, Luca (2020): "Nature's Externality: Hegel's Non-Naturalistic Naturalism". In: *Problemi International* 4, pp. 51–73.

Jacobi, Friedrich Heinrich (1994): *The Main Philosophical Writings and the Novel Alwill*. Edited and translated by George di Giovanni. Quebec: McGuill-Queen's University Press.

Longuenesse, Beatrice (2007): *Hegel's Critique of Metaphysics*. Translated by Nicole J. Simek. Cambridge: Cambridge University Press.

Marx, Karl (1990): *Capital. A Critique of Political Economy. Volume One*. Translated by Ben Fowkes. London and New York: Penguin.

Rödl, Sebastian (2018): "Die innere Negativität des Denkens". In: Thomas Khurana/Dirk Quadflieg/Francesca Raimondi/Juliane Rebentisch/Dirk Setton (Eds.): *Negativität: Kunst, Recht, Politik*. Berlin: Suhrkamp, pp. 401–424.

Robert B. Pippin
Idealism and the Problem of Finitude: Heidegger and Hegel

Abstract: Idealism in Kant, Fichte, and Hegel has nothing to do with the mind-dependence of the world or a mind-imposed structure in experience, or a so-called objective idealism (a claim about the nonmaterial nature of the real, in favor of its ideal nature). Instead, it is a claim about the capacity of pure (empirically unaided) reason to determine of all that is knowable that it is knowable, and how it is knowable. Human reason can thus be understood to be self-authorizing, a tribunal unto itself. In the Hegelian version, this determination of the knowable is a determination of all that there is in its knowability, and so a metaphysics. For Hegel, the determination of the knowable is not the determination of a limitation, as in a limitation just to the knowable-for-us. Or, in Hegel's famous and controversial phrase, this determination is "absolute". Since Hegel, this claim has been subjected to a wide range of criticisms, the most important of which insist on the finitude of human reason. The most important critics are Schelling and Heidegger, and in this paper I begin to assess those criticisms.

1 The idealism problem

Heidegger's interest in Hegel is prepared for and accompanied by a growing attention in his Marburg and early Freiburg years to Kant, as well as the entire German idealist tradition. He lectured on German idealism in 1929, the same year as his remarkable book on Kant, *Kant and the Problem of Metaphysics*, appeared. He lectured on Hegel's *Phenomenology* in 1930/31, on Kant's transcendental principles in 1935/6 (this would become the basis of his book *The Question Concerning the Thing*), on Schelling's *On the Essence of Human Freedom* in 1936, and on *The Metaphysics of German Idealism* in 1941. He continued to publish on the idealists in the later phases of his career as well, as in his acute formulations of his differences with Hegel in *Identity and Difference* in 1957. He continued to publish on Hegel and Kant late into the 1950s, and his evaluation of the importance of "overcoming Hegel", and Hegel's idealism, became more and more prominent. He was already saying such things as the following in *The Basic Problems of Phenomenology* (1927):

Robert B. Pippin, University of Chicago.

> And this means always that Hegel must be overcome by radicalizing the way in which the problem is put; and at the same time he must be appropriated. This overcoming of Hegel is the intrinsically necessary step in the development of Western philosophy which must be made for it to remain at all alive. (BP, p. 178)

This is a sentiment often expressed by Heidegger, that German idealism and especially the thought of Hegel represent the culmination of all philosophy and must be overcome for philosophy to have a future. "Fulfillment" is another translation for "*Vollendung*", and it could mean that the basic problems posed by Greek philosophy were "solved" by Hegel, so that there is no longer any philosophical work to do. But it could also mean that the distortions and obscurities inherent in the metaphysical tradition were taken on and thought through by Hegel to a point where it became clear (not to him, but retrospectively) that the whole tradition had "culminated" in a dead end, and this in a way that might suggest the necessity for and the possible direction of a new beginning. Heidegger of course means the latter, "dead end" view, as is obvious from his claim about "perishing", the translation of "going to the ground" (*geht ... zugrunde*). ("Where history is genuine, it does not perish merely by ending and expiring like an animal; it perishes only historically" [IM, p. 202]. We must understand, says Heidegger, "that Hegel himself has come to an end with philosophy because he moves in the circle of philosophical problems" [BP, p. 282].)

Heidegger's claims about Hegel will be our main focus, but as noted, Heidegger also folds his account of Hegel as culmination into a general account of German idealism, which includes his coming to terms with the work of Kant, Fichte, and Schelling as well. This means that the general position he wants to oppose, free us from, is idealism, "culminating" in "speculative idealism", and we should begin by saying something about the idealism that Heidegger is interested in, the general importance he gives it.

Idealism in this tradition (for Heidegger and, in my view, in itself) should not be understood as a claim about the mind-dependence of the world or about mind-imposed structure in experience or as a so-called objective idealism (a claim about the nonmaterial nature of the real, in favor of its "ideal" or immaterial nature), but first and foremost as an objection to empiricism, the claim that all knowledge is or must be based on empirical experience. By contrast, idealism in Kant, Fichte, and Hegel is a claim about the capacity of pure (empirically unaided) reason to determine of all that is knowable that it is knowable, and how it is knowable. Since this amounts to a claim about the normative authority of knowledge claims, and since it is pure reason alone that demonstrates such normative authority, this must mean that human reason is to be understood to be self-authorizing, a tribunal unto itself. As Heidegger notes in *Kant and the Prob-*

lem of Metaphysics, the idealist move results in a paradoxical self-reflection: "a philosophizing laying the ground for philosophy" (KPM, p. 26). Heidegger is echoing the Kantian claim that in pure critique, we are dealing with "what reason brings forth entirely from out of itself" (CPR, Axx). In the Hegelian version, which will ultimately be the main focus in the following, this determination of the knowable is a determination of *all that there is* in its knowability, and so a metaphysics. For Hegel, the determination of the knowable is not the determination of a limitation, as in a limitation just to the knowable-for-us. Or, in Hegel's famous and controversial phrase, this determination, this self-determination by reason of its own requirements, is "absolute", and so a determination of the Absolute, of all that is in its knowability; and that "leaves nothing out". Reason's self-imposed requirements define and delimit all that there is and can be. In other words, idealism in this sense invokes the deepest principle of Western rationalism, "to be is to be rationally intelligible"; there can *be* nothing *alogos*, or unintelligible. (Another famous way of putting this, which will loom large in what follows: there is an "identity of thinking and being".) This is the founding principle of Greek metaphysics, as Heidegger understands it, thought through to its culmination in Hegel, and it will be the heart of Heidegger's critique of the metaphysical tradition.

Heidegger formulates the issue this way in *The Fundamental Concepts of Metaphysics*:

> The question concerning the essence of world is a fundamental question of metaphysics. The problem of world as a fundamental problem of metaphysics finds itself led back to logic. Logic is therefore the proper basis of metaphysics. The connection here is so insistently obvious that we would be amazed if it had not insistently forced itself upon the attention of philosophy from time immemorial. And indeed, as we have briefly shown with respect to the problem of world, this connection provides the basis and path for the whole of Western metaphysics and its questions, insofar as it is logic that prescribes the examination of all problems with respect to the *logos*; and its truth as problems of metaphysics. (FCM, p. 289)

Kant and Hegel both agree that there is pure thinking, philosophical knowledge not derived from experience, and that the proper subject of pure thinking is thinking itself, or "logic". This is obviously not a system of truth-preserving inferences, but a theory of the concepts necessary for any thinking to have content (what Kant called transcendental logic), to relate to objects such that judgments having such form can be true or false. For Kant, such categories provided the necessary conditions for the possibility of sense experience, and this made possible a "metaphysics of experience". For Hegel, concepts necessary for contentful thinking determined *what could be* in general.

Heidegger makes just as clear his objections to this presupposition about the priority of logic for metaphysics, for the meaning of being.

> In spite of this, we must pose the question of whether this connection between logic and metaphysics, which has utterly ossified into self-evidence for us, is justified; whether there is, or must be, a more originary problematic; and whether or not precisely the usual way of asking metaphysical questions orients itself toward logic in the broadest sense precisely because insight into the peculiar character of the problem of world has hitherto been obstructed. (FCM, p. 289)

For our future discussion of the issue announced in the notion of a "culmination", we might also note how important the idealists, and Hegel in particular, are for Heidegger in this scheme.

> This phenomenon of the λόγος is not only familiar in philosophy in general, and especially in logic, but λόγος in the broadest sense as reason, as *ratio*, is the dimension from within which the problematic of being comes to be developed. That is why for Hegel—the last great metaphysician in Western metaphysics—metaphysics coincides with logic as the science of reason. (FCM, p. 290)

Now, Heidegger obviously understands that one prominent understanding of idealism has to do with the question of whether the external world exists, or whether it can be known in itself, questions that assume our primary access in experience is to the contents of consciousness, understood as "in me", or that this world is "structured" by a form-imposing mind. But in §43a of *Being and Time*, when he notes that "in principle", idealism when properly understood has an "advantage" over subjective idealism, he begins to make clear his own understanding of idealism and its connection to what we have been saying:

> If what the term "idealism" says, amounts to the understanding that Being can never be explained by entities but is already that which is "transcendental" for every entity, then idealism affords the only correct possibility for a philosophical problematic. If so, Aristotle was no less an idealist than Kant. (BT, p. 251)[1]

Obviously, this rests everything of significance on the idealist determination of the *necessary* requirements of intelligibility, what Hegel called a logic. We should think that such a determination sets out what Kant in another context called the

---

[1] For an extended defense of this claim, especially with respect to Aristotle (and the differences between Hegel and Aristotle even so), see Pippin 2018. See also: "Viewed with minute exactitude, the anxiety that prevails today in the face of idealism is an anxiety in the face of philosophy ..." (BP, p. 167). And the discussion in *Heidegger and the Subject* (Raffoul 1998, p. 52).

"really" and not merely logically possible. If there is no way to defend such a claim to necessity, then there is no idealism in this "German" sense. The position obviously does not hold that there is nothing unknown, but rather that there is nothing in principle unknowable, and that the logic of the form of the knowable can be fully determined. This, then, would clearly amount to a claim about the conceptual structure or logic of *what there is*. Formulated differently, to be is to be determinate; just what something is, delimited from what it is not. The idealist claim is that pure thinking can specify the possibility of the determinability of anything at all. In so doing, idealism is a metaphysics. For Heidegger, this all indicates an "errancy", a distortion from the start since, for one thing, a thought's focus is on "the beings", what is required for a being to be the being it is. It leaves unanswered, "unthought", the meaning of being itself, how it is that any being can be, or can be available for thought at all. What is errant for Heidegger is the idealist indifference to finitude, and he thinks Kant has appreciated this far more than the later idealists. However, even for Heidegger's Kant, such finitude is not a matter of some restriction on what could be known but is out of our reach (the standard view of Kant's results), and the spirit of Kantian idealism remains for him a kind of realism as well. Heidegger's interpretation of Kant's highest principle of synthetic judgments resonates with Hegel's denial of any gap between subject and object that needs to be overcome.

> [W]hat makes an experiencing possible at the same time makes possible the experienceable, or rather experiencing [an experienceable] [*Erfahrbare bzw. Erfahrene*] as such. This means: transcendence makes the being in itself accessible to a finite creature. (KPM, p. 84)

Many of the most influential figures in European philosophy in this period (from roughly 1807 until the present) considered Hegel and something like this idealism (the self-sufficiency and autonomy of pure thinking; or, one might say, the autonomy of philosophy itself) as their chief opponent, and they often explicitly did so in the way Heidegger did—by identifying Hegel as the epitome or culmination of all Western philosophy. In part, this also had something to do with a kind of frustration that Hegel, especially in his *Phenomenology of Spirit*, his *Philosophy of Objective Spirit*, and his *Realphilosophie* lectures, seemed, on the one hand, to turn philosophy away from purely ideal theory to what he himself insisted on, which was *Wirklichkeit*, historical actuality. But on the other hand, he seemed to take back with one hand what he had given with the other, not only insisting that philosophy is bound to its own time, comprehends its own time in thought, but also claiming that a rational core and structure is developing in time, ultimately available only to pure philosophy or pure thinking. He seemed to be saying that major historical change, widespread social practices, and institutions were all subject to a supreme invocation of the principle of sufficient reason. This did not merely mean that their existence could be empirically explained, but that there was a reason for them being as they were, progressively better and better reasons when compared with what had gone before. In the understandable reactions ensuing from such frustration, the dispute in one way or another concerns an attack on the idealist claim about the autonomy, self-sufficiency, and "self-authorizing" character of rational reflection (a feature common to Kant, Fichte, and Hegel) as a foundation for all such accounts, a necessary presupposition for any account of actuality. What seemed especially outlandish to his critics was Hegel's claim to the absolute status of the results, which was attacked in favor of various versions of the finitude or limitation of any such reflection.

Now, some of these "finitist" critiques often draw large implications from what I believe to be a distorted interpretation of Hegel. However, the proposal here is not that all of modern continental philosophy, or Heidegger's critiques, through Hegel, of the entire metaphysical tradition, rests on a mistaken interpretation of Hegel. Many other issues were certainly at play, and the figure I have focused on as the most effective challenger to Hegel's version, Heidegger, provides with some glaring exceptions, a sophisticated, deep, highly accurate, and insightful reading of what Hegel was trying to do. I will explain what I mean by this later. But the contestation between idealism and anti-idealism, understood as that between a claim about the self-sufficiency of reason and a contrary claim about its putative radical finitude, is of major philosophical importance in itself. There is a way of genuinely understanding Hegel such that this long critical reaction certainly has some real grip on a real problem in Hegel. In other words, while it is true that the received interpretation of Hegel is largely inaccurate,[2] pointing this out hardly settles the issue. The central general challenge to idealism is still a powerful one. The basic claim in this long tradition about the insufficiency of idealism, or "pure thinking", or even philosophy itself (as in Heidegger's notion of a culmination), is important enough to warrant sustained interrogation. Eventually, I want to say that Hegel's most important potential contributions to this discussion have been both misunderstood and under-

---

[2] I am certainly aware of what might well seem to be the arrogance of such a claim, but in this context, all I can do is to invoke the case for such a claim made in *Hegel's Idealism* (Pippin 1989) and *Hegel's Realm of Shadows* (Pippin 2018). While Heidegger might appear to have interpreted Hegel in quite a traditional way, theologically, his understanding of theology is distinctive enough that it is consistent with the core of his reading of Hegel: that, for Hegel, metaphysics is logic, a "science of pure thinking", and that a completely self-reflective logic, the Absolute, has been achieved.

valued, even by Heidegger, for all the depth and power of his interpretation. The central claim is that when the ambitions of what Hegel calls "pure thinking" (which are admittedly considerable) are properly identified, the criticisms embodied in the "finitist" argument form that I want to identify do not hold; paradigmatically so in Heidegger's treatment. Let me proceed to a simplified summation of the idealist ambition.[3]

The central idealist claim began with Kant's *Critique of Pure Reason* and his assumption that reason was capable of determining what it was entitled to claim, and capable also of restricting itself if it could not provide such authority. This almost immediately generated the concern that such an enterprise would end not only in a destructive skepticism but in an all destructive "nihilism" (F. H. Jacobi's original coinage), with nothing of moral substance or objective status left standing. But a deeper and more long-standing issue arose in the thought of Hegel, especially in the attempt made in his major theoretical work *The Science of Logic*, a book that has not enjoyed much of a reception in either anglophone or European philosophy until very recently. The said issue looks like this.

Hegel's claim in that book has three components. The first is the claim that *a priori* knowledge of the world, the ordinary spatio-temporal world, is possible; knowledge about that world, but achieved independently of empirical experience. The second component is where all the interpretive controversies begin. It is the claim that this *a priori* knowledge, while in some sense to be specified and ultimately about the world, consists in thinking's or reason's *knowledge of itself*; thinking's determination of thinking or, as Hegel designates it, a "science of pure thinking". This is what distinguishes classical rationalism from idealism, as Hegel (and Kant) understood it. The former holds that reason has access to its proper objects outside itself; the latter, that the object of pure thinking is itself. But there is clearly a question to be answered: *How* could the first two components—*a priori* knowledge of being and the object of pure thinking being itself—possibly be jointly true? One long dominant interpretation of Hegel on this point, the third component, and the putative resolution of this tension, holds that these two claims can both be assertable only if what there "really" is, the "really real world", what is accessible only to pure reason alone, is itself *thought*, that is, "thinking moments"; something like the Absolute or God thinking itself, an inherent, evolving noetic structure, unfolding in time from the human perspective, in itself a *nunc stans*, a Spinoza-like absolute. Pure thought thinking itself is the manifestation of the *noesis noeseos*, God thinking himself, or it is the

---

[3] A full defense of the interpretation of Hegel's *Logic* sketched out here may be found in Pippin 2018.

divine-like apprehension of the noetic reality that underlies experienced appearances. I cannot do so here, but I have argued for some time that this interpretation does not fit the text. So an alternative interpretation is necessary, and I will discuss it in a moment.

But apart from the interpretation issue, the most important critiques of idealism in this sense all hold that any such project is doomed from the start, that there is not and cannot be any self-sufficient "pure thinking". I noted that such a broad counter claim is often summarized as a doctrine of "radical finitude". This is an apt title since Hegel insists that, to use an Aristotelian formulation, "thinking thinking thinking"[4] is not the thinking of any object, and when he wants to summarize such an unusual reflective self-relation, he notes the "infinity" of thinking's relation to itself. Pure thinking's object is itself, but not as an object or event; rather, its object is the thinking also interrogating thinking; a circle, not a dyadic relation; hence the provocative notion of "infinity", without beginning or end. The anti-idealist criticism holds that thinking must always be understood as grounded on, or dependent on, or an epiphenomenon of, some sort of non-thinking ground, or Absolute, or materiality or contingency or the unconscious instinct or drive of the thinker, or an always already implicitly orienting understanding of the meaning of Being. Hegel's comment on the matter in *The Science of Logic* is a perfect indication of the difference between idealism and anti-idealism:

> The claim that the *finite is an idealization* defines *idealism*. The idealism of philosophy consists in nothing else than in the recognition that the finite is not truly an existent. Every philosophy is essentially idealism or at least has idealism for its principle, and the question then is only how far this principle is carried out. (SL, p. 124 [21.142])

In the most decisive case in the tradition for Heidegger, the dependence in question is what Kant emphasized, the dependence of thinking on sensible intuition, of pure thinking on pure intuition. (The significance of this for Heidegger is also existential: "[M]an is, at the same time, not master of the being which he himself is" [KPM, p. 160].) Schelling's early formulation is also apt. The distinction between thinking and what is other than thinking, between subject and object, can itself be neither a subjective nor an objective distinction. If it were either, there would actually be no distinction. So what there really is can be characterized neither as absolute subject nor absolute object, but—and here the difficulties begin—somehow "the neither subject nor object". Hegel's prioritization of the Concept, in his terms, the identification of the Absolute as the Concept, is

---

[4] This is the apt formulation of Ariyeh Kosman (see Kosman 2013).

said to be a prioritization of absolute subjectivity and so to require a relation to what is other than thought, which is nature, as pure domination. It would be hard to overstate the influence of such an argument form (the details vary a great deal of course, but this form of skepticism remains) from Schelling to Heidegger, and Adorno.[5]

In Hegel's treatment, the topic of pure thinking is presented as having nothing to do with the existing human thinker, the subject, consciousness, the mind. The topic rather raises as a problem the possibility of the intelligibility of even whatever is being touted as the pre-conscious source or hidden origin, the intelligibility of what is assumed in any such determinate identification as a knowledge claim, even of "the neither subject nor object". That is either something available for some kind of apprehension or it is not. If it is, it must be subject to some regime of intelligibility for this determinacy to be accounted for. This is what Heidegger denies when he insists that the meaning of being, being as such, is not "a" being, and not subject to the requirements of determinacy. Insisting this does beg the question. (This is not to mention that *Dasein*'s access to the meaning of its own being is not access to anything determinate. What it is to be *Dasein* is, precisely, not to be a being.) So, Hegel's project is thought's determination of what thought must be, its moments (*Denkbestimmungen*), in order to be a possible truth-bearer, a result that for Hegel immediately involves what could be the object of any truth claim. (Kant distinguished general and transcendental logic this way. General logic determines the rules necessary for thinking to be coherent thinking at all; transcendental logic "introduces" possible content, considers thinking as having content other than thinking.) In the face of this, if someone simply persists in asking, "But *where* is all this thinking and explaining happening?" all one can reply is, "wherever there is thinking". This is not to say

---

[5] For the most part, Heidegger wants to say that what German idealism leaves unthought is the problem of the meaning of Being, but he has a number of ways of making that point. As we shall see, some of the most striking and accessible stem from his use of Kant. Heidegger attributes the primacy of imagination claim to the first edition of the *Critique*. Consider: "All reinterpretation [*Umdeutung*] of the pure power of imagination as a function of pure thinking—a re-interpretation which 'German Idealism' even accentuated subsequent to the second edition of the *Critique of Pure Reason*—misunderstands its specific essence" (KPM, p. 138). Also: "And yet, in the second edition of the *Critique of Pure Reason*, did Kant not give mastery back to the understanding? And is it not a consequence of this that with Hegel metaphysics became 'Logic' more radically than ever before? ... What has the outcome of the Kantian effort been if Hegel explains metaphysics as logic thusly: 'Logic is consequently to be grasped as the system of pure reason, as the realm of pure thought. This realm is truth, as it is without a veil, in and for itself' ... Can there be more compelling proof for how little the metaphysics which belongs to human nature, and hence how little 'human nature' itself, is self-evident?" (KPM, p. 171)

that there is not always a thinker or subject of thought; it is to say that thought that can be truth-bearing is constituted by what is necessary for truth-bearing, by any being of whatever sort capable of objective (possible true or false) judgment.[6] Any such determination of a source or ground or subject-object, must still, so goes the case for the possible explication of absolute intelligibility, make sense within a general regime of sense-making, or nothing has been claimed by the putative claim for an *Ungrund*, or non-ground; an empty place in logical space would have just been suggested. Any such criticism, in so far as it is a thinking, a judging, a claim to know, is always already a manifestation of a dependence on pure thinking and its conditions, and such "moments" of pure thinking are to delimit (but not limit) the normative domain of intelligibility (what can *rightly* be distinguished from something else, or rightly posited as "ground", for example) and not any process or series of events that goes on in supposed independence of the empirical world. Pure thinking, as Hegel understands it, is neither dependent on nor independent from the empirical, or from materiality or the brain or the "indifference point" or whatever new "absolute" comes into fashion. His position would be better understood by rough analogy with Frege or Wittgenstein of the *Tractatus* or the early Husserl in his account of logic as metaphysics. That anti-Hegelian question already manifests (for the Hegelian) a misunderstanding of the question of pure thinking itself. This is not to deny that any reference to thinking presumes a thinker, indeed a living, purposive, finite, embodied rational thinker. (Hegel addresses this issue in his *Philosophy of Subjective Spirit* and elsewhere.) It is, rather, to argue for the autonomy of the question of "any thinking at all", whatever the existential status of the thinker. (While, as we have seen, Heidegger does not claim that pure thinking is an epiphenomenon of something else, something "material", he will want to argue that the status of the subject in Kant and post-Kantian thought is seriously under-theorized and remains obscure.) That is, it is to insist on the priority and autonomy of "logic", and that means, for Hegel, its complete self-determination of its own "moments". Hegel's enterprise in the *Logic* takes as

---

6 There is a similar sentiment in Kant: "Pure reason, as a faculty which is merely intelligible, is not subject to the form of time, or, consequently, to the conditions of the succession of time" (CPR, A551/B579). This must mean that the subject is in no ordinary sense a substance. But given the dependence of thinking on the pure forms of intuition (essentially on time), this cannot be the whole story either, as Heidegger is at pains to point out in *Kant and the Problem of Metaphysics*. Thinking is not to be understood as an attribute of a mental substance, a thing, but how we should understand the subject will require a great deal of attention. Consider Heidegger's summary: "Rather this 'from-out-of-itself-toward ... and back-to-itself' first constitutes the mental character of the mind as a finite self" (KPM, p. 134).

its topic the categories or "thought determinations" (*Denkbestimmungen*) necessary for thought to have determinate objective content, an enterprise that at the same time specifies the determinations inherent in the possible determinacy of being itself. It is true that it would seem that Hegel is subject to his own criticism, that pure thinking must already assume a determination of what pure thinking amounts to, but Hegel's innovation here, partly derived from Fichte, is that pure thinking comes to self-consciousness about itself *by thinking*, in the sense that one understands what one believes in believing it, understands what one is doing in doing it. This is all still much too telegraphic, but it forms the core of the idealist response to anti-idealism, and it will recur as an issue often in what follows.

There is a good summation of the conceptual structure of the problem this raised for Heidegger in Gadamer's study *Hegel's Dialectic*:

> Thus Heidegger's ambiguous formulation, "the consummation of Metaphysics", leads us finally to an ambiguity common to Hegel and Heidegger. Concisely stated, the issue here is whether or not the comprehensive mediation of every conceivable path of thought, which Hegel undertook, might not of necessity give the lie to every attempt to break out of the circle of reflection in which thought thinks itself. In the end, is even the position which Heidegger tries to establish in opposition to Hegel trapped within the sphere of the inner infinity of reflection? (Gadamer 1976, pp. 101–102)

Put a different way, if Hegel were making a claim about the mind's thinking nature, how we must think about the world, knowledge would be limited by its "instrument", something Hegel had been vigorously denying since the Introduction to the *Phenomenology*. In knowing itself, what pure thought knows is the possible intelligibility, the knowability, of anything that is. But the intelligibility of anything is just what it is to be that thing, to be determinately "this-such" (*tode ti*), the answer to the "what is it" (*ti esti*) question, definitive of metaphysics since Aristotle. To be is to be intelligibly, determinately, "what it is". So in knowing itself, thought knows of all things, *what it is* to be anything. As for Aristotle, the task of metaphysics is not to say of any particular thing what it is. It is to determine what must be true of *anything at all* (what used to be called *transcendentalia* in scholasticism), so that what it is in particular *can* be determined by the special sciences. Of course, the *Physics* and the *De anima* are also philosophical sciences for Aristotle, and therein lies the beginning of a problem for both Hegel and Heidegger. One of the ways Heidegger characterizes traditional metaphysics is that it does indeed try to determine *a priori* what it is to be some kind of being or other. In traditional language, it confuses the tasks of a *Metaphysica generalis* and a *Metaphysica specialis*. In his terms, it assumes there can be *a priori* ontic knowledge, knowledge of beings or a region of beings, or knowledge of Being itself as if it were a knowledge of beings. (Hegel, I want to claim, agrees with him about this.) This, according to Heidegger, is what Kant was trying to avoid by insisting that ontology give way to a Transcendental Analytic. Kant was only insisting that our original openness to Being, which Heidegger characterizes as "letting-things-stand-against" us, is of a completely different order of "knowing" ("pre-ontological") than the one appreciated by traditional metaphysics, and in the proper register of "finitude", Kant means to recuperate ontology as a *Metaphysica generalis*. Heidegger cites Kant's first *Critique*, A845/B873, and the discussion in Kant's *Über die Fortschritte der Metaphysik* (KPM, p. 88). This "set up" by Kant, followed by Heidegger, will pose a misleading problem for Hegel. Kant and Heidegger agree that at the most basic level, thought is finite because thought, understanding, knowledge, cannot create its own objects; it depends on a comportment toward what is other than the subject. With things set up that way, it looks like Hegel's claim about the infinity of thought says that thought *does* create its own objects. That is not at all his position, but it remains a common interpretation of Hegel on metaphysics. The other Kantian claim that is of massive importance to Heidegger's critique of idealism is his argument that he has shown, or rather Kant has shown and he has exfoliated the point, that pure thinking can arrive nowhere, certainly not at the determination of the "horizon" of all possible objectivity, without being everywhere not only intertwined with but also dependent on sensibility, especially the "sensible" faculty of the imagination. This is true of pure thinking as well, and so requires an explanation of pure intuition/sensibility. All of this is supposed to dislodge "Ratio and Logos" from their central role in the history of metaphysics, to deny "the primacy of logic", most evident in the culmination of that tradition in Hegel. See KPM, p. 117.

The analogy with such things as Frege's and Husserl's critiques of psychologism in a theory of pure thinking only goes so far, not only because Hegel's account of how pure thinking determines the necessary "moments" of the intelligibility of anything at all is already a distinctive and unprecedented position that would obviously have to be explained and defended, but also because it involves a further argument about the bearing of such results on the intelligibility of the natural world and human practices. This feature of Hegel's position, referred to earlier as an understandable frustration (textually, the relation between his *Logic* and the *Philosophy of Nature* and *Philosophy of Spirit*) touches on another major dimension of the anti-idealist critique, one most associated with Schelling, Kierkegaard, and the Heidegger of *Being and Time*. It is that thought, paradigmatically Hegel's pure thinking (or even philosophy itself, as traditionally understood), cannot contribute to any understanding of, cannot in effect even "reach", the most vital, concrete issues faced in a human life, existential issues, especially the "meaning" of its own death. This is all another implication of the finitude of thought, and it is argued that more and more radical ways of somehow addressing, illuminating, understanding concrete existential issues are needed. Hegel certainly cannot contribute to this, so goes the criticism,[7] if Hegel is understood as he seems to require: interrogating the role of reason, some normative order, in the changing socio-political, religious, and artistic practices of an age. Since Hegel's Spirit, *Geist* (Hegelian *Dasein* in some sense), is self-positing, a "product of itself", according to Hegel, the development of this self-positing depends on a collective self-understanding, which in turn requires a continuing attempt by *Geist* to justify itself to itself, which Hegel regards as progressively more satisfactory. In this sense, the self-understanding at issue must be "rational". Since any such justification must be incomplete and must also depend on assumptions about justification and meaning that *Dasein* cannot reflectively redeem, but must always already assume, Heidegger has no faith in such an insistence. Of course, this all depends on the proper understanding of what Hegel means by such an appeal to reason in such practices, and my claim is that once the proper form of the structure of rationality or account-giving and justification in the *Logic* is understood, its bearing on the issues Hegel himself brilliantly brought it to bear on—ethical life, art, religion—can be properly appreciated. For Adorno and Heidegger, Hegel's claim about the absolute delimitation of rationality, and so practical justifiability, is not a mere philosophical mistake, but an act of hubristic self-assertion typical of Western thought, and one that has had and continues to have catastrophic real-world consequences.

Some quotations from Hegel are relevant here to get our final bearings on the position Heidegger will try to "free us from", or "overcome".

> Thus *logic* coincides with *metaphysics*, with the science of *things* grasped in *thoughts*, which used to be taken to express the *essentialities of the things*. (EL, §24)[8]

We should note the change in emphasis insisted on by Hegel. The new metaphysics, logic, concerns things as grasped, *gefaßt*, in thought, whereas the old met-

---

[7] The criticism can sound like a capacity limitation, that there is something just outside our grasp, which we could obtain were our capacity not limited, but it could also be put as a limitation that descends from the object of any thought because that object itself is unthinkable, either because infinite (e.g., God) or because finite, of a sort that allows no discursive articulation, and so in that sense no intelligible account (e.g., the meaning of Being in Heidegger's critique).
[8] See the original: "Die *Logik* fällt daher mit der *Metaphysik* zusammen, der Wissenschaft der *Dinge* in *Gedanken* gefaßt, welche dafür galten, die *Wesenheiten der Dinge* auszudrücken."

aphysics was a thing-metaphysics, used to think of its subject matter as the "essence of things".
And:

> The objective logic thus takes the place rather of the former *metaphysics* which was supposed to be the scientific edifice of the world as constructed by *thoughts* alone. (SL, p. 42 [21.48])

Again, objective logic alone takes the place of the former metaphysics, *tritt damit vielmehr an die Stelle der vormaligen Metaphysik*, which thought of its object as the scientific edifice of the world.
And finally,

> The older metaphysics had in this respect a higher concept of thinking than now passes as the accepted opinion. For it presupposed as its principle that only what is known of things and in things by thought is really true [*wahrhaft Wahre*] in them, that is, what is known in them not in their immediacy but as first elevated to the form of thinking, as things of thought. This metaphysics thus held that thinking and the determination of thinking are not something alien to the subject matters, but are rather their essence, or that the *things* and the *thinking* of them agree in and for themselves (also our language expresses a kinship between them); that thinking in its immanent determinations, and the true nature of things, are one and the same content. (SL, p. 25 [21.29])

I can't imagine a more definitive confirmation of the "logic as metaphysics" interpretation.

2 Heidegger's distinction

This all only sets a very general context of anti-idealism, in favor of a "finitude of thought" thesis. I have been suggesting that far and away the deepest, most thoughtful engagement with idealist and especially Hegelian thought in post-Hegelian philosophy is Heidegger's. In fact, a good case can be made that Heidegger's distinction among all such anti-idealist positions is that his is the first genuine confrontation with Hegel in all of the post-Hegelian European tradition. For our purposes, which at this point is merely to sketch the general tenor of Heidegger's approach, the discussion that is especially important is what was published as the second part of *Identity and Difference* (1957), originally the end of a seminar and later also a lecture, called "The Onto-Theological Constitution of Metaphysics". This is because Heidegger goes immediately and directly to the heart of Hegel's enterprise and states it accurately as just what it is. Heidegger tells us that the subject matter, the *Sache*, of thinking for Hegel is "thinking as such", *Denken als solches*. And he immediately adds exactly the right qualification:

> In order not to misinterpret this definition of the matter—thinking as such—in psychological or epistemological terms, we must add by way of explanation: thinking as such—in the developed fullness in which what has been thought [*in der entwickelten Fülle der Gedachtheit des Gedachten*], has been and now is thought. (ID, p. 42)

Thinking in the fullness of what has been thought is Heidegger's formulation of the Hegelian claim that logic, properly understood, is metaphysics. The thinking of pure thinking is at the same time the thinking of the world in its thinkability, *what* has been and is now being thought. Heidegger reminds us that we can only understand this from Kant's viewpoint, although not like Kant, transcendentally, but speculatively. That is, Hegel thinks thinking as *Being*, and not as a subjective epistemological condition; or, said conversely, Being is only possibly available in any sense in its thinkability. Heidegger realizes that pure thinking's taking itself as object does not result in a mere theory of thinking, or the rules of thinking, or a "philosophy of pure cognition". As Heidegger says directly, for Hegel, "Being is the absolute self-thinking of thinking" (ID, p. 43). The last thing Heidegger means by this is that Being is mental activity, whether human or divine. That would merely be an account of one of the beings, a subject matter of one of the special sciences, and would so presuppose a logic of intelligibility. Because of his own approach, Heidegger is in a unique position to realize that the subject matter of the *Logic* is not in any sense whatsoever a being, not "the" Absolute's self-positing, not the noetic substructure of the world, not abstract objects, not the mind of the Christian God, not a substance, but, in his language, the meaning of Being, the *Sinn des Seins*. As he puts it in his distinctive language,

> the Being of beings reveals itself as the ground that gives itself ground and accounts for itself. The ground, the *ratio* by their essential origin are the λόγος, in the sense of the gathering of beings and letting them be. They are the ἓν πάντα. Thus "science", that is, metaphysics, is in truth "logic". (ID, p. 56)

And he tells us what he thinks Hegel means by logic:

> We now understand the name "logic" in the essential sense which includes also the title used by Hegel, and only thus explains it: as the name for that kind of thinking which everywhere provides and accounts for the ground of beings as such within the whole in terms of being as ground (λόγος). The fundamental character is onto-theo-logic. (ID, p. 59)

The "divine" at stake in what Heidegger means by theo-logic is, he constantly explains, not a being, not anyone to whom we can pray or play music to or dance for, he notes with a hint of contempt. He means: because, in Hegel as the culmination of all metaphysical thinking, thinking is self-grounding and thereby serves as ground (for any being being intelligibly what it is), this thinking is also "theology" because it concerns the *causa sui*. Pure thinking is productive self-generating.

So in summation:

> Metaphysics responds to Being as logic, and is accordingly in its basic characteristics everywhere logic, but a logic that thinks the Being of beings, and thus logic which is determined by what differs in the difference: onto-theo-logic. (ID, p. 70)

As we shall shortly see, Heidegger means that metaphysics is determined by this difference (between Being and the beings) without being able to think the difference; it is and must remain unthought in metaphysical thinking. Compare what Heidegger is saying to what Hegel says, and the accuracy of his characterization will be immediately clear:

> [T]he logical is to be sought in a system of thought-determinations in which the antithesis between subjective and objective (in its usual meaning) disappears. This meaning of thinking and of its determinations is more precisely expressed by the ancients when they say that *nous* governs the world, or by our own saying that there is reason in the world, by which we mean that reason is the soul of the world, inhabits it, and is immanent in it as its own innermost nature, its universal. (EL, §24)

So, Hegel is said to reanimate the Platonic-Aristotelian "logical" ontology, which holds that to be is to be intelligible, in principle knowable. For Hegel, again as Heidegger understood him, to be is necessarily to be determinate (a this-such, discriminable from any other "such"), and the requirements of determinacy are also the requirements for anything to count as a being. Anything putatively indeterminate—an object, an event, a state of affairs, a meaning, Being—that cannot be distinguished from anything else "isn't anything".[9] That is, the basis of Hegel's claim for his logical idealism, or the identity of thinking and being, is that thinking's self-constitution of the requirements for any determinacy must already just count thereby as the only possible meaning of any being *being the being it is*; its delimitability from other beings. This is supposed to be shown in the *Logic*'s opening claim that the mere thinking of "being" is not a thought at all. The indeterminacy of mere being, its indistinguishability

---

[9] See *The Basic Problems of Phenomenology* (BP, p. 170) for an excellent summary.

from what is not being, makes it indistinguishable from "nothing". Therewith follows the spontaneous self-constitution by pure thinking of what *would* satisfy the determinacy conditions without which nothing could be a determinate anything. The beginning of wisdom for the early Heidegger is that, on the contrary, there *was* clearly a being not at all comprehensible as, not at all being, "determinate"—the being Heidegger called "*Dasein*" precisely to indicate that it was not a determinate this-such. *Dasein* is openness to the meaning of being itself, "being there" at the site of any manifestation of such meaning.[10] There could be no logos in the Hegelian sense to a being, *Dasein*, that was what it took itself to be, a being whose mode of being is *to-be*, existence, a self-interpreting being, especially not one whose mode of being was to be constantly faced with its own non-being, the possibility of the random, arbitrary end of its being in death. Such a being could never be simply "what it is".[11] But this was only the beginning of the larger claim most associated with Heidegger: that the meaning of being itself would be forever hidden, even forgotten, if Hegel's views about the "infinity" of pure thinking, there being nothing "outside" the conceptually determinable, were accepted. Being would be rendered a determinate object like any other, a position which would assume and not account for the meaning of being itself. It would presume an understanding of the meaning of being in an "ontic" way, as a being, which again would presuppose rather than address the meaning of being as such. Further down the road in the Hegelian development, as we shall see, the same is true of "life".

This is Heidegger's problem with "metaphysical thinking". He notes approvingly that Hegel's approach is developmental, not deductive, and that this developing thought thinking thinking is intertwined with the history of thought, with the history of philosophy. Herein, one of the deepest affinities between Hegel and Heidegger: that dealing with figures in the history of philosophy is not preparatory to philosophy or exemplary for philosophy, but is the highest form of philosophy itself. As Heidegger put it in his essay "Anaximander's Saying" (1946): "The only Western thinker who has thoughtfully experienced the history of thought is Hegel" (AS, p. 243). In his engagement with this thinking, Hegel tries to think rightly what really has been thought in the developing positions, and Hegel's attempt is an *Aufhebung*, a preserving and raising up of all that has been rightly but partly thought into a whole. Heidegger accepts this inter-

---

10 See Carmen (forthcoming) on "Existentialism as Anti-Rationalism" for a compelling picture of Heidegger's position.
11 Any claim that, nevertheless, *that* sort of being is just that, determinacy enough, is a mere debater's point. *Dasein*'s mode of being is not-being, ungrounded, the "basis of a nullity". That *Dasein*'s determinate being, what sets it off as what it is, *is such indeterminacy*, is nonsense.

twining with the history of thought, but says that his approach is to think what is *unthought*, what remains hidden in the history of thinking as *logos*. Hegel's self-determining thinking always misses something essential to its possibility, and Heidegger's life-long task was to help us identify what is always missing and why. Accordingly, his engagement is not an elevation, not progressive, but a "step back", a *Schritt zurück*. While Hegel thinks the ultimate identity of thinking and being, Heidegger's basic thought is difference, *Differenz*. Thinking's determination of absolute intelligibility actually "recedes" before the true subject matter of thought, Being. Something remains "unasked", the difference between Being and beings. All of these are claims we need to explore and assess in what follows.

Even so, even given this claim about the exfoliation of what is "unthought" in the history of pure thinking, of metaphysics, it is important that Heidegger thinks the unthought (by which he basically means the true appreciation of the ontological difference, the priority of the question of being) *in pure thinking*. In this sense, his topic is the same as Hegel's: pure thinking's reflection on its own possibility.

> The term denoting this character by which being precedes beings is the expression a priori, *apriority*, being earlier. As a priori, being is earlier than beings. The meaning of this a priori, the sense of the earlier and its possibility, has never been cleared up. (BP, p. 20)

And:

> The a priori character of being and of all the structures of being accordingly calls for a specific kind of approach and way of apprehending being—*a priori cognition*. (BP, p. 20)[12]

So, in conclusion, if Heidegger has rightly characterized the nature of Hegel's project in the *Logic*, and I think he has, what is it in the "logic as metaphysics" project that remains unasked, unthought? If we take our bearings only from *Being and Time*, then we can put the point in Schelling's way: we would have

---

12 This *a priori* cognition is, at this period in Heidegger's thought, phenomenology, but already a distinctly Heideggerian phenomenology. It is characterized this way: "Being does not become accessible like a being. We do not simply find it in front of us. As is to be shown, it must always be brought to view in a free projection. This projecting of the antecedently given being upon its being and the structures of its being we call phenomenological construction" (BP pp. 21–22). He aligns himself with Hegel again when he elaborates on this projection: "Because destruction belongs to construction, philosophical cognition is essentially at the same time, in a certain sense, historical cognition. 'History of philosophy,' as it is called, belongs to the concept of philosophy as science, to the concept of phenomenological investigation" (BP, p. 23).

it that the mark of thinking's finitude is the "unreachability" of human existence itself, i.e., that such concrete existence can never be rendered fully intelligible. Not only is existence an unfinishable temporal (or "temporalizing") project, and so never something that can be taken in as an object of thought, one of its most distinctive characteristics is its very *unintelligibility* to itself. It finds itself uncanny, not at home anywhere, the anxious, null basis of a nullity, something it cannot help but flee in a tranquilizing ("falling") everydayness. But once Heidegger has fully shifted attention to the problem of metaphysics, another issue looms much larger: the absolute difference between Being and beings, our inevitable confusing the question of "what is it to be" with "what is it to be this or that being". This is, of course, Heidegger's master thought throughout his career, even in *Being and Time*. But what do the thought and the criticism (if that is the right word to characterize what Heidegger has noted) mean in Hegel's terms?

The first thing one can say is that Heidegger is generally right about the *Logic*. Hegel does insist that the question of being necessarily always amounts to a question about what it is to be this or that being. This is the result of the first moment of the *Being Logic* ("The Doctrine of Being"), and it is that moment where the deepest "confrontation" (*Auseinandersetzung*) with Heidegger must take place.[13] In this, as in so much else, Hegel follows Aristotle. Being is said in many ways, but there is some primacy to being as *tode ti*, a this-such, determinate being. I noted that this does not mean that it is the job of the *Logic* to determine what it is to be any particular determinate being, but to determine what anything at all must be to determine what any determinate being is. But this last formulation does not seem to reach the question Heidegger is interested in since it is still directed to beings, *die Seienden*. As Heidegger realizes, the closest formulation in Hegel for the "Being of beings" question is simply pure thinking, determinate intelligibility. But that topic, which Heidegger wants to treat as Being's own manifestation, its unconcealing or happening, and so as what any pure thinking as judging must presuppose, is not a topic or moment for pure thinking.

And while Heidegger agrees that there is nothing empirical about the theory of pure thinking at the center of German idealism, he does note that such a theory never went deep enough. Again, he gets Hegel right when he notes,

---

13 Heidegger does not call his treatment of past philosophers an interpretation or an assessment but an *Auseinandersetzung*. This, he thinks, requires him to excavate what is "unthought" in the thought of a philosopher. Both of these features, the confrontation and the reliance on the unthought, result, quite consciously, in something that does not look much like the history of ideas or the history of philosophy as it is usually practiced, or even like textual interpretation.

> In Hegel this determination of the subject as *hupokeimenon* undergoes sublation into the interpretation of the subject as self-consciousness-as self-conceiving, as concept or notion [*Begriff*]. For him the essential nature of substance lies in its being the concept of its own self. (BP, p. 153)

But, he goes on to say,

> it must be acknowledged equally that the being of the subject does not consist merely in self-knowing—not to mention that the mode of being of this self-knowing remains undetermined—but rather that the being of the *Dasein* is at the same time determined by its being in some sense—employing the expression with suitable caution—extant [*vorhanden*] and in fact in such a way that it has not brought itself into existence by its own power ... The subject remains with the indifferent characterization of being an extant entity. And defining the subject as self-consciousness states nothing about the mode of being of the ego. (BP, p. 153)

What he means here is that it is one thing to have successfully warded off possible interpretations of the subject of thought as empirical, as in psychologism, or as metaphysical substance, as in immaterialism or the *res cogitans*, but that just tells us what the distinct mode of being of the ego *is not*, and we still need to investigate this mode of being, a major "unthought" thought in German idealism. Kant, Hegel, and Fichte wanted to say that the sole assumption necessary for an account of pure thinking is only (and non-committingly) the "I or he or it" that thinks, but Heidegger insists that this leaves out the question of the mode of being of the subject, and he is certainly right. The notion of a "transcendental-logical" subject is merely a way to avoid the question.

This is a decisive and distorting absence because of the way Heidegger wants us to understand the task of a properly reconceived metaphysics. He puts it this way in his lectures *The Fundamental Concepts of Metaphysics:*

> Metaphysics is a questioning in which we inquire into beings as a whole, and inquire in such a way that in so doing we ourselves, the questioners, are thereby also included in the question, placed into question. (FCM, p. 9)

However, it is also true that he does not mean his version of the metaphysical question to be like the alternatives proposed by psychologism and immaterialism. Those pose the question as about *Dasein*'s "what-being", as a question of substance, a kind of thing. And Heidegger's "meaning of Being" question assumes the contrary, and so calls for a new mode of interrogation. When he wants to explain how metaphysical questions are comprehensive (*inbegriffen*), he says,

Idealism and the Problem of Finitude: Heidegger and Hegel — 147

they also in each case always comprehend within themselves the comprehending human being and his or her *Dasein*—not as an addition, but in such a way that these concepts are not comprehensive without there being a comprehending in this second sense, and vice-versa. No concept of the whole without the comprehending of philosophizing existence. (FCM, p. 9)

Although we have reached the point where a very great deal would have to be said about Heidegger's unusual language, it is here that we do seem to reach some sort of absence in Hegel's enterprise, even if whether that means that something crucial is "missing" or not is a separate question. If the Being of beings, the Absolute, is thinkability, have we asked *in* the *Logic* what it is, what it means, to be thinkable? Thinkability, or even thinking itself, is not one of the determinate moments of the *Logic*, and when the characteristics of thought or judgment become self-conscious in the *Concept Logic* ("The Doctrine of the Concept"), it is the forms of judging this or that, in their determinate possible inferential relations, that are attended to. I noted before that Hegel thinks we cannot provide an independent theory of the thinkable as such. We can merely manifest thinking by pure thinking. We know what pure thinking is by thinking. Any other formulation would presuppose and so elude itself. But this means that the "science of pure thinking" does and cannot count pure thinking itself as one of its moments. And from Heidegger's point of view, this is not adequate. What we learn in the process of trying to think anything at all determinately is the possible determinacy of any being. "Thinking thinking thinking" is the enacting of thinking, and the reflective self-consciousness at the end of the *Logic*, the Concept of the concept, of intelligibility itself, is a form of self-consciousness about the intelligibility *of any being*, not something like "being as intelligibility itself". That is always unasked, unthought, presupposed, even if manifested, or enacted. The *Concept Logic* is supposed to allow the inclusion of the *Logic* itself inside "the Concept". But that just covers what we have been through, what the thinking of any being amounts to. It does not and cannot include what Heidegger seems to be after: "what it means for Being to be thinking's self-determination of thinking". That question both must be and cannot be "inside" the Concept. Put another way, logic itself, or the question "What is logic?" is not a possible moment. And we know from Heidegger's 1928 lecture course, now published as *The Metaphysical Foundations of Logic*, that Heidegger thinks that question is deeply intertwined with the "meaning of Being" question. So Heidegger is right that the question remains unasked, even unthought.

This is all not to deny that there is something also quite limited and often tendentious about Heidegger's assessment of Hegel. There are other passages where he does not charge that the question of the mode of being of the thinker has been left unthought by Hegel, but that Hegel did "think" it, and did so as a Cartesian, with the subject understood as nothing more than an individual center of consciousness. Here is the charge:

> The theory according to which man is initially subject and consciousness, and is given to himself primarily and most indubitably as consciousness, basically arose from quite different intentions and perspectives in connection with Descartes and his attempt to lay the foundations of metaphysics. It is a theory which has come to pervade all philosophy in the modern age and was subjected by Kant to a peculiar, although not an essential, transformation. This led finally to the Hegelian attempt to absolutize the approach which takes the isolated ego-subject as its point of departure, which is why we describe this philosophy as absolute idealism. (FCM, p. 208)[14]

This all also raises the question of whether Heidegger is right to draw the rather apocalyptic consequences he does from this "forgetting" or not asking this question; in a word, his word, "technology". But it also raises what might seem like an unusual question from Heidegger's point of view. Is this all actually a *problem?* It is not as if Heidegger thinks this elusive topic *should* have been itself a moment within the *Logic*. He is, in many other works, asking for other modes of interrogation, from a "fundamental ontology" form of phenomenology, to *Gelassenheit*, to *Andenken*, to the four-fold. But from Hegel's point of view, there is no reason to believe that these attempts would not generate their own form of "difference", and so elusiveness. And for Hegel, this would be because the only kind of interrogation of being-there could be is the interrogation of any determinate being, and the mode of being of those determinations, thought determinations, *Denkbestimmungen*. It might be Heideggerian enough for Hegel to invoke another formulation of the same problem, i.e., that thinkability as the meaning of being can only be shown, not said.

Moreover, from Hegel's point of view, there is another source of unclarity in Heidegger's basic position. At the start of *The Basic Problems of Phenomenology*, when he is trying very hard to distinguish his understanding of the always presupposed, implicit orientation from the meaning of Being from any "world view" (*Weltanschauung*) philosophy (his target is Jaspers), Heidegger characterizes his conception of a philosophical science quite conventionally:

> Philosophy is the theoretical conceptual interpretation of being, of being's structure and its possibilities. Philosophy is ontological. (BP, p. 11)

---

[14] See also Pippin 1997, pp. 375–394 for a defense of Hegel's anti-Cartesianism.

But Heidegger does not at this point discuss any of the modal questions involved in philosophical conceptuality, although that is crucial for any "scientific" philosophy. There is clearly a borrowed Kantian structure here: Being is available, manifest, and so the question is, how is this possible? Even, as Heidegger will formulate it, what makes it possible? ("Unveiledness of being first makes possible the manifestness of Being" (EG, p. 103). Or in *Being and Time:*

> But in significance [*Bedeutsamkeit*] itself, with which *Dasein* is always familiar, there lurks the ontological condition which makes it possible for *Dasein*, as something which understands and interprets, to disclose such things as "significances" [*Bedeutungen*]; upon these in turn is founded the Being of words and language. (BT, p. 121)

Fair enough, but the results, if actually "theoretical-conceptual", make a claim to *necessity*. A resulting formulation of a condition that could not be otherwise. Not just this or that element makes it possibly available; that would not be scientific, would give us mere sufficient conditions. We want necessary conditions. We want elements in place without which this availability would not be possible; it is possible only on assumption of these elements. In Kant, necessity is tied to necessary conditions of experience. That means, necessary for a unity of consciousness, the transcendental unity of apperception, to be possible. In Hegel, necessity is internal to the development of the Concept. Any conceptual moment or "thought determination" is necessary for anything at all to be determinate, a condition of it being at all, and only possible if determinacy is supplemented by the concept of finitude. Whether this is defensible or not, we can at least see the basis of necessity in this internal self-negation and developmental necessity. And in Heidegger? Without *what* would there be no availability, no manifestness, clearing? Perhaps without *Dasein* as Heidegger understands it, as being-there, a possible site for meaningfulness; perhaps eventually without beings being an *Ereignis*, an event or happening of meaning? All of this is not to say that Heidegger wants simply to reject Hegel, to charge Hegel with the kind of irrelevance that, say, Hobbes claimed for Aristotle or the scholastics. But the logical space treated by *The Science of Logic*, the domain of determinate intelligibility and its conditions, becomes a regional ontology, as dependent on the unasked question of the meaning of being as all such ontologies. So Hegel can launch and perhaps even complete "the science of pure thinking" and claim some ontological relevance for it, but he cannot claim that the Concept, that model of intelligibility and determinate being, is the Absolute.

This kind of demarcation of a regional ontology (which alone is a fit subject for an assertion) is not a result that either would accept; Hegel because it is unsystematic and would leave unclarified the relation between such a region and any other region (in fact, the result would preclude any such question), and Heidegger because it would still be the case that such a region presupposed some availability of the meaning of Being and would leave that dependence unclarified. But it may be the most consistent result of taking on board Heidegger's concerns.

Bibliography

Carmen, Taylor (forthcoming): "Existentialism as Anti-Rationalism". Forthcoming in: *Markus Gabriel's New Realism*. Springer.

Gadamer, Hans (1976): *Hegel's Dialectic: Five Hermeneutical Studies*. Translated by P. Christopher Smith. New Haven: Yale University Press.

Kant, Immanuel (1910–): *Gesammelte Schriften*. Berlin: Preussische Akademie der Wissenschaften.

Kosman, Ariyeh (2013): *The Activity of Being: An Essay on Aristotle's Ontology*. Cambridge, MA: Harvard University Press.

Pippin, Robert (1989): *Hegel's Idealism: The Satisfactions of Self-Consciousness*. Cambridge: Cambridge University Press.

Pippin, Robert (1997): *Idealism as Modernism: Hegelian Variations*. Cambridge: Cambridge University Press.

Pippin, Robert (2018): *Hegel's Realm of Shadows: Logic as Metaphysics in Hegel's Science of Logic*. Chicago: University of Chicago Press.

Raffoul, François (1998): *Heidegger and the Subject*. Translated by David Pettigrew and Gregory Recco. Atlantic Highlands: Humanities Press.

Paul Redding
Hegel's Metaphysical Alternative to the Choice between an Unrealistic Platonic Realism and an Opposing Skeptical Anti-realism

Abstract: In this paper I argue for an interpretation of Hegel's philosophy beyond a choice between two distinctly "unrealistic" options: Robert Brandom's "robust" realism and Richard Rorty's skeptical *anti*-realism. I thus interpret Hegel's idealism as a form of weakened Platonic realism (a realism *about ideas*, or realistic *idealism*) that falls between the interpretations of Rorty and Brandom. This position broadly coincides with the "actualism" found within debates over modality within analytic philosophy and represented there by Arthur Prior and Robert Stalnaker. For the actualist, there is a sense in which the actual world necessarily contains "mind" and its ideational contents, but this is a trivial sense. What we mean by the actual world, in contrast to some of the non-actual possible alternatives to it, is the world as containing *us*, and we have no option other than to think of ourselves as "minded".

A contribution to the field of the philosophy of economics in which is propounded a "realistic realism" (Mäki 2009) neatly captures the worry that lies behind many critics of *philosophical* realism as well as my own concern with the now popular "realist" interpretations of Hegel's philosophy. Philosophical positions described as "realist" can often be considered as *unrealistic* when put forward as approaches to the world suited to beings such as ourselves, at least on the view of ourselves as broadly belonging to the natural world, and as such, as in some ways continuous with other natural entities. How could it be, it might be asked, that beings that developed in a way that prioritized the development of capacities to find food or avoid predators evolved the type of cognitive capacities relevant to various philosophical realisms? Speculative realists, for example, typically conceive of the world as it is "anyway" as "mind-independent": the world would have the characteristics that it is known to have, even were there no beings in the universe capable of knowledge of its nature. This characteristic is shared, however, by those who interpret Hegel's "absolute *idealism*" as a type

Paul Redding, University of Sydney.

of realism in the more Platonic sense, as does, for example, James Kreines (Kreines 2015). According to this type of realism, the world has features typically attributed to the mind. Thus, for Kreines, "reason" is "in the world" in a way that is independent of the existence of *reasoners* within it, Platonic ideas being seen, in a way reminiscent of Aristotle, as the *natures* or *essences* of things. In relation to this type of realism, naturalistically inclined critics are likely to have worries about "reason" or "concepts" being part of the objective fabric of the world. For example, how could the evolved brain have acquired the capacity to know the nature of mathematical entities when understood, as in Platonic realism, as abstract mind-independent idealities that somehow give form to the objective world?

Standardly, those with worries about such a realism are likely to be grouped as occupying the opposing stance of a skeptical "anti-realism" that has other problems. (Hegel, of course, is supposedly able to somehow slip through the nets of such dichotomies, but showing how this occurs rather than simply repeating the claim is seldom simple.) In this essay I begin with a dispute between two analytic philosophers sympathetic to the spirit of Hegel and who otherwise share many assumptions, Robert Brandom and his former teacher, the late Richard Rorty. Rorty had popularized the work of the American philosopher Wilfrid Sellars, whose views Brandom would systematically elaborate and apply in his interpretation of Hegel (e. g., Brandom 2019). But while Rorty derived consequences from Sellars critical of philosophical realism, Brandom would come to advocate a *strongly* realist interpretation of the same doctrines. In relation to this dispute, I will then go on to propose, both in its own terms and as appropriate for Hegel, a form of weakened Platonic realism that might be thought to fall between a form of skeptical anti-realism that Rorty is commonly (but perhaps mistakenly) taken to advocate and the "robust" realism of Brandom. This is a position found within broader debates over modality within analytic philosophy from the second half of the twentieth century, "actualism" or "modal actualism".

The position thus described was first applied in the 1960s and 70s to the work of Arthur Prior and was later embraced by Robert Stalnaker. Both opposed a version of realism that many regarded as *massively* unrealistic—specifically the "modal realism" that David Lewis propounded from the late 1950s until his death in 2001. While the modal realism embraced by Brandom is not that of Lewis, it was nevertheless subjected by Rorty to the criticism of being, from a naturalistic perspective, unrealistic. While the actualist shares Rorty's critique of all such realisms, a reorientation of metaphysics itself from a focus on "reality" to "actuality" allows the actualist to avoid the sorts of skeptical consequences thought to constitute the anti-realism that push opponents in the realist direction.

1 Modal metaphysics and the tension between naturalism and realism

The analytic revolution of the first half of the twentieth century aimed at dispelling the type of traditional metaphysical debates that had dominated previous philosophy by virtue of a logical analysis of philosophical claims. Crucial here had been the logical revolution of the late nineteenth century initiated by Gottlob Frege and developed and popularized in the twentieth by Bertrand Russell. One of the casualties of this new way of thinking about philosophy had been Hegel himself,[1] but more broadly, the new philosophy withdrew interest in the area of modality and other traditional metaphysical topics. Rorty's broadly anti-metaphysical stance, influenced especially by Carnap, together with his naturalism had made him skeptical of modal talk such as talk about mere possibilities—those things, events or states of the world that *might have* existed but in actuality do not. How could a naturalist about the world find something in it for modal talk to be *about?* The natural world might include many puzzling things, but it is hard to see how it could find a place for ones that simply *don't exist*. Must not modal talk go the way of much other earlier metaphysics or the theological talk with which, say, seventeenth-century philosophy had been inseparable? Rorty had thought of Hegel as a thinker liberating us from such ideas. Brandom, drawing on the same Sellarsian resources as Rorty, would however, come to interpret him as a "robust" realist about modality and, moreover, about the objective reality of concepts, facts and truths as well.

Around the middle of the twentieth century modal issues once more came to assume an importance for many analytic philosophers, especially in the wake of technical developments in *modal logic*. Here, new life had been given to the analysis of talk of possibility in terms of "possible worlds" as found in the seventeenth century in Leibniz. As reintroduced by Saul Kripke (Kripke 1959), this was a technical term operating within a mathematical model, but debate would come to be centered on David Lewis' "modal realist" *ontological* interpretation of the notion. Lewis' "realism" here, however, seems misleadingly qualified *as* "modal". What Lewis had a realistic view *about* were the *possible worlds themselves* invoked in the effort to show the meaningfulness of talk about what *might have been* but in fact is *not* the case. Wanting to do justice to claims such as "Hilary Clinton *might have* won the 2016 US Presidential election had she not

---

[1] See Redding 2007, Introduction, for the way Russell had used the revolution in logic against Hegel.

described some voters as 'deplorables'", Lewis' solution was to affirm the reality of non-actual but *possible worlds* in which some counterpart of Hilary *did* win the election.[2] However, because the modal features of *any one world* depended on the existence of others, this means that each of the possible worlds of Lewis' bizarre metaphysical cosmology taken individually, and thus including our own world, the *actual* world, are themselves curiously *amodal*.[3] I will call *this* realism "possible world realism", leaving "modal realism" for versions that *do not* rely on the realism of possible worlds, as in Brandom's version.

Leibniz's original version of the doctrine of possible worlds had been elaborated within an overtly God-centered view of the world that at that time had been generally accepted. In the context of a more secular culture in which individuals are more likely to have a naturalistic view of themselves, Lewis' version was received with a generally incredulous response. While Lewis himself considered his own realism about possible worlds *compatible* with naturalism, such a combination many other philosophers found incredible, raising the question, for example, of how natural creatures such as ourselves could ever know anything about alternative realities with which they were spatio-temporally and causally disconnected.

Hegel had lived and philosophized at a time that might be thought of as pivoting between the theocentric world of Leibniz and our own more secular times, and Hegel's metaphysical commitments had been interpreted in both ways, his followers dividing after his death broadly into "right", God-centric and "left" more secular, naturalistic followers. Rorty might be thought to be in the tradition of the left-Hegelians, suspicious of the theological inheritance of the type of unrealistic realism of which Lewis' philosophy can be seen as providing a contemporary manifestation. Significantly Brandom had both Rorty *and* Lewis as the advisors of the PhD dissertation within which his interpretation of Hegel had first developed. He would eventually develop a variety of *modal realism*, different to that of Lewis but a realism, nevertheless, and Rorty would criticize that aspect of his account as unrealistic for intelligent but natural creatures such as ourselves.

While discussions of modality had been broadly off-limits within analytic philosophy during the first half of the twentieth century, modal issues had nevertheless been central to the work of the Austrian "object theorist" Alexius Meinong, and in the 1950s, the Hegel interpreter John N. Findlay would attempt

---

[2] In Lewis' system, the *actual* Hilary cannot exist in other worlds, but a type of close *Doppelgänger* can.
[3] Lewis had been greatly influenced by Quine for whom the world was amodal. Lewis's individual worlds are themselves somewhat Quinean.

to interpret Hegel in ways that had benefited from Meinong's account of intentionality, but divesting that account from its modal realism (Findlay 1958, Redding 2017). In his PhD on Meinong carried out in the early 1930s, Findlay had attempted to use the implicit *logic* of Meinong's modal insights in a way that freed them from a type of possible-worlds realism even more extravagant than that of Lewis (Findlay 1963).[4] While Findlay did not label his own position as "actualist" he was an important precursor to the *later* actualist responses to Lewis' modal metaphysics, the term later being applied to Findlay's former student, the creator of the modal logic of *time* ("tense" or "temporal" logic), Arthur N. Prior (e.g., Prior 1967).

In this essay I will attempt to situate such an actualist approach to modal logic between Brandom's unrealistic realism and the form of skeptical anti-realism to which realism is usually opposed. In particular, I will draw upon Rorty's fundamental intuition that any aspiration to an entirely *non-contextual* or *non-perspectival* account of human cognition—the traditional "God's-eye" point of view—is, both in itself and in Hegel's view, unrealistic. But this does not have the generally skeptical consequences usually attributed to it. When the task of metaphysics is narrowed down to capturing the nature of the *actual world* rather than what is *necessarily the case* in the actual world, there should be no concern with its being understood as a type of "realism". Capturing this intuition was, I suggest, at the heart of Hegel's idealism and in particular, his approach to judgment and inference in the "Subjective Logic" of his *Science of Logic*.

2 Sellarsian Hegelianism

In an autobiographical essay, Richard Rorty described the intellectual disillusion that had been induced by his historically inflected passion for philosophy:

> The more philosophers I read, the clearer it seemed that each could carry their views back to first principles which were incompatible with the first principles of their opponents, and that none of them ever got to that fabled place "beyond hypotheses". (Rorty 1999, p. 10)

Hegel, he claimed, had enabled him to see philosophy in a different way. From reading Hegel's *Phenomenology of Spirit* he came to see philosophy as "a matter of out-describing the last philosopher" but this did not deprive the activity of philosophizing of meaning because, in accord with Hegel's idea of the "cunning

---

4 Meinong included in his ontology even *impossible* worlds.

of reason", such competition could serve another purpose so as "to weave the conceptual fabric of a freer, better, more just society" (Rorty 1999, p. 11).

Rather than a search for ultimate truths, philosophy had become what he would later describe as an "edifying conversation", but many would find the verbal dialectic that Rorty characterized in this way as anything but conversational. One of the sources of this characterization had been Hans-Georg Gadamer who also drew on Hegelian ideas but who gave the notion of philosophical conversation a type of Kantian *moral* twist. Rather than simply subject the views of another to logical scrutiny, Gadamer's philosophical conversationalist was a hermeneutic one: the goal of such dialogical engagement was to enable, *via* the recognition of others as *differently located* in culture and history, a grasp of the unthought presuppositions informing *one's own*. Like Kant's invocation to take others as genuine *subjects* rather than explainable empirical phenomena —that is, broadly as natural worldly objects—the Kantian hermeneut was to recognize others as, like herself, sources of rationally evaluable *claims* about the world. Moreover, this had to be extended from individual claims to the *criteria* for evaluation implicit in those claims themselves. Not only first-order claims about the world could be contested, so too could the criteria being appealed to in the course of disputes over such first-order claims.

While in his account of such a "conversation" Gadamer had relied upon a quasi-Kantian moral imperative to treat one's conversationalist as an equal partner, any such imperative, Rorty thought, *unrealistically* presupposed the capacity to step beyond the contextually specific determiners of an agent's actions, including the actions of interpretation. In this context, Rorty's views were generally parallel to Hegel's critique of the formalism of Kant's moral philosophy. However, reflecting more evolutionary-based naturalistic ideas similar to those found in Nietzsche, Rorty characterized the "edifying conversation" more as a battle among ego-centric "conversationalists", motivated to trumping their interlocutors by re-interpreting their claims and re-characterizing the underlying criteria of those claims. He found a *Hegelian* model for this in the "struggle for recognition" between master and slave in Hegel's *Phenomenology of Spirit* as interpreted by the likes of Kojève and Sartre, (Kojève 1969; Sartre 1956). This struggle for recognition was meant to represent a struggle among humans in which each attempted to impose his or her interpretations onto others. Further employing Hegel's idea of the "cunning of reason", this type of cultural struggle could be seen as having the entirely *unintended* beneficial effects of enriching the conceptual fabric with which humankind as a whole interpreted the world. It was such a view that he linked to the views developed by Wilfrid Sellars in the mid-twentieth century. Rorty's interpretations of Hegel in this regard, I believe, had combined insights and errors, and his adoption of a type of generalized naturalism and embrace of Nietzsche had contributed to a generally skeptical "anti-realist" tone within which his criticism of unrealistic realism has been taken. Reducing the scope of philosophy to the actual world, however, allows this tone to dissipate.

Attracted to Kant's idea of the role played in perception by concepts articulated into holistic networks, Sellars had been opposed to the broadly empiricist epistemological orientation that he saw as dominating analytic philosophy in the first half of the twentieth century, summing up its inadequacy with the idea of the "myth of the given" (Sellars 1997). This myth was seen as giving to humans the reassurance that they could be confident in the knowledge attained in the world as long as it was ultimately based on that which was *given* in perceptual experience and elaborated in logically valid ways. But Sellars rejected the type of parallelism between words and world presupposed in such a view. Effectively, he believed that the *holistic* nature of the logical breakthroughs of the early twentieth century, continuous more with the Kantian than the empiricist tradition, had undercut the atomistic assumptions about the nature of perceptual experience inherited by empiricists from the seventeenth century.

Modern logic had broken the grip of Aristotelian logic, from the perspective of which a judgment had paradigmatically been thought of as involving some sort of combination of independently meaningful subject and predicate terms, encouraging the idea of a translation into relations among atomistic "ideas"—the "givens" of perceptual experience. In the logic of George Boole, for example, in which modern algebra had been applied to Aristotle's subject–predicate logic, a sentence such as "the sun shines" could be thought of as classifying an object, the sun, as a member of the class of shining things. Its perceivable *shine* might thereby be thought of as something "given". But Aristotle's subject–predicate view had already come under strain with the approach to judgment by Immanuel Kant in the late eighteenth century, and in the late nineteenth, Gottlob Frege had challenged even more deeply the traditional subject–predicate structure of judgment. In Frege's view the content of judgments, assertions or beliefs were better thought of as non-composite entities—*propositions* capable of being either true or false. Frege's view was thus much closer to the ancient *Stoic* propositional logic than the Aristotelian logic of terms, but it was also closer to the *Platonist* conception of the mind-independent reality of *abstract entities* or *idealities* such as the propositions in question. According to Sellars, epistemological ideas of givenness were effectively tied to pre-Fregean ways of thinking about logic. Rather than built up from smaller meaningful sub-propositional parts that could somehow accommodate atomic givens, propositions had to be understood as acquiring meaning in virtue of their relations to *other propositions*, an idea perhaps prefigured by Kant's idea of the "transcendental unity" of apperceptive (that is, conceptualized perceptual) beliefs. On the other hand, Sellars clearly rejected the type of Platonist conception of propositions as fundamentally abstract, mind-independent entities, as favored by Frege. Such entities were thought to be typical of those unrealistic objects posited by traditional metaphysics. How could otherwise *natural, finite* beings with natural and finite cognitive capacities come to engage epistemically with non-concrete, mind-independent entities?

In the place of any such ultimately Platonic account Sellars gave a broadly *meta-linguistic* interpretation of propositions as well as the other abstract entities seemingly required by philosophy. We should direct our attention to the functional roles played within speech of distinct *kinds* of expression. Asserted sentences come to stand in inferential relations to other sentences within the distinctive "language games" that are the bedrock of rationality. These are games in which a speaker can be asked to provide justifications for a claim, should an interlocutor feel the need. Justifications thus take the form of further sentences meant to settle the interlocutor's doubt, leading him or her to accept the earlier sentences in question. Disputes about the criteria for the evaluation of such claims would in turn be settled in the same way. In this way, "language games", in the course of which reasons for what had earlier been said could be asked for and provided, constituted the linguistic infrastructure within which the modern logicians' "propositions" come to stand to each other in non-causal, "rational" relations.

Sellars' program was immensely complex and ambitious (see, for example, DeVries 2005 and O'Shea 2007). While appealing to the *actual* linguistic practices of a community, in a way not unlike that of the later Wittgenstein, Sellars nevertheless wished to keep in play more of the traditional tasks of philosophy, but without theological or Platonic commitments. In this regard he specified the *normative, rule-following,* nature of linguistic behavior that could not be simply reduced to naturalistic causal processes but that nevertheless was compatible with such a naturalistic view. What distinguished Sellars' naturalism from the naturalism of others was that it had a "normative turn" (O'Shea 2007). The question of how to understand the "binocular vision" meant to combine normative and naturalistic views is one of the most difficult and controversial aspects of Sellars' philosophy, sorting his followers into "right" and "left" Sellarsians echoing the subsequent history of Hegel's philosophy. Rorty was, predictably, on the "left" and was critical of what he regarded as remnants of an unacceptable realism in Sellars' philosophy which he attempted to expunge.

Sellars had limited his critique of realism to the reality of traditional Platonic abstracta but had embraced a realism about empirical *science: scientific* realism. Rorty's attitude to this was complex. His idea of "rational debate" as a type of battle of wills seemed to rule out issues of truth and rationality, but he disputed this. Unlike the caricature sketched by many of his analytic critics, he was not a *skeptic* about either everyday or scientific knowledge. Such an *anti*-skepticism about science he clearly shared with Sellars.[5] But he was skeptical of claims concerning any type of second-order knowledge *about* this knowledge, affording it a justificatory status above being just another move within the struggle over interpretation. He thus opposed Sellars' scientific realism, which he considered a philosophical stance rather than a scientific one. A physicist's claims about the physical world were *limited* to theories about the physical world. These theories do not extend to meta-level ones about the relation between the theories and the physical world itself. A similar opposition would be extended to Brandom's *modal* realist claims erected on a Sellarsian basis.

3 The Rorty–Brandom clash over modality

In an essay on Rorty, Brandom had described his former teacher's master strategy in *Philosophy and the Mirror of Nature* (Rorty 1979) as his having used "a Kantian conceptual tool to undermine a (broadly) Kantian representationalist picture". The tool was the Sellarsian one insisting on "the distinction between *causal* considerations and *justificatory* considerations" (Brandom 2000, p. 160). This had been the strategy that Kant had used against Locke, but in Rorty it was expressed in *linguistic* form as the claim "that inferential or justificatory relations obtain only between items *within* a vocabulary", while in contrast, "relations between applications of a vocabulary and the environing world of things that are not applications of a vocabulary must be understood exclusively in non-normative causal terms". In short: "Normative relations are exclusively intravocabulary. Extravocabulary relations are exclusively causal" (Brandom 2000, p. 160). However, Brandom then criticizes Rorty for unnecessarily muddying the waters by rejecting "the idea of facts as a kind of thing that *makes* claims true". Brandom quotes from Rorty that "since truth is a property of sentences, since sentences are dependent for their existence upon vocabularies, and since vocabularies are made by human beings, so are truths". Brandom then adds that "at this point something has gone wrong" (Brandom 2000, p. 161).

According to Brandom, nothing in Rorty's underlying position entails that there are no facts prior to the existence of claim-making, vocabulary-employing

---

5 This anti-skepticism must be kept in mind when considering Rorty's *anti-realism* which is often taken to be a skeptical doctrine.

humans. We can "understand facts as true claims, acknowledge that claiming is not intelligible apart from vocabularies and still insist that there were true claims, and hence true facts, before there were vocabularies" (Brandom 2000, p. 162). Brandom reminds the reader of Sellars's distinction between two senses of "claim": a "claim" can refer to an *act* of claiming on the one hand or the *content* of what is claimed on the other. Of course, there were no *claimings* prior to humans but this does not extend to "claimables". "If we had never existed, there would not have been any true claimings, but there would have been facts (truths) going unexpressed, and in *our* situation, in which there *are* claimings, we can say a fair bit about what they would have been" (Brandom 2000, p. 163).

In response, Rorty reasserted his belief "that there were no truths before human beings began using language: for all true sentences S, it was back then that S, but there were no 'worldly items'—no facts, no truths—of the sort Brandom believes in" (Rorty 2000, p. 184). Rorty's reply had not moved Brandom from this position, which is re-expressed in his recent book on Hegel's *Phenomenology of Spirit* (Brandom 2019). There he appeals to Frege's distinction between *sense* (*Sinn*) and *reference* (*Bedeutung*) as analogous to that between claimings and claimables. Acknowledging that for such "response-dependent" concepts such as *beauty*, in which the "property of being beautiful is sense-dependent on that of pleasure" such that "one could not *understand* the concept beautiful* unless one *understood* the concept pleasure",[6] he denies that this dependence extends to *reference*.

> It does not at all follow that something could not *be* beautiful* unless something responded with pleasure. On this definition, there were sunsets that were beautiful* before there were any suitable pleasure-capable responders, and they would still have been beautiful* even if there never had been such responders. For it still could be the case that *if* there *were* such responders present, they *would* respond (or *would have* responded) with pleasure. (Brandom 2019, p. 83)

Here it becomes clear that this distinction between "sense-dependence" and "reference-dependence" is bound up with the modal talk of which Rorty had been skeptical. "Possibilities", he had declared, "are cheap" and "not worldly enough to do anything". To say that there were unexpressed truths about anything before the existence of human claimings is "like saying that the rules of

---

6 Brandom employs underlining to designate that he is referring to concepts—here the concepts beautiful and pleasure. The concept "beautiful*" refers to the concept beautiful specifically understood *as* response-dependent.

baseball were there, but unexpressed, before baseball was played" (Rorty 2000, p. 184).

Adopting for a moment the language of possible-world semantics, one can say that what would allow Brandom's modal claim that "*if* there *were* [beauty-] responders present they *would* respond (or *would have* responded) with pleasure" to be meaningful, would be the existence of a *possible* world in which there *were* no beauty-responders (and so no *us*) but in which there *are* sunsets like the ones *we* find beautiful in the actual world. *Were* we, or beings like us, to exist in that possible world, they would be found beautiful *there, as well*. Brandom does not, of course, like Lewis, believe that such an analysis depends upon the *reality* of those possible worlds as *really existing* worlds, just like our own. Without Lewis' realism, possible-world semanticists treat a "possible world" is something abstract—some set of consistent propositions, where the plurality of propositions is needed to capture the fact that talk of any *particular* possibility will link it to others because of that holistic feature of concepts that Brandom discusses as their "sense-dependence". Brandom does not need Lewis' possible-world realism here because he has at his disposal Sellars' meta-linguistic treatment of propositions, including *modal* propositions. But Brandom's painted scenario looks odd. Isn't speculating about a possible world without us, and then asking what it would be like *with us*, simply referring once more to the *actual world* in which it is uncontroversial that sunsets are beautiful?

Brandom's way of posing the question here is actually the reverse of the way possibilities are typically discussed in possible-world semantics. What is meaningfully discussed as a possibility for the actual world is formulated in a description of what is the case in some possible alternative world. Brandom, however, starts with a possible world, and asks about *alternative possibilities* for that world, but the idea that questions of alternative possibilities further iterated for non-actual possible worlds has been criticized as a meaningful move by Stalnaker (Stalnaker 2012, ch. 1.5). This will turn out to be significant for Brandom's approach to modality.

Brandom's Sellars-inspired *pragmatist* approach to modality that is meant to be free from the metaphysical snares of possible-worlds semantics is implicit in his more generally "inferentialist semantics". Following Sellars' strategy of treating the meaning of propositions in terms of their relations to other propositions, Brandom works from a basis of the sentence–sentence relation of *incompatibility*. With the idea of incompatibility in place, one can derive the notion of implication by the idea that "p implies q" can be read as saying that everything *incompatible* with q is thereby necessarily incompatible with p (Brandom 2008, pp. 119–121). This is the "incompatibility semantics" that he applies to modal assertions with the claim that "to be incompatible with *necessarily-p* is to be compatible with something that *does not entail p*" and "to be incompatible with *possibly-p* is to be incompatible with *everything* that is *compatible* with something *compatible* with p" (Brandom 2008, p. 129). Treating incompatibility as a modal semantic primitive in this way allows the introduction of "*modal* logical vocabulary in the very same setting, and the very same terms, in which we introduce the classical *non*-modal logical vocabulary" (Brandom 2008, p. 128).

Brandom links his attitude to modality to the *Kantian* dimension of Sellars's own philosophizing—what he calls the "Kant-Sellars thesis" about modality. The basic idea here is that "the ability to use ordinary empirical descriptive terms such as 'green', 'rigid', and 'mass' already presupposes grasp of the kinds of properties and relations made explicit by modal vocabulary" (Brandom 2008, pp. 96–97). We might think of this as Kantian inasmuch as Kant's insistence that in order to achieve objectivity the contents of all judgments need to be brought under the "pure categories of the understanding", which include the *modal* categories.[7]

As Brandom himself indicates, his "incompatibility semantics" turns out to have many of the features of Kripke's use of possible worlds (Brandom 2008, p. 129), but as others have pointed out, there is one important difference. While Kripke had fixed the truth conditions of 'necessarily p' by starting from *one possible world* which is taken to be the actual world and then treating other possible worlds in terms of their accessibility from the former, "Brandom defines necessity in a global way by talking about the entirety of all sentences at once. Thus, Brandom's account lacks anything like a particular perspective from which a formula like 'necessarily p' is evaluated" (Göcke/Pleitz/von Wulfen 2008, p. 137). We have seen this at work in the shape of his reply to Rorty in which he effectively starts with a conception of a merely possible world, one without us, and then treats the actual world as a possibility *for it*. But while his incompatibility approach may allow him to avoid the metaphysical traps of Lewisian possible-worlds semantics, I suggest that this change to the "accessibility" relation puts him on the Lewis–Leibniz "possibilist" side of the debate about

---

7 We might here remember Sellars's argument in *Empiricism and the Philosophy of Mind* about the reporting on the color of ties under different lighting conditions. In learning to use the concept "blue", say, one has to learn that a particular blue thing may not always *look* the same way. Under odd sorts of lighting a blue tie might look *green*. Thus the very capacity to correctly apply the concept "blue" must include the capacity to make inferences of the type, "were I observing this under such and such conditions this blue thing would indeed look green", or "if I am actually observing this under such and such conditions this thing that *looks* green might actually *be* blue".

the nature of possible worlds, opposing him to the "actualist" interpretations of Kripke, Prior and Stalnaker, as well as Hegel.

4 Hegel's non-Fregean approach to judgment and its consequences for modal thought

Brandom's distinction between sense-dependence and reference-dependence, of course, hangs on the Fregean distinction between sense and reference and the basic Fregean idea that sense *determines* reference. Brandom attributes analogues of this distinction to Hegel on the basis of his interpretation of passages from Hegel's *Phenomenology of Spirit* (e.g., Brandom 2019, ch. 12). However, I suggest, Hegel's explicit account of judgment and inference as given in Book III of *The Science of Logic* does not reflect this Fregean distinction. There is a limited role for something like the sense–reference distinction in as much as Hegel's account of judgment has a place for those sorts of judgments in which the judgment content could be understood as a complete proposition—an abstract entity with a stable truth value. But Hegel is insistent that this *cannot* be the only logical form a judgment can take for it to have a content.

The account of judgment one finds in Section 1 of Book III is one that has *more* in common with George Boole's account in *Laws of Thought* than it does with Frege's. In contrast to the Frege–Russell conception of a singular underlying judgment form, Boole worked with two different judgment forms, distinguishing "primary propositions" as in "the sun shines" which relates *an object* (the sun), *to a group of objects* (things that shine) from *secondary* propositions such as "it is true that the sun shines" (Boole 1854, p. 38). Unlike "the sun shines", which is a de re proposition *about* the sun, the secondary proposition here is not about the sun, but is about the primary proposition (that is in turn about the sun), saying *of* it *that* it is true. Being about the *dictum*, it is what is traditionally described as de dicto.

In his account of judgment Hegel distinguishes two broad types of judgment he describes as *qualitative* and *quantitative* or as judgments of *inherence* and judgments of *subsumption* (Hegel 2010, pp. 557, 570) that broadly coincide with the de re/de dicto distinction. The authority in logic at the *Tübinger Stift* while Hegel was there, Gottfried Ploucquet, had followed Leibniz in his attempt to modernize the Aristotelian syllogism by the use of algebra, an approach independently discovered in the nineteenth century by Boole. Both Leibniz and Boole had mixed elements from Aristotle's *term logic* with a more *propositional* form of logic found earlier in the ancient Stoics, and both struggled to unify these different approaches to judgment. Hegel had inherited this dual analysis of judgment structure and his account of judgment in *The Science of Logic* reveals an attempt to combine them in a systematic way.

The fact that judgments of inherence, with their Aristotelian *term-logical* structure, can be differentiated from judgments of subsumption, with more "modern" propositional content, is demonstrated by the fact that each handle negation in a different way. In negating a judgment of inherence, such as "the rose is red", the scope of negation extended only to the predicate: to deny that the rose is red is to imply that it is nevertheless a rose that has some *non-red* color (Hegel 2010, p. 565). This leaves the negated judgment ("the rose is non-red") as, "still positive" and so open to a further, "second" negation that "negates the determinateness of the predicate of the positive judgment" (Hegel 2010, p. 566)—that is, it negates the form of its relatively determinate predicate, such as of a red or non-red inhering color, so as to result in a *subsuming* predicate. In this resulting judgment form, any *link* between singular and universal (as in "inherence") has been broken. Hegel's discussion of the resulting "infinite judgment", which is clearly linked to the judgment form found later in his discussion of the judgments of Leibniz's *characteristica universalis* (Hegel 2010, pp. 607–608), shows a total loss of subject–predicate form characteristic of the type of "external negation" that extends to the *entire* content of the judgment as found in the Stoics (Bobzien 2020) as well as modern logics like Kant's transcendental logic or Frege's *Begriffsschrift*.[8]

In contrast to judgments of inherence as de re, there is a *sense* in which his judgments of subsumption may be conceived as de dicto like Boole's secondary propositions. The idea of the judgment of inherence's *second* negation clearly suggests that what is denied is *the dictum*, that is, the complete contents of what the other *said*. This means that, in now opposing the critic's claim that the original judgment was false, the first judge might be understood as *affirming* the complete judgment—affirming that it is *true*. In short, the process of double negation has transformed the original judgment into something like a Boolean secondary one. However, as defenders of the "redundancy theory of truth" point out, to say "It is true that *p*" is really to say no more than "*p*" itself, and Hegel clearly thinks of the judgment of subsumption into which the judgment of inherence has been transformed is a judgment purporting to be about the

---

8 On the Fregean form of the sentences of Leibniz's *characteristica universalis*, see Angelelli 1990. Hegel clearly recognized Leibniz's strategy here of effectively converting the subject of a sentence to a predicate, such that both subject and predicate *predicates* are equated in virtue of both being *true of* some third term. See his description of Leibniz's "mathematical syllogism" (Hegel 2010, pp. 602–604).

world rather than *about* a judgment. I suggest the underlying form of a judgment of subsumption would be better understood as *de facto*—a judgment that is meant to be about some abstract "state of affairs" or "way things are", rather than some specific qualified object. There is thus set up a type of equivalence between the two otherwise *opposed* logical forms that a sentence such as "The rose is red" can be understood as having.

Russell had *denied* that everyday judgments like Boole's "the sun shines" or Hegel's "the rose is red" were *in fact* proper judgments. Without complete propositional content—a proposition the truth or falsity of which did not change with time—Russell came to treat such judgments as *incapable* of truth or falsity. Frege's early criticism of Boole's dualistic account of judgment form had been more moderate, acknowledging that he employed two different term-based and proposition-based accounts of content, but complaining that these "ran alongside one another" and stood in no "organic" or systematic relation (Frege 1979, p. 14). Brandom implicitly aligns Hegel's account of judgment here with *Russell's* monistic account, stressing that Hegel was deeply critical of any "*two-stage* representational story". As both Boole's and Hegel's accounts of judgment as dualistic are, in some sense, "two-staged", Brandom's claim is too general. The paradigm of the "*two-stage* representational story" he has in mind is the early modern one in which a mind is immediately acquainted with its own intrinsically intelligible *representings*, as found in the early modern "way of ideas" tradition, and on the basis of which it can in turn come to know other things, "paradigmatically physical, material, extended things" as what is *represented* in those representings (Brandom 2019, pp. 40 – 44). It is true that Hegel is indeed a critic of this view and it is this that gives to his epistemology features of Sellars' "critique of the Myth of the Given". However, Brandom over-extends this parallel so as to ignore aspects of the "two-stage representational story" that survives in Hegel.

There is a sense in which Hegel would be critical of Boole's version of the two-stage model in as much as Boole seems to think of singular statements such as "the sun shines" as capable of being understood independently and so without reference to statements with properly propositional contents. While Hegel treats simple perceptually based "judgments of existence" such as "the rose is red" at the outset of his account of judgments, this does not imply that such judgments are independently intelligible, providing the firm basis for the understanding of *further* judgments as Boole's approach suggests. Hegel's demonstrative procedure works in the opposite way: he will first present an "immediate" account of what is being explained, show the conceptual problems that such an account faces, and then will replace it by a further account which resolves these conceptual difficulties. Characteristically, however, the immediate account being "*aufgehoben*" means that it is *negated but preserved* within the succeeding account. The simple "judgment of existence" with its *inherence* form of predication should not be *permanently* superseded, and neither is it, as the two basic predicative forms of inherence and subsumption can be seen as oscillating as Hegel's analysis passes through several cycles (Redding 2019). The last of these cycles will involve judgments in which a *specific* individual thing is now judged in terms of the criteria determining its *kind*, as in Hegel's example, "This house is good", in which the predicate 'good' is determined by normative aspects of our conception of a house. Here, the superseded earlier de re form of the simple perceptual judgment has returned, now within a more complex structure.

In short, while Hegel doesn't employ the two-stage model in ways it is employed by either Descartes or Boole, the distinction between simple judgments about substances and their "inhering" qualities and more abstract judgments with properly propositional contents about states of affairs is still importantly in play. Moreover, the preservation of de re judgment form is incompatible with the idea that Hegel holds to Frege's sense-reference distinction in any *general* way. This, I suggest, will be especially crucial for his account of modality as can be seen by parallels between Hegel's account and Robert Stalnaker's attempt to rescue possible-world semantics from David Lewis' metaphysics. Like Kripke in *Naming and Necessity* (Kripke 1972), where Kripke invoked the modal distinction between proper names and definite descriptions, Hegel distinguishes between reference to a thing as *singular* (*einzeln*), as by the use of a proper name or a demonstrative phrase, and as a *particular* (*besonder*) as "subsumed" under a predicate. Such a distinction is not recognized by Russell, Quine or Lewis, nor seemingly by Brandom, but it is crucial for Stalnaker's criticism of Lewis' use of possible-world semantics.

In his debate with Lewis, in not accepting the ontological reality of possible worlds, Stalnaker falls back on the idea that possible worlds are simply sets of "maximal propositions", a proposition being maximal "in the sense that for every (actual) proposition, either it or its contradictory is entailed by it". But Stalnaker then notes that "a proposition might be maximal in this sense while failing to be fully *specific*, where a proposition is fully specific only if for every existential proposition that it entails, it also entails a singular proposition that is a witness to that existential proposition" (Stalnaker 2012, p. 19). While Stalnaker does not mention intuitionistic logic (the logic developed in relation to "intuitionistic" or "constructive" mathematics), intuitionism is the home of the notion of a witness or "proof object" required for the truth of any *abstractly* propositional claim (Bridges/Palmgren 2018, section III). The link to intuitionism is here relevant, as like Hegel's, and for similar reasons, intuitionistic logic does not hold the *classical laws of logic* to be axiomatic.

Like Kripke, and in contrast to Brandom, Stalnaker treats possible worlds in terms of their "accessibility" from the *actual* world. Crucially, the difference between propositions pertaining to merely possible worlds and those pertaining to the actual world concerns the possibility for the latter to be accompanied by singular witness statements—a distinction hinging on the type of distinction Hegel describes between judgments of inherence and judgments of subsumption. In talking abstractly about the actual roses in my garden, it is possible to point to some specific rose, "this rose". But this, of course, does not apply in the case of discussing *possible* roses—perhaps a new variety that I envisage crossbreeding and planting. Such roses don't yet exist. The propositions constituting the possible world in which my garden is populated by the new rose cannot be accompanied by Stalnaker's witness statements or Hegel's judgments of *inherence*. The idea of the accessibility of possible world *from* the actual coincides with the idea that the meaningfulness of talk of possible worlds depends upon specific semantic resources that only find a place in talk about *the actual world* (Stalnaker 2012, p. 13).

5 Conclusion: Actualism as a more modest and realistic realism

One of the many virtues of Brandom's "inferentialist" reading of Hegel is that it shows how realism about *concepts* is linked to realism about *modality*, but Brandom's *interpretation* of this realism is, I believe, rightly criticized by Rorty as an unrealistic view of the cognitive capacities of otherwise natural beings.[9] Stalnaker's actualist account of modality, however, reveals the possibility of a more modest realism that grounds modal concepts in cognition of the *actual* world. In such a view, human cognition is never *entirely* freed from contextual or indexical features and does not rely on any "god's-eye view" from nowhere. Contextually specific "indexical" de re judgments cannot be eliminated from inquiry and even the actual world is itself understood in a type of "indexical" way: it is a world to which we language users belong and from which we can gain cognitive access to its alternate possible states. The actual world contains alternate possi-

---

9 Like Brandom, Rorty seems broadly to accept the modern Frege–Russell account of judgment. Without an account of the truth of non-general judgments, this pushes his critique of unrealistic realism towards an opposing skeptical anti-realism.

bilities, concepts and truths only because it contains entities *for whom* such things exist—us. There is a sense in which it *necessarily* contains us, but this is a trivial sense: what we *mean* by the actual or real world is just what we gesture at when we wave our arm about indicating what is "out there". Exclude us from it and we are already in the realm of some non-actual alternative.

Elsewhere (Redding 2015), I have argued that Hegel's inferentialism is weaker than Brandom's in that it implies a representationalist dimension to cognition: the inferential relations among assertive speech acts while necessary are not sufficient for our thoughts to bear upon the world. The eliminable role of Hegel's judgments of inherence that signaled this representational dimension here signal his actualist approach to modal issues. Anything stronger than this is incompatible with a view of ourselves as beings belonging to nature rather to some lost Platonic heaven.

Bibliography

Angelelli, Ignacio (1990): "On Johannes Raue's Logic". In: Ingrid Marchlewitz/Albert Heinekamp (Eds.): *Leibniz' Auseinandersetzung mit Vogängern und Zeitgenossen*. Stuttgart: Franz Steiner, pp. 184–190.

Boole, George (1854): *An Investigation of the Laws of Thought, on Which Are Founded the Mathematical Theories of Logic and Probabilities*. London: Macmillan and Co.

Brandom, Robert B. (2000): "Vocabularies of Pragmatism: Synthesizing Naturalism and Historicism". In: Robert B. Brandom (Ed.): *Rorty and His Critics*. Malden, MA: Blackwell, pp. 156–183.

Brandom, Robert B. (2008): *Between Saying and Doing: Towards an Analytic Pragmatism*. Oxford: Oxford University Press.

Brandom, Robert B. (2019): *A Spirit of Trust: A Reading of Hegel's Phenomenology*. Cambridge, MA: Harvard University Press.

Bridges, Douglas/Palmgren, Erik (2018): "Constructive Mathematics". In: Edward N. Zalta (Ed.): *The Stanford Encyclopedia of Philosophy* (Summer 2018 Edition). https://plato.stanford.edu/archives/sum2018/entries/mathematics-constructive, visited on 1 October 2021.

DeVries, Willem A. (2005): *Wilfrid Sellars*. Chesham, Bucks: Acumen.

Findlay, John N. (1958): *Hegel: A Re-examination*. London: Routledge.

Findlay, John N. (1963): *Meinong's Theory of Objects and Values*. 2nd edn. Oxford: Oxford University Press.

Göcke, Benedikt/Pleitz, Martin/von Wulfen, Hanno (2008): "How to Kripke Brandom's Notion of Necessity". In: Bernd Prien/David P. Schweikard (Eds.): *Robert Brandom: Analytic Pragmatist*. Frankfurt: Ontos, pp. 135–148.

Kant, Immanuel (1998): *Critique of Pure Reason*. Edited and translated by Paul Guyer and Allen W. Wood. Cambridge: Cambridge University Press.

Kojève, Alexandre (1969): *Introduction to the Reading of Hegel*. Edited by A. Bloom. Translated by J. H. Nichols Jr. New York: Basic Books.

Kreines, James (2015): *Reason in the World: Hegel's Metaphysics and Its Philosophical Appeal.* Oxford: Oxford University Press.
Kripke, Saul A. (1959): "A Completeness Theorem in Modal Logic". In: *The Journal of Symbolic Logic* 24, pp. 1–14.
Kripke, Saul A. (1972): *Naming and Necessity.* Cambridge, MA: Harvard University Press.
Lewis, David K. (1986): *On the Plurality of Worlds.* Oxford: Blackwell.
Mäki, Uskali (2009): "Realistic Realism about Unrealistic Models". In: Don Ross/Harold Kincaid (Eds.): *The Oxford Handbook of Philosophical Economics.* Oxford: Oxford University Press, pp. 68–98.
O'Shea, James R. (2007): *Wilfrid Sellars: Naturalism with a Normative Turn.* Cambridge and Malden, MA: Polity Press.
Prior, Arthur N. (1967): *Past, Present and Future.* Oxford: Clarendon Press.
Redding, Paul (2007): *Analytic Philosophy and the Return of Hegelian Thought.* Cambridge: Cambridge University Press.
Redding, Paul (2014): "Pragmatism, Idealism and the Modal Menace: Rorty, Brandom and Truths about Photons". In: *The European Legacy* 19. No 2, pp. 174–186.
Redding, Paul (2015): "An Hegelian Solution to a Tangle of Problems Facing Brandom's Analytic Pragmatism". In: *The British Journal for the History of Philosophy* 23. No. 4, pp. 657–680.
Redding, Paul (2019): "Time and Modality in Hegel's Account of Judgment". In: Brian Ball/Christoph Schuringa (Eds.): *The Act and Object of Judgment.* London: Routledge, pp. 91–109.
Rorty, Richard (1979): *Philosophy and the Mirror of Nature.* Princeton: Princeton University Press.
Rorty, Richard (1989): *Contingency, Irony and Solidarity.* Cambridge: Cambridge University Press.
Rorty, Richard (1999): "Trotsky and the Wild Orchids". In: *Philosophy and Social Hope.* London: Penguin, pp. 3–20.
Rorty, Richard (2000): "Response to Robert Brandom". In: Robert B. Brandom (Ed.): *Rorty and His Critics.* Malden, MA: Blackwell, pp. 183–190.
Sartre, Jean-Paul (1956): *Being and Nothingness: An Essay on Phenomenological Ontology.* New York: The Philosophical Library.
Sellars, Wilfrid (1997): *Empiricism and the Philosophy of Mind.* With an Introduction by Richard Rorty and a Study Guide by Robert Brandom. Cambridge, MA: Harvard University Press.
Stalnaker, Robert C. (2012): *Mere Possibilities: Metaphysical Foundations of Modal Semantics.* Princeton, NJ: Princeton University Press.

Part II: Contemporary Impulses for a New Idealism

Slavoj Žižek
A Materialist Defense of an Idealist Subjectivity

Abstract: In light of the threat of post-humanism as yet another "death of the subject", this chapter is in search of the vestiges of the survival and new proliferation of subjectivity in the most unexpected places. First, the possibility of the formation of a revolutionary self in Buddhism is discussed, arising from the destitution of the human, humanist self. Then, even contemporary Hollywood film production can be of aid. Todd Phillips's *Joker* is interpreted as an implicitly political film, inasmuch as it knows how to circumvent and subvert the common psycho-social genesis. The hero rather enacts a transition from madness to becoming a stand-in for the pure form of subjectivity. A direct emancipatory political project is absent from the film's storyline: we, the spectators, are solicited to fill the absence that the hero in his inner void represents. It will be shown that what makes *Joker* so unsettling is that it does not engage in calling for political action, but ultimately leaves the decision to us.

In times of realism enjoying great popularity in philosophy and post-humanism threatening to dissolve the bulwarks of humanity, it is the function of subjectivity in its old-fashioned Cartesian, Kantian, Hegelian, Freudian, and Lacanian traditions that is proving to be strangely ineradicable, almost tenacious in both contemporary philosophy and the artifacts of popular culture of the twenty-first century. Why does it seem that we cannot do without the purely logical entity of the subject? And what is the conceptual frame in which to account for this great "undead" of Western, and increasingly global, thought? A case should be made for the emergence of the subject at the interstice of an irreducibly idealist element taking shape within the ontological priority of reality. The subject will be interpreted not as an entity which somehow "is", but rather as a function which arises as the name for "what is not" in a given situation, hence as a form of nothingness. It is the endurance, the survival of the subject in the era of post-human-

---

Funding note: The research included in this chapter was funded by the Slovenian Research Agency (ARRS) under the research project "The Possibility of Idealism for the Twenty-First Century" (J6–1811).

Slavoj Žižek, University of Ljubljana.

ity that perhaps testifies to the need to rehabilitate idealism, a stance which never fully recovered after the death of Hegel. The implications of this stance affect even today's popular culture: Can we really presume to explain the success of, say, Todd Phillips's film *Joker* without recourse to the logical operations immanent to the form of subjectivity?

1 Revolutionary self-destitution ...

Far from being constrained to the clinical experience, what Lacan called subjective destitution, the concluding moment of the psychoanalytic process, also has a political dimension described by Brecht. In his *Beggar's Opera*, Brecht condenses four basic existential stances (the longing for everyday joys, brutal reality, religious feeling, and cynical wisdom) into two (longing for joyful happiness versus cynical acceptance of reality), with joyful cynicism as "the last word". However, this was not Brecht's own last word: with a breath-taking consequence, Brecht added in his learning plays (*Der Jasager, Die Maßnahme*) another subjective position, that of a purely formal gesture of self-sacrifice grounded in no deeper meaning or goal. The implicit logic here is that one cannot overcome cynical wisdom with some positive ethical ideal: cynicism can undermine them all, it is only a totally meaningless self-sacrificial act that undermines the cynical distance itself. The Freudian name for such an act is, of course, "the death drive", and its Hegelian name is "self-relating negativity". However, we should be very careful here: Brecht makes it clear that this act is not a kind of pure excessive suicidal gesture of stepping out of the symbolic space (something that rather belongs to the theory of Bataille). In yet another case of "infinite judgment", the death drive coincides with its opposite, with radical alienation in the symbolic order. Along these same lines, Saroj Giri describes "revolutionary self-destitution, self-objectification", as a specific form of subjectivity:

> A specific, individual life, a unique human being, is now an object, a mere object who can be taken down any time. ...
> The "comrade as object" is a continuation of de-classing and de-personification, now taken to the point of revolutionary destitution, involving the courage to die, death. To the extent that the comrade is a living human being, his or her objectification will and must involve the openness to death. Life is hanging in a balance, and the vulnerability to death is a constant presence. You are never safe and the willingness to sacrifice life is best embraced graciously. (Giri 2020, p. 11)

What Giri establishes here is a double link with the past, recent and more ancient. Recent past refers to the idea of objectification and destitution, which is close to Fanon's idea of declivity: "an utterly naked declivity is where an authentic upheaval is born". Or when he says, "the Negro is a zone of non-being, an extraordinarily sterile and arid region, an utterly declining declivity" (Giri 2020, p. 20). Ancient past refers to the Buddhist revolutionary self (see Giri 2018). The void (of destitution) "as the 'path,' the rupture/opening to a 'new world' can be found in the Buddha's *nibbana*. *Nibbana* is often known as Awakening or Enlightenment, but actually *nibbana* is, in the first instance, extinction, the blowing out, the vanishing" (Giri 2020, p. 13).

What Giri calls subjective destitution is therefore not just a new form of political subjectivity but simultaneously something that concerns our basic existential level, "*a different way of being, involving a different modality of life and death*" (Giri 2020, p. 14). In his afterword to Peter Hallward's collection *Think Again*, Badiou approvingly quotes Lin Biao: "The essence of revisionism is the fear of death" (Badiou 2004, p. 237). This existential radicalization of the political opposition between orthodoxy and revisionism throws a new light on the old 1968 motto "the personal is political": here, the political becomes personal, the ultimate root of political revisionism is located in the intimate experience of the fear of death. Badiou's version of it would be that, since "revisionism" is, at its most basic, the failure to subjectivize oneself, to assume fidelity to a Truth-Event, being a revisionist means remaining within the survivalist horizon of the "human animal".

There is, however, an ambiguity that clings to Lin Biao's statement: it can be read as saying that the root of political revisionism lies in human nature, which makes us fear death; but it can also be read as saying that, since there is no unchangeable human nature, our very intimate fear of death is already politically overdetermined, for it arises in an individualist and egotistical society with little sense of communal solidarity; which is why, in a communist society, people would no longer fear death.

"Comrade as object" does not imply that we should observe and manipulate ourselves from a cold "objective" distance. It is to be supplemented by its inversion, "object as comrade":

> Instead of going over to the fetishistic powers of the commodity, one had to go towards the "hidden" engineering/artistic powers of things, objects and materials: this would, as it were, allow the object to commune and speak, providing us the *first contours of the "object as comrade"*. (Giri 2020, pp. 5–6)

This "object as comrade" displays what Giri calls idealism in the (material) thing itself, of what we may call spiritual corporeality as opposed to the fetishist idealism which imposes on a thing, from outside, a social dimension as its reified property: to treat an object as "comrade" means to open oneself up to the virtual potentials of an object in an intense interaction with it. Maybe, a surprising link can help us understand what is meant by "object as comrade", which supplements "comrade as object": today's object-oriented ontology (OOO). This is Graham Harman's concise description of the OOO's basic stance:

> The arena of the world is packed with diverse objects, their forces unleashed and mostly unloved. Red billiard ball smacks green billiard ball. Snowflakes glitter in the light that cruelly annihilates them, while damaged submarines rust along the ocean floor. As flour emerges from mills and blocks of limestone are compressed by earthquakes, gigantic mushrooms spread in the Michigan forest. While human philosophers bludgeon each other over the very possibility of "access" to the world, sharks bludgeon tuna fish and icebergs smash into coastlines. (Harman 2010, p. 94)

Such a way of treating an object as a "comrade" also opens up a new way of being ecological: to accept our environment in all of its complex mixture, which includes what we perceive as trash or pollution, as well as what we cannot directly perceive since it is too large or too minuscule (Timothy Morton's "hyperobjects"). Along these lines, for Morton, being ecological

> is not about spending time in a pristine nature preserve but about appreciating the weed working its way through a crack in the concrete, and then appreciating the concrete. It's also part of the world, and part of us. ...
> Reality is populated with 'strange strangers'—things that are 'knowable yet uncanny.' This strange strangeness, Morton writes, is an irreducible part of every rock, tree, terrarium, plastic Statue of Liberty, quasar, black hole, or marmoset one might encounter; by acknowledging it, we shift away from trying to master objects and toward learning to respect them in their elusiveness. Whereas the Romantic poets rhapsodized about nature's beauty and sublimity, Morton responds to its all-pervading weirdness; they include in the category of the natural everything that is scary, ugly, artificial, harmful, and disturbing. (Meis 2021)

Is not a perfect example of such a mixture the fate of rats in Manhattan during the COVID-19 pandemic? Manhattan is a living system of humans, cockroaches ... and millions of rats. The lockdown at the peak of the pandemic meant that since all restaurants were closed, the rats that lived off the trash from those restaurants were deprived of the source of their food. This caused mass starvation: many rats were found eating their offspring. The closure of restaurants, which changed the eating habits of humans but posed no threat to them, was a catastrophe for the rats, rats as comrades. Another similar accident from recent history could be called "sparrow as comrade". In 1958, at the beginning of the Great Leap Forward, the Chinese government declared that "birds are public animals of capitalism" and set in motion a large campaign to eliminate sparrows, which were suspected of consuming approximately four pounds of grain per sparrow per year. Sparrow nests were destroyed, eggs were broken, and chicks were killed; millions of people organized into groups and hit noisy pots and pans to prevent sparrows from resting in their nests, with the goal of causing them to drop dead from exhaustion. These mass attacks depleted the sparrow population, pushing it to near extinction. However, by April 1960, Chinese leaders were forced to realize that the sparrows also ate a large number of insects on the fields, so that rather than increasing, rice yields fell substantially after the campaign: the extermination of sparrows upset the ecological balance, and insects destroyed crops as a result of the absence of natural predators. By this time, however, it was too late: with no sparrows to eat them, locust populations ballooned, swarming the country and compounding the ecological problems already caused by the Great Leap Forward, including widespread deforestation and misuse of poisons and pesticides. This ecological imbalance is credited with exacerbating the Great Chinese Famine, in which 15–45 million people died of starvation. The Chinese government eventually resorted to importing 250,000 sparrows from the Soviet Union to replenish their population (see the "Four Pests campaign" entry on Wikipedia).[1]

However, we have to bear in mind something that OOO ignores and Giri is fully aware of: while subjective destitution (a term Giri took from Lacan), i.e., reduction to an object, does not mean de-subjectivization, it DOES mean de-humanization: after subjective destitution, the subject is no longer "human" in the sense of a depth of personality, a "rich inner life" as opposed to external reality, and similar psychic baggage. Only in and through destitution does the subject in its purity (a capitalized Subject) emerge:

> The activist-comrade *as object* is still a Subject—a subject who perhaps speaks in the name of History and invokes the "metanarrative" of the "stages of History", but whose self-destitution and self-objectification open up a revolutionary possibility by creating a null point, a void in History itself. (Giri 2020, p. 13)

---

[1] Three examples from the cinema of Joris Ivens perfectly exemplify this dimension of object as comrade. Is his documentary *Regen* (*Rain*, 1929), a portrayal of Amsterdam during rainfall, not a portrait of "rain as comrade"? One should also mention Hanns Eisler's *Fourteen Ways of Describing the Rain*, a twelve-minute exercise in dodecaphony for flute, clarinet, string trio, and piano, written as a musical accompaniment to Ivens's *Regen*. Then, there is Ivens's *Pour le Mistral* (*The Mistral*, 1966), representing "wind as comrade": scenes of life and landscape in Provence, where a chilly wind called the mistral blows down the valley of the Rhône to the Mediterranean. Finally, there is one more portrayal of "wind as comrade": *Une histoire de vent* (*A Tale of the Wind*, 1988), shot in China, where an old and ill Ivens attempts to depict the insight that "the secret of breathing lies in the rhythm of the autumn wind".

Through subjective destitution, we do not enter a happy interaction of "object as comrade" and "comrade as object", in which a destitute subject deals with objects that surround him as his equal interlocutors, renouncing to act as their master who exploits them. In subjective destitution, the subject is not simply immersed in the flux of reality, he is rather reduced to a void, a null point, a gap in reality. It is only through this reduction to a void, from the subjective position of that void, that a subject can perceive and experience the interaction of "comrade as object" and "object as comrade". In other words, through subjective destitution, the subject is radically divided: into a pure void and the object that she is. In this way, we overcome mortality and enter undeadness: not life after death but death in life, not dis-alienation but extreme, self-abolishing alienation—we leave behind the very standard by which we measure alienation, the notion of a normal, warm daily life, of our full immersion in a safe and stable world of customs. The way to overcome a topsy-turvy world is not to return to normality but to embrace the turvy without the topsy.

Already from this brief description, it is clear that the phenomenon of subjective destitution assumes many forms, which cannot be reduced to the same inner experience. There is the Buddhist nirvana, a disconnection from external reality which enables us to acquire a distance towards our cravings and desires—I assume a kind of impersonal stance, my thoughts are thoughts without a thinker. Then there are so-called mystical experiences, which should not be confused with nirvana: although they also involve a kind of subjective destitution, this destitution takes the form of a direct identity between me and a higher Absolute (typical formula: the eyes through which I see god are the eyes through which god sees himself)—my innermost desire gets depersonalized, it overlaps with the will of god himself, so that the big Other lives through me. In short, while in nirvana one steps out of the "wheel of desire", the mystical experience enacts the overlapping of our enjoyment with the enjoyment of the big Other. Then there is the subjective stance described by Giri: the destitution of a revolutionary agent who reduces herself to an instrument-object of the process of radical social change—she obliterates her personality, including the fear of death, so that revolution lives through her. Then there is the explosion of self-destructive social nihilism—think of Todd Phillips's film *Joker* (2019), but also of the scene from Eisenstein's *October* in which the revolutionary mob penetrates the wine cellar of the Winter Palace and engages in an orgy of massive destruction of hundreds of bottles of expensive champagne. And, last but not least, there is subjective destitution in its psychoanalytic (Lacanian) sense of traversing the fantasy, which is a much more radical gesture than it may appear: for Lacan, fantasy is not opposed to reality but provides the coordinates of what we experience as reality, plus the coordinates of what we desire—the two sets of coordinates are not the same, but they are intertwined: when our fundamental fantasy dissolves, we experience the loss of reality, which also impedes our ability to desire. We should also recall that traversing the fantasy is not Lacan's final word: in the last years of his teaching, he proposed the final moment of the analytic process to be identification with the symptom, a gesture that enables us a moderately acceptable form of life.

How are these versions related? They seem to form a kind of Greimasian semiotic square, since there are two axes along which they are disposed: active engagement (self-destructive social explosion, revolutionary destitution described by Giri) versus disengagement (nirvana, mystical experience); self-contraction (destructive explosion against external reality, nirvana) versus reliance on a big Other (God in mystical experience, History in revolutionary destitution). In a destructive explosion, we contract into ourselves by way of destroying our environment; in nirvana, we just withdraw into ourselves, leaving reality the way it is. In a mystical experience, we disengage from reality by immersing ourselves in divinity; in revolutionary destitution, we renounce our Self by engaging in the historical process of revolutionary change. (From the Lacanian standpoint, these last two stances court the danger of falling into the perverse position of conceiving of oneself as an object-instrument of the big Other.)

What Lacan calls subjective destitution is the zero level, the neutral abyss in the center of this square. One should be very precise here: what we reach in subjective destitution is not the absolute Void, out of which everything springs, but the very disturbance of this Void, not the inner peace of withdrawal but the imbalance of the Void—not the fall of the Void into finite material reality but the antagonism/tension in the very heart of the Void, which causes the emergence of material reality out of the Void. Structurally, the other four versions of subjective destitution come second, they are attempts to pacify the antagonism ("self-contradiction") of the Void.

The question that arises here is: How should destitution in its politically engaged form avoid the fall into perversity? The answer is clear: it should suspend its reliance on the big Other (on historical necessity, etc.). Hegel constrained philosophy to grasping "what is", but for Hegel "what is" is not just a stable state of things, it is an open historical situation full of tensions and potentials—one should therefore link this insight with Saint-Just's claim: *Ceux qui font des révolutions ressemblent au premier navigateur instruit par son audace*, "Revolutionaries are akin to a first navigator guided by his audacity alone." Isn't this the implication of Hegel's confinement of the conceptual grasp to the past? As engaged subjects, we have to act with a view to the future, but for *a priori* reasons we cannot base our decisions on a rational pattern of historical progress (as Marx thought), so we have to improvise and take risks. Was this also the lesson

Lenin learned from reading Hegel in 1915? The paradox is that what Lenin took from Hegel—who is usually decried as *the* philosopher of historical teleology, of inexorable and regular progress towards freedom—was the utter contingency of the historical process.

The common-sense counter-argument that arises here is: subjective destitution is such a radical gesture that it is limited to an enlightened elite and remains an impossible ethical ideal for the masses, except in rare episodes of revolutionary enthusiasm. But I think that this reproach misses the point: Giri emphasizes that subjective destitution is not an elitist stance of leaders but, on the contrary, a stance displayed by numerous ordinary combatants, such as the thousands who risk their lives in the struggle against COVID-19.

2 ... versus destructive nihilism

It is crucial to note at this point that subjective destitution as the emergence of a radical gap in the continuity of History is here not an explosion of destructive violence which can be transformed into a pragmatic and realist construction of a new order only at a later stage: Giri describes subjective destitution as a stance which enables us to engage in the construction of a new social order. As such, revolutionary subjective destitution should be strictly separated from the outbursts of radical negativity that appear as self-destructive political nihilism. There is no better example of this topic in art than Todd Phillips's *Joker*—one cannot but express admiration for a Hollywood in which it is possible to make a movie such as *Joker*, and for the public that turned it into a mega blockbuster.

However, the reason for the film's popularity resides in its metafictional dimension: it provides the dark genesis of the Batman story, a genesis that has to remain invisible for the Batman myth to function. Let's try to imagine *Joker* without this reference to the Batman myth, just as the story of a victimized kid who adopts the mask of a clown to survive his predicament—it simply wouldn't work, it would be just another realist drama. *Time Out* characterized *Joker* as "a truly nightmarish vision of late-era capitalism" and categorized it as a "social horror film" (De Semlyen 2019)—something unimaginable until recently, a combination of two genres that are perceived as totally disparate, a realist depiction of social misery and fantasized horror, a combination which, of course, only works when social reality acquires dimensions of horror fiction.

The three main stances towards the film in our media perfectly mirror the tripartite division of our political space: conservatives worry that it may incite viewers to acts of violence; politically correct liberals discern in it racist and other clichés (already in the opening scene, a group of boys who beat up Arthur appear to be black), but also an ambiguous fascination with blind violence; leftists celebrate it for faithfully rendering the conditions of the rise of violence in our societies. But does *Joker* really incite spectators to imitate Arthur's acts in real life? Emphatically no—for the simple reason that Arthur-Joker is not presented as a figure of identification—the whole film works on the premise that it is impossible for us, the viewers, to identify with him.[2] He remains a stranger until the end.

Before *Joker* was released, the media already warned the public that it may incite violence; the FBI itself specifically warned that the film may inspire violence from clowncels, a subgroup of incels obsessed with clowns such as Pennywise from *It* and the Joker. (There were no reports of violence inspired by the film.) After the film was released, critics were not sure how to categorize it: is *Joker* just a piece of entertainment (as is the entire Batman series), an in-depth study of the genesis of pathological violence, or an exercise in social criticism?

Since *Joker* depicts radical rebellion against the existing order as a self-destructive orgy of violence with no positive vision underlying it, it can also be read as anti-leftist—for Tyler Cowen, the film "quite explicitly portrays the egalitarian instinct as a kind of barbaric violent atavism, and it is pointedly critical of Antifa and related movements, showing them as representing a literal end of civilization. Only the wealthy are genteel and urbane and proper" (Cowen 2019). The lesson of the film is thus: no radical steps, we can only count on the benevolent charity of the rich to gradually improve things. The leftist answer to this reading is that the self-destructive rebellion portrayed in *Joker* is such that the nihilist explosion of brutal rage signals precisely that we remain within the coordinates of the existing order and that a more radical shift of the political imagination is needed. From his radical leftist standpoint, Michael Moore found *Joker* to be a timely piece of social criticism and a perfect illustration of the consequences of America's current social ills: when it explores how Arthur Fleck became the Joker, it brings up the role of bankers, the collapse of the healthcare system, and the divide between the rich and the poor. Moore is therefore right to mock those who feared the film's release:

> Our country is in deep despair, our constitution is in shreds, a rogue maniac from Queens has access to the nuclear codes—but for some reason, it's a movie we should be afraid of. ... The greater danger to society may be if you DON'T go see this movie. ... This movie is not

---

[2] The most one can argue is that the film incites us, the viewers, to act through the Joker: the Joker acts for us, he actualizes our brutal rage against the social order, thus enabling us to go on living as usual since we vented out our frustration through him.

> about Trump. It's about the America that gave us Trump—the America which feels no need to help the outcast, the destitute. ...
> The fear and outcry over *Joker* is a ruse. It's a distraction so that we don't look at the real violence tearing up our fellow human beings—30 million Americans who don't have health insurance is an act of violence. Millions of abused women and children living in fear is an act of violence. (Moore 2019)

However, *Joker* does not only depict this America, it also raises a "discomfiting question":

> What if one day the dispossessed decide to fight back? And I don't mean with a clipboard registering people to vote. People are worried this movie may be too violent for them. Really? Considering everything we're living through in real life? ...
> *Joker* makes it clear we don't really want to get to the bottom of this, or to try to understand why innocent people turn into Jokers after they can no longer keep it together. Not because of the (minimal) blood on the screen, but because deep down, you were cheering him on—and if you're honest when that happens, you will thank this movie for connecting you to a new desire—not to run to the nearest exit to save your own ass but rather to stand and fight and focus your attention on the nonviolent power you hold in your hands every single day. (Moore 2019)

But does it really work like that? The "new desire" Moore mentions is not the Joker's desire—to see this, one has to introduce the psychoanalytic distinction between drive and desire. Drive is compulsively repetitive; in it, we are caught in the loop of turning around the same point again and again, while desire enacts a cut, it opens up a new dimension. The Joker remains a being of drive: at the end of the movie, he is powerless and his violent outbursts are just impotent explosions of rage, actings-out of his basic powerlessness. In order for the desire described by Moore to arise, one step further is needed: an additional change of the subjective stance has to be accomplished if you are to pass from the Joker's outbursts to becoming able to "stand and fight and focus your attention on the nonviolent power you hold in your hands every single day"—when you become aware of this power, you can renounce brutal bodily violence. The paradox is that you become truly violent (in the sense of posing a threat to the existing system) only when you renounce physical violence.

This does not mean that the Joker's act is a dead-end to be avoided—it is rather a kind of Malevich-moment, a reduction to the zero point of the minimal frame of protest. Malevich's famous black square on a white surface is not some kind of self-destructive abyss we should beware not to be swallowed by, but a point through which we should pass to gain a new beginning. It is the moment of the death drive, which opens up the space for sublimation. And in the same way that, in his minimalist paintings such as *Black Square*, Malevich reduced a painting to its minimal opposition of frame and background, the Joker reduced protest to its minimal content-less self-destructive form. An additional twist is needed to pass from drive to desire, to leave behind the nihilist point of self-destruction, to make this zero point function as a new beginning. However, the lesson of *Joker* is that we have to go through this zero point to get rid of the illusions that pertain to the existing order.

This zero point is today's version of what was once called a proletarian position, the experience of those who have nothing to lose—or, to quote Arthur from the film, "I've got nothing left to lose. Nothing can hurt me anymore. My life is nothing but a comedy." This is where the idea that Trump is a kind of Joker in power finds its limit: Trump definitely did not go through this zero point. He may be an obscene clown in his own way, but he is not a Joker figure—it's an insult to the Joker to compare him with Trump. In the film, Wayne the father is a "joker" in the simple sense of an agent who displays the obscenity of power.

Now we can see where M. L. Clark, relying on Thomas Moller-Nielse, goes ridiculously wrong when he reads my own philosophy as a version of the Joker's nihilist stance: "Žižek's Hegelian-philosophy-meets-flimsy-pop-science relentlessly insists that the only objective reality is not the Nothingness from which Something was created, but rather the tension between the true nothing-burger underpinning existence, and the moral depravity of our every, inevitable attempt to impose meaning upon it" (Clark 2019). In short, the position ascribed to me is one of the basic ontological fact consisting in the tension between the ultimate meaningless void/crack and our (i.e., humanity's) attempts to impose some universal meaning on this chaotic crack—such a position is nothing special, it simply reproduces a certain existential humanism, which perceives humans as beings who heroically endeavor to impose some meaning upon the chaos of the world into which we are thrown. However, according to Clark, I make a step further in the Joker's direction: since all attempts to impose meaning on the primordial chaotic Void obfuscate this void and are thus hypocritical, i.e., since they escape from the basic nonsense of existence, they are acts of moral depravity —or, to bring this point to the extreme, morality itself (attempts to impose a universal meaning upon reality) is a form of moral depravity. The only consequent moral stance is thus one of full nihilism, of joyfully endorsing the violent destruction of every attempt to impose a moral order on our chaotic lives, of renouncing every universal humanist project that would enable us to surmount our discord:

> As such, no matter how much we might want to insist that our shared humanity is stronger than our momentary discords and our abiding individual differences, the Jokers and Žižeks

are never quite going to be persuaded. Their respective ideological frameworks require them to keep pointing to the social tensions that remain: the chaos that will always be a part of our collective press towards a better-synthesized societal whole. (Clark 2019)

I of course consider this stance of radical nihilism not only totally at odds with my clear political engagement but also self-contradictory: it needs its fake-moral opponent to assert itself in its nihilistic destruction and in the unmasking of its hypocrisy. Therein resides the limit of all the desperate attempts to reverse tragedy into triumphant comedy practiced by incels, clowncels, and the Joker himself, who, just before shooting Murray, his TV host, tells him:

> Have you seen what it's like out there, Murray? Do you ever actually leave the studio? Everybody just yells and screams at each other. Nobody's civil anymore! Nobody thinks what it's like to be the other guy. You think men like Thomas Wayne ever think what it's like to be someone like me? To be somebody but themselves? They don't. They think that we'll just sit down and take it like good little boys! That we won't werewolf and go wild!

The assertion of joyful destruction remains parasitic on this complaint. The Joker doesn't go "too far" in the destruction of the existing order, he remains stuck in what Hegel called "abstract negativity", unable as he is to propose its concrete negation.

Insofar as the Freudian name for this negativity is "death drive", we should be careful not to characterize Donald Trump's self-destructive defense against attempts to impeach him as manifestations of the death drive (see Butler 2019). Yes, while Trump rejected the accusations against him, he simultaneously confirmed (and even boasted with) the very crimes he was accused of and broke the law in his very defense. But did he not thereby just enact (more openly than usual, true) the paradox that is constitutive of the rule of law, i.e., the fact that the very agency that regulates the application of the law has to exempt itself from its reign? So yes, Trump was obscene in acting the way he acted, but in this way he merely brought out the obscenity that is the obverse of the law itself; the "negativity" of his acts was totally subordinated to (his perception of) his ambitions and well-being, he was far from the self-destruction of the existing order enacted by the Joker. There was nothing suicidal about Trump's boasting about his breaking the rules, it was simply part of his message that he was a tough guy president beset by corrupt elites while boosting the US abroad, and that his transgressions were necessary because only a rule breaker could crush the power of the Washington swamp. To read this well-planned and very rational strategy in terms of the death drive is yet another example of how it is left liberals who are really on a suicidal mission, giving rise to the impression that they are engaged in bureaucratic-legal nagging, while the President was doing a good job for the country.

In Christopher Nolan's *The Dark Knight*, the Joker is the only figure of truth: the goal of his terrorist attacks on Gotham City is made clear: they will stop when Batman takes off his mask and reveals his true identity. What, then, is the Joker who wants to disclose the truth beneath the mask, convinced that this disclosure will destroy the social order? He is not a man without a mask; on the contrary, he is a man fully identified with his mask, a man who IS his mask—there is nothing, no "ordinary guy", beneath the mask. This is why the Joker has no back-story and lacks any clear motivation: he tells different people different stories about his scars, mocking the idea that he should have some deep-rooted trauma that drives him. It may appear that *Joker* aims precisely at providing a kind of socio-psychological genesis of the Joker, depicting the traumatic events which made him the figure he is.[3] The problem is that thousands of young boys who grew up in ruined families and were bullied by their peers suffered the same fate, but only one "synthesized" these circumstances into the unique figure of the Joker. In other words, yes, the Joker is the result of a set of pathogenic circumstances, but these circumstances can be described as the causes of this unique figure only retroactively, once the Joker is already there. In one of the early novels about Hannibal Lecter, the claim that Hannibal's monstrosity is the result of unfortunate circumstances is rejected: "Nothing happened *to* him. *He* happened."

However, one can (and should) read *Joker* also in the opposite sense and claim that the act that constitutes the main figure as "the Joker" is an autonomous act by means of which he surpasses the objective circumstances of his situation. He identifies with his fate, but this identification is a free act: in it, he posits himself as a unique figure of subjectivity.[4] We can locate this reversal at the precise moment in the film when the hero says, "You know what really makes me laugh? I used to think that my life was a tragedy. But now I realize, it's a fucking comedy." One should take note of the exact moment Arthur says this: while, standing by his mother's bedside, he takes her pillow and uses it

---

[3] Before seeing the movie and knowing only critical reactions to it, I thought it provided the social genesis of the figure of the Joker; now, after seeing it, I must admit, in the spirit of communist self-criticism, that I was wrong: the passage from passive victimhood to a new form of subjectivity is the pivotal moment of the film.

[4] Clowncels are also not just determined by their circumstances: even more so than incels in general, they enact a symbolic gesture of turning their suffering into a form of enjoyment—they obviously enjoy their predicament, parading it proudly, and are therefore responsible for it rather than being mere victims of unfortunate circumstances.

to smother her to death. Who, then, is his mother? Here is how Arthur describes her presence: "She always tells me to smile and put on a happy face. She says I was put here to spread joy and laughter." Is this not the maternal superego at its purest? No wonder she calls him Happy, not Arthur. He gets rid of his mother's hold on him (by killing her) through fully identifying with her command to laugh.

This, however, does not mean that the Joker lives in a maternal world: his mother is a half-dead impassive victim of paternal violence, obsessed with the ultra-rich Wayne as the father of her child, hoping until the end that he will help her and Arthur.[5] (The film elegantly leaves it open whether Wayne effectively is Arthur's father or not.) Arthur's sad fate is thus not the result of a too-strong maternal presence—far from being guilty, his mother is herself the victim of extreme male brutality. Apart from Wayne, there is another paternal figure in the film: Murray, the comedian who invites Arthur to his popular TV show and thus gives him a chance at social integration and public recognition. One is almost tempted to say that this duality of Wayne and Murray enacts the opposition between the "bad" and the "good" father (in this case, the father who ignores Arthur and the father who recognizes him), but the integration fails, Arthur sees through Murray's hypocrisy and shoots him in the middle of the TV show, and it is only after this, after repeating the murder of his mother in the public murder of a paternal figure, that he fully becomes the Joker. (In yet another elegant move, Arthur does not kill Wayne, his putative father, himself—this act is left to an anonymous man wearing a clown mask, a member of the Joker's new tribe. Both Oedipal enigmas, the question of who is Arthur's father and the question of who enacts the parricide, are thus left in the dark.)

Because of his act, the Joker may not be moral, but he definitely is ethical. Morality regulates how we relate to others with regard to our shared common Good, while ethics concerns our fidelity to the Cause which defines our desire, a fidelity which reaches beyond the pleasure principle. Morality in its basic sense is not opposed to social customs, it is an affair of what was called *eumonia* in ancient Greece, the harmonious well-being of the community. One should recall here how at the beginning of *Antigone*, the chorus reacts to the news that someone (at this point one doesn't yet know who) violated Creon's prohibition and performed funeral rites on Polynices' body—it is Antigone herself who is implicitly castigated as the "cityless outcast" engaged in excessive demonic acts that disturb the *eumonia* of the state, fully reasserted in the last lines of the play:

---

5 I rely here on Matthew Flisfeder (private exchange).

> The most important part of happiness
> is therefore wisdom—not to act impiously
> towards the gods, for boasts of arrogant men
> bring on great blows of punishment
> so in old age men can discover wisdom. (Sophocles 2007, p. 201)

From the standpoint of *eumonia*, Antigone is definitely demonic/uncanny: her defying act expresses a stance of de-measured excessive insistence, which disturbs the "beautiful order" of the city; her unconditional ethics violate the harmony of the *polis* and are as such "beyond human boundary". The irony is that while Antigone presents herself as the guardian of the immemorial laws which sustain human order, she acts as a freakish and ruthless abomination—there definitely is something cold and monstrous about her, as is rendered by the contrast between her and her warmly human sister Ismene. And it is in this same sense that the Joker is ethical but not moral.

One should also take note of Arthur's family name, Fleck, which is German for stain/spot. Arthur is a disharmonious stain in the social edifice, something with no proper place in it. Yet what makes him a stain is not just his miserable marginal existence but primarily a feature of his subjectivity, his propensity to compulsive and uncontrollable outbursts of laughter. The status of this laughter is paradoxical: it is quite literally extimate (to use Lacan's neologism), intimate and external. Arthur insists that it forms the very core of his subjectivity: "Remember you used to tell me that my laugh was a condition, that there was something wrong with me? It isn't. That's the real me." But precisely as such, it is external to him, to his personality, experienced by him as an autonomized partial object that he cannot control and that he ends up fully identifying with—a clear case of what Lacan called "identification with a symptom" (or rather "sinthome": not a bearer of meaning, of a coded message from the unconscious, but a cipher of enjoyment, the elementary formula of the subject's enjoyment). The paradox here is that in the standard Oedipal scenario, it is the Name-of-the-Father which enables an individual to escape the clutches of maternal desire; with the Joker, the paternal function is nowhere to be seen, so the subject can outdo the mother only by over-identifying with her superego command.

Not only does the film provide the socio-psychological genesis of the Joker, it also implies condemnation of a society in which protest can only assume the form of a new tribe led by the Joker. There is a subjective act in this move made by the Joker, but no new political subjectivity arises through it: at the end of the movie, we get the Joker as a new tribal leader, but one with no political program, just an explosion of negativity—in his conversation with Murray, Arthur insists twice that his act is not political. Referring to his clown makeup,

Murray asks him, "What's with the face? I mean, are you part of the protest?" Arthur's reply: "No, I don't believe any of that. I don't believe in anything. I just thought it'd be good for my act." And again later: "I'm not political. I'm just trying to make people laugh."

A. O. Scott, writing in *The New York Times*, therefore misses the point when he dismisses *Joker* as "a story about nothing": "The look and the sound ... connote gravity and depth, but the movie is weightless and shallow" (Scott 2019). There effectively is no "gravity and depth" in the Joker's final stance—his revolt is "weightless and shallow", and that's the utterly desperate point of the film. There is no militant Left in the film's universe, it's just a flat world of globalized violence and corruption. Charity events are depicted as what they are: if a mother Theresa figure were to be there, she would for sure participate in the charity event organized by Wayne, for the humanitarian amusement of the privileged rich. However, it's difficult to imagine a more stupid critique of *Joker* than the reproach that it doesn't portray a positive alternative to the Joker's revolt. Just imagine a film shot along these lines: an edifying story about how the poor, the unemployed, those with no healthcare coverage, victims of street gangs and police brutality, etc., organize non-violent protests and strikes to mobilize public opinion—a new non-racial version of Martin Luther King ... and an extremely boring film, lacking the crazy excesses of the Joker, which make the film so attractive for the viewers.

Here we get to the crux of the matter: Since it seems obvious to a leftist that such non-violent protests and strikes are the only way to proceed, i.e., to exert efficient pressure on those in power, is what we are dealing with here a simple gap between political logic and narrative efficiency (to put it bluntly, brutal outbursts such as those of the Joker are politically a deadlock but they make a story interesting) or is there also an immanent political necessity in the self-destructive stance embodied by the Joker? My hypothesis is that one has to go through the self-destructive zero level for which the Joker stands—not actually, but one has to experience it as a threat, as a possibility. Only in this way can one break out of the coordinates of the existing system and envisage something really new. The Joker's stance is a blind alley, a total deadlock, superfluous and non-productive, but the paradox is that one has to go through it to perceive its superfluous character—there is no direct way from the existing misery to its constructive overcoming. Or, insofar as the Joker obviously is a kind of madman, one should recall Hegel, for whom madness is not an accidental lapse, distortion, or "illness" of the human spirit, but something which is inscribed into the individual spirit's basic ontological constitution: to be human means to be potentially mad:

> This conception of derangement as a *necessarily* emerging form or stage in the development of the soul is naturally not to be understood as if we were asserting that *every* mind, *every* soul, must go through this stage of extreme disruption. Such an assertion would be as absurd as to assume that because *crime* is considered in the *Philosophy of Right* as a *necessary* appearance of the human will, therefore the commission of crime is supposed to be made an inevitable necessity for *every* individual. Crime and derangement are *extremes* which the human mind *in general* has to overcome in the course of its development, but which do not appear as *extremes* in *every* individual but only in the shape of *limitations, errors, follies*, and of *non-criminal wrongdoing*. (Hegel 2007, p. 116; §408, Zusatz)

Although not a factual necessity, madness is a formal possibility constitutive of the human mind: it is a threat that has to be overcome if we are to emerge as "normal" subjects, which means that "normality" can only arise as the overcoming of this threat. This is why, as Hegel put it a couple of pages later, "derangement must be dealt with *before* the *healthy, intellectual* consciousness, although it has the intellect for its *presupposition*" (Hegel 2007, p. 116; §408, *Zusatz*). In short, we do not all have to be mad in reality, but madness is the real of our psychic lives, a point to which our psychic lives necessarily refer in order to assert themselves as "normal". And it is the same with the Joker: we are not all Jokers in reality, but the position of the Joker is something the human mind *in general* has to overcome in the course of its development. The elegance of *Joker* is that, in order to articulate a new positive political vision, we don't have to actually become Jokers—the film does it for us. The film stages the madness, confronts us with it, and thereby enables us to overcome it.

In his interpretation of the fall of East European communism, Habermas proved to be the ultimate left Fukuyamaist, silently accepting that the existing liberal democratic order is the best possible, and that while we should strive to make it more just, etc., we should not challenge its basic premises. This is why he welcomed precisely what many leftists saw as the big deficiency of anti-communist protests in Eastern Europe: the fact that these protests were not motivated by any new visions of a post-communist future—as he put it, Central and Eastern European revolutions were just so-called "rectifying" or "catch-up" revolutions: their aim was to enable Central and Eastern European societies to gain what Western Europeans already possessed, i.e., to rejoin West European normality. However, although the Hong Kong protests may appear to fit this frame, the ongoing wave of protests in different parts of the world tends to question it—and this is why these protests are accompanied by "joker-like" figures. When a movement questions the fundamentals of the existing order, its basic normative foundations, it is almost impossible to get just peaceful protests without violent excess.

The elegance of *Joker* resides in how the crucial move from the self-destructive drive to what Moore called a "new desire" for an emancipatory political project is absent from the film's storyline: we, the spectators, are solicited to fill in this absence. Are we, though? Will *Joker* not turn out to be yet another proof that today's sphere of culture and entertainment can easily integrate even the most "subversive" anti-capitalist messages and practices? Just imagine a biennale, such as *La Biennale di Venezia*, where the program does not question Eurocentrism or the all-pervasive reign of financial capital or our destruction of the environment. Why should *Joker* be any different from paintings that destroy themselves, from galleries that "make us think" by displaying rotten animal corpses or sacred images soaked in urine? Maybe it is not as simple as that. Maybe, what makes *Joker* so unsettling is that it does not engage in calling for political action—it leaves the decision to us. Visiting an "anti-capitalist" art performance or engaging in social charity makes us feel good—seeing *Joker* definitely does not do that, and that's our hope. The Joker practices what Giorgio Agamben called the courage of hopelessness—in short, he enacts a version of subjective destitution.

Bibliography

Badiou, Alain (2004): "Afterword: Some Replies to a Demanding Friend". In: Peter Hallward (Ed.): *Think Again: Alain Badiou and the Future of Philosophy*. London: Continuum, pp. 232–237.
Butler, Judith (2019): "Genius or Suicide". In: *London Review of Books* 41. No. 2. https://www.lrb.co.uk/the-paper/v41/n20/judith-butler/genius-or-suicide, visited on 22 November 2021.
Clark, M. L. (2019): "Secular God-of-the-Gaps: Žižek, Joker, & Tribes Built on Tribelessness". In: *Another White Atheist in Colombia*. https://www.patheos.com/blogs/anotherwhiteatheistincolombia/2019/10/tribelessness-secular-zizek-joker, visited on 22 November 2021.
Cowen, Tyler (2019): "*Joker*". https://marginalrevolution.com/marginalrevolution/2019/10/the-joker.html, visited on 13 July 2022.
De Semlyen, Phil (2019): "Joker". In: *Time Out*. https://www.timeout.com/movies/joker-1, visited on 22 November 2021.
"Four Pests Campaign". In: *Wikipedia*. https://en.wikipedia.org/wiki/Four_Pests_campaign, visited on 22 November 2021.
Giri, Saroj (2018): "The Buddhist Ineffable Self and a Possible Indian Political Subject". In: *Political Theology* 19. No. 8, pp. 734–750.
Giri, Saroj (2020): "Introduction: From the October Revolution to the Naxalbari Movement: Understanding Political Subjectivity". In: K. Murali: *Of Concepts and Methods. 'On Postisms' and Other Essays*. Paris: Foreign Languages Press, pp. 1–32.

Harman, Graham (2010): *Towards Speculative Realism: Essays and Lectures*. Winchester and Washington: Zero Books.
Hegel, Georg Wilhelm Friedrich (2007): *The Philosophy of Mind*. Translated by W. Wallace and A. V. Miller. Oxford: Clarendon Press.
Meis, Morgan (2021): "Timothy Morton's Hyper-Pandemic". In: *The New Yorker*. https://www.newyorker.com/culture/persons-of-interest/timothy-mortons-hyper-pandemic?fbclid=IwAR0qbxs2y57TIQsOloIW9MrBtqIeIMIFK3SsfBQeCcWXiGIKRpnUmRAiNTk, visited on 22 November 2021.
Moore, Michael (2019): Facebook post. https://www.facebook.com/permalink.php?story_fbid=10156278766436857&id=24674986856, visited on 21 November 2021.
Scott, A. O. (2019): "'Joker' Review: Are You Kidding Me?" In: *The New York Times*. https://www.nytimes.com/2019/10/03/movies/joker-review.html, visited on 21 November 2021.
Sophocles (2007): "Antigone". In: *The Oedipus Trilogy*. Translated by George Young. Charleston: Biblio Bazaar.

Sebastian Rödl
Philosophy and Its History

Abstract: The paper is an idealist attempt at reconciling the tension between the historical, time-bound emergence of metaphysical truths and their timeless validity. Proceeding from the Aristotelian definition of metaphysics as a science which studies being insofar as it is being, and from Plato's notion from the *Theaetetus* that the soul does not grasp being by way of an organ but only through itself, the paper defines knowledge of what is insofar as it is as the knowledge of the absolute, hence, an absolute knowledge. Nevertheless, metaphysics passes through a contingent process of being constituted by persons living in a certain society under certain material conditions; in short, metaphysics possesses a history. Thus, a judgment which apprehends itself through itself, hence, a judgment on being qua being, does not lie outside time, but performs a perpetual annihilation of time and its difference between this and that temporal existence thinking it.

Introduction

She who holds that what is—is most truly, most beingly—is an idea may on that account be called an idealist. The idea, here, is what is apprehended not by the senses, but in thought. The idealist is the one with whom alone Socrates will enter into a conversation, while those who hold that only what they can touch with their hands is real are too brutish to speak to.

It may seem that, while what is seen and touched, the object of the senses, resides in time and is thus subjected to becoming and passing away, the idea, the object of thought, lies outside time, holding out eternally, lifting her who apprehends the idea out of the dung of the ephemeral, giving her something worthy and enduring to which to attach herself. While this is not completely wrong—and how could it be?—it is awfully misleading.

In opposition to the apparently naïve desire to contemplate the eternal idea, the heavenly form, it has come to be received as a superior consciousness of more modern times to recognize that thoughts, concepts, ideas have a history, and that there can and should be a study of this history, the history of ideas. This study reveals the idea in each case to be a creature of a time, a society, a

---

Sebastian Rödl, University of Leipzig.

https://doi.org/10.1515/9783110760767-011

form of reproduction, political struggles, an economic order, and so on. While this is not completely wrong—and how could it be?—it is awfully misleading.

I want to engage the question raised by these two notions of the idea and time, the idea and its history, by considering philosophy and time, and philosophy and its history. It will transpire that it is impossible to place philosophy inside time, and that this impossibility resides in the historicity of philosophy, in philosophy's being nothing but its own history.

In order to understand philosophy to be historical, it is necessary first to convince oneself of the timelessness of philosophy. It will be the task of the first section to engender this conviction. The second section will reveal its timelessness to be the historicity of philosophy. I hope that will shed light on idealism, the idealism that philosophy is.

1 Philosophy

By "philosophy" I designate the science described by Aristotle in Book Gamma of his *Metaphysics*. I thus also call that science metaphysics. One may hold that metaphysics is only one of the many fields of philosophy, alongside epistemology, moral philosophy, and others. I do not think that this is right, but I will not speak further on this point. Even those who do not believe that philosophy is metaphysics will admit that metaphysics is philosophy; to this extent, what I say will be relevant to them as well.

Metaphysics is the science of what is insofar as it is. It investigates what belongs to what is in itself and belongs to it precisely insofar as it is (*Metaph.* 1003a21–22, 1005a14); it apprehends the truth with respect to what determines what is, determines it solely insofar as it is (*Metaph.* 1004b15–17). Metaphysics discerns the principles, the highest, or first, causes of what is, again, insofar as it is (*Metaph.* 1003a28–31). The concept of being thus designates the object of metaphysics, and it designates the character with respect to which metaphysics studies this object. In order to see what metaphysics is, then, we must examine this concept, the concept of being.

The passage from the *Theaetetus* that finally refutes the idea that knowledge is perception explains that the soul does not apprehend being through an organ, but rather through itself (*Theaet.* 185d). Negatively: not through an organ; positively: through itself. First, the negative determination. The soul apprehends a thing through an organ as that organ makes that thing accessible to it; an organ, through which the soul apprehends, delimits a domain of what is apprehended through it. The power of representing through organs—sensibility—is thus divided into senses, each with an organ and a corresponding domain of objects.

A given sense with its organ apprehends a determinate domain of objects. We can form the concept of something that belongs to this domain. This represents the formal object of the sense in question: through it we think of something exclusively as the object of this sense. Thus, color is the formal object of vision; the concept of color, the concept of an object of the sense of vision. The concept of the formal object of a sense and the concept of this sense are *one* concept, for the formal object is defined as the object of the sense in question, and the sense as the power of apprehending this object.

The activity in which the soul apprehends being is judging. A judgment states how things stand, how they are, how it is. "So it is", says the judgment. What color is to vision, being is to judgment. Being is the formal object of judgment and its concept is the formal concept of the object of judgment. It is the concept of an object of judgment *überhaupt*.

It is easy to see that being is not apprehended through an organ; judging has no organ. For what we always apprehend, through whatever sense, indeed, regardless of which senses we have, we apprehend it, necessarily apprehend it, as something that is. What we apprehend through an organ, however, falls within a limited domain. It would be contingent if there were nothing that lay outside this domain. By contrast, it is not contingent that nothing lies beyond what is. It is not contingent that everything—thus, everything that there is, everything that is—is. This is tautological. It shows that, in the concept of being, we have always already exceeded every limit, thought beyond every limit. The notion that being is apprehended through an organ is empty.

The soul does not apprehend being through an organ. For being is unlimited, infinite. It is occasionally suggested that we do judge through an organ, the brain perhaps, or the knee. (Joseph Boyce claimed to think with his knee.) Then judgment is a special sense, a sense for being, one could say. A given organ, however, its given nature, limits the domain of what is apprehended through it. When we think we judge through an organ, this thus suggests to us that there are certain things—consciousness, let's say—which we don't comprehend, because the organ through which we comprehend things—be it the brain or the knee—is so constituted as to fail to render them accessible. Determinate things—consciousness, say—lie beyond judgment, just as determinate things—sounds—lie outside vision. This is nonsense, since the concept of being, the concept of the formal object of judgment, is unconditionally universal. It is always already beyond any limit that we think in the concept of a given organ, its determinate nature, its limited domain.

Metaphysics is the knowledge of what is and of what determines it insofar as it is. Therein it is, further, the knowledge of the principle of what is. Metaphysics is the knowledge of what explains whatever is—it apprehends that by which it is necessary—again, insofar as it is. We can determine the character of this principle and the knowledge of it to the extent that its character is determined by the unconditional universality of the concept of being. Then we see that the principle of what is insofar as it is, is unconditionally necessary. For since the concept of being is unconditionally universal, there is nothing beyond this principle upon which it could depend and which could make it necessary. We see, further, that knowledge of the principle is absolutely apodictic. Indeed, it is impossible that it be grounded in any other knowledge. The knowledge of the principle of what is insofar as it is recognizes this principle as unconditionally necessary and is thus in itself the knowledge that things cannot be otherwise than they are known to be in that knowledge. It is in itself knowledge of itself as knowledge and therein absolute. So, the knowledge of what is insofar as it is, is knowledge of the absolute and thus absolute knowledge.

This may incline one to declare that the idea of knowledge of what is insofar as it is, thus, metaphysics, is meaningless. This has been attempted. I will not go into this. I will only remark that the result of this is frequently that the consciousness of the unconditioned, since it is not supposed to be knowledge, is located in other powers of the mind, for example, in a feeling that can only be expressed in music. This is anti-philosophy. Philosophy is the effort to live through reason, thus, to think the ultimate ground and not merely to feel it.

In fact, everyone who judges at all aspires beyond every limited knowledge to knowledge of what is insofar as it is. Aristotle thus remarks that the *physikoi*, who search for the elements of beings and find them, for example, in water or fire, must believe that their elements are elements of what is insofar as it is (*Metaph.* 1003a28–32). And Williamson remarks that the *physikoi* of the present day, naturalists, envision an unconditional, as he puts it, an absolute universality when they declare that everything is a part of nature (Williamson 2003, p. 416).

The object of metaphysics—what is insofar as it is—is infinite. Its ground is thus unconditionally necessary and the knowledge of it is absolutely apodictic. What, however, should such knowledge be? If we don't know the answer to this question, this is because we have thus far only considered Plato's negative determination: the soul does not apprehend being through an organ. Plato continues: the soul apprehends being through itself. That is the positive determination. The negative is grounded in the positive. If we come to understand how this is so, we will have a positive concept of the knowledge of what is insofar as it is.

The formal object of judgment, being, and therefore judgment, is infinite. The infinity of judgment must have its ground in this: what judgment apprehends, it apprehends through itself. We said that being is to judgment as color is to vision. The cases are different because the soul apprehends being through itself. No organ limits the object of judgment. What determines the formal object of judgment, says Plato, is nothing other than judgment. Judgment determines its own formal object, and this means it determines itself, its own nature. We must clarify this point.

In judging, I am conscious of judging as indeed I judge. It is not the case that I judge, and additionally, in a second act, that I am conscious of so judging. If I were not conscious of judging, I would not judge. Judging and being conscious of judging are one act; every judgment comprehends itself through the concept of judgment. In this way, judgment apprehends what it does so through itself: It apprehends what it apprehends *through its own concept*, the concept of judgment. Now, the concept of judgment is the same as the formal object of judgment. By apprehending what I apprehend through the concept of judgment, I am conscious of apprehending it in the manner of judging, and this means: as something that is. A judgment represents its object through the concept of the object of judgment *überhaupt:* through the concept of being.

The concept of the formal object of judgment does not reflect, it is not bound to, the given nature of an organ, a nature that limits what is apprehended by this organ. The soul apprehends being through itself, says Plato; I have said that judgment represents its object through its own concept, the concept of judgment. The concept of judgment thus does not reflect, it is not bound to, a given nature of judging. There is no nature which judgments exhibit anyway, and which then comes to be thought in the concept of judgment, and is thought therein to be as it is anyway.

Judgment has no given nature corresponding to a limited formal object: the object that an act of this kind, judgment, apprehends. (Indeed, we can put this by saying that judgment is not *of a kind*.) Judgment has no nature that is as it is and that then may be known in a suitable concept. The concept of judgment does not derive its content from the given nature of a certain activity of the soul, whose nature it captures. The concept of judgment is itself the source of its content. The concept of judgment determines itself. Therefore, the nature of judgment, which is thought in the concept of judgment, is not a character that judgment has anyway. Rather, it is nothing other than the self-determining concept of judgment. Therefore, the nature of judgment is unconditionally necessary. A given nature would be a brute fact, a ground for which must be sought in something other than itself, which determines it to be the way that it is. A given nature, as such, is not necessary in itself, but rather through something other, which *makes* it necessary. The nature of judgment, however, is nothing other than the self-determining concept; it is not determined through something other, but rather only through itself and is thus unconditionally necessary.

The concept of being is infinite, I have said. Being is not represented through an organ, says Plato. That is the negative determination. The soul apprehends being through itself, says Plato. The concept of judgment determines itself, I have said. That is the positive determination. It explains the negative. The concept of being is infinite *because* it determines itself. Once again: judgment is not a given, limited power of the soul with a given, limited object. Judgment is for itself its own concept; thus, its nature is nothing given, limited. Judgment is the self-determination of its nature and thus always already beyond every limitation of its object. The determination of its object, as it is thought in the concept of being, is not something given, limited, to which judgment must conform in order to apprehend what is. This determination is the self-determination of judgment. The soul apprehends being through itself. The concept of being is: the soul, reason, judgment, thought.

We have noted that the principle of what is insofar as it is, is unconditionally necessary and the knowledge thereof absolutely apodictic. Knowledge of the absolute is absolute knowledge. We do not understand what that should be when, and so long as, we represent the principle of what is insofar as it is as something which is there, which is as it happens to be, and which then is, or fails to be, known. For something, in other words, that is there, which is as it happens to be, as such is not unconditionally necessary. The knowledge of it is not in itself the knowledge of its own ground, and precisely therein it is a brute fact. The unconditionally necessary is only that whose concept is determined through itself and which therefore is nothing other than this self-determining concept. The self-determining concept is absolutely apodictic knowledge because what it knows is not something that exists independently of it, but rather is nothing other than its own self-determination. Knowledge of the absolute is absolute knowledge, and it can be this because it is the self-knowledge of the absolute, and hence nothing other than what it knows. When we wondered what knowledge of the absolute, knowledge of what is unconditionally necessary, should be, we thought that the absolute is over there and the knowledge must approach it and go to it. In truth, the absolute is always already with the knowledge. It is knowledge itself.

Judgment is infinite; it is infinite because it is self-conscious. Judgment is the act that determines its own nature; indeed, this act is nothing other than the concept of its very nature, and precisely therein it is absolute knowledge of the absolute, the highest principle of what is insofar as it is. The first thing that we think, the first thing that thought thinks of itself, is this: judgment is the original singular act, and this act is being. Metaphysics is the self-explication of this act, of judgment, of *nous*, of reason.

2 History

Having determined what metaphysics, what philosophy is, we can now ask how the difference of time appears in it. Metaphysics, so it seems, has a history. There are people who lived in particular times in particular places under particular circumstances, and whose thoughts have been handed down to us in texts, thoughts that present themselves as metaphysical knowledge. The temporal sequence of these people and their thoughts comprises the history of metaphysics. Since we recognize the thoughts in question as ostensible, or alleged, metaphysical knowledge, we have apparently understood them. We will thus first consider what it means, and how it is possible, to understand expressions of metaphysical knowledge.

To this end, we will take a step back and consider how, in general, it is possible to understand a judgment. We will distinguish internal understanding from external understanding. Internal understanding explains why someone judges as she judges by *what* she judges. External understanding explains why someone judges as she judges while leaving out of account what she judges. More precisely, an understanding is internal *to the extent that* it explains a judgment by what it judges. Likewise for external understanding. For it is possible that a judgment cannot be fully understood from the inside. And no judgment can be fully understood from the outside.

We can bring out the distinction in this way. Suppose that someone judges B because she judges A, in such a way that she grounds the former judgment in the latter. Then one can understand why she judges B by recognizing that it follows from A. In understanding the judgment in this way, one understands it internally. Admittedly, one thereby understands it only conditionally. For it has not yet been explained why she judges A, on which ground she rests her judgment B. When one understands this internally, as well, one has understood her judgment B internally.[1]

Internal understanding understands why someone judges by what she judges. The internal understanding of a judgment therefore does not appeal to any determination of the one who judges aside from her judging what indeed she judges. External understanding, by contrast, cites causes that lie in determinations of the one who judges, determinations that do lie in her judging what

---

[1] It may be that someone grounds something in something from which the former something does not follow. Even then, the understanding is not completely external. One may notice, for instance, that it would follow according to a pattern that is valid elsewhere, but not here. And to this extent, one understands internally.

she judges. If someone deliberates cogently, I understand why she thinks as she does by making clear to myself what it is that she thinks. When someone speaks nonsense, I look for external causes, such as his being drunk.

The judgment that is internally understood is knowledge. For knowledge is judgment that is non-accidentally true. That is still imprecise. A judgment is knowledge if what explains the judgment shows it to be true, and not *per accidens*, but in virtue of the form of the explanation: what explains the judgment as such, *as what explains the judgment*, shows that the judgment is true. When a judgment can be completely explained in this way, then it is completely explained by its truth. This is the internal understanding, which explains the judgment by what it judges. A judgment can be understood externally only if and to the extent that it is not knowledge, but rather false or true by accident.

To the extent that I understand internally why someone judges what she judges, to this extent I judge as she does. And not only this, but, furthermore, what explains her judgment, explaining it internally, also explains mine, and does so equally internally. One may be inclined to think that this means that I judge, on the one hand, and she judges, on the other hand, and that our judgments share the same content. *Two acts* of judgment with *one content*. This notion can be reduced *ad absurdum* in more than one way; here, however, in the following way: since I understand your judgment internally and thereby judge as you do, what explains my judgment is the same as what explains yours, namely, *what* I judge explains it, which is what you judge. Nothing in the cause of my judging characterizes it as mine in contrast to yours. However, when there is no difference in the cause, there is none in the effect. Through my understanding of your judgment, we understand our judgment. Better still, the judgment understands itself. For anyone who understands why we judge as we do, it is with him as it is with me and you: he has no act of judging distinct from ours. When and to the extent that a judgment is explained through what it judges, it explains itself. One need not consider anything outside of it, one need only consider the judgment itself as the judgment that it is, in order to comprehend why it is. Further, this comprehension is nothing other than the judgment itself; the judgment is the internal understanding of itself.

It is a familiar truth, it is the most familiar truth, that we understand a judgment internally. If someone says something and one answers, "I understand", this ordinarily expresses an internal understanding. One does not mean, "I understand, you are drunk", but rather, "I understand, I see why it is as you say". Conversely, by "I don't understand", one ordinarily does not mean, "I don't know if you are drunk or hypnotized", but rather, "I cannot follow your thought; I don't see how what you say shows that it is as you say". It is a familiar truth, it is the most familiar truth, that a judgment explains itself. That a judgment can explain itself indeed means nothing other than this, that it is possible to ascertain how things are by thinking. This is no mere assumption or plea, no hypothesis to be confirmed by further contemplation or even empirical evidence. It is not something that I learn from somewhere. It is the original knowledge that judging itself is. If I say that judgment understands itself, that is, internally, I do not put forward any thesis, not in a sense in which there it would then be a possible act of the intellect that denied this thesis.

Now, someone could say:

> Good, that is so, I can understand why someone thinks what she thinks by attending to what it is that she thinks. This does happen. But the other thing you have said, that I and you, as I understand you in this way, share in one act of judging, that surely can't be right.

Now, no one simply says this. For one surely must ask why that cannot be so. Therefore, whoever says this will think something that he believes shows that it cannot be so. He will say: That surely cannot be, that I and you, that we share in one act of judging, because ... However, whatever follows that "because" will be meaningless. For example, one could assert that an act of judgment consists in the fact that the brain of the one who judges suffers a particular change or is in a particular state. That, however, is nonsense; judgment has no organ, for its object is infinite.

Someone could further say:

> What you are claiming is that my understanding you is nothing other than judgment explaining itself. But those who judge are human beings who live in a particular time in a particular society under particular material conditions. You move about in your lofty sphere of the self-determining concept, whose sublime activity is carried out over the heads of human beings who, given what you say, are completely irrelevant to that activity.

In fact, the opposite is true. In what we are saying here we are thinking of actual human beings and of nothing else. It is not good to be certain that one knows what the actual human being is. The human being, the actual human being, as everyone knows, is wonderful, and what she actually is: that nobody knows. Within the limits of our aims, we can elaborate a little further on what the actual human being is, as she is judgment.

When someone judges $6 + 8 = 11$, this can be explained by the fact that she has taken the "8" for a "5". When, by contrast, he judges $6 + 8 = 14$, then this is explained, is fully explained, by the fact that $6 + 8 = 14$. One might object that the fact he judges that $6 + 8 = 14$ has further conditions, particularly the fact that he can count, further, that someone taught him this, that there was a school in which he could learn it, that the society in which he was raised provided such schools, and so on. In this way, we encounter historical, cultural, social conditions, which, so it seems, must be taken into consideration in order to comprehend how it can come about that someone judges 6 + 8 = 14.

That someone can calculate is a condition for him calculating. When Damian says 6 + 8 = 14, he does not calculate, and when he says 6 + 8 = 11 he does not miscalculate. Why doesn't he calculate? Because what he does is not of a sort that can be explained in the manner described. That someone can calculate means that he can do something that can be internally understood. The fact that a child can calculate, and all that this presupposes, is therefore not an external cause of his judgment that 6 + 8 = 14. Rather, it falls within the internal understanding of this judgment. Though Damian's school and what underlies such an institution must be there for him to learn to calculate and then to judge 6 + 8 = 14, in general the capacity and its conditions are not prior to the act. A society that maintains schools in which children learn to calculate is one in which the knowledge 6 + 8 = 14 is actual. The presuppositions for a child learning to calculate (school, etc.) are based on this knowledge, not the other way around. The fact that a child can calculate and everything that is necessary for this, is explained through the knowledge, which for this very reason is explained completely internally.

This pertains equally to the practical knowledge of how to act well. One often hears that someone must be raised correctly in a well-ordered society in order to be virtuous. That is true. Here too, however, the act is prior to the capacity. One can only raise a child to be virtuous through virtue, and a society so ordered that this can come about is the actuality of the knowledge of the good, not an external cause of this knowledge.

Judgment is internally understood when and to the extent that the judgment is understood through what it judges. One might object that according to this definition no empirical judgment can be fully internally understood. For in order for someone to perform an empirical judgment, it is always ultimately necessary for the object of her judgment to have affected someone's senses. And thus, here the truth of the judgment can never be recognized from the content of the judgment alone. Now, the latter is true, but it does not mean that the empirical judgment cannot be completely internally understood. It means that the empirical judgment cannot be unconditionally internally understood, but rather only under a condition. Given that a tomato affects the senses, the judgment that there is a red tomato is explained by there being a red tomato. That is, the affection is a condition of the possibility of internally explaining the judgment. It is not a cause to which an external understanding may appeal. The judgment is not an effect evoked by a stimulation of nerve endings. One can see this by the fact that someone who says, "That is a red tomato", expresses the same act of judging if he later, when there is no longer any red tomato there, says, "That was a red tomato". One might think this shows that a judgment is a state evoked by a stimulus, a state that is enduring, or inert. That is false. Judging is not a state that endures, but rather, as the example shows, is itself a consciousness of its duration. Conversely, a subsequent stimulus does not nullify the judgment; rather, a new judgment can only nullify an old one by means of a new stimulus in the event that it understands itself as the insight into a mistake that it, the new judgment, corrects.

Since the empirical judgment can only be conditionally internally understood, ignorance is possible in this domain. Further, the advancement of knowledge here is not only possible, but essential to this form of knowing. And thus it is possible to incorporate the given empirical knowledge into a superior standpoint.

Empirical knowledge understands itself internally, but only conditionally. That is a defect of empirical knowledge as knowledge. The archetype of knowledge is the unconditionally internally understood judgment, thus, the judgment that is understood unconditionally from what it judges. Such a judgment is absolute knowledge, the original knowledge, in which knowledge, reason, *nous*, determines itself.[2]

Now we can return to our question how temporal difference appears in philosophy by considering what it means to understand metaphysical knowledge, as such knowledge is present in the text of an author from the past. And here we can in general say that it is not possible to understand metaphysical knowledge from the outside. One can only understand absolute knowledge, metaphysics, through itself and as itself. We shall go through several meanings of "not from the outside".

The first is the one we have just developed: not from the outside means that the understanding is not external. It holds generally that understanding a judgment externally, we therewith decide that it is not knowledge. One might think that there is a historical understanding of a philosophical thought, which would be an external one, one that understands the thought not through what it thinks, thus through the thought itself, but rather through the circumstances of the time in which someone thought it. The supposition that there is such an understanding does not open up any way in which philosophy might reflect

---

[2] It is thus not correct to treat empirical knowledge as the paradigm of knowledge in epistemology. And it is not correct, indeed, it is absurd to take unconditional knowledge to be incomprehensible because and to the extent that it differs from empirical knowledge in that it does not presuppose affection by its object.

on its history, for it is the supposition that there is no philosophy. That doesn't mean that someone's philosophical thought has no historical, social, cultural conditions. We have discussed this above on the example of the knowledge 6 + 8 = 14, and on the example of the knowledge of how to act well. What we said there can also be said here: the historical, social, cultural conditions of philosophical knowledge lend themselves to being internally understood as such conditions, namely, as the actuality, the self-actualization, of that knowledge.

Knowledge can never be externally understood. Empirical knowledge, however, can be considered from the outside and still be regarded as knowledge in the manner of being incorporated into more advanced knowledge. The knowledge of philosophy, however, is not empirical but unconditional. Thus, it is impossible to apprehend metaphysical knowledge from a superior standpoint, which has advanced beyond it.

The fact that there is no progress in philosophy distinguishes philosophy from empirical knowledge. This is compatible with the fact that, as Aristotle states, the *physikoi* do not understand the nature of their investigation, since they seek the principle of what is insofar as it is, in elements rather than in its unconditional unity determined through itself. And it is compatible with the fact that, as Kant states, the metaphysics of the time does not understand the ground of the possibility of metaphysical knowledge, since it does not find it in the self-legislation of reason. Now, it is progress when one is in the dark and the light turns on. That is not at issue. Rather, the point is that a temporal progression in which what is later is superior to what is earlier does not belong to the form of metaphysical knowledge.

The fact that philosophy does not know progress distinguishes it from empirical knowledge. Philosophy is not the only human activity that repels the idea of progress. All human activities that are a consciousness of the unconditional and thus themselves unconditional do so. In one respect, all of the humanities have that character. They also have an empirical side. When a new source is found, this yields the possibility of progress in the study of history. For precisely this reason, the essence of the study of history emerges particularly clearly in ancient history, in which the body of (written) sources has remained largely unchanged for decades. Another striking field in which there is no advance, in which what is valid is always valid, is art.

A third way to apprehend a judgment from the outside is to contradict it, to oppose it. Of all of the forms of being outside a judgment that we have spoken of, this one is the most inner outer, for it confronts the judgment immediately as judgment; it confronts it as something whose nature it is to explain itself. The philosophical judgment, however, excludes this outer as well. In philosophy, there is no position and counter-position, opinion and counter-opinion. Philosophical knowledge is not a possible judgment that confronts another possible judgment. A philosophical statement cannot be understood as a more or less plausible hypothesis to be measured against others. This is the character of metaphysical knowledge, namely, of the unconditional judgment that is understood through itself, or internally. Wittgenstein says, "If one tried to advance *theses* in philosophy, it would never be possible to debate them, because everyone would agree to them" (Wittgenstein 2009, p. 50e [PU 128]). When I read a text, I only understand it as philosophical knowledge if I recognize what it says as something that has this character: it is that which everyone agrees upon and which cannot come up for discussion. For this reason, every investigation into the influences on an author or a thought—who influenced him, from whom did he get this?—stands in the way of philosophical understanding by suggesting that the thought in question has an explanation other than its truth.

It is a philosophical experience that certain philosophical texts are infinite in the sense that the limits of the knowledge I find in them are none other than the limits of the knowledge that I bring to them. If I find such a text limited in any way—not clear enough, incomplete, etc.—this does not show a defect in the text, but rather a defect in my thinking. I call this an experience because it is an encounter with philosophical texts and also because it takes time. One must experience several times that the supposed stupidity of the author was one's own. In another sense, however, it is not an experience: it cannot be vindicated by any given interpretation of the text. It is a principle of interpretation, the principle through which alone a text can be apprehended as the expression of philosophical knowledge. In this way, it is a necessary philosophical experience.

This may sound like devoutly kneeling down before tradition as the holy scripture. The association is not entirely misguided, for bending the knee is a form of consciousness of the unconditional. Not the one, however, that philosophy is. This shows that it is not only misguided to seek to bring to light influences on a philosopher of the tradition, but just as misguided to find oneself influenced by the texts of the tradition. Wittgenstein explains, in the preface to the *Tractatus Logico-Philosophicus*: "Perhaps this book will be understood only by someone who has himself already had the thoughts that are expressed in it— or at least similar thoughts" (Wittgenstein 2001, p. 3). This holds for philosophy in general. There is thus no occasion to ascribe the thoughts here, for instance, to Hegel. There is such an occasion only as these thoughts are muddled and confused. If they are true, then they are no more his than they are mine.

Since metaphysical knowledge has no outer, time does not affect it as a form of externality. A thought that can be internally understood is not then and not there. It does not belong to the time of the one who thinks it, nor to the time of the one who understands it. The internal understanding of this thought is a unity of both times. I tried to say in the first section what Plato thought and what Aristotle thought, and I did so in such a way as to explain the thoughts in question solely through themselves. I have not spoken about the circumstances of Plato and Aristotle. I have not taken into consideration what cultural and social conditions were prevalent when Plato and Aristotle lived. Further, I have, verbatim and by paraphrase, repeated sentences from Hegel and Parmenides. For instance, judgment is the original singular act, which is nothing other than being. And, judgment is for itself its own concept. I have not cited these isolated sentences, but rather the interconnection of thoughts in which they stand, not the whole of it, but pieces. One can begin to lay out Parmenides' didactic poem and the introduction to *The Phenomenology of Spirit* working from what I have said.

When we spoke above about what it means to understand a judgment internally, we saw: when I understand internally why you judge as you do, then I judge the same, and what explains my judgment is the same as what explains yours. And we have concluded that my judgment and your judgment are but one act, and that, as I understand you, the judgment understands itself. Now, this does not mean: you must not say that I understand you; you should instead say that the judgment understands itself. Rather, we correctly apprehend what it means that I understand you when we see that it is nothing other than this: the judgment understands itself. For this reason, the converse equally holds: we correctly apprehend what it means that the judgment understands itself when we see that it is nothing other than this: I understand you. And this applies to me and Hegel, to you and Parmenides. When is that thought: being and thinking are the same? It does not belong to the time of Parmenides, for I have thought it, and have thought it in the same act, as I have internally understood that thought. Is the thought therefore not in any time, or nowhen? No, it is not outside time. Rather, it is the continual annihilation of time and its difference. It is the annihilation of time in the sense that it reveals the nullity of temporal difference through this difference itself. The philosophical knowledge is in Parmenides and is in me and thus it includes the temporal difference, but includes it precisely in the manner of being nothing other than the consciousness of the nullity of this difference. The existence of the temporal difference is its annihilation; its annihilation, its existence.

The history of philosophy is perfectly and completely irrelevant in this sense: what someone else thought elsewhere and in earlier times is, so conceived, without the least interest for philosophy. Yet the history of philosophy is infinitely significant because philosophizing is nothing other than the actuality of this history as an unconditional present.

Bibliography

Aristotle (1984): "Metaphysics". Translated by W. D. Ross. In: *The Complete Works of Aristotle*. The revised Oxford translation. Edited by Johnathan Barnes. Vol. 2. Princeton: Princeton University Press.
Plato (1997): "Theaetetus". Translated by M. J. Levett and Myles Burnyeat. In: *Complete Works*. Edited by John M. Cooper. Indianapolis and Cambridge: Hackett, pp. 157–234.
Williamson, Timothy (2003): "Everything". In: *Philosophical Perspectives* 17. No. 1, pp. 415–465.
Wittgenstein, Ludwig (2001): *Tractatus Logico-Philosophicus*. Translated by D. F. Pears and B. F. McGuiness. London and New York: Routledge.
Wittgenstein, Ludwig (2009): *Philosophische Untersuchungen/Philosophical Investigations*. 4th edn. Translated by G. E. M. Anscombe, P. M. S. Hacker and Joachim Schulte. Oxford: Wiley-Blackwell.

Isabelle Thomas-Fogiel
Beyond Realism and Correlationism, the Idealist Path

Abstract: We have recently witnessed a radical bipartition of the philosophical field: on the one hand, correlationism, which indiscriminately encompasses idealism, skepticism, constructivism, and relativism, and on the other hand, the bloc of contemporary realists. *Tertium non datur.* The aim of my intervention is to overcome this dilemma, in which we have been trapped by the contemporary concern to set up realism as the "unsurpassable horizon of our time", and to show how idealism, far from being one of the two members of the opposition, represents a third solution. To do so, I start with the opposition between realism and correlationism as it has been re-staged by the debate between Meillassoux's *Après la finitude* (2006), which claims to represent a radical and rigorous realism, and Bitbol's *Maintenant la finitude* (2019), which intends to defend a consequent correlationism. This will allow me to bring out the difference with the principle that structures any idealist enterprise, namely, a certain definition of truth.

Almost all the philosophers of the last 30 years have rallied to realism, each one endeavoring to exhibit within this great common genre its specific difference: "metaphysical and analytical" realism (Armstrong, Lowe, Tiercelin, etc.), "speculative" (Meillassoux, Harman, etc.), "ordinary" (Diamond, Cavell, and its innumerable variants, such as Travis's pragmatic contextualism) or "phenomenological" (Romano) or simply "new" (Ferraris, Gabriel). All determination being negation, these realists define themselves in opposition to an X that they determine as the object to struggle against. Significantly, all of them, beyond the diversity of adjectives by which they particularize their realism, attack the same adversary: idealism, which they associate with subjectivism and a form of relativism, terms that Meillassoux has synthesized under the practical label of "correlationism". Thus, we have recently witnessed a radical bipartition of the philosophical field: on the one hand, correlationism, which indiscriminately encompasses idealism, skepticism, constructivism and relativism, and on the other hand, the bloc of contemporary realists. *Tertium non datur.* The aim of my intervention is to overcome this dilemma in which we have been trapped by the contemporary concern to set up realism as the "unsurpassable horizon

Isabelle Thomas-Fogiel, University of Ottawa.

https://doi.org/10.1515/9783110760767-012

of our time", and to show how idealism, far from being one of two members of the opposition, represents a third solution. To do so, I will start with the opposition between realism and correlationism as it has been re-staged by the debate between Meillassoux's *Après la finitude* (2006), which claims to represent a radical and rigorous realism, and Bitbol's *Maintenant la finitude* (2019), which intends to defend a consequent correlationism. The analysis of this recent confrontation is particularly instructive in that, on the one hand, the opposition between these two texts constitutes a condensed version of the dilemma that all contemporary realist positions strive to set up, an opposition that Meillassoux has undeniably brought to its maximum intensity; on the other hand, it makes it possible to demonstrate the flaws in the dilemma and thus to identify the missing tertium. Indeed, analyzing the exact nature of the correlationism as put forward by Bitbol will make it possible to highlight its most fundamental difference compared to idealism, to which, however, his constant reference to authors such as Kant, Fichte and Husserl might, at first reading, seem to associate him. Everything unfolds as if both Bitbol and Meillassoux, beyond their undoubtedly frontal opposition, agreed to reject the principles upon which all idealism rests in order to offer our contemporaries only the choice between two exclusive options: correlationism or realism.

But, one may ask, what is this intrinsic dimension of idealism that is obscured in this current confrontation? Is it legitimate, in fact, to claim that there are structuring features of idealism beyond the diversity of its historical incarnations? Moreover, if we do not want to be satisfied with simply establishing that Bitbol and Meillassoux are not idealists, a perfectly vain undertaking insofar as this is indeed their right, how can we demonstrate that the very dynamics of their opposition outlines the necessity of this third way? These are the questions I will have to answer in the course of my elucidation. To do so, I will first question the opposition between Meillassoux and Bitbol by highlighting both the most general principles on which it rests and the different definitions of truth that this contemporary gigantomachy makes available to us. This will allow me to bring out the difference with the principle that structures any idealist enterprise, namely a certain definition of truth, which, significantly, these two authors and, beyond them, most of the contemporary philosophical field, leave out. Finally, after having highlighted the specificity of idealism, which in no way fits into the opposition but transcends it, it will remain for me to test the fruitfulness of the idealist principle for the ghost of philosophy "yet to come".

1 A questionable dilemma

1.1 The principles on which the opposition realism/correlationism rests

Let us approach the most general principle which is also the essential one. The realist conception is characterized by three principal theses, which unify contemporary realist philosophies and give them, beyond their undeniable diversity, an identical structure. First of all, an ontological thesis: reality is everything that is independent of me because it is external and prior or posterior to my representations, aims or cognitive schemas. Then an epistemological thesis: we can have knowledge of this independent reality. Finally, a philosophical thesis about the definition of truth. Saying the true is defined by the conformity of my proposition to an external thing (states of affairs or facts of a world posited as independent from my judgment). Reality outside me is what confers its truth on my proposition; in this sense, the real *makes* the truth of my proposition (this is the "truth-maker" of current analytic metaphysicians). Truth is so subordinated to reality that to define the former necessarily means referring to the latter. In short, for every realist, reality is defined as independent, knowable and "maker of the true". Of course, while the different realist currents agree on what the real is (independent and knowable) and the definition of truth (subordinated to an antecedent real), they nevertheless continue to declare themselves different from each other. In fact, they agree on what the real is (definition or intension of the concept) but not on what sort of things are real, that is, on the cases or individuals that the concept subsumes (its extension). Is the real only what is perceived (the heirs of Austin), the material thing or state of physical facts (the physicalists, materialists, naturalists) or the famous given of the phenomenologists, the forms of life of the Wittgensteinians, the essences of certain analytic metaphysicians or any object whatsoever, including the unicorn, as the partisans of flat ontology and certain neo-realists want it. These differences, however, do not alter the profound unanimity which, through their three common theses, has made the real (defined as independent, knowable and truth-making) the new Eldorado of philosophy.

Meillassoux fulfills precisely these three clauses:
- First, ontological realism, since he refers to a "great outdoors", which he also determines as a thing-in-itself, which is, for him, matter; such is the meaning of his claim to a "speculative materialism". More precisely, his general approach in *After Finitude* consists in positing a thing "in itself" by subtraction; what he calls in *Principe du signe creux* (2016) his subtractive realism.

It is a question of subtracting our modes of access from the statements and then positing the remainder thus obtained as "real", i.e. for him, that which, prior and posterior to us, is independent, unbound, etymologically: ab/solute.

– Next up, epistemological realism. For Meillassoux, philosophy is a rational and even scientific exercise that delivers positive knowledge (namely "the necessity of contingency") about what is independent of us ("the great outdoors" or matter). In his text, science is mobilized at a triple level: on the one hand, the philosophical enquiry begins with the content, which Meillassoux intends as "literal" (Meillassoux 2008, p. 14), of the claims of the experimental sciences; on the other hand, it is a science, mathematics, that makes it possible to determine the most general structure of all material things; finally, philosophy delivers by rational means (and not by sensible, religious means, etc.) positive contents about things in themselves. This is the ultimate meaning of the term "speculative", which designates a scientific philosophy because it is able to determine the exact properties of the independent thing. In short, on the one hand we have a clear ontological commitment to what is, namely the great outdoors or matter, and on the other hand, the determination of its main knowable property: necessary contingency.

– From these two theses follows his philosophical thesis about truth: it is what is "in itself" that makes our statements true. Thus, statements that are, he tells us (Meillassoux 2008, p. 12), "ideal" relate to referents (e.g. ancestral facts) that are "real". The real referent, as a state of independent matter, *makes* our ideal judgment true.

Against this fundamental structure of realism, which remains invariable whatever the multiplicity of its present-day figures, Bitbol's position, in *Maintenant la finitude*, can be expressed, very broadly, as follows:

1) An absolute independence of the real (as a total "non-relation") cannot be asserted without contradiction; hence ontology, which cannot be conceived as the doctrine of things that would be in themselves, becomes a philosophy of the relation, that is, of the interdependence between a subject and an object. Here Bitbol lays claim to ontological correlationism.

2) As a corollary, scientific propositions cannot be the account of an independent and already self-structured reality, but are the ceaselessly renewed acts of giving meaning to correlations, for example theory/experiments, observer/observed, etc. This is the principle of his epistemological correlationism. But, although he relies on Kant, Bitbol does not intend to reveal a priori and universal subjective forms that would impose their norms on an inchoate material from the outside, but rather to show how every known object is

the ever-recurring crystallization of the interaction, which is constantly modifiable, of a subjective pole and an objective pole. This epistemic thesis is established, in *Maintenant la finitude*, from an in-depth analysis of scientific practice, in particular of quantum physics, which can be explained, in his eyes, as a calculation aiming to establish the probability of our anticipations, a sort of bet that only makes sense within the techniques available to us at a given moment of scientific evolution. Moreover, science's concern to establish connections between phenomena is nothing other than a "vital need to legalize what happens" (Bitbol 2019, p. 192[1]). Hence our connections, even the most general ones, are the result of successive and always revisable attempts by a finite subject, which, forced to adapt to its environment, must increase its technical mastery in order to survive.

To this science, which he identifies with all rational knowledge, Bitbol opposes the endo-ontology that he borrows from Merleau-Ponty. This new part of phenomenology does not intend to know the being or the absolute, by objectifying it, but rather to approach its lived experience and thus to unveil a new field of investigation, that of the I "in the present of its enunciation" (Bitbol 2019, p. 111). This "I" is no longer Husserl's universal subject but becomes the individual *hic et nunc* concretely immersed in a totality in which he participates. Bitbol's epistemological doctrine, which limits rational knowledge to the scientific sphere alone, thus opens up a particular type of phenomenology which, unlike Husserl, is no longer about knowledge, no longer evaluated in terms of truth and falsity, but is similar, as Bitbol repeatedly emphasizes, to the "mysticism" of the early Wittgenstein.

This device models Bitbol's philosophical thesis about truth. At the level of rational and objective knowledge, our truth claims remain mere bets. The criterion for selecting one belief as more likely to succeed than another is that of utility. In short, Bitbol discards the realist thesis of a truth subordinate to a prior and independent reality (which I will henceforth call, for the sake of brevity, the "truth: reality" thesis) by appealing to a pragmatic criterion, namely the interest of the species in organizing a world that is ultimately possibly chaotic (which is the "truth: utility" thesis). If we now consider his conception of truth no longer at the level of objectifying reason but at the level of endo-ontology, we must recognize that the question is clearly no longer that of truth and falsehood. Following Wittgenstein's example, any assertion with a claim to truth will be therapeutically deconstructed, with a view to accessing the singular experience of the

---

[1] All translations of this book are mine.

"fulfilment of being in the living present" (Bitbol 2019, p. 150). Bitbol's project can therefore be summed up in one sentence: I had to deny knowledge in order to make room for an endo-ontology, which is neither proven nor said, but is experienced in the solitude of an irremediably singular "I".

Hence, even if the arguments of *Maintenant la finitude* against Meillassoux's realism are still striking, the fact remains that Bitbol ratifies, in spite of himself, Meillassoux's ultimate aim. Indeed, Meillassoux's argumentative strategy consisted in showing that there is no possible alternative to the opposition between, on the one hand, a realism for which reality is independent, knowable and truth-making and, on the other hand, a philosophy of the subject–object relationship, which increasingly values finitude (from Kant to Nietzsche, from Husserl to Heidegger and up to Wittgenstein) and is forced to promote various more or less sophisticated forms of epistemological relativism, inevitably leading to a non-rational approach that Meillassoux, in his Chapter 2, stigmatizes under the general term of "fideism" (Meillassoux 2008, p. 28), which, in his opinion, is the hallmark of philosophy since Kant. Because for him all idealism necessarily leads to relativism, the opposition between the two blocks, realism and correlationism, becomes inevitable: *tertium non datur*. Bitbol thus falls into the trap set by Meillassoux's realism, itself an epitome of the argumentative strategy of contemporary realists. Bitbol's consequent correlationism, apparently nourished by Kant and Husserl, leads him to a relativist conception of knowledge. And in fact, if we confront the first two theses, ontological and epistemological, the possibility of a third way seems compromised: either reality is independent of our cognitive schemas or it is not. Either we can have a knowledge of what is totally independent of us, or we must give up talking about things in themselves and only be interested in what things are for us; a world "for us" which, in the course of the rearrangements of idealism (which, in Meillassoux's eyes, have all historically proved to be relativistic) becomes a "for me", which itself inevitably metamorphoses into a singular subject "in the present of its enunciation".

Nevertheless, perhaps my above attempt to highlight the third thesis—the thesis that relates to the definition of truth—offers us a way to break out of this stranglehold.

1.2 The status of truth in contemporary discussion

Let us resume the debate by focusing on the notion of truth. On Meillassoux's side, we have a notion of truth which is always subordinated to an antecedent reality; this allows him to claim to restore a robust conception of truth and thus to have abolished any risk of relativism. Bitbol, on the other hand, renounces any strong notion of truth. Truth is only plausibility, that which works in a specific context and with regard to a specific purpose: the struggle for survival.

Meillassoux and Bitbol endorse two historical definitions of truth: "truth: reality" on the one hand and "truth: utility" on the other. Moreover, they admit, even if they do not thematize it, that truth also has to do with the notion of coherence between propositions. But for them this is a clause which, on its own, cannot fully define truth. And certainly the problem of the identification between truth and coherence is known since Plato: this truth, entirely dependent on the starting axioms which, as Hilbert said, are arbitrary, leads to a form of relativism. We therefore have three definitions of truth: "truth *qua* reality", "truth *qua* utility", "truth *qua* coherence".

Now, here again, this clarification of the definitions of truth available today seems to lead us to validate part of Meillassoux's device: if we wish to maintain a strong notion of truth, realism appears to be our only option, since "truth qua utility" and "truth qua coherence" inevitably degenerate into relativism.

But are these really the only definitions of truth at our disposal? Yes, if we follow our two authors; yes, again, if we trust Pascal Engel, who retains only these three possibilities in his book *Truth* (2000), a vast survey of the different definitions of truth in the course of the (analytic) history of philosophy; yes, finally, if we believe the odes to realism, intoned by almost all the philosophers of the last 30 years.

1.3 The fallacy on which the realist fight against relativism is based

In fact, all these realists presuppose from the outset that relativism can only be fought by restoring the notion of an independent real, which guarantees the truth of our propositions. For them, "to have" the real is automatically to recover a robust definition of truth. Affirming the real becomes the necessary and sufficient condition for fighting relativism. This is evidenced by the global dynamic of realism over the last 30 years, which has consisted in expanding the sphere of what is real and populating it, sometimes to the extreme, with the most diverse entities: from the perceived shoe (Ferraris 2012) to the essences of the analytic metaphysicians (Armstrong 1997; Tiercelin 2011) to the unicorn of flat ontology (Harman 2011). With this simple act, they believe that they have defeated correlationism in all its forms. Because it is postulated at the outset that only the real is the maker of truth, the philosophical task now consists only in filling the domain of real being by extending it ever further. "Let us find an independent real and truth will follow", such is their surreptitious presupposition. Because the history of philosophy is supposed to have made only three definitions available to us (reality, utility, coherence), embracing some form of realism has become the only way to restore a strong notion of truth and to combat the unbridled relativism of the previous era. Yet far from the realist implication that if one cannot access independent things, then no truth is possible, the whole of idealism, beyond the diversity of its concrete incarnations, has precisely the particularity of daring another strong definition of truth.

2 The idealist breakthrough

2.1 The common structure to all idealisms

Is there a univocal definition of idealism? One could be forgiven for doubting this, since even specialists in the field acknowledge that this term is attended by great confusion. To escape this impasse, we need to look at the historical occurrences of the term, and the meanings that have been attributed to it. In another text (Thomas-Fogiel 2017), I have traced the history of the meaning of this term at length, since its creation in 1702, and followed the tribulations of its use through the texts of authors who identify themselves as "idealist". Kant was the first philosopher to declare himself "idealist"; before him, the term had been used to designate thinkers who did not call themselves idealists: Leibniz, who inaugurated the use of the term in 1702, used it to refer to Plato and defined idealists as "the supporters of Ideas" (Leibniz 1994 [1702], p. 198) as opposed to those of matter (the materialists). Wolff and then Diderot use it to designate Berkeley (who never called himself an idealist); D'Argens, Baumgarten, Tetens and some others extend it to the doctrines of Leibniz and Malebranche. In short, before Kant, no one called himself an idealist. A study of Kant's use of the term "idealist" (both in his pre-critical works, wherein he speaks of idealism in general, and in his critical works, wherein he claims for himself a particular type of idealism that he calls "transcendental"), clearly shows that he defines idealism (non-transcendental and transcendental) from its strict etymology: the idea and more precisely in his case: ideality, a term that allows him to dissociate himself from both Plato's Ideas and the ideas of the empiricists, which are only associated with the psychological representations of an empirical subject. Whether in Leibniz's proponents of Ideas or in Kant's proponents of ideality, the term "idealism" is never dissociated from its strict etymology. It is this same etymological definition of idealism that Hegel puts forward, for whom the use of the term "idealism" is always correlated with the notion of ideality (Tinland 2013, p. 9). Certainly, Hegel's conception of ideality is different from Kant's, since ideality no longer refers to the normativity of a subjective instance but becomes the immanent characteristic of life in all its dimensions: "the continuous agency of life is therefore absolute idealism" (Hegel 1969–1971, vol. 9, p. 339 [2]). Nevertheless, a longer historical investigation can demonstrate this permanence of the definition in all authors who declared themselves idealists, from Kant to Fichte, from Schelling to Hegel, from Bradley to Husserl. This definition of idealism is declined in four moments. I have already largely evoked the first one, namely:

1) It is the terms ideas or idealities that constitute the common genus of all idealisms, beyond their specific difference: transcendental, empirical, problematic, dogmatic in Kant, or objective, subjective and absolute in Hegel. In this way, the definition of the term idealism is not necessarily dependent on the notion of subjectivity.
2) This ideality is likely to be characterized by different dimensions which all portray a different order than the one that the contemporary realists intend to bring to light under the indeterminate term of reality. Among these dimensions, we find, first of all:
    a) a non-materiality that we can, if we want to, interpret as non-reality (*Irrealität* said Husserl 1974, p. 227), but this term would then be understood, etymologically as "non *res*", that is, a non-spatiotemporal object. To use a trivial example, addition is not a *res* but an operation that always has a certain number of properties (associativity, commutativity). This arithmetical legality is of a different order than the laws that are supposed to govern the objects of nature. Mathematical entities and the relations between them are valid regardless of the consideration of material things. Any ideality is an abstraction, in the strict sense of what is likely to retain a determinable meaning even once all reference to an existing particular has been removed: whether the triangle is isosceles or scalene is of little importance when it comes to determining its meaning or essence, i.e. the property which, if removed, would make the notion itself disappear. However, ideality does not have as its absolute opposite the term reality, in the mode: "if ideality *then* no reality". Historically, idealism is not directly opposed to all notions of reality, but to the monist and materialist metaphysical thesis that reduces all manifestations to matter or its laws. Conversely, the idealist establishes that idealities have a specific structure and a dynamic of their own, whose au-

---

[2] This translation is mine.

tonomy from material constraints alone is proclaimed. Idealism does not deny the order of reality—"the real series", as Fichte said (Fichte 1982, p. 46)—but asserts the independence of the ideal series. This is why the idealist can just as easily conceive a system in which there would be an unbridgeable gulf between the series of idealities and that of material or natural reality, as he or she can, on the contrary, posit a strict identity between the ideal and real orders, or again as he or she can envisage relations of participation, harmony, realization (ideality having to be accomplished in what is not itself), etc. Therefore, it is clear that idealism has never implied the negation of everything commonly understood as having the rank of reality (the perceived thing, the world or nature in general, matter, etc.), a foolish, albeit common, interpretation that Hegel already denounced: "If idealism is as this crude mode of representation defines it, there have in fact never been any idealists among the philosophers" (Hegel 1969–71, vol. 19, p. 11[3]). Idealism lies in the thesis of an autonomous dynamic of the ideal series. This ideality is also characterized by:

b) the possibility of accessing a specific type of temporality that could be called metatemporality, in that it is defined at least as the possibility for an ideality to be reactivated identically or re-actualized at any time.
c) an omnisubjectivity: idealities are likely to be knowable, *de jure*, by a subject wherever the place (the culture or the context) in which this subject is punctually immersed. It follows that:

3) The idealist affirms that true knowledge is possible. This is what differentiates him or her from the skepticism and relativism with which he is mistakenly associated today. An idealist is someone who maintains a strong notion of truth but who, for all that, no longer links this true knowledge to a prior ontological option that would determine the being or the real (independent and in itself) as the guarantor of a true proposition.
4) This truth is defined as the realization of universality and is thus resolutely detached from the definitions of truth previously listed. Truth is now correlated to that of universality, which itself is specified as that which is, *de jure*, valid in all places and at all times. To use a trivial example: truth in mathematics can be based on the fact that in solving a problem X, I will perform the same acts today and reach the same result as the slave-boy in *Meno* (meta-temporality and omnisubjectivity of certain mathematical operations). The question here is not to look for a being-in-itself that is independent of

---

[3] This translation is mine.

such and such an operation X or such and such a result Y, but to determine whether the operation and what results from it can claim to be repeatable at all times and in all places.

In short, there is, historically, an alternative to the challenge set by all contemporary realism: either embrace ontological realism or renounce the notion of truth, which, without the support of the independent thing, would be condemned to disappear or dwindle into probability or utility. Moreover, not only has the history of philosophy offered us, with the idealists, another definition of truth, but the very approach of the realists attests, albeit against their will, to the strength of this definition.

2.2 "All philosophy is idealist, or it is not philosophy": The proof by the realists

Polarized on the unique notion of reality, the restoration of which is supposed to resolve all philosophical impasses that modernity has bequeathed to us since Kant and postulating from the outset that this reality makes the truth, the realists have hardly dwelt on the possible aporias of their conception of truth. Of the many aporias, I will mention only the most serious.

First of all, their definition may seem empty, since it does not tell us how we can concretely apply it. From it we cannot answer the question: How do I know that my statement says the truly independent thing? By what means, then, can we list what is real and what is not: matter but not unicorn, caloric but not phlogiston? We would have a definition of truth but would not be able to derive any criteria of truth from it.

But even more seriously, if we remain at the level of the definition of truth alone, it seems circular. Indeed, to say that our proposition is true by the nature of a real X implies that we must first determine what this "real" or independent fact consists of. Therefore, we must first identify the external fact as "real" before we can have any definition of truth. However, determining what this fact or reality is presupposes that we do so in a true manner; but in order to do so in a true manner, we must have already determined the fact, since it is what makes our statement true, etc. In short, this subordination of the truth of the proposition to an external and independent X, however trivial it may be, is by no means self-evident once analyzed. "So one goes round in a circle. Consequently, it is probable that the content of the word " true " is unique and indefinable", sighed Frege (Frege 1956, p.291), who was not readily suspected of relativism.

Finally, the definition of truth as universality is, in fact, at the heart of the philosophical practice of the realists themselves. Indeed, what do they claim when they define truth as subordinate to reality? They claim the truth of this definition, it being understood that they cannot, without sinking into relativism, accept the idea that their definition is only valid for them, their tribe or their society. But this truth which the realist claims by giving this definition only makes sense as the "truth: universality" (valid in all places and at all times) and not the "truth: reality" (in conformity with an independent X). To claim: "the truth of a proposition is subordinate to an independent *res*" is not comparable to the kind of truth one claims by saying: "the cat is on the doormat". To decide whether or not to validate the latter proposition is, of course, to refer to the external fact and to note that it is indeed, for the moment, i.e. in the particular time and place where I am stating it, as my proposition says it is ("now, it is night", etc.). But for the definition: all truth is subordinate to an external fact, I cannot say that this proposition is true because it conforms to an external fact. In short, truth is conformity to an external fact, except for this definition of truth. What the realists say—their *Sagen*, as Fichte said (1986)—has as its content the definition of truth as subordinate to a reality X, but what they do (their *Tun*) is to implement surreptitiously another definition of truth, namely: my definition of truth is valid in all places and at all times. Their whole position thus sinks into pragmatic or reflexive contradictions, unless they remove all notion of truth from their vocabulary. They always presuppose another definition of truth than the one on which they base their realism. By doing so, they relativize or even cancel the content of their own definition and thereby attest to the impossibility of presenting only one face of truth ("truth: reality"). This is why contemporary realists, in their inevitable claim to universality, seem to be another possible illustration of Hegel's proposition that "all philosophy is idealist, or it is not philosophy". Faced with this pragmatic contradiction that collapses the central pillar that supports any realist edifice (the real as truth-maker), it becomes clear that maintaining a strong notion of truth does not necessarily imply the notion of real, independent things or of being-in-itself, but can also be authorized by the notion of universality. Universality is not what is there, given, first, outside and without us, but what is defined as valid, *de jure*, at all times and in all places. Universality is not a correct proposition at the moment when I say it, in the place (context) where I am, it is not found but becomes what is to be realized (Fichte) or has to happen (Hegel) at the end of a process or a rational dynamic (whether this dynamic is conceived as that of a subjective instance, as in Husserl, or as the very movement of the totality, as in Hegel). Truth as universality, the key to all idealism, is thus paradoxically revealed to be that which is always already presupposed by realist philosophers insofar as they philosophize, i.e. insofar as they claim to give a definition of truth and not merely to list particular and punctual contents without end.

The impossibility of the contemporary realist position about "truth" having been demonstrated, it remains to consider the fecundity of the idealist definition of truth. Are we too going to turn in a circle and find no criteria to apply it?

3 Ideality, universality, truth

3.1 Do idealities exist independently of us? A futile question

Great are the dangers lurking in this definition of truth as universality. I will limit myself here to the most general ones, in order to remove some suspicions about its viability.

The first would be to produce a theory of the universality that is merely an amplification of "truth: reality". We would say, for example, that exists Idealities X (the triangle, humanity, etc.) in general and that individuals are the concrete instantiations of this already existing "type" or "genre". We would judge the conformity of such concrete groups or individuals by this abstract and unchanging measure and in so doing assume the classical notion of truth as the adequacy of our judgment to a prior being-in-itself. It is this movement of reification of idealities that has led some to say that Husserl professed a realism of essences or that Platonism could be read as a realism of Ideas.

However, it is by no means inevitable that the question of a real resurfaces at a higher level, i.e. that of the idealities. Indeed, when faced with an ideal, the question is not whether an independent being corresponds to it but whether it is valid in all places and at all times. An ideality can be said to be true if and only if it is valid in all places and at all times, but false, incomplete—or not yet true—in the opposite case. Its characteristic is not to exist in an independent world but to remain identical whatever the time and place in which it has been understood or will be actualized again. The Pythagorean theorem can be said to be true because it is reproducible in the same terms today as yesterday. Therefore, whether a philosopher, such as Frege, after having established the universality of this theorem decides to posit a third realm to house the idealities that he identifies, or, on the contrary, another philosopher refuses to hypostatize these X's by extraposing them in a world independent of us, changes absolutely nothing since this has no incidence on their possibility of being true or false. In both cases, the characteristic "being true" will precede the question of reference as being independent or not.

But a question which, no matter how it is answered, does not change the nature of the theory being examined is a meaningless question, even futile. More exactly, it can only have relevance at a level other than that of truth, since the truth of X can be determined prior to answering this question.

In fact, the problem was only posed because one remained implicitly attached to "truth: reality": there must be a being independent of us who makes the truth ("truth-maker") of our proposition. But the question that arises concerning ideality is not that of its independent being, but that of its universality. The question of universality is prior; it precedes any determination of reality or being-in-itself. If such and such a proposition (the theorem) is universal, then, in the end, it is of little concern where it is, as long as I continue to examine the question of its truth.

This is why we must not confuse the universality whose fruitfulness I am trying to test with the theory of "universals" from the Middle Ages. Let us assume, by following temporarily an empiricist hypothesis, that the triangle just like "horsehood" or humanity are concepts produced by the human species for the purpose of pure utility, and generated by abstraction from the finite given (such as this horse in front of me); an abstraction that we then take, by a reflexive gesture, as an object of analysis. These concepts, even if produced in this way, can claim the status of idealities, because if the problem of their truth or falsity is at stake, the first question to ask is not whether these concepts exist somewhere, but whether they can be the object of a proposition of the type: the triangle or humanity is in all places and times X and not Y. I first determine the "truth: universality" of X, then I may or may not ask the question of where these concepts exist (in nature, in an intelligible world, in my mind?), taking care, however, that the question "where?" is not a trap when it comes to ruling on *what* is in all places. In short, the question of the truth of the concept precedes the question of its reality outside me. Moreover, this question precedes the question of whether truth is in the subject, because it does not have to be bothered with questions of "prior" or "posterior" to me, intern or extern, of linked or unlinked, questions which, conversely, suppose that one surreptitiously reintroduces the subject–object duality as the primary frame of reference: what is prior *to* my cognitive schemes, what is external *to* the human species, what is before us?, etc. The independent reality of the realists, because it is always determined from these notions of anterior and posterior (cosmological time which precedes human time, in Meillassoux), and of exterior to me ("the great outdoors"), implies the implicit acceptance of the subject–object duality in order to be defined. The question of the truth of idealities, on the contrary, is independent of this duality. Therefore, Meillassoux, with his relational notions (anterior, exterior), cannot go beyond the general framework of the subject/object opposition; on the other hand, Hegel seems better able to transcend it since his notion of truth does not presuppose it.

But, the reader will object, even if one were to concede that there are fewer vicious circles or contradictions in the idealist definition than in the realist one, the question of the criterion of truth remains. We use, you say, concepts which are general because they abstract from the particular in order to retain only the most essential determination. These concepts can also be articulated according to a precise dynamic (whether it is called life or law). Among this multiplicity of general concepts that we use (starting with the word itself, which is already an abstraction), those that can be reactivated at any time and in any place without undergoing decisive modifications (e. g. Pythagoras' theorem), or those for which we can establish the law of transformation can claim the rank of idealities. But then how will you determine that you are dealing with an ideality that you can claim is universal, and not with an incomplete abstraction, variable or changing according to the contexts? By what criteria or procedures are you going to posit that humanity is X and not Y without being contradicted by various alternative solutions, such as saying that "humanity is X" is not a proposition that applies at all times and in all places but the expression of a dominant and colonialist society? or again that "the essence of the triangle is to be a three-sided figure" can be said to be true only by virtue of its definition alone, as can the "unmarried bachelor" ; there is no ideality here but the simple use of a conventional sign.

Finally, the notion of universal (that which holds good in all places and at all times) seems to bring with it the notions of completeness and totality which are closed. By what criteria can you claim to have attained it?

3.2 The process of universalization

In order to answer, a few clarifications are required. Each of them would deserve a more in-depth treatment but I can only suggest them, in the context of this article.

1) The notion of universality does not intrinsically refer to the notion of a closed and completed totality but is also linked to that of an "unlimited domain". Brice Halimi (2013, p. 7) proposes this definition, which can be found as the first entry many ordinary dictionaries. There is no obligation to privilege one dimension over another.
2) Just as the universality I am trying to apprehend differs significantly from the medieval model of the "universals", so it does not fall under the definition of the universal given by certain analytical philosophers. In the wake of Frege, the universal is, for them, the form of a judgment: "to be a man im-

plies to be mortal", i.e. whatever x is, if x is Man, then x is Mortal". It is a logical form of judgment (conditional, as we can see) among others (for example, singular judgment: "Socrates is Greek"). In this case, the universal is said to be simply logical or theoretical, and the broader notion of universality is relegated to the practical domain, which is considered irrelevant when it comes to questioning the truth. Nevertheless, nothing obliges us to confine reflection on the notion of universality to the logical analysis of judgment. To say that the Pythagorean theorem is true because it can be repeated in the same terms and with the same results today as yesterday is not to say that the theorem has the form: "for all X, if etc." Aristotle, so much appreciated by contemporary realists, uses the term "universal" in two distinct senses, one in the *Metaphysics* (universality), the other in the *Analytics* (logical type of judgment), without commentators feeling obliged to say that only the one in the *Analytics* is admissible, making the other one the chimerical ideal of poets.

3) Moreover, as previously demonstrated, knowing that the question of the independent thing outside of us is irrelevant for judging the truth of a proposition, I am entitled, in what follows, to take as my guiding thread what is usually called the order of thought. I will therefore ask the following question: why not focus our attention on the process of universalization, i.e. on what is required to form the universal? So let us change our perspective, and rather than start by trying to directly fill the notion of universality with an X that could exemplify it, let us focus on the conditions that allow its formation. In short, let us look at the dynamics of universalization.

Universalization requires an operation that consists, at least, in expanding the finite given by going beyond it. Many everyday judgments could not take place without this process of enlarging the limits, which we can define as the infinitization of the finite. This is the process we find exemplarily at work in the act of rising from the singular (Socrates, here, at such and such a moment) to the particular (Socrates' friends as a group of a few people, here, at such and such a moment), to the universal (humanity, and therefore what is beyond the "here" and "now"). Here again, the operation consists in going beyond what is given to me (Socrates, such and such a group), in transcending the particular in order to infinitize the finite. Of course, in this maximizing process, through which I move from Socrates to humanity, we cannot fulfill our expectations through the effective apprehension of the totality. Indeed, I am confronted with the unlimited, whereas in the enlargement process that I engage in by saying there is a cube (beyond the facets that are given to me), I can stop the process by going, for instance, around the cube. The difference is certainly radical, but as

I have said, I am concerned with the process that underlies the possibility of forming a universal, which is, for the moment, simply an aim. Universal is, strictly speaking, an ideal. The act or condition required is thus an aggrandizing movement towards a required but not given universality. Because this enlargement consists in increasing the perspectives and moving back the imposed limits, universalization can be defined as the dynamics of the envelopment of different elements in a space that is not given.

Following from this highlighting of the conditions of formation of the universal, it seems justified to say that the universal is, at the very least, the space of envelopment to be realized (or to come) in order to pluralize perspectives, i.e. to put oneself in new place than one's own, and through this act to move beyond one's finite perspective. By thought, I aim at a space greater than the one given to me (my tribe) and this aiming leads to a process of unlimiting limits.

3.3 The criterion of truth

Now, and this is what is decisive, this process of unlimiting limits and perspective pluralization may well be exactly that which fulfills the aim of universality and attests to or refutes its accomplishment. Indeed, a process of universalization can be said to be more or less well carried out. Taking aim at universality does not condemn us to failure (as in the case of the "bad infinity" denounced by Hegel), but it does give us a precise methodical rule: to determine the degree of encompassment of a judgment or a theory and to evaluate them by this standard. Thus, if the judgment or theory excludes more than it integrates, if it constantly assumes, in order to build itself up, an "other" that it is not and relegates it to nothingness, the conception will lack universality and may be disqualified. In this sense, different theories or judgments can be ordered according to truth, according to their greater or lesser degree of universality, i.e. according to their capacity to encompass, to welcome and not to reject or exclude.

Consequently, considering this process of forming the universal provides us with a criterion, a rule, a means of fulfilling our aim, i.e. of realizing the ideal and honoring our claim to universality. The aspiration for universality is no longer a simple demand condemned to failure but an ideal that can be realized, accomplished. Let us give a concrete illustration of this process of universalization within a field of knowledge, namely mathematics.

Indeed, many of their procedures can exemplify this theoretical activity that always expands and thus infinitizes the finite. When we are examining different paradigms (e.g. Euclidean and then non-Euclidean geometry) we are not obliged to declare the former theory entirely false in itself, but rather to push back the limits of the previous space, in order to encompass, in a wider space, each universe (Euclidean, non-Euclidean). This is, for example, what Felix Klein did in the 1870s in his *Erlangen programm*. It is a question of creating a new intelligible space in which to situate the various propositions, without making them absolute or fixed contradictions or denying their differences and particularities. The truth of a mathematical theory is judged less by what it says about a referent, external and already structured without us, than by the theory's capacity to encompass different particular points of view, by making them neighbors. To achieve this, it is always necessary to modify and reconfigure the space that accommodates these different particulars, by enlarging it. It is this ability to integrate and expand that can be considered a criterion of truth; corollary to this, the error is to declare a particular state (e.g. Euclidean geometry) as definitive and "in itself". Error consists in freezing, fixing, closing; truth, in widening, encompassing, disenclosing. Error is linked to finiteness, truth to infinitization. The fact that the sciences are evolving does not mean that we are, by nature, missing our object (because of radical finitude), but that we are expanding it more and more, pushing back its limits. Knowledge, in this example, is not so much unfinished since it positively "unfinishes" what is initially finite and given. This operation of "unfinishing", in the sense of always going beyond the fixed limits, the established codes, the bounded given, signals the entry into a process of truth. Claiming truth consists in wanting to encompass more and more and to exclude less and less. Truth itself is attested to or recognized by the enlargement that has taken place. It is not absurd, indeed it is necessary, to measure the validity of a theory by its capacity to encompass, and by contrast, its poverty by the number of things it excludes. Consequently, the notion of universality in no way condemns us to the frenzied pursuit of a chimera but it is the very thing that permits us to inaugurate a process of knowledge and truth. Through the notion of the unlimited we can produce, in the different fields of knowledge (whether theoretical, practical, historical, political, etc.) a series of judgments to be ordered according to their greater or lesser capacity to be universalized. Universality thus becomes this ever-widening space that we must constantly shape in order to make differences coexist, without reducing them to a simple identity or freezing them into absolute contradictions. Truth even becomes synonymous with this process of enlargement and infinitization. Each ideality as moments or figures of universality (Euclid's geometry, Riemann, etc.) tends to be encompassed again in a wider space. "When one speaks of the absolute idea, one can think that here finally the substantive must come to the fore, that here everything must become clear. One can, to be sure, vacuously spout on end about the absolute idea" (Hegel 2010, p. 300). "Vacuously spout about" because true knowledge is not attained where we "see" an ultimate entity but resides in the process of infinitization itself.

No doubt the reader will think that we have reached the precise moment when we fall under the objection that Schelling and Hegel made to Fichte. In considering the process of the idealization and formation of universality, we have analyzed the movement by which thought forms this notion. Remaining in the realm of thought, we have renounced any philosophy of nature and again introduced a gulf between the world of the subject (thought) and that of the object (matter). But in what way would it be irremediably mad to take as a hypothesis to be tested that nature, like thought, could have something to do with the notion of infinity, if we want to create a philosophy of nature or rely on sciences of nature? It is no madder than to start from the principle that nature is contingency (Meillassoux). From a philosophical point of view, these two very general hypotheses can claim the same dignity. If we wanted to create a philosophy of nature, we would have to ask ourselves which one is more fruitful. It is certain that the hypothesis that there is a process of infinitization of the finite (for example, a punctual x in continuous expansion, to use a metaphor) or, conversely, of finitization of the infinite (an individualization of X from a larger space), is only a conceptual possibility, but it is no less so than is the contingency of matter. Moreover, even if we wanted to keep Meillassoux's idea (and that of current physics), that mathematics can better express nature outside of us, how could taking infinity and infinitization as a starting point be less fruitful than the thesis of a radical contingency of everything? These two hypotheses are not contradictory, we simply have to establish their greater or lesser fruitfulness if we want to create a philosophy of nature.

However, the debate about the philosophy of nature is not over, and I had no intention, in this article, of claiming that it was. I only intended to suggest the possibilities for future reflection that the idealist path has outlined.

4 Conclusion

At the end of this journey, the weakness of the dilemma realism/correlationism, in which contemporary realism has sought to confine philosophical debate, is clear. Surreptitiously assuming a single definition of truth, realists leave out the notion of universality, by which all idealists have defined the notion of truth. In this refusal of universality, our contemporary realists paradoxically find themselves in perfect agreement with the relativism of the 1970s. Both give up the ideal of universality. The conception of truth, suggested to us by the idealist opening, allows three results:

1) It allows us to relativize the realist definition of truth, as an expression of a particular outside of myself. If this ordinary and narrow definition of truth as correctness (i.e., as conformity to a thing) does not have to be challenged in all circumstances, it must nevertheless not be absolutized, as realists do. Reconnecting with universality as truth allows us to situate this ordinary conception of correctness on a relevant level, and thus to encompass it in a wider sphere, whereas the reverse is not possible: subordinating the theory of truth to a fact would exclude any coherent recourse to the ideal. To think in accordance with truth is not only to observe "what is the case" (correctness), nor simply to have a grip on what is already there, but to think is also to produce new spaces, to open up new worlds, and to do so, to unfinish the given, the finite, the real. In short, thinking according to truth consists in accomplishing universality, which requires the implementation of acts or processes that can be rigorously defined and verified.

2) It allows us to overcome the theory/practice split. The maxim: do not exclude but always seek to enlarge by bringing together particulars, is a requirement of theoretical as well as of practical thinking and a criterion of its truth. To tie truth back to an ideal (universality) allows us to no longer confine the procedures of truth to the only disciplines that would have to deal with facts (for example physics) while others (for example ethics) would be relegated to the sphere of conventions whose rules we would be content to apply.

3) It allows us to overcome the tragic figure of a humanity condemned to pursue an inaccessible ideal (truth), and thereby authorizes us to dare to think beyond finitude, without, however, like Meillassoux, rushing towards a supposedly salvific great outdoors. It is thanks to the ideal (as a claim to universality) that we can implement the process of infinitization and arrive, by its very effectuation, at a concrete truth in such and such a domain, theoretical or practical. Certainly, and ultimately the desire for truth as universality (as an ideal) could disappear and with it the whole philosophical activity of humanity. We could very well return to a state where it would only be a question of us as individuals and our immediate environment; we could return to the finiteness of the given, to the narrowness of what is. The claim to truth as a concern for universality is in fact a nondeductible instance because it is independent of any antecedent. The notions of "independence" and therefore the "absolute" do not characterize the thing, but freedom. In this sense, the real name of the absolute is not contingency of nature, but freedom of mind. Nevertheless, once this claim to universality has been asserted, its success or failure obeys precise rules: to infinitize the finite, to widen the space of perspectives in order to open up new dimensions that will be

authentic places of truth and hospitality. While the world does hold different places, philosophy must preserve a single home, that of truth. This is the ideal of universality.

Bibliography

Armstrong, D. M. (1997): *A World of State Affairs*. Cambridge: Cambridge University Press.
Bitbol, Michel (2019): *Maintenant la finitude*. Paris: Flammarion.
Engel, Pascal (2000): *Truth*. London: Routledge.
Ferraris, Maurizio (2012): *Manifesto del nuovo realismo*. Rome and Bari: Laterza.
Fichte, Johann Gottlieb (1982): *Wissenschaftslehre nova methodo*. Hamburg: Meiner.
Fichte, Johann Gottlieb (1986): *Die Wissenschaftslehre: Zweiter Vortrag im Jahre 1804*. Hamburg: Meiner.
Frege, Gottlob (1956): *The Thought: A Logical Inquiry*. Translated by P. T. Geach: Mind, New Series, Vol. 65, No. 259. Oxford University Press.
Halimi, Brice (2013): *Le nécessaire et l'universel: analyse et critique de leur corrélation*. Paris: Vrin.
Harman, Graham (2011): *The Quadruple Object*. Winchester: Zero Books.
Hegel, Georg Wilhelm Friedrich (1969–1971): *Werke*. 20 vols. Edited by Eva Moldenhauer und Karl Markus Michel. Frankfurt am Main: Suhrkamp.
Hegel, Georg Wilhelm Friedrich (2010): *Encyclopedia of the Philosophical Sciences in Basic Outline, Part I: Science of Logic*. Translated by Klaus Brinkmann and Daniel O. Dahlstrom. Cambridge: Cambridge University Press.
Husserl, Edmund (1974): *Formale und transzendentale Logik: Versuch einer Kritik der logischen Vernunft* (Husserliana, vol. 17). Haag: M. Nijhoff.
Leibniz, Gottfried Wilhelm: (1994 [1702]): *Système de la nature et de la communication des substances et autres textes*. Paris: Flammarion.
Meillassoux, Quentin (2008): *After Finitude: An Essay on the Necessity of Contingency*. Translated by Ray Brassier. London and New York: Continuum.
Meillassoux, Quentin (2012): *Principe du signe creux*. Ecole normale supérieure de Paris. https://www.youtube.com/watch?v=Ic8h23MNVWU, visited on 1 November 2021.
Thomas-Fogiel, Isabelle (2017): "L'Opposition entre réalisme et idéalisme? Genèse et structure d'un contresens". In: *Revue de métaphysique et de morale* 95. No. 3, pp. 393–426.
Tiercelin, Claudine (2011): *Le ciment des choses: Petit traité de métaphysique scientifique réaliste*. Paris: Ithaque.
Tinland, Olivier (2013): *L'idéalisme hégélien*. Paris: CNRS.

Paul Guyer
A Typology of Idealism

Abstract: Kant conceived of idealism as the view that only minds exist, as did other eighteenth-century philosophers, both those who accepted idealism under some name and those who rejected it. In view of this definition, Kant denied that he was an idealist, and was right to do so. But there is another tradition in idealism, going back to Plato, according to which matter as well as mind exists, but mind or the mind-like is more real or more valuable than matter. Kant's idealism is part of this tradition, although he comes to it on practical rather than theoretical grounds.

a) Introduction

Samuel Johnson thought to refute Berkeley by kicking a stone and feeling the ensuing pain. Surely that temptation must have occurred to all of us at some time, even though Dr. Johnson's "refutation" is riddled with problems—to start with a conundrum that must also occur to us all: how could Berkeley have felt Johnson's pain? There does seem to be something ridiculous about idealism. Yet it is also a recurring theme in the history of philosophy that must have some truth buried in it.

I say "theme" rather than "thesis" or "position" because there have been many ideas that have sailed under the flag of idealism, some more *outré* than others and some more plausible than others.[1] My first aim in this paper is to provide some classification. I do not want to say immediately classification of *types* of idealism, because my argument will be that we must distinguish types of *arguments for* idealism as well as types of idealism itself. Following A. C. Ewing, we can distinguish epistemological from metaphysical arguments for idealism (see Ewing 1934, ch. II). But we can also distinguish monistic from dualistic versions of idealism itself: the former is the view that nothing exists except minds and their ideas, the latter that there is matter as well as mind, or ideas, but that the latter are in some way or ways more real or important than the latter, the sort of view that does not deny the existence of matter but holds, in Ewing's

---
[1] Nicholas Stang writes that "there is a certain historical naivety (*sic*) in thinking that 'idealism' means one particular doctrine" (Stang 2017, p. 100).

Paul Guyer, Brown University.

words, that "spiritual values have a determining voice in the ordering of the universe" (Ewing 1934, p. 3).² In principle, then, there are at least four possible types of idealism: monistic idealism arrived at by epistemological arguments, monistic idealism arrived at by metaphysical arguments, dualistic idealism arrived at by epistemological arguments, and dualistic idealism arrived at by metaphysical arguments. In what follows I adduce examples of each of these. But there is one more possibility that I will mention, namely that a dualistic idealism might be advanced on practical grounds rather than any theoretical grounds at all, epistemological or metaphysical. This possibility must be recognized if Kant's overall philosophical position is to be counted as any version of idealism.

One version of idealism, famously associated with the aforementioned Bishop Berkeley, although he himself called it "immaterialism", is that all that exists are ideas and the minds or spirits that have them, in his case both finite minds like human minds and an infinite mind, the mind of God. This is how Berkeley's contemporaries such as Christian Wolff and Alexander Gottlieb Baumgarten understood idealism, and it is also how Kant defined idealism antecedent to his own, although none of these German philosophers endorsed idealism so understood. One who did, however, at least in some expositions of his philosophy, is Leibniz, but the view has also had later defenders, notably the British philosopher J. McT. E. McTaggart, the teacher of G. E. Moore and Bertrand Russell, in the early twentieth century.³ But an alternative position that is also reasonably called idealism is that there is another type of existent than minds and their ideas, call it matter, but—and here is the difference between this version of idealism and mind-body dualism *sans phrase*—non-material reality is in some way *more* real than mere matter, or in some way more important than the latter. This is the idealism of Plato and Hegel, of the British idealists whose views Ewing did not want to discuss—and of Kant.⁴ But Kant's view, insofar as it is

---

2 Stang continues the passage previously quoted thus: "Originally coined to refer to the Platonic view that what is ultimately real are 'ideas'—intelligible archetypes of which sensible objects are imperfect replicas—'idealism' came to mean, in the early modern period, the view that everything ontologically depends on minds and their ideas (states). This is correlated with a shift in the meaning of 'idea' itself: from intelligible Platonic archetypes (*eidos*) to the immediately available mental contents (often sensible ones) of the early modern 'way of ideas'" (Stang 2017, p. 100).
3 It is also the version of idealism recently defended by Aaron Segal and Tyron Goldschmidt, who write that "Idealism is the view that the world is in some sense mental. But not just mental: *thoroughly* mental, *wholly* mental, mental *through-and-through*" (Segal/Goldschmidt 2017, p. 35).
4 A contemporary statement of this form of idealism is offered by Thomas Hofweber: "The real issue about idealism is not simply about matter and how it relates to minds, but about the place of minds in reality. Idealism is better seen as a label for the vision that minds are central in re-

to be considered dualistic idealism in this sense, does not depend on theoretical considerations, such as what I will suggest are the metaphysical arguments of Plato and the epistemological arguments of Hegel, but on practical grounds. My underlying assumption is that it is only in that form that idealism would be worth defending, but I will not attempt to argue that large point in this primarily classificatory paper.[5]

The dividing line between metaphysical and epistemological modes of argumentation for idealism may not always be entirely sharp. Nevertheless, the general difference between them will be clear enough. We will see, for example, that some of Berkeley's arguments for his immaterialism are metaphysical, in the sense that they turn on claims about the nature of things, while others are epistemological in character, turning on claims about the possibility of knowledge. Leibniz's arguments for the reality only of monads and God, that is, for his version of the view that all that is real is mind, are clearly metaphysical, and McTaggart's arguments for the unreality of time and for the reality only of mind are likewise clearly metaphysical. As for the other idealist ontology, that matter as well as mind or something more like mind than like matter are both real, but the latter is more real than the former, Plato's arguments are both metaphysical and epistemological, at least if his myth of pre-natal acquaintance of how we know the Forms can be considered epistemological, while Hegel's argument is more purely epistemological, turning on the claim that the history of human knowledge is the history of the *self-knowledge* of spirit, that is, the phenomenology of spirit. Finally, Kant's basic argument for the thesis of transcendental idealism that space and time and everything in them are mere appearance is clearly epistemological, but this does not lead him to deny the existence of something real outside our ideas and minds, and thus to what he would regard as idealism, namely monistic idealism. He does end up with a version of dualistic idealism,

---

ality. In particular, on the idealist vision, minds are metaphysically central for reality" (Hofweber 2017, p. 125).

5 One possible form, or family of forms, of idealism that I will not consider here is what may be called conceptual or linguistic idealism. This has been a common view in twentieth-century philosophy of many stripes, from Cassirer in the 1920s to Collingwood in the 1930s to much analytic philosophy. Two recent versions of it are offered by Nicholas Stang, who interprets Kant's transcendental idealism, and counts it as a genuine version of idealism, as the view that what concepts we can have are limited by what intuitions we can have (Stang 2017), and Thomas Hofweber, who argues that what facts there are and what is the case, as opposed simply to what is, is determined by our, human language (Hofweber 2017). I believe that these positions are trivially true and do not have genuine metaphysical implications of either the monistically idealist or dualistically idealist sort. But I will not attempt to demonstrate that here.

but, as I have said, on practical grounds rather than any theoretical grounds at all.

b) Idealist dualism: Mind is more real than matter

To keep some kind of chronological order, let's begin with the version of idealism that we can associate with both Plato and Hegel, the view that does not deny the reality of matter but that considers some form of mind or something mind-like more real and/or more important than mere matter—the view that I have called dualistic idealism, or what we might also call something like "mind-emphasizing dualism".

One clarification: Plato's Forms, as they now tend to be called, or in the older, more literal translation, "Ideas" (*eidōs*), are definitely not material, but he does not seem to think of them as states of mind, accidents of mental substances, representations in or by a mind, or in any of the ways that ideas have been conceived in modern philosophy. They exist apart from minds, certainly any ordinary minds, as well as apart from matter, although the nature of their existence is not otherwise specified. That may well have seemed an untenable position to later philosophers who were attracted to the Forms but could understand them only as properties or products of some mind or *nous*, for example as emanations of the divine mind in Neo-Platonism. Still, that they are not material is enough to make them ideal for Plato, if not ideas in a modern sense—ideas in Locke's sense, or representations (*Vorstellungen*) in Kant's. What I want to emphasize here, however, is that Plato never denies that there are ordinary objects like rocks and tables, but he does think that the Forms are more perfect and more real than these. He, or his Socrates, has metaphysical arguments for that position, and then adds an epistemological supplement, namely that we could not have acquired knowledge that we clearly do have from acquaintance with merely material objects. We might regard this as the inference from knowledge of necessary truth to *a priori* knowledge in its most elementary form.

As Plato presents the theory of Forms in dialogues such as *Phaedo* and the *Republic*, his emphasis is that they have a kind of perfection that their material counterparts can never have, and thus cannot be any kind of material objects; in the *Meno* he adds his epistemological argument that since knowledge of such extraordinary objects cannot be acquired by ordinary acquaintance with physical objects, it must have been acquired, by acquaintance with the Forms themselves, in a pre-natal and better existence, then forgotten upon (or in the trauma of) birth, but is able to be recaptured by proper questioning and reasoning in response. The argument for the Forms is that, for example, ordinary equal things, such as sticks and stones equal in length or size, can "appear to one to be equal and to another to be unequal", because they are only approximately equal, but the Equal itself, or as we would say, though it might not carry Plato's connotation of self-predication, equality, cannot be both equal and unequal (*Phaedo* 74b–c; Plato 1997, p. 65). It is neither approximately equal nor changeable in any way, thus from equal to unequal or back again. It is a better form of equality than that of ordinary, physical objects, thus it is the very Form of equality itself. The idea of the perfection of the Forms greater than that of any ordinary physical object is expressed in the *Republic* by the metaphor of the cave: our ordinary acquaintance with physical objects is at multiple removes; in the cave where we humans normally live, we are acquainted only with flickering shadows of objects that are themselves crude copies of the more real and perfect objects that exist outside the cave, fully illuminated by the sun instead of by the mere flames of torches—but that realm is not really physical, but itself a metaphor for the kind of truth that can be reached only by reasoning. The ultimate Form is the Form of the good, for each Form is the form of a good or the best version of what it is, but it is not a visible object known by acquaintance; it is an intelligible object known by reasoning.

> The visible realm should be likened to the prison dwelling ... And if you interpret the upward journey and the study of things above as the upward journey of the soul to the intelligible realm, you'll grasp what I hope to convey ... In the knowable realm, the Form of the good is the last thing to be seen, and it is reached only with difficulty. (*Republic*, Book VIII, 517b; Plato 1997, p. 1135)

This is because it is not *seen* at all, but can only be reached by difficult reasoning.

This reasoning, however, is not merely dialectic, or a kind of argumentation, but is ultimately some sort of insight or intuition, what Plato calls *noēsis*. This is because his model of knowledge is knowledge by acquaintance. But his underlying assumption is that ordinary acquaintance with physical objects won't do, *because physical objects won't do:* that is, they don't have the degree of perfection that we nevertheless know the Forms to have. So this knowledge must be some sort of non-sensory acquaintance with something non-physical, such as the pre-natal knowledge that the slave boy has of geometry in the *Meno*, which "If he has not acquired ... in his present state", he must have "learned them at some other time" (*Meno* 82b–86a; Plato 1997, pp. 882–886), or the *noēsis* of the *Republic*. One point to note here is that Plato never seems to think that a Form such as the Form of equality is a *construct* or *product* of an ordinary mind; it cannot be constructed out of the materials available to an ordinary mind because those materials never have the perfection that the Form has. The idea that we ourselves could idealize the perfect out of our experience of the imperfect is not part of Plato's model. The Forms must be something nonphysical and therefore not imperfect. Yet they must be available to the ordinary mind by *some* kind of acquaintance, because that is Plato's model of knowledge-acquisition, although again not ordinary sensory acquaintance, because that is always acquaintance with the imperfect. Finally, this epistemology cannot be considered an epistemological argument *for* Plato's form of idealism—the doctrine that there are Forms more perfect than any merely physical reality, although it does not deny the admittedly lesser existence of ordinary physical reality—but is rather the *consequence* of Plato's version of idealism. Any form of idealism requires some form of epistemology, but the latter is not necessarily an epistemological argument for idealism.

Hegel also affirms the greater reality of mind—"spirit"—without denying the reality of physical objects, but his argument, or perhaps better approach, is more directly epistemological than Plato's. His famous slogan, from the Preface to the *Philosophy of Right*, that "What is rational is actual, and what is actual is rational", which indeed he presents as a description of Plato's own philosophy, might suggest that nothing exists that is not rational, so if rationality and physical existence are ontologically distinct, the latter is nevertheless entirely permeated by the former (Hegel 1991, Preface, p. 20). In fact, Hegel explicitly says that he does *not* mean that everything that exists is rational. He does hold that

> the rational, which is synonymous with the Idea, becomes actual by entering into external existence [Existenz], it emerges in an infinite wealth of forms, appearances, and shapes and surrounds its core with a brightly coloured covering in which consciousness at first resides, but which only the concept can penetrate in order to find the inner pulse, and detect its continued beat even within the external shapes. But the infinitely varied circumstances which take shape within this externality as the essence manifests itself within it, this infinite material and its organization, are not the subject-matter of philosophy. To deal with them would be to interfere in things with which philosophy has no concern ... (Hegel 1991, Preface, p. 21)

Hegel makes fun of Plato for getting into the details of child-rearing and of Fichte for detailing passport regulations; these things are not philosophical, for they involve too much contingency to be entirely rational. At the same time, he makes it clear that reason or "the Idea" is not totally isolated from physical or material existence, and indeed in some way *needs* to be expressed in such reality, although that will bring contingency and the non-rational, if not the irrational, along with it. So he does have a dualistic ontology, with some sort of intelligible reality on the one hand and physical, material existence on the other, but insists that the former must become manifest in the overall structure if not every detail of the latter. His position is like Plato's in its dualism, but perhaps is also a criticism of Plato's in its insistence that the spiritual *must* express itself in the physical; Plato had left physical reality's "participation" in the Forms unexplained and apparently entirely contingent.

Still, Hegel makes it clear that the rational is not just the proper subject-matter of philosophy, which might be trivially true, if philosophy is simply defined as the study of or cognition of the rational. He clearly also holds that the spiritual, the Idea or reason itself, is more important and more valuable than mere physical reality or nature. One place where this is clear is in his famous argument in the *Lectures on Fine Art* that aesthetics concerns only the beauty of fine art, not the beauty of nature, not because there is no such thing as the latter, but because nature as such is not a product of spirit. "The beauty of art is beauty *born of the spirit and born again*", and precisely because of that "the beauty of art is *higher* than nature" (Hegel 1975, Introduction, vol. 1, p. 2). This is an explicitly evaluative claim that the spiritual reality of thought is better than mere physical reality, even if it is necessary for spiritual reality to express itself in physical reality: "Art liberates the true content of phenomena from the pure appearance and deception of this bad, transitory world, and gives them a higher reality, born of the spirit" (Hegel 1975, Introduction, vol. 1, p. 9). And this evaluation is reflected in the fact that art itself must be transcended first by religion and then by philosophy—where religion seems to be something like philosophy still bound down by sensuous imagery, for example by mythology and iconography—so that the physical expression of the spiritual and intelligible is necessary but only as a stage in spirit's progress toward complete self-knowledge. "[N]either in content nor in form is art the highest and absolute mode of bringing to our minds the true interests of the spirit. For precisely on account of its [sensuous] form, art is limited to a specific content" (Hegel 1975, Introduction, vol. 1, p. 9).

Hegel's version of dualistic idealism—the form of idealism that recognizes the reality of both matter and mind, but valorizes the latter over the former—is more epistemological in approach than Plato's in that epistemology is not a mere complement to a metaphysical argument, for example the argument that only something immaterial can be perfectly equal because physical equals are always only approximate; rather, Hegel's philosophy is driven by the epistemological assumption that the only real knowledge is self-knowledge, which obviously must be mind's or spirit's knowledge of itself because what other sort of thing could know anything at all? But further, Hegel also assumes, spirit *must* succeed in coming to know itself, so the dialectic—in which spirit first manifests itself in nature without any self-knowledge at all, then in human social institutions, but finally then, with the glimmering of self-knowledge, in art and religion, which are finally superseded by philosophy, spirit's ultimately adequate self-knowledge—is a necessary process, that is, one that must take place. These are the assumptions of Hegel's formula that spirit is not merely "in itself" but "for itself", that is, known to itself; this is the process that begins with art but culminates in philosophy. "For the truly actual is only that which has being in and for itself, the substance of nature and spirit", the in itself and the for itself, "which indeed gives itself presence and existence, but in this existence remains in and for itself and only so is truly actual". That is, spirit becomes itself only in becoming for itself, that is, coming to know itself. "It is precisely the dominion of these universal powers which art emphasizes and reveals" (Hegel 1975, Introduction, vol. 1, p. 8); but at the same time "Only one sphere and stage of truth is capable of being represented in the element of art", namely a physicalized conception of spiritual reality suitable for expression in the physical imagery of sculpture, in other words, classical art. But "there is a deeper comprehension of truth which is no longer so akin and friendly to sense as to be capable of appropriate adoption and expression in this medium" (Hegel 1975, Introduction, vol. 1, p. 8), that is, the medium of sensuously accessible physical reality. The dialectic marches on from art to religion but beyond that to pure, that is, purely intellectual philosophy, all driven by the assumption that knowledge is the product of mind or spirit, but the only proper knowledge is self-knowledge, so the only real knowledge is spirit's ultimate self-knowledge.

A less portentous but even more clearly epistemological argument for a dualist idealism can be found in the American Hegelian Josiah Royce—at least he was a Hegelian in his earlier years, before he came more under the influence of Charles Sanders Peirce and tried to effect a compromise between idealism and pragmatism. The basis of Royce's idealism, already presented in his first book, *The Religious Aspect of Philosophy*, published in 1885 when Royce was just thirty, was what he called the argument from error. Royce's argument is, if you like, a version of the Cartesian argument that even doubt proves the existence of thought, but with a stronger epistemological assumption: according to him, skepticism begins with insistence upon the possibility of error, but the recognition of that possibility presupposes not only that there *is* "absolute truth", in comparison to which error is error, but also that this absolute truth must be known by some mind, and even that we, that is, finite, human minds, have to have some sort of access to it in order to recognize error as error. "Either then there is no error, or else judgments are true and false only in reference to a higher inclusive thought, which they presuppose, and which must, in the last analysis, be assumed as Infinite and all-inclusive" (Royce 1885, p. 393). So there must exist a mind capable of knowledge of the absolute truth, and our finite human minds must stand in some relation to that mind sufficient to allow us to recognize error as such. The former mind certainly goes beyond anything ever perceived, and even finite human minds turn out to have a capacity that exceeds sense-perception and what one might have thought of as ordinary intellectual operations upon the data of sense-perception. None of this is to say that human minds and the meta-mind that knows absolute truth in all its glory are all that exist, and Royce never casts doubt on the existence of ordinary physical objects. So he counts as a dualist, but certainly one who ascribes to mind powers not merely different from but far greater than any that matter alone could have. In this regard he stands in the dualist idealist tradition of Plato and Hegel. His argument for this form of idealism is based on epistemological assumptions and inferences, like Hegel's, although he reaches his conclusion not through Hegel's assumption that the only genuine knowledge is self-knowledge but through the different epistemological assumption that even recognition of error presupposes some sort of apprehension of the truth.

Now let us turn from these forms of idealism that are also forms of dualism to what eighteenth-century philosophers considered idealism, namely what Berkeley called immaterialism and what we might call monistic idealism or mental monism—the view that all that exists are ideas and the minds, although one of these minds may be greater than all the others.

c) Mental monism: Minds are all there is, but one is greater than the others

Berkeley used the term immaterialism for his doctrine that all that exists are minds and their ideas, and that among the minds there is one infinite mind and many finite minds. Germans such as Wolff, Baumgarten, and Kant called this idealism, in Kant's case, "subjective idealism" and "material idealism". For example, Baumgarten identified idealism with the position that there are only mental substances: "An intellectual substance, i.e., a substance endowed with intellect, is a spirit (an intelligence, a person). ... Whoever admits only spirits in this world is an idealist" (Baumgarten 2013, §402, pp. 175–176). Kant took this definition of the kind of idealism he rejected over from Baumgarten, whose textbook Kant used for his course on metaphysics throughout his career: "Idealism consists in the claim that there are none other than thinking beings; the other things that we believe we perceive in intuition are only representations in thinking beings, to which in fact no object existing outside these beings corresponds." Kant would claim that his own position was the "very opposite" of that, meaning that he does assert the existence of objects existing outside our representations, although not corresponding to the way in which we represent them (Kant 2004, §13, Note III, 4:288–289);[6] that will raise the question whether Kant's "transcendental idealism" should count as a form of idealism at all. But we will come back to that.

While Berkeley advanced both metaphysical and epistemological arguments for his position, Leibniz, the *pater familias* of the other German philosophers just named, advanced a purely metaphysical argument for his position, although he did not call it idealism either—it was (one version of) his monadology. Without ever clearly avowing idealism under that or any other name, Leibniz was completely committed to one metaphysical argument from which he drew an undeniably idealist interpretation of his "monadology". This was his argument, stated in the late, eponymous paper, that everything composite must ultimately be composed of simple substances but that everything that is spatio-temporally extended is infinitely divisible, so nothing spatio-temporally extended can be an ultimately simple substance; therefore the simple substances out of which everything else is composed must be mental rather than physical in nature. As he puts it at the start of the *Monadology*, "The *monad* which we are here to discuss is nothing but a simple substance which enters into compounds"; "There must be simple substances, since there are compounds, [and] the compounded is but a collection or *aggregate* of simples"; but "where there are no parts, it is impossible to have either extension, or figure, or divisibility", or conversely where there is simplicity there cannot be extension or figure or divisibility— thus no spatially extended or physical matter (Leibniz, *Monadology*, §§1–3; in Leibniz 1969, pp. 643–644). I call this argument strictly metaphysical because it turns entirely on claims about the nature of simplicity and composition, without any consideration of how we might know these claims to be true. In other places, such as the 1686 paper on "Primary Truths" and his exchange with Antoine Arnauld that became known as the *Discourse on Metaphysics*—although these sources were not known during the period of Leibniz's greatest influence in the first part of the eighteenth century—Leibniz offered a truth-theoretical argument, namely that everything that is true of a substance is true in virtue of some property contained in it alone, that everything in the universe is the subject of infinitely many true statements appearing to relate it to everything else in the universe, but that the only form in which any substance could contain all those relations as its own is as *representations*, so substances must be representers,

---

[6] The Cambridge Edition of Kant includes the pagination of the Academy Edition (volume and page), so only that pagination will be cited here.

that is, minds. The idea of each substance "already contains all its predicates or events and expresses the whole universe. In fact, nothing can happen to us except our thoughts and perceptions ..." (Leibniz, *Discourse on Metaphysics*, §14, in Leibniz 1989, p. 47); indeed, on Leibniz's account nothing can happen to *anything* except thoughts and perceptions. Again, though, this argument does not turn on an epistemological premise such as that all we can *know* are our own thoughts and perceptions; it turns on the claim that the only way in which any substance, which according to the previous argument must be simple, can incorporate into itself all of the complexity of the universe is by (somehow) representing it. Any epistemological qualms about that premise are eased with the wave of the hand that of course most of these perceptions, even in the most intelligent finite creatures like ourselves, are "obscure"; only in God as the supreme mind is the representation of the universe completely clear and distinct throughout. What we might call *human* epistemology plays no role in Leibniz's argument for the monadology.

Speaking of obscurity, perhaps Leibniz obscured the completely idealist implications of his monadology from himself and some followers as well by the ambiguity of his conception of the pre-established harmony among all substances, an assumption that itself does not turn on any epistemological premise but on a theological premise, that of God's benevolence, which might also be considered metaphysical.[7] In many places, Leibniz considers the appearance of spatial relation to be nothing but the way in which the pre-established harmony between monads that properly speaking have only mental properties appears to those monads, and thus considers space and everything insofar as it seems spatial to be *phaenomena bene fundata*, an obvious source for Kant's later conception of the spatio-temporal realm as merely phenomenal. Sometimes, however, Leibniz wrote as if the mental and the physical, that is, the spatially extended, are two separate realms, each of which evolves according to its own internal principles, but with a pre-established harmony between *them* creating the appearance of interaction between them. Sometimes Leibniz interpreted his pre-established harmony in a monistically idealist way, sometimes in defense of metaphysical dualism. But his basic conception of the monads, which did not seem to vary much between 1686 and 1714, entailed idealism, whether Leibniz liked this result or not.

Berkeley's argumentation for his immaterialism was much more of a mix of epistemological and metaphysical considerations than Leibniz's purely metaphysical arguments. When Berkeley makes arguments in his *Three Dialogues be-

---

[7] On the difficulties of interpreting Leibniz's monadology, see Garber 2009.

tween *Hylas and Philonous* (1713) such as that heat might be thought to exist outside the mind, pain is surely thought to exist only within the mind, but "they are both immediately perceived at the same time, and the fire affects you with only one simple, or uncompounded idea", so that "the intense heat immediately perceived, is nothing distinct from a particular sort of pain" (Berkeley, *Three Dialogues*, in Berkeley 1949, vol. 2, p. 176), and is thus as mental as the pain is, this might be considered a metaphysical argument, namely that since heat and pain cannot be separated, they must be one and the same thing, and since pain is clearly mental, so must be heat. But it might also be considered an epistemological argument, that if we cannot know heat without knowing pain, then heat and pain must be the same thing, and since the latter is mental, or an idea, the former, and in due course other supposedly physical properties, must also be mental. Some of Berkeley's arguments in the somewhat more technical *Treatise concerning the Principles of Human Knowledge* (1710) might also be considered epistemological, such as the one which he claims he is "content to put the whole upon", namely that you cannot conceive of anything existing unconceived because you cannot do this without conceiving yourself conceiving it, so in fact no conceiving or perceiving is ever anything more than "framing in your mind certain ideas" (Berkeley, *Treatise*, §§22–23, in Berkeley 1949, vol. 2, p. 50), that too turns on claims about what we can conceive or perceive. But when Berkeley claims that "the existence of an idea consists in being perceived" and "an idea can be like nothing but an idea" (Berkeley, *Treatise*, §3, §8, in Berkeley 1949, vol. 2, pp. 42, 44), those are metaphysical claims, made on the basis of assumptions about the very nature of ideas. It is not that we have no way of knowing whether an idea could exist without being perceived, or whether it could be like something that is not an idea; it is that these are not even possible, at least in Berkeley's view. His further claim that ideas are passive, causally inert, thus that they can neither produce nor alter another idea (Berkeley, *Treatise*, §25, in Berkeley 1949, vol. 2, p. 51), is also a metaphysical rather than epistemological claim, although it might also lead only to a parasitical argument: it could ground an argument that nothing outside our ideas could cause them only if it were already supposed that the only candidate for anything outside our ideas were more ideas, which by the metaphysical premise could then not cause our ideas. But idealism would already have been presupposed in such an argument.

This argument might also cause difficulties for Berkeley's theology. Faced with the question of why we think objects have continued existence when our ideas of them do not, Berkeley appeals to the divine mind, infinite in capacity, that has all ideas all the time. But if one idea does not cause another, God's ideas cannot cause our ideas, so the solution can only be that of Nicolas Malebranche:

that we humans directly perceive, though only intermittently, the ideas in the mind of God. Of course, then we are perceiving something outside our own ideas, so this may be problematic for Berkeley. But in any case, this is not the place to pursue detailed issues about Berkeley further; the relevant point here is just that he offers epistemological as well as metaphysical arguments for idealism. Having seen that, let's now turn back to another purely metaphysical line of argument for idealism, namely that of the early twentieth-century British philosopher John McTaggart Ellis McTaggart.[8]

Unlike other British idealists who may have affirmed some form of dualist idealism, or unlike F. H. Bradley, who affirmed the existence of the "Absolute" without equating it with mind, McTaggart affirmed idealism in its monistic form throughout his career. In his earliest publication, at age twenty-four, he wrote that "The progress of an idealistic philosophy may, from some points of view, be divided into three stages. The problem of the first is to prove that reality is not exclusively matter. The problem of the second is to prove that reality is exclusively spirit. The problem of the third is to determine what is the fundamental nature of spirit" (McTaggart 1934 [1890], pp. 210 ff.). In the last paper published during his lifetime, he wrote "Ontologically I am an idealist, since I believe that all that exists is spiritual" (McTaggart 1934 [1924], p. 273). His main argument for this conclusion proceeds, like Leibniz's, by positing criteria for genuine substancehood that only minds can satisfy. He considers three candidates: physical, spatio-temporally extended matter, sensa, or objects of perception considered to exist separately from perception, and minds themselves. Contrary to Leibniz, McTaggart supposes that genuine substance must be infinitely divisible, but then, closer to Leibniz, that their infinite parts must be related by "determining correspondence", each part determining every other; he then argues that neither spatio-temporal matter nor sensa can satisfy this requirement: matter "cannot be divided into parts of parts to infinity either in respect of its spatial dimensions, or of that dimension which appears as temporal. And matter, as usually defined, and as we have defined it, has no other dimensions. ... And therefore it cannot exist" (McTaggart 1927, §362, p. 43). Sensa, meanwhile, are both derivative for their content on matter, and also have no parts at all, *a fortiori* are not infinitely divisible (McTaggart 1927, §375, pp. 57–58). With matter and sensa out of the way, he then concludes that mind or spirit, which can represent infinite divisibility and determining correspondence as well, is the only candidate left for genuine

---

[8] The terms of an inheritance required McTaggart to adopt "McTaggart" as his surname, even though it was already his middle name. Instead of then just reversing the order of his middle and last names, he added the second "McTaggart"!

substancehood, and the only thing that really exists.[9] In further similarity to Leibniz, he supposes that there is a multiplicity of minds, harmoniously related, although by their own love for one another rather than by an external act of God (McTaggart 1927, ch. XLI, pp. 144–169). McTaggart admits that there is something provisional about his argument by elimination, for it is only our "experience" and our "imagination" that suggest that matter, sensa, and mind are the only candidates for reality, thus that there is no *a priori* proof that his enumeration is complete, so "we are entitled to hold all substance to be spiritual, not as a proposition which has been rigorously demonstrated, but as one which it is reasonable to believe and unreasonable to disbelieve" (McTaggart 1927, §428, p. 115). So he does employ what might be considered an epistemological rule of inference in his metaphysical argument—crudely put, don't worry about possibilities you can't even imagine—but he is not troubled by any doubt about this principle.

We have now seen, to be sure in the merest sketches, metaphysical arguments for idealism as mental monism from Leibniz, Berkeley, and McTaggart, as well as epistemological arguments. Adding these results to those of the previous section, we have seen idealism understood as a form of dualism but one that privileges mind over matter, and that this can be argued for on metaphysical grounds, as in Plato, or on epistemological grounds, as in Hegel, and now that idealism understood as a form of monism, which recognizes the existence of mind alone, can also be argued for on either metaphysical or epistemological grounds. The time has now come to ask where the "transcendental idealism" on which Kant prided himself fits into this model of idealism.

We noted earlier that Kant considered his own doctrine the "very opposite" of idealism understood as Berkeley (favorably) and Baumgarten (unfavorably) understood it, namely the view that all that exists is minds and their ideas. His basis for this claim was that he did not deny the existence of something other than mind. McTaggart shared Kant's self-assessment, stating that "Kant did not assert that all reality was spiritual, and Berkeley did", and for this reason he held that his own "position is idealist, in that sense in which Leibniz, Berkeley, and Hegel were idealists", but Kant was not (McTaggart 1927, §432, p. 119). He was right about this. In contrasting his own position to traditional idealism, Kant was more focused on Berkeley than on Leibniz; but the difference between his position and Leibniz's monadology too can be expressed in Leibnizian terms: while he agrees with Leibniz that space and time and objects represented in

---

9 Like McTaggart, Aaron Segal and Tyron Goldschmidt attempt to argue for monistic idealism by elimination, in their case by eliminating physicalism and property-dualism from the framework of philosophy of mind (Segal/Goldschmidt 2017). Their argument appears question-begging to me, assuming from the outset that physicalism is inadequate to comprehend thought.

space and time are merely *phaenomena bene fundata*, he does not hold that we have any reason at all, even a reason as good as McTaggart's provisional reason, for thinking that the *noumena* that appear to us in this phenomenal form are themselves mental in nature. Of course, *some* noumena, namely *ourselves*, must be at least partly mental in ultimate nature, in order to be able to represent anything at all, but it does not follow on his account that all noumena are mental, or even that we ourselves are exclusively mental in character. What does follow, according to Kant, is that we must *conceive* of some reality as being different than how we *perceive* it, although we cannot say more about it. This might be considered a doctrine of learned ignorance, but not genuine idealism, at least in the sense of mental monism. However, we might conclude that Kant's position *is* a version of idealism in the dualist, Platonic tradition, for it does hold that *rational* being, present in our ability to set our own ends freely, is more *valuable* than anything else in the universe. So Kant's own position might be considered a *practically* rather than *theoretically* grounded version of idealist dualism.

d) Kant

Let's consider Kant's theoretical grounds for his rejection of the monistic idealism of Berkeley and Leibniz, and then, although briefly, his practical form of dualistic idealism. My theses here are: (1) Kant's argument for the merely phenomenal character of space and time, thus his denial of their characterization of ultimate reality, is primarily epistemological in character; (2) Kant's argument that there must nevertheless be something ontologically distinct from our own representations, thus for a version of dualism rather than mental monism, is also primarily epistemological in character; (3) but Kant's practical philosophy is founded upon the supposition of the unconditional value of rational being, and of rational being alone, and in that sense his transcendental idealism, while not a version of mental monism, is a version of idealistic dualism.

The precise interpretation of Kant's transcendental idealism is of course a deeply vexed matter, and there is no room here to get into details.[10] For present purposes, here I will just adopt the account of transcendental idealism that Kant offers in the *Prolegomena*, published just two years after the first edition of the *Critique of Pure Reason* and presumably *not* representing any radical change in his self-understanding:

---

[10] See Guyer 1983, 1987, 2016, and 2017, as well as Allais 2015. For the contrary view, see Allison 1983, 2004.

> I therefore grant their reality to the things that we represent to ourselves through the senses, and limit our sensory intuition of these things only to the extent that in no instance whatsoever, not even in the pure intuitions of space and time, does it represent anything more than the mere appearances of these things, and never their quality in themselves … For what I called idealism did not concern the existence of things (the doubting of which, however, properly constitutes idealism according to the received meaning), for it never came into my mind to doubt that, but only the sensory representation of things, to which above all space and time belong; … these last … are not things (but mere ways of representing), nor are they determinations that belong to things in themselves. (Kant 2004, §13, Note III, 4:289–293).

Kant's argument for this position, clearly stated in the *Prolegomena* but also in the first edition of the *Critique*, is based on epistemological premises: (1) we know various truths about space, time, and the things in them, both general things and the specific truths of geometry and arithmetic, to be universally and necessarily true, thus we know them *a priori*; (2) in order to know them *a priori*, we must know them as properties of our own representations; (3) but—and this is the crucial move—they cannot *also* be properties of things as they are in themselves, for in that case we could only *know* them to be such contingently, not necessarily; (4) therefore the spatial and temporal properties that we know *a priori* to be true of our representations cannot be true of things in themselves at all; whatever their properties are, they are non-spatial and temporal. As Kant puts the key move in this argument in the *Critique of Pure Reason*,

> if the object ([e.g.,] the triangle) were something in itself without relation to your subject: then how could you say that what necessarily lies in your subjective conditions for constructing a triangle must also necessarily pertain to the triangle in itself? … If, therefore, space (and time as well) were not a mere form of your intuition that contains *a priori* conditions under which alone things could be outer objects for your, which are nothing in themselves without these subjective conditions, then you could make out absolutely nothing synthetic and a priori about outer objects. (Kant 1998, A 48/B 65–66).

Likewise, in the *Prolegomena* he argues that space (and the same applies to time) cannot be a property of things in themselves, for in that case "The space of the geometer would be taken for mere fabrication and would be credited with no objective validity", that is, universal and necessary truth, "because it is simply not to be seen how things would have to agree necessarily with the image that we form of them by ourselves and in advance" (Kant 2004, §13, Note I, 4:287). Nevertheless, Kant makes it very clear, *avant la lettre*, that he is not offering an argument by elimination, in the style of McTaggart, for the conclusion that reality is ultimately mental rather than physical; rather, what follows, in his view, is simply that we know nothing at all about the ultimate nature of (external) reality:

"the strictness of critique" proves "the impossibility of settling anything dogmatically about an object of experience beyond the bounds of experience" (Kant 1998, B 424). As far as theoretical philosophy is concerned, Kant sees no prospect for proving that all reality is mental or spiritual.

Of course Kant's master argument for transcendental idealism is open to a fatal objection: it relies on *modus ponens*, but is open to *modus tollens:* that is, it argues that since we know what we know about space and time *a priori*, space and time cannot be properties of things outside our representations of them; but we could equally well argue that since space and time *could* be properties of things outside our representations of them, we *do not* after all know what we know about them *a priori*. The epistemic assumption on which the argument turns is open to question. However, since my aim here is only typology, not assessment, I will not pursue this point further. Instead, I will turn to my second point about Kant's transcendental idealism, namely that his argument that even though we (supposedly) do know that things in themselves are not spatial and temporal, we also know that things other than our representations exist *do* exist, is also epistemological in character. This is the argument of Kant's "Refutation of Idealism", added to the second edition of the *Critique of Pure Reason*.

Once again there is no room here to defend my interpretation of the "Refutation" in any detail.[11] But the gist of Kant's argument is a variation on the argument of the Second Analogy, his proof of the universal law that every event must have some cause: there his argument is that because we can always vary the order of any representations of states of affairs of external objects in our imagination, the only way that we can determine—that is, know—that there has been an event in the external world, that is, an irreversible sequence of states of affairs, is by conceiving of the order of those states of affairs (and hence of our representations of them) as bound down by some causal law or other (Kant 1998, A 198/B 243). Similarly, the argument of the "Refutation" is that even "empirically determined consciousness of my own existence proves the existence of objects in space outside me", because on the basis of imagination alone I could order apparent memories of my own inner states in any order, and can have knowledge of their determinate order only by correlating them with the rule-governed sequence of states of objects other than, that is, ontologically distinct from, my mere representations. The "determination of my existence in time is possible only by means of the existence of actual things that I perceive outside of myself" (Kant 1998, B 275–276). In his treatment of idealism in the Fourth Paralogism of Pure Reason in the first edition of the *Critique*, Kant

---

11 In addition to Guyer 1983 and 1987, see also Guyer 2018a and 2018b.

had argued that it is no problem to refute "problematic idealism" at all, because all that it takes to prove the existence of objects *in space* is acquaintance with their phenomenology, immediately given by the pure form of our intuition. But he had also observed that the expression "outside me" or "outside us" is ambiguous, able to mean either phenomenologically spatial in appearance or ontologically distinct from our representations and ourselves (Kant 1998, A 373); and the expression "in space outside me" would be redundant unless the second edition Refutation were intended to prove that my representations of objects in space or as spatial are also representations of objects ontologically distinct from myself, although, as the *Prolegomena* had said, in representing their ontologically independent existence spatially I am representing them in a manner that is necessary for me, or for any human being, but not in a way that represents those objects as they actually are. That is Kant's transcendental idealism from a theoretical point of view: that our representations of outer objects are necessarily spatial, but that outer objects themselves are necessarily non-spatial, although we do not know anything more about them, at least on theoretical grounds (and *mutatis mutandis* for time). Theoretically, Kant's position is a form of dualism, positing both our own representations and something ontologically distinct from them, otherwise unspecified, thus with no reason to hold them to be mental. For that reason, McTaggart was correct to distinguish Kant's position from that of Leibniz, Berkeley, and himself. And Kant's arguments for both the negative and the positive aspects of his transcendental idealism, as we have seen, are epistemological in character.

But this is not the last word about Kant's transcendental idealism, as I suggested. While from a theoretical point of view Kant's position is that both spatial and temporal properties are appearances of some ultimate reality, or realities that we can assert to be non-spatio-temporal, but about which we can otherwise say nothing more, from a practical point of view we can say more about ultimate reality. Specifically, we can say that at least we ourselves, that is, we humans, are free and rational beings, and further that our own, ultimate, free and rational being is intrinsically and unconditionally valuable in a way that nothing else is—thus Kant affirms a version of the dualistic but mind-preferring idealism pioneered by Plato. The first part of Kant's practical dualistic idealism, as we can call it, is asserted both in the *Groundwork for the Metaphysics of Morals* and the *Critique of Practical Reason*. In Part III of the *Groundwork* Kant claims that "a human being really finds in himself a capacity by which he distinguishes himself from all other things, even from himself insofar he is affected by objects, and that is *reason*", which is a form of "self-activity" or a "spontaneity so pure that it thereby goes far beyond anything that sensibility can ever afford it" (Kant 1996, 4:452); in the *Critique of Practical Reason*, his "fact of reason" argument is that "by attending to the necessity with which reason prescribes" "pure moral laws" to us "and to the setting aside of all empirical conditions to which reason directs us" we also become aware of our possession of a "pure will" (Kant 1996, 5:30). The value of the good will is then asserted in the *Groundwork*, both in its opening claim that a good will is the only thing "that could be considered good without limitation" (Kant 1996, 4:393) and in the claim, which Kant indeed says is the "ground of a possible categorical imperative", that "their nature already marks out" rational beings as ends in themselves, something true of nothing else (Kant 1996, 4:428–429). So the core of Kant's moral philosophy, and of his philosophy as a whole, for the sake of which the theoretical limits of our knowledge were established, is that free and rational being, manifest to us in the form of our own humanity, is valuable in a way that nothing else is. This is Kant's version of Platonic, value-based dualistic idealism.

So there is a substantive conclusion to our exercise in classification. Idealism comes in two forms, monistic and dualistic; the former asserts that the only reality is mental in character, the latter that there is matter as well as mind, but that mind is more important than matter. Kant's version of the latter recognizes its intrinsically normative or moral character; he offers no purely metaphysical argument for the superiority of the non-material to the material, as Plato did, but an explicitly moral argument for both the specification and the valuation of the non-material. Later writers, such as Hegel, had this in their background even if they did not make explicitly moral arguments for their versions of idealism. And since the theoretical arguments for idealism, whether metaphysical or epistemological, are deeply problematic, perhaps the conclusion to draw is that if idealism has any claim to plausibility at all it is as a moral doctrine, or as a colorful expression of a moral doctrine of the incomparable value of human beings, and other rational beings should there be any.

Bibliography

Allais, Lucy (2015): *Manifest Reality*. Oxford: Oxford University Press.
Allison, Henry E. (2004): *Kant's Transcendental Idealism: An Interpretation and Defense*. 2nd edn. New Haven: Yale University Press.
Baumgarten, Alexander Gottlieb (2013): *Metaphysics*. Translated by Courtney Fugate and John Hymers. London: Bloomsbury.
Berkeley, George (1949): *The Works of George Berkeley, Bishop of Cloyne*. Edited by A. A. Luce and T. E. Jessop. 7 vols. London: Thomas Nelson and Sons.
Ewing, A. C. (1934): *Idealism: A Critical Survey*. London: Methuen.
Garber, Daniel (2009): *Leibniz: Body, Substance, Monad*. Oxford: Oxford University Press.

Guyer, Paul (1983): "Kant's Intentions in the Refutation of Idealism". In: *Philosophical Review* 92: 329–382.
Guyer, Paul (1987): *Kant and the Claims of Knowledge*. Cambridge: Cambridge University Press.
Guyer, Paul (2016): "Arguing for Transcendental Idealism: Lucy Allais on *Manifest Reality*". In: *Kantian Review* 2: 261–272.
Guyer, Paul (2018a): "Mendelssohn, Kant, and the Refutation of Idealism". In: Corey Dyck/Falk Wunderlich (Eds.): *Kant and His German Contemporaries*. Vol. 1 (*Logic, Mind, Epistemology, Science and Ethics*). Cambridge: Cambridge University Press, pp. 134–154.
Guyer, Paul (2018b): "Baumgarten, Kant, and the Refutation of Idealism". In: Courtney Fugate/John Hymers (Eds.): *Baumgarten and Kant on Metaphysics*. Oxford: Oxford University Press, pp. 154–170.
Hegel, Georg Wilhelm Friedrich (1975): *Aesthetics: Lecture in Fine Art*. Translated (from the posthumous edition by H. G. Hotho) by T. M. Knox. 2 vols. Oxford: Clarendon Press.
Hegel, Georg Wilhelm Friedrich (1991): *Elements of the Philosophy of Right*. Edited by Allen W. Wood. Translated by H. B. Nisbet. Cambridge: Cambridge University Press.
Hofweber, Thomas (2017): "Conceptual Idealism without Ontological Idealism: Why Idealism Is True After All". In: Tyron Goldschmidt/Kenneth L. Pearce (Eds.): *Idealism: New Essays in Metaphysics*. Oxford: Oxford University Press, pp. 124–141.
Kant, Immanuel (1996): *Practical Philosophy*. Edited and translated by Mary J. Gregor. Cambridge: Cambridge University Press.
Kant, Immanuel (1998): *Critique of Pure Reason*. Edited and translated by Paul Guyer and Allen W. Wood. Cambridge: Cambridge University Press.
Kant, Immanuel (2004): *Prolegomena to Any Future Metaphysics that Will Be Able to Come Forward as Science*. Translated by Gary Hatfield. Cambridge: Cambridge University Press.
Leibniz, Gottfried Wilhelm (1969): *Philosophical Papers and Letters*. Edited by Leroy Loemker. 2nd edn. Dordrecht: D. Reidel.
Leibniz, Gottfried Wilhelm (1989): *Philosophical Essays*. Edited by Roger Ariew and Daniel Garber. Indianapolis: Hackett.
McTaggart, John McTaggart Ellis (1927): *The Nature of Existence*. Vol. 2. Edited by C. D. Broad. Cambridge: Cambridge University Press.
McTaggart, John McTaggart Ellis (1934 [1890]): "The Further Determination of the Absolute". Reprinted in: J. McT. Ellis McTaggart: *Philosophical Studies*. Edited by S. V. Keeling. London: Edward Arnold, pp. 210–72.
McTaggart, John McTaggart Ellis (1934 [1924]): "An Ontological Idealism". Reprinted in: J. McT. Ellis McTaggart: *Philosophical Studies*. Edited by S. V. Keeling. London: Edward Arnold., pp. 273–92.
Plato (1997): *Complete Works*. Edited by John M. Cooper. Indianapolis: Hackett.
Royce, Josiah (1885): *The Religious Aspect of Philosophy: A Critique of the Bases of Conduct and Faith*. Boston: Houghton, Mifflin & Co.
Segal, Aaron/Goldschmidt, Tyron (2017): "The Necessity of Idealism". In: Tyron Goldschmidt/Kenneth L. Pearce (Eds.): *Idealism: New Essays in Metaphysics*. Oxford: Oxford University Press, pp. 34–49.
Stang, Nicholas F. (2017): "Transcendental Idealism without Tears". In: Tyron Goldschmidt/Kenneth L. Pearce (Eds.): *Idealism: New Essays in Metaphysics*. Oxford: Oxford University Press, pp. 82–103.

Jela Krečič
Fiction: The Truth of Idealism and Realism

Abstract: For some time, we have been witnessing a turn to realism in popular culture. By contrast, the distinguishing mark of classical Hollywood cinema was to place an idealizing frame before reality to produce the effect of truth. Thus, my main thesis is that this disavowal of the artistry of idealization in Hollywood, which can also be traced to the currently widespread philosophical endorsement of realism, has little to do with the real or the truth. Accordingly, I aim to prove that genres, especially classical Hollywood comedy not only create challenging theoretical and political ideas but also provide a new perspective on the dispute between realism and idealism. An analysis of the use of *mise en abyme* (in art as well as in popular culture) provides an insight into the complex relationship between idealism and realism, fiction and truth.

Ours is said to be an era of realism. Not only in philosophy, marked by the advent of speculative or new realism, but in popular culture as well, we are witnessing a growing obsession with getting in touch with a sort of "reality-in-itself", divested of any kind of ideal mediation. In opposition to these almost juvenile tendencies, I will argue that the "real of reality" can never be gotten for free. The seemingly direct contact with reality will be unmasked as always already caught in an unrecognized and thus neglected ideological frame. Inversely, I will claim that in order to catch a glimpse of reality beyond ideological constraints, there is always a price to pay, one of inventing the ideal frames of indirectness.

The twentieth century brought about the rise of the entertainment industry, dedicated to providing meaningless fun and joy for the masses and in this way distracting them from their miserable lives. Movies, especially, took on the role of creating ideals to which individuals or communities aspired. However, it is curious that from the 1950s onward the opposite tendency emerged in the heart of show business: Hollywood started to aspire to a more realistic depiction of reality. There was an attempt to disavow generic frameworks and to offer something

---

Funding note: The research included in this chapter was funded by the Slovenian Research Agency (ARRS) under the research project "Truth and Indirectness. Toward a New Theory of Truth" (J6–3138).

Jela Krečič, University of Ljubljana.

more real, authentic instead: life and heroes as they supposedly really are, in all their misery and misfortune. It seems this tendency became quite powerful; it never really ceased to this day. Current popular production (movies and television) is based on a similar premise that there is an authentic real life and that popular content should faithfully reflect it in its raw immediacy.

Such a naive approach contains a grain of philosophical or, better said, pre-philosophical thought. Realism in popular culture is, probably unknowingly, conceived on a pre-Platonic, commonsensical basis: there is a hierarchy of being whereby things in themselves or things as they supposedly are enjoy ontological primacy over the images of such things. Real, unmediated life overweighs the entire sphere devoted to producing appearances. As opposed to such spontaneous philosophy, Plato's ontological hierarchy entails an additional, third element and is therefore much more sophisticated. According to Plato, the original entities, governing the hierarchy of being, are ideas and not reality as it appears to or is experienced by us. Reality as we experience it is therefore already an appearance imitating the true reality of ideas. Within this tripartite structure, art as the *mimesis* of *mimesis* represents the third, basest element. But Plato's own disparaging attitude toward all kinds of mimetic arts, foremost (epic) poetry, discloses that this ontological inferiority of art nevertheless reveals a certain repressed, almost traumatic truth at the core of Plato's idealism. It can be argued that art as imitation of imitation brings to light the very ideality which enables an ontological connection between otherworldly ideas and this-worldly things in the first place.[1]

The implicit assumption of the present-day obsession with authenticity is thus based on a simplified version of this hierarchy, where our raw feelings, sensations, experiences already stand as the truth behind all appearances: for example, the truth behind the social roles we play. Part of the same impulse is the fixation on the direct approach to reality, on immediate experience versus indirectness, on authenticity as opposed to falsity or phoniness. These dichoto-

---

[1] According to Slavoj Žižek, the Platonic ideas do not reside in the other world but *arise* within the difference between things and their imitations in works of art: "When Plato dismisses art as the 'copy of a copy,' when he introduces three ontological levels (ideas, their material copies, and copies of these copies), what gets lost is that the Idea can only emerge in the distance that separates our ordinary material reality (second level) from its copy" (Žižek/Gabriel 2009, p. 132). "Therein resides Plato's deep insight: Ideas are not the hidden reality beneath appearances (Plato was well aware that this hidden reality is that of ever-changing corruptive and corrupted matter); Ideas are nothing but the very form of appearance, this form as such—or, as Lacan succinctly rendered Plato's point: the Suprasensible is appearance as appearance" (Žižek/Gabriel 2009, p. 134).

mies—real/imaginary, truth/falsehood, realism/idealism, directness/indirectness—play an important part in the definition and self-understanding of contemporary popular production.

One can wonder how movie production, created as a form of escapism (but never merely that), once proudly bearing the title of the dream factory, tries to faithfully portray real life today and live up to all its uninspiring aspects.

I will try to address this issue in two ways: on the one hand, I will concentrate on the phenomena of reality TV and the rise of quality television in the 1990s. As different as they are, the two share the same tendency: devotion to realism. I will analyze the strategies they employ to create a realistic depiction of "life as it is", and I will demonstrate what the limits of such attempts at realism are.

On the other hand, I will analyze the classic Hollywood comedy *Sullivan's Travels* as an example of a genre that affirms the importance of escapism and mere fun while also producing a harsh critique of social injustice. This film—constructed as metafiction, as a comedy within a comedy—also offers a complex and important insight into the problem of realism and idealism.

I will dedicate the final part of this paper to a short philosophical introspection on metafiction or *mise en abyme* and its relation to truth and fiction.

1 Escape to realism

Reality shows (like the pioneering *Big Brother*)[2] should be understood in the context of a general cultural turn to realism: it is presumed that we should rid ourselves of false images, including old TV genres and their artificiality, and with it also of our naivety. We should focus our attention on real people with real problems and film them without censorship. Not only are these shows carefully con-

---

[2] The idea behind reality television—as is well known—is to gather ordinary individuals at an isolated location and continuously record them. They have no access to the outside world, so the "appeal" of the show lies in the challenges the group is faced with. The viewers get to decide who will remain in the Big Brother "house" by televoting. The winner, who is finally chosen by the audience, gets a handsome cash prize. Let us remind the reader that reality TV and so-called reality shows emerged in the late 1990s. The first *Big Brother*, which went on to become the blueprint for a plethora of related content, was shot in the Netherlands in 1997. The name "Big Brother" is an ironic reinterpretation of Orwell's *1984*. However, I am tempted to say that Orwell's literary dystopia gets its twisted postmodern turn in reality shows. Money and fame or a potential new career in show business motivate common people to voluntarily submit to the omnipresent eye of Big Brother, placing themselves on exhibit for the entire TV audience to see and subjecting themselves to the viewers' decisions.

structed, but, more importantly, what this sort of philosophizing forgets is that uncensored reality is already a form of illusion. The ordinary mortals chosen to live in the Big Brother house are playing the part of themselves, or rather a version of themselves, for the cameras. So the lesson to be learned from them is that the face behind the deceiving mask is nonetheless a new mask.

What was supposed to be reality (in itself) is always already constructed—or, as proposed by Lacan, reality has the structure of fiction.[3] The turn to reality is a new form of escapism, with reality shows being a good example of this escape. Or, as Alenka Zupančič has elaborated with precision:

> It is therefore no coincidence that reality shows function as the prominent form of escapism (as entertainment): there seems to be nothing as comforting and reassuring as this showing off of realism, watching "real" people on "real" locations doing whatever they do in "real" life. Is there any better proof and illustration of Lacan's thesis that "reality is always and necessarily fantasmatical" than the popularity and mesmerism of reality shows? Reality is fantasmatic, and if we want to get to some real we need recourse to some artifice. (Zupančič 2020, p. 284)

The problem with reality shows is therefore not only that they are just as fake as other productions. Quite the contrary, what they show us is the very construction of "real" reality in all its uninteresting dullness. Moreover, they demonstrate that revealing life as it (presumably) is has no inspiring edge, no emancipatory potential. It is—at best—a firm ally of the hegemonic ideology and *status quo*. In other words, we witness a concession to reality (to what is) as the ultimate horizon of possible personal and communal experience.

2 Reality according to quality TV

The production of reality shows represents only one part of the late twentieth- and early twenty-first-century viewing experience. The same historical moment that saw traditional TV networks gladly adopt the reality TV format also led to the emergence of so-called quality television.[4] Cable networks, such as HBO, introduced a different type of programming, the kind that was previously reserved

---

[3] Lacan introduced this thought in his seminar on *Hamlet*. Cf. Lacan 1958–1959. I will return to this slogan in another context later.
[4] That the series represents the principal narrative form, the form of our era, is one of the main theses proposed by Wajcman in *Les séries, le monde, la crise, les femmes* (Wajcman 2018, p. 10). Although the medium of television produced great shows and series even beforehand, "quality" had not yet become a commonplace standard defining the entire sphere of television.

for (art) cinema. *The Sopranos* (1999 – 2007), *The Wire* (2002 – 2008), and *Six Feet Under* (2001 – 2005) are the first heralds of several crucial changes in the landscape of TV series,[5] which we can view primarily as an answer to the reality TV boom. With its simple concept, the latter considerably lowered the production costs incurred by TV networks. Quality television, on the other hand, bet on the opposite: it offered well-scripted, refined, and demanding productions, which aspired to cinematic brilliance in terms of form and content (as well as costs).

At first glance, it seems the two TV phenomena could not stand further apart. Despite their obvious differences, however, we can see both reality and quality television as part of a similar impulse: the pursuit of reality and authenticity. The fact that quality television became the privileged site of serious drama alone points to the rejection of phony Hollywood genres or genres that had dominated the TV landscape for so long.[6]

The turn to realism is further reflected in the new types of heroes populating these TV shows, who are no longer decent people or model citizens. Instead, they are depicted in all their weakness, regardless of whether they are criminals, law enforcement professionals, or "ordinary" people. All their unflattering aspects are exposed and emphasized. They lack any moral compass, which in many respects, especially compared to classic TV genres, makes them anti-heroes. Instead of phony, polished, unequivocal characters, we are now faced with complex, ambiguous protagonists.

---

[5] HBO can be considered the key entity contributing to the improved quality of twenty-first-century television. Even its erstwhile slogan, "It's not TV, it's HBO", suggests that we are dealing with something more meaningful. As opposed to nineties' TV networks, this cable provider specialized in programs regular networks couldn't air because of various legal restrictions (the ban on swearwords, obscenities, etc.). In the nineties, HBO started producing its own content, trusting in the kind of stories, dialogues, and heroes that would not have made it on air on regular TV channels. The history of HBO and its operational policies are examined in detail in the book *It's Not TV* (Cf. Leverette/Ott/Buckley 2008). Around the time of HBO's first great triumphs, other networks or providers also started to produce similar content. It is worth mentioning FX, now perhaps most famous for producing *Louie*, Showtime, which rose to fame with *Dexter* and *Weeds*, and AMC, which made a name for itself with *Mad Men*. Today, these networks are joined by even less conventional producers: Amazon, perhaps the largest online retailer of goods in general, has started making its own TV series, and Netflix was the first to provide a video streaming service for movies and series. As a producer of series, Netflix was the first to transform viewing habits (leading to, for example, binge-watching) by publishing their series all at once, that is, with all the episodes of a given series becoming immediately available.

[6] Many contemporary television comedy shows also testify to this general move towards realism. They are characterized by a turn to drama and tragedy, to the point that we are bound to call them dramedies or sadcoms rather than sitcoms.

Let's take a quick look at some of these new types of heroes: David Chase's *The Sopranos* focuses on the life of Tony Soprano (James Gandolfini), who might be considered an anti-hero solely for being a New Jersey mafia boss. In the series, however, we also get to see him as a family man suffering from panic attacks, henceforth going to therapy (albeit in secret). *The Wire* by David Simon is a painfully realistic portrait of Baltimore, where inefficient and bureaucratized state institutions are shown as no less problematic than their adversaries, the drug gangs, the talented but utterly flawed detective Jimmy McNulty (Dominic West) being the most ambiguous one of them all. Vince Gilligan's *Breaking Bad* centers on chemistry teacher and father Walter White (Brian Cranston), who is diagnosed with cancer and starts to sell drugs out of desperation, which leads to his fully embracing the world of crime. Matthew Weiner's *Mad Men* revolve around Don Draper (John Hamm), an advertising guru and family man who is at the same time a promiscuous character nurturing a dark secret.

Adam Kotsko explores this new kind of television hero in *Why We Love Sociopaths: A Guide to Late Capitalism Television* (Kotsko 2012). He designates the many anti-heroes that have taken over quality television as sociopaths, and he considers the viewers' love of them as a symptom of the present-day social order falling apart—consequently, in the eyes of the audience, social success can only be achieved through antisocial behavior, a scrupulousness in achieving one's goals.[7]

While I may agree with the claim that the sociopath has become the predominant model of hero (although it appears that by resorting to such a classification Kotsko falls victim to moralizing), I cannot agree with the diagnosis as to why these heroes are predominant and also so popular. The very fact that these kinds of dubious characters step into the forefront of the golden age of television with all their pathologies can be viewed as a turn to realism and the pursuit of an authentic portrayal of complex individuals and their lives. All the above-mentioned characters featuring in now already classic TV series are at least in part Hamlet-like subjects grappling with anxieties, ghosts from the past, feelings of powerlessness, and worries about their inadequacy—they depict how an ordinary mortal might act if pushed into extraordinary circumstances (which they usually help create). Moreover, the viewers' love of these sketchy heroes can be seen not as their moral decline but as the opposite: a new form of puritanism. The

---

7 Cf. Kotsko 2012.

viewers' enjoyment is at least partially due to the moral superiority they feel when faced with the "problematic" protagonists.[8]

There are scores of other substantial and formal characteristics of modern series that fall under the same realistic impulse. In terms of form, modern quality television series combine two traditional TV formats: the serial and the series (the episodic procedural). The first tells a single continuous story throughout multiple episodes, while the second tells multiple stories, each resolved in a single episode. The most prominent variant of the serial format used to be the soap opera. Now, however, with complex characters, a large cast facilitating expansion into various subplots, and the relativization of moral categories (i.e., the absence of unequivocally good or bad characters), TV series have gained new credibility. While they retain the structure of the episodic procedural insofar as an episode can stand alone, the main overarching story still unfolds over several episodes, intertwining with side story arcs in a novelistic fashion in the manner of a serial.

Quality serials follow a complex hero, be it male or female, and they usually also address a specific social trauma. *The Sopranos* explore the world of crime through the existential anxieties of the main protagonist; *The Wire* addresses the systemic issues of American capitalism and racism; *Breaking Bad* confronts us with the workings of the American healthcare system, or rather the American health insurance system, which will not cover the cancer treatment costs of an ordinary chemistry teacher, thus pushing him into a life of crime. *Mad Men* can be interpreted as a critical examination of the 1960s in the USA. There are numerous examples of such a forthright approach to American contemporaneity. This limited list of quality TV series serves to illustrate what devices these shows use to incite a sense of authenticity and to portray reality in all its brutal aspects (be it individual or systemic—preferably both). So we are no longer dealing with television or mere entertainment but with serious drama, which is supposed to get us in touch with authentic psychological and social traumas.

This sort of production is often complemented by another, more obvious and pervasive form of directness: deploying explicit violence, sex, and profanity. This is another sign of modern TV series trying to achieve the greatest possible effect of authenticity and realism on all levels.[9]

---

8 Petra Kettl and Robert Pfaller propose a similar reading in "The End of Cinema as We Used to Know It: Or How a Medium Turned from a Promising Graduate Into an Old Folk". Cf. Kettl/Pfaller 2020.

9 Its "cinematic" style is what contributed to the effectiveness of modern television: shooting on location, visual sophistication, dynamic framing, and innovative montage.

But what is the real reach of these shows, which are so obviously opposed to old conventions and phoniness and instead aim for a realistic effect? Analyzing HBO production, Marc Leverette gave an insightful comment on HBO's shifting the borders of established television products: "However, while HBO has from the beginning claimed to eschew formula in its programming, it is now rather obvious that eschewing formula is just as formulaic ..." (Leverette 2008, p. 145). Quality television, which emerged against established genres and proven formulas with the above-mentioned formal attributes and those pertaining to new intriguing content, at some point became its own genre and formula, similar to how Hollywood's anti-genre realist movies of the 1950s eventually began to function as a new genre in themselves.[10] Several radical, groundbreaking series paved the way for a new prevalent model, which is reflected in the fact that many features previously characteristic only of special cable productions (ambiguous, complex protagonists, violence, sex, profanity) have already penetrated into the mainstream production of traditional TV networks (and their evening programming). Quality has become the predominant pattern, so that initially revolutionary narratives are already perceived as something domesticated, neutralized, something that can no longer shock or provoke us.

While quality television's turn to authenticity might have appeared shocking and subversive at the moment of its origin more than 20 years ago, its true political reach remains questionable. All the previously mentioned features characteristic of quality television in no way undermine contemporary Western capitalism or its ideology. To a large extent, quality series are normalizing subversion, finally turning their subversive and revolutionary aspects into a new brand and the dominant pop culture trend.

I would like to emphasize that the purpose of this criticism isn't to undermine the value of the quality TV produced in the past 20 years. It is rather directed against the praising of its supposedly disruptive and groundbreaking realism and political radicalism. If these series are radical, it is not because of their excessive form, their realistic portrayals of contemporary American life, but on account of their aesthetic properties: from an intriguing screenplay and skilled plotting to the actors' performances and elaborate production. These features are also the reason why, in contrast to reality TV, quality TV is considered worthy of lengthy elaborations and interpretations. What makes several of these series valuable is not a faithful depiction of life in itself but exactly the meticulous artistic approach to it.

---

10 See Harvey 2001, pp. 141–142.

3 The trouble with authenticity

We can address the problem of meticulous fiction aspiring to ring true from another angle. Let's take Preston Sturges's highly acclaimed comedy *Sullivan's Travels* (1941), which focuses on Hollywood's famous director of light comedies John L. Sullivan (Joel McCrea). At the height of his fame, Sullivan begins to question whether his talent has not been wasted on worthless genre products intended solely for entertainment. Using this wide-reaching medium, could he not communicate something more relevant to his large audience? Is it not his duty as an artist to address the pressing issues society is fraught with?[11] As he tells his incredulous producers, he now wants to switch from frivolous topics to a realistic drama adaptation of the novel *O Brother, Where Art Thou*.[12]

The producers are, of course, less than thrilled about his idea, arguing that nobody will want to watch such grimness on the screen, but Sullivan takes his mission seriously and decides to acquaint himself with life in poverty. If he is to tackle a fundamental social issue such as deprivation or homelessness, he needs to become familiar with it firsthand, through direct experience. He is led by the naive philosophical presupposition that the immediate experience of homelessness and poverty can provide a convincing cinematic representation of these pressing issues. Sullivan's butler,[13] who has experienced deprivation in a much more genuine manner, is also opposed to Sullivan's decision, but Sullivan persists. To make a long story (and a complex plot) short, after a couple of failed attempts to get a genuine taste of poverty, the director unexpectedly finds himself among the poor, and finally, following an unfortunate series of events, even lands in jail. In the end, he succeeds too much, excessively; he ends up among the most degraded class of them all, behind bars with very little hope of getting out.

The experience of poverty and prison-bound hopelessness eventually leads to Sullivan changing his artistic credo. He realizes the error of his ways during one of the movie's key scenes, as a community of black worshippers invites the prisoners to their church to watch slapstick cartoons. At this point, the direc-

---

[11] It's worth mentioning that Sullivan acts like a reader of Walter Benjamin, who celebrates the art of filmmaking in his essay "The Work of Art in the Age of Mechanical Reproduction". He places his bet on the educational revolutionary film, which could reach the masses and raise their political awareness, instead of pulp Hollywood productions.
[12] This novel does not exist, but the Cohen brothers did make a movie with the same title in 2000 as an homage to Sturges.
[13] For the importance of this dialogue, see Zupančič 2020, p. 280.

tor shows scenes from the cartoon and cuts to shots of the audience laughing.[14] We witness several close-ups of prisoners laughing excessively—their laughter is almost disturbing. At first, Sullivan is skeptical about the idea of spending a relaxed evening watching a comedy, but then, at some point, he gives in and becomes part of the laughing community. At first glance, the scene does look naive since it suggests that all the poor need is some harmless fun and laughter. However, the idea of a community bound by laughter, as suggested by Zupančič, contains the germ of political engagement.[15] The political power of collective laughter emerges from its excessiveness, its utter uselessness. Sturges takes care to cut from one laughing face to another to emphasize the importance of this meaningless fun of the collective body. And the denouement of the movie is even more complex and theoretically refined.

When the hero manages to prove who he really is after protesting his innocence, he is acquitted and finally released from prison. But now he no longer wants to make a realistic movie about poverty—he claims that he doesn't know enough about it. This is a rather surprising twist as it seems that the filmmaker has been through more than enough to provide audiences with an "honest", genuine truth about the most vulnerable social groups. As Zupančič convincingly argues, Sturges's point is that "being a poor person" is not only a sociological category, it is also an ontological one. And this ontological dimension of poverty is bound to the very structure of the system—to the systemic production of the class struggle and the production of the poor. In other words, someone who has spent some time among the deprived only as a tourist or as part of his sociological experiment does not qualify as poor because he cannot have experienced the systemic exclusion from the world of comfort and leisure. Sullivan gets out of jail exactly on account of his celebrity and his social status (connected to his wealth), while the marginalized poor classes are tied to their pole of the class division without the possibility of breaking through. Or, to put it in yet another way: social justice as practiced in the USA is not blind to one's social standing.[16]

---

14 The idea of a black religious community welcoming the prisoners would demand a separate treatise. It suffices to note that even when showing people of color, Sturges goes for a discrete but, in the light of the compromise-heavy Hollywood, still rather bold depiction. The black show pity for people from the margins of society and generously accept them in their community. They are shown to be much more enlightened, humane, and cultivated than, for example, the white prison guards.
15 Cf. Zupančič 2020, p. 281.
16 The mere fact that the poor cannot afford expansive legal representation puts them in an utterly unequal position in relation to those who can. See also Zupančič 2020, pp. 279–280.

Sturges's point is therefore quite subtle. A realistic "portrayal" of poverty would lose touch with the systemic dimension of the production of inequality. Moreover, such a seemingly authentic representation of poverty would be much more mendacious and fake than comedies, which at least do not pretend to be anything more than carefree entertainment. In the end, Sullivan decides that from now on, he is going to make nothing but comedies.[17]

One of the messages of *Sullivan's Travels* is the affirmation of genre products which harbor no pretensions about tackling socially relevant topics.[18] Sturges implies that comedy and (collective) laughter serve a function—they make the hard lives of tired, exploited people easier. However, at the same time, the movie also suggests that innocent fun is not necessarily completely innocent. If we take (collective) laughter as something that serves no purpose, something that is not entangled in the production of *the status quo*, it is perhaps also something that marks the site of emergence of the (collective) subject, which can result in emancipatory politics.

That said, one has to point out another, even more important dimension of the movie. No matter how hard *Sullivan's Travels* affirms comedy as pure entertainment, the movie itself is anything but. It is not just another genre product providing us with meaningless fun. Quite the contrary, it ventures a statement on the nature of its comic narration in the shape of a movie within a movie. On the one hand, it communicates that there is nothing wrong with comedy being mere entertainment, but on the other hand, it contradicts this thesis by actually addressing a very serious social issue: the movie is filled with scenes of masses of poor and homeless people, of dirt and filth, in which the underprivileged are deemed to live. Also, the close-ups of no-name prisoners keep the audience in touch with the raw brutality of American reality. This attitude differs substantially from the beautiful leftist soul which satisfies itself with lamenting about the cruel world while secretly expecting nothing to change and at the same time congratulating itself for its nobility and charity. Sturges, on the contrary, shows that inequality, the radical break between the classes, has nothing to do with a kind and noble heart—at no time does he try to romanticize or glorify the poor—but he rather delegates the question to the system of injustice itself. He solicits us to see poverty and inequality as a systemic problem and not

---

[17] This, by the way, does not sit well with his producers, who wanted to profit nicely from *O Brother, Where Art Thou?* given the media hype surrounding their director.

[18] Movies glorifying the poor as incredibly brave and noble people were made by Frank Capra. No matter how well-intentioned this great American director might have been, the function of such movies is to erase the class struggle as a social problem and re-articulate it as an issue of individual moral propriety, helping the reproduction of systemic injustices.

as a moralistic one (of the noble poor). As previously mentioned, all these subtle messages can be relayed only as a comedy about a comedy.

Moreover, a comedy that declares itself in opposition to a direct realistic portrayal of the class struggle can—as a comedy about a comedy—still say something relevant about this very topic. It might be worth noting that the metafictional form of *Sullivan's Travels* is not deployed as a function of postmodernist play or the celebration of its self-reflexivity. It is rather a tool for the movie to approach what is inevitably overlooked if one tries to address it directly, namely, the class struggle and the phony attitude toward systemic social issues (which Sullivan embodies at the beginning of the movie).

The movie suggests that it is all too easy to be critical of popular culture only because it employs the means of fiction and cinematic illusion. The real error lies in the belief that we may come closer to the truth by opting for the realist genre, although—one might add—realism is also a genre relying on artistic rules. Sometimes comedy (especially a comedy within a comedy) constructs a stage where a certain social truth becomes visible. Or better yet, it constructs a perspective on this truth that would otherwise stay hidden or appropriated by sentimental lamentation.

Movies such as *Sullivan's Travels* ultimately help us acknowledge that reality in itself is not something neutral, it is not a given ontological entity independent of our cognition and perception, but is always already constructed through the ways we approach it. This has, of course, dire epistemological implications, but it also points to what was mentioned earlier: the idea of a direct approach to reality is nothing less than ideology in its pure state.[19] On the one hand, metafiction can expose reality in its problematic, traumatic aspects. On the other hand, revealing its own fictional exploration of it also suggests that reality itself is nothing but fiction.

4 Mise en abyme

This brings us back to Lacan's slogan: reality has the structure of fiction. Interestingly enough, he introduces this famous thought in his seminar on *Hamlet* while contemplating its notorious *mise en abyme*, the so-called play-scene in

---

[19] The concept of ideology opens up a large field of inquiry, which I cannot go into in detail. I am referring to Althusser's conception of ideology, which, among other things, implies that what we perceive as neutral objective reality is in fact a sign of our (the subject's) immersion in ideology.

which the main protagonist re-enacts the events of his father's death.[20] The only way to introduce the traumatic truth about his father's murder is through a play, a fiction. One might wonder why Hamlet doesn't reproach his uncle, the new king, directly. The direct approach would probably result in the king's denial or even in his campaign against Hamlet as a madman. A play (within a play), on the other hand, presents itself as fiction and cannot be denied so swiftly— it is, after all, a mere play. However, its effect is the effect of truth. In other words, since truth is framed in the form of make-believe, it can trigger a reaction that can be perceived as an admission of guilt.

To put it in philosophical terms, the relation between the regime of truth (as a medium of ideal forms of the human mind) and the regime of reality (as a medium of what happened objectively and cannot be simply undone by way of ideological circumvention) must be rearranged. There are two limits which can hardly be trespassed. On the one hand, one can never fully grasp reality-in-itself; one's propositional attitudes tend to approximate to it endlessly. On the other hand, one can also never become subject to a sudden revelation of absolute truth; this one is usually deferred to the transcendent spheres of Platonic heavens and mystical inclinations. The best one can hope for in this world is setting up those frames of indirect contact between the two where truth and reality will, to an extent, "magically" coincide and perhaps reveal themselves fully.

This does not by any means imply that truth and reality are both mere fiction, but rather that they are dependent on the mode of their disclosure, their delivery. The idea of experiencing truth as untouched by our cognitive abilities is a sign of our immersion in a specific ideology (as *Sullivan's Travels* implies), and a pure philosophical fiction at that, a blatant case of abstract idealism. Instead, to make any sense of reality, to deliver any kind of truth, one has to find means of addressing it, and these means are an inseparable part of the truth one is trying to unveil.

This thesis, based on Lacan's slogan, beseeches another conclusion. Fiction (or art) is never mere fiction separated from reality or truth. It is rather a form of grasping it. If we take another look at *Hamlet*, we can discern two important issues: the first concerns the status of the truth of its plot. We are dealing with a traumatic event (murder, violent seizure of power) that threatens the law and order in Denmark and also the well-being of its main protagonist. So Shake-

---

20 Cf. Lacan 1958–1959.

speare's play deals with truth as something traumatic, as "out of joint" or out of place—something that destabilizes a political community.[21]

The second important issue concerns the introduction of a play within a play, which brings about another theoretical challenge. In fictional redoubling, the fiction posits itself as the topic of its own story; it is a medium that addresses itself as a medium, a mode of representation and the subject of the same representation. One could therefore argue that the redoubling of fiction produces a division (a differentiation) within the fiction itself: there is a cut between the fictional story and the story about the story within the same fictional realm. This gap does not simply belong to the realm of fiction or reality, it disrupts or traverses both of them. To put it another way, when dealing with "ordinary" fiction (without an obvious metafictional frame), the plot usually revolves around a certain kernel of reality (the traumatic truth or the Real, as Lacan calls it) and strives to somehow resolve it, or at least to provide a fictional way of tackling it. *Mise en abyme*, on the other hand, exposes this unbearable element and makes it visible, sometimes literally.

Michel Foucault offers an interesting insight into this problem in *The Order of Things,* when he is dealing with Diego Velázquez's Las Meninas.[22] As is well known, *Las Meninas* is a meticulously crafted portrait of Spanish princess Margaret and her staff witnessing Velázquez at work, presumably making a portrait of the royal couple, Philip IV and Marianna of Austria. Foucault focuses on the figure of the painter and his gaze, which is directed outside the picture's frame. He elaborates who (or what) occupies this space outside the frame:

---

[21] I am tempted to say that art and fiction usually revolve around the truth as cracked, or around reality as stained by a certain traumatic dimension. This also goes for the fictional works that manage to provide a smooth solution for the exposed cracks. The classical detective novels come to mind: the murder that destabilizes a well-functioning community is in the end accounted for so that life can go on as usual.

[22] He also discusses Miguel Cervantes's *Don Quixote and* points out that in the second part of the novel, Don Quixote "meets characters who have read the first part of his story and recognize him, the real man, as the hero of the book. Cervantes's text turns back upon itself, thrusts itself back into its density, and becomes the object of its narrative" (Foucault 2002, p. 53). "Between the first and second parts of the novel, in the narrow gap between those two volumes, and by their power alone, Don Quixote has achieved his reality—a reality he owes to language alone, and which resides entirely inside the words" (Foucault 2002, p. 54). It is interesting that, at the dawn of modern literature, Cervantes needs to address its fictional frame and include it in its own story, as if to state that, in the modern age, any metaphysical warrant of truth and reality simply overlapping is lacking, so reality can only be "brought to light" by way of the intricate idealist mechanisms of truth—hence, by way of fiction.

> The painter is turning his eyes towards us only in so far as we happen to occupy the same position as his subject. We, the spectators, are an additional factor. Though greeted by that gaze, we are also dismissed by it, replaced by that which was always there before we were: the model itself. But, inversely, the painter's gaze, addressed to the void confronting him outside the picture, accepts as many models as there are spectators; in this precise but neutral place, the observer and the observed take part in a ceaseless exchange. (Foucault 2002, p. 5)

Las Meninas points to a certain spot occupied by every single spectator of the painting. But in the realm of the painting, this spot is also occupied by Velázquez's models. The mirror in the back of the painting reveals that the object of the painter's gaze (and not only his but that of the majority of the king's household) is the royal couple, the king and queen.

The power couple is—judging by the gazes of others—central, but it is hidden in the painting twice: it is positioned outside the picture's frame as well as hidden on the painter's canvas (we only see its back), so it only shows up in the reflection of the canvas in the mirror. "The mirror provides a metathesis of visibility that affects both the space represented in the picture and its nature as representation; it allows us to see, in the center of the canvas, what in the painting is of necessity doubly invisible." Foucault concludes this paragraph with a quote: "'The image should stand out from the frame'" (Foucault 2002, p. 9).

The idea of the "doubly invisible" deserves further elaboration. In the realm of the painting, its main topic is twice excluded but introduced through a mirror image. The royal couple's erasure from the spotlight reveals instead the backstage of the main event (a "behind the scenes"), putting the observers of the painting (the princess and her staff) in the spotlight. The painting hints at the outside of its frame but finally manages to include the excluded element in the mirror. By doing so, Velázquez already suspends the "natural order" of painting: he destabilizes the contours of painting since his painting is "reaching out of the frame". It marks a fragile line between the fictional and non-fictional realms by including the outside of the painting in the painting itself. But this maneuver is possible only on account of another invisible spot that occupies the same structural spot as the royal couple—us, the spectators.

This spot remains excluded from the painting. Only the painter's gaze makes us aware of it or, at least, hints at it. More precisely, it makes us aware of the fact that as seeing beings we are not only gazing (at the world or at a painting) but are also an object of (a picture's, painter's) gaze. It implies that every painting depends on such a spot and its exclusion. It must stay hidden for fiction to work—to effectively deceive us, to make us believe (if nothing else) that we can see everything there is to see, although our gaze (our point of view) literally remains hidden from us. One cannot overlook the epistemological implications of the painting: not only is our perspective constitutive for the interpretation of it, but the painting also has the means to transform spectators (their gazes) into a picture in its own right. Velázquez's painting includes this dimension of the visual field in itself.

The hint at the blind spot is the way a painting steps out of its frame and nevertheless addresses its missing element. The image of the royal couple in the back is an attempt at neutralizing the spectator's precarious position. This image seems, at least for a while, to stabilize all the fleeing gazes, gaps, and positions within and outside the frame, and in effect to cover up the blind spot.

However, as Foucault points out, the situation is even more complex: the exteriority of the painting is also the position the painter occupies. To be able to grasp the painting's scene, he would have to step out of the painting and share the spot with his models and his spectators, making himself both into the gaze and into the object of his own gaze. In this way, *Las Meninas* points to its hidden, impossible, but formative element: the off-field, the field usually excluded from the picture's frame. This dimension is invoked by the painting, by its reflexive dimension, and is not simply present in it. It is an element of the destruction of traditional relations within the painting, of the traditional relations between the canvas and the spectator, but also of traditional epistemological relations: we are not only omnipotent observers, we are also being observed and therefore inscribed in the visual field as such. This destructive element, one destroying the realm of fiction as the realm of the spectator's reality, does not belong to the realm of fiction. The limit between the interior and the exterior, between the visible and the invisible, is integrated into the painting, making it much more than a portrait of "las meninas". We are not dealing only with fiction. This work of fiction introduces a gap as a disruptive force that subverts the realms of fiction and reality.

5 Conclusion

Why this long detour through *Las Meninas* in my examination of the dialectics of truth and fiction in recent, and not-so-recent, popular culture? My aim was to show how the *mise en abyme*, which characterizes the acme of classical art, is fully operative also in contemporary cinema and TV fiction. In all these cases, the self-reflexivity of fiction paradoxically points towards something that is less fictitious than even reality as we perceive it directly, with our own senses amidst our quotidian lives, hence, something more real than reality itself. It is the dimension of the Real, as Lacan calls it, namely, the very gap within reality which establishes it from within as a consistent, phantasmatic, perceivable screen. To conclude, I would thus like to further elaborate the thesis that truth is constitutively bound to the mode of its examination, and in this way delineate a possible forthcoming debate.

For this purpose, I would like to propose a small mental exercise, reminiscent of Lacan's fantasy of the Café de Flore after the extinction of humanity, or his image of a mountain lake which no one perceives (see Lacan 1991, p. 46). Imagine there is a global catastrophe that leads to the extinction of the entire human race. And imagine that the majority of the artworks (including *Las Meninas*) were to remain intact, although there would be no one to perceive them, to look at them, to enjoy them. What would be their status? Would the dialectics triggered by these works as proposed above still apply? Would *Las Meninas* entail all the above-mentioned layers and dimensions or would the painting regress to a mere piece of canvas with some oil paint on it? Would that be the ultimate reality of *Las Meninas*? And would fiction ultimately melt into reality? I am inclined to say yes. Without the human apparatus, the status of this painting changes radically. However, this does not render its truth, its immanent dialectics, relative or non-consequential, but it rather stands to show that the ideal forms of truth, and hence the subjectivity ensuing from the human existence with its cognitive powers, are a constitutive part of the reality in which human beings are immersed. In other words, the existence of people with their intellectual investigations and examinations is part of the truth people are seeking out. The reality of the world would be radically different without the idealist strategies of truth intervening in it. I am tempted to say that the existence of subjectivity as such triggers the dialectics of fiction and truth, directness and indirectness, the real and the imaginary. In this sense, it is the human being itself, this "entity of minimal idealism", entailing its position in epistemological relations, its production of idealizing linguistic forms, propositional attitudes, negative sentences, which open up the possibility of truth and falsity, etc., which represents the Real that disturbs the "natural order of things", thereby allowing reality to appear as reality in the first place.

Bibliography

Foucault, Michel (2002): *The Order of Things: An Archaeology of the Human Sciences*. London and New York: Routledge.
Harvey, James (2001): *Movie Love in the Fifties*. New York: Da Capo Press.
Kettl, Petra/Pfaller, Robert (2020): "The End of Cinema as We Used to Know It: Or How a Medium Turned from a Promising Graduate into an Old Folk". In: *Crisis and Critique* 7.

No. 2, pp. 129–159. https://crisiscritique.org/2020/july/complete.pdf, visited on 31 March 2021.
Kotsko, Adam (2012): *Why We Love Sociopaths: A Guide to Late Capitalism Television*. Winchester in Washington: Zero Books.
Lacan, Jacques (1958–1959): *Desire and Its Interpretation. Unedited seminar translated by Cormac Gallagher*. http://www.lacaninireland.com/web/wp-content/uploads/2010/06/THE-SEMINAR-OF-JACQUES-LACAN-VI.pdf, visited on 31 March 2021.
Lacan, Jacques (1991): *The Seminar, Book II: The Ego in Freud's Theory and in the Technique of Psychoanalysis, 1954–1955*. Translated by Sylvana Tomaselli. New York and London: W. W. Norton.
Lacan, Jacques (1998): *The Four Fundamental Concepts of Psycho-Analysis*. Translated by Alan Sheridan. New York and London: W. W. Norton.
Leverette, Marc (2008): *"Cocksucker, Motherfucker, Tits"*. In: Marc Leverette/Brian Ott/Cara Louise Buckley (Eds.): *It's Not TV: Watching HBO in Post-television Era*. London and New York: Routledge, pp. 123–152.
Leverette, Marc/Ott Brian/Buckley, Cara Louise (Eds.) (2008): *It's Not TV: Watching HBO in Post-television Era*. London and New York: Routledge.
Wajcman, Gerard (2018): *Les séries, le monde, la crise, les femmes*. Paris: Verdier.
Žižek, Slavoj/Gabriel, Markus (2009): *Mythology, Madness, and Laughter: Subjectivity in German Idealism*. London and New York: Continuum.
Zupančič, Alenka (2020): "Preston Sturges and The End of Laughter". In: *Crisis and Critique* 7. No. 2, pp. 272–290. https://crisiscritique.org/2020/july/complete.pdf, visited on 31 March 2021.

Mladen Dolar
Virus and Idea

Abstract: In the times of the present pandemic the paper attempts to look at the virus as a philosophical problem. The first use of virus in the sense of an agent causing infectious diseases stems from the time of the Enlightenment and happens to coincide with the introduction of the term materialism in the philosophical sense. The first line of inquiry scrutinizes the infectious quality that was traditionally ascribed to the powers of sensuality, the body, ultimately matter and the material, supposed to be endowed with viral capacity. This line leads back to Plato and the problems he had with the contagious nature of mimesis, a paradigmatic case for this stance. Hegel, as opposed to this, ascribed viral powers to spirit itself and saw contagion (*Ansteckung*) as the key force in the spread of the ideas of the Enlightenment, eventually leading to revolution. The paper proposes a new 'viral ontology' that attempts to single out the virus as an entity inhabiting both matter/body and spirit, and ultimately stands at the core of being human.

What, if anything, is a virus? What kind of ontological entity is it, if it's appropriate to speak about ontology here? Or rather, what kind of nonentity? Is it the verge between entity and nonentity? It's not to be seen or perceived, not without some sophisticated scientific equipment, it's too trivial to be considered by ontology, yet this nonentity, this almost nothing, has the power to bring to a halt entire cities, countries, continents, to ruin people's lives, devastate the economy, produce millions of victims, derail the world. One could pose the Leibnizian question: Why is there virus rather than nothing? Or, is the virus an ominous sign that there would rather be nothing? Is being always infested by some viral almost nothingness?

1 Virus and materialism

The term stems from Latin, where *virus* means "poison". The word made its way into a number of languages, as Latin words frequently did; the first English use is documented around the year 1400. At the time, it just meant "poison". In 1728, after the word had been around for a couple of centuries, we have the first use of virus not merely in the sense of "poison", but of "an agent causing infectious

---

Mladen Dolar, University of Ljubljana.

https://doi.org/10.1515/9783110760767-015

diseases". The diseases in question were (what else but) venereal diseases, sexually transmitted diseases—there is something like a secret phantasmatic connection between the virus and Venus, a peculiar mix of poison, sex, enjoyment, and infection. By sheer coincidence, the first documented mention of the word "materialism", taken as a philosophical current, appeared in 1726, at exactly the same moment, in Johann Georg Walch's *Philosophisches Lexicon* (with many reprints). The word would quickly spread, indeed it became viral and deeply marked the century. Virus and materialism both oddly coincide in the heyday of the age of Enlightenment.

If I continue for a bit in a textbook manner—the virus such as it is known today was first discovered, described, and isolated by Dmitri Iosifovich Ivanovsky, a Russian botanist who was sent to Ukraine, Crimea, and Bessarabia in the 1880s to investigate a mysterious disease attacking and ruining tobacco plantations. In 1892 he published a paper marking the discovery of the first virus, which was to become known as the "tobacco mosaic virus", TMV, the founding father of all viruses. "Mosaic" because it produced mosaic patterns on tobacco leaves, lovely and fatal. So the first known virus was assaulting tobacco, the virus-poison was ruining this other poison, it was actually trying to protect our health, shielding us from poisonous enjoyment and its spread (well, it didn't quite succeed). While Ivanovsky described the first virus, he didn't yet give it that name. The discovery couldn't be complete without the name, namely "virus", which was accomplished by Dutch micro-biologist Martinus Beijerinck in 1898, inaugurating the twentieth century—the century that was to be fraught with so many viruses couldn't quite begin without that word. Speaking of historic coincidences, the invention of the term virus in its current usage coincided almost exactly with Freud's publication of *The Interpretation of Dreams* in 1899, another viral book for the century. Another theme to ponder on, virus and psychoanalysis.

If I pursue this biological thread a bit further, at a very basic level (I have no proper expertise on that),[1] a virus is like the lowest form of life, strictly speaking not even life, for it doesn't possess the capacity of self-replication on its own. It is not even a cell, just genetic material (DNA or RNA enveloped in a protein wrap) which has to find a host, a proper cell, in order to be able to replicate at all. Viruses get hold of cells and force them to reproduce their genetic material in vast quantities, thereby exploding and annihilating their hosts while outsourcing their reproduction. They are like replicating machines, parasites that need a vic-

---

[1] The summary information about viruses is gathered from various internet sources, with no ambition for completeness or thoroughness. I am only interested in a couple of points of some theoretic interest.

tim for their own replication, a host to then be discarded. In themselves they are not really alive, they cannot self-replicate, which is the crucial requirement of life. They are like the refuse of life, a side-product, fragments of life, rubble, the flotsam and jetsam of life—but flotsam and jetsam that is not a remainder of something else, but coextensive with life. Biologists can't quite agree on their origin. One theory maintains that viruses are atrophied and emaciated cells; they were once cells but then degraded to this primitive form (taking advantage of the parasitic habitus). The other, more intriguing (and more widespread) theory maintains that they are co-originary with cells, that they emerged together with cells in a process of co-evolution. They evolved as their counterpart and supplement, as the waste and rubbish of life, its reduced mechanical parasitic anti-image, but still coterminous with life, not a residue of something prior. They are a degenerate surplus of life, its trash and scum, but there is no life without them. "Viruses co-exist with life wherever it occurs", says our wiki-oracle. Here is an elementary point of philosophical interest: There is no life without this element that derails life but has no consistency in itself and is itself not really alive. There is, ontologically, at a minimum, life plus that something, or rather almost nothing, which disrupts life and threatens with its ruin, its contaminating discharge. No life without a derailing minuscule surplus based on replication and repetition.[2] One could say: life in the age of mechanical reproduction—but this age has always already started.

As already mentioned, the term "virus" in the sense of an agent of infection emerged at the same time as the term "materialism" in the sense of a philosophical stance, in the heyday of the Enlightenment (1726–1728). The introduction of the term "materialism" produced the effect that, in retrospect, it seems as if it has always been there, ever since ancient times, and that the history of philosophy could be conceived as a perpetual antagonism between the two camps of idealism and materialism. Walch, as the author of the *Lexicon*, should have shown objectivity and impartiality, or at least a semblance of them, in treating all philosophical currents with an equal eye, but he couldn't quite hide his indignation and outrage at materialism (cf. Walch 1726, pp. 1735–1736). Matter, promoted by materialism, immediately appears as something threatening, dangerous, on the one hand due to its merely mechanical nature, and on the other hand due to being potentially infectious, contagious, virulent, so that materialism, swearing

---

[2] Given that the virus appears like a repetitive replicating machine grafted upon life, one cannot quite resist a very crude association with Freud's death drive, in line with Freud's ambition to base both life and death drives on the biological (protozoa etc.). The growth, expansion, and proliferation of life vs. the deadly mechanically repetitive counterpart of sub-life?

only by matter and the body, knows no transcendence, no morals, no free will, no immortal soul—it promotes the mechanical instead of the spiritual. There is a confluence of two strands in this anxiety: on the one hand, the immediate concern was with the mechanical materialism which gained currency at the time (following Descartes and culminating with La Mettrie's *Man a Machine* etc.),[3] and on the other hand, there was a much older distrust and resistance in relation to the body and its spurious enjoyment, going back to the very origins of philosophy. Thus, materialism is a current that was defined as an enemy from the outset, with the implicit assumption that matter has to be contained and the spirit is what should confine, enclose, hold in check the contagion by matter and the body. This is based on a longstanding philosophical fantasy, which, in a simplified form, implies that matter is like an infectious disease, threatening to spread if left unchecked, and in which spirit appears as an immunological problem: it plays the role of the vaccine and the quarantine, the disinfectant, the prohibition of close contact, etc., to counteract this contagion. There is a quasi-biopolitical agenda underpinning the notions of matter and spirit.

Materialism was never just an epistemological problem, a problem of knowledge and cognition, merely a philosophical view that matter is the only substance. It always entailed an affective attitude, an anguish produced by tackling matter and the body, their potential contagiousness, their filth, their viral nature, and references to spirit were always calls for purification.[4] One could propose the odd couple epistemology vs. epidemiology. The virus would then figure as matter in its extreme and reduced form, its refuse, and therefore matter in its pure state, matter brought to the gist, matter at its minimum, the invisible matter being more matter than the visible one. The virus would thus be like the "real" atom of matter, its minimal particle, the affective and "biopolitical" counterpart to the atoms of physics (as well as those conceived by the ancient atomists). In this view, it doesn't even have the status of a proper entity, it is a pure capacity of infection and infinite reproduction, replication and mechanical repetition. The virus is like the truth of the matter. We can never quite say, "We are materialists, of course, we moderns are not concerned with transcendence, the beyond, the

---

[3] For a more detailed argument, cf. Dolar 2020.

[4] Cf. Jankélévitch (1960), who persuasively argues, with an array of historical examples, that spirit is inherently based on a primal anxiety of infection and contagion, which threaten with expropriation and disintegration. Mere contact is enough to pollute the whole, and spirit has always functioned as a rampart of purification, a shield against the impure. Spirit is coupled with decontamination. Is there a "biopolitical" subplot always tacitly present in the concept of spirit? This also extends to the term "catharsis", based on *katharos*, pure, *kathairein*, to cleanse.

soul, and spiritual elevation"—we can't say it because of this viral sting that always inhabits matter, a sting which inspires anxiety, unease, disgust, but also, as their obverse side, enjoyment and its excess (and enjoyment always spills into excess).[5] It affects us in ways other than cognitive ones. This is the prevailing, if simplified, traditional representation—matter and body as a potential (viral) disease, and spirit as the cure. One could tentatively maintain that every philosophy is, in some aspect, the philosophy of the virus, that the virus is always underpinned by an ontological background. Tell me what you think of the virus and I'll tell you ...

2 Virus and idealism: Plato

Let's have a look at what Plato and Hegel have to say about the virus, and let's keep to just these two giants. Consider the way Plato treats the problem of mimesis, or rather what one could call his panic fear of mimesis. There is the vast problem of how art should be treated in the ideal community of Plato's *Republic* (one third of this dialogue is curiously devoted to art, "aesthetics" is immediately taken to be a political issue, a source of possible contagion), and of course we cannot properly deal with this here, nor with the larger problem of mimesis and its key function in art (defining much of the traditional view of art, which modernism, allegedly, has done away with), so very briefly: In theater, to take just this example, actors mimetically impersonate various personalities, they assume someone else's voice and posture, their behavior, they imitate them—this is what defines acting. "Now, to make oneself like someone else in voice or appearance is to imitate the person one makes oneself like" (Plato 1997, p. 1031 [393c]). But this imitation entails consequences. The problem is that it always leaves a mark, one cannot imitate innocently, without being stained by what one imitates. So the question arises, "whether or not we'll allow tragedy and comedy into our city", "whether our guardians should be imitators or not" (Plato 1997, p. 1032 [394d]).

> They mustn't be clever at doing or imitating slavish or shameful actions, lest from enjoying the imitation, they come to enjoy reality. Or haven't you noticed that imitations practiced from youth become part of nature and settle into habits of gesture, voice, and thought?—

---

[5] Is disgust an elementary form of enjoyment, or rather the rudimentary cell of both enjoyment and its proscription "in one"? A proscription inscribed in the guts before one ever gets to a cognitive (di)stance, a visceral epistemology and social theory. Cf. Miller 1997 and Menninghaus 2003.

> I have indeed.—Then we won't allow them to imitate either a young woman or an older one or one abusing her husband, quarrelling with the gods, or bragging because she thinks herself happy, or one suffering misfortune and possessed by sorrows and lamentations, and even less one who is ill, in love, or in labor.—That's absolutely right. (Plato 1997, p. 1033 [395c–e])

They should by no means imitate women ("ill, in love, or in labor"—note the sequence!), they shouldn't imitate slaves, bad men, perverts, cowards, drunkards, madmen, and furthermore, just in case, they should also refrain from imitating "neighing horses, bellowing bulls, roaring rivers, the crashing sea, thunder or anything of that sort" (Plato 1997, p. 1033 [396b]). In a word, one shouldn't imitate anything lowly, from villains, women, and slaves to animality and nature, anything below the rank of a free citizen, for one is necessarily affected by it, whether one wants to or not. One never knows; imitation informs and permeates our being, so one might not be able to stop neighing, roaring, bellowing, thundering, or crying out in labor. It catches us unawares, without our conscious consent. There is no innocent or neutral imitation, imitation always sticks; people are like wax, mimesis is like a knife. Theater appears as a particularly dangerous source of epidemic. We contract what we imitate, we may become what we enact, notwithstanding that acting is just a material emulation of words and behavior. But why should one fear that? It all seems as if the material has the power to affect the immaterial, to contaminate the realm of ideas and our spirit. Touch possesses the secret power to infect the untouchable. It appears as if Plato doesn't quite believe in his own theory of ideas, but secretly believes that they can be infested and put in jeopardy by the material, by mere imitation. The material is viral. Actors are particularly at risk since they imitate in their body and voice, but the audience, which watches the spectacle with empathy, with horror and pity, is equally exposed since models and examples attract and mold our spirit. We become what we watch, watching is already being in touch, in contact, if at distance, but no distance is distant enough to prevent one being affected by what one sees. Examples irresistibly call for emulation.[6]

Is Plato's fear of mimesis based on a secret belief in magic or on a secret belief in materialism? How to tell the two apart? There is something like a "materialism" of magic, which works by material means of contact (if at distance) to effect the contamination of the non-material. This secret "materialist" belief is based on ascribing magical powers to matter, its capacity to work in ways that defy the usual material causality, thus being able to cause much more havoc than mere matter ever could. (Like in the canonical formula of disavowal: "I

---

[6] For a more detailed account, cf. Dolar 2017.

know very well that material imitation has no power over the ideas, yet I firmly believe it does.") But then again, can there ever be a neutral concept of matter, reducing it to its accountable physical properties and nothing else? Matter and nothing more? Can there be an espousal of materialism based solely on a clear-cut epistemic decision and causality? Couldn't one say that "magic" is both an obfuscation of what is at stake in matter and an indication of the impossible effectivity that is involved? A mixture of delusion and insight? The materialist superstition as not quite separable from materialist knowledge? Matter is always "matter plus". There is always a surplus over matter that forms the gist of matter.

But where does this secret power come from, the power of the corporeal (imitation) to infect the spiritual? Perhaps the problem ultimately lies in enjoyment as the secret mover of the corporeal and the material. When imitating, something in us starts enjoying it—it just enjoys and it doesn't want to know (which is, by the way, one of Lacan's definitions of the unconscious, or rather its "it"). There is an enjoyment that we cannot control and contain. "It" starts enjoying mimesis, and particularly imitating questionable models, "it" forces its way to satisfaction regardless of any other considerations.[7] "It" enjoys at our expense. One cannot quite oppose and fight "its" enjoyment by better knowledge, by cognition, epistemologically. The episteme seems powerless in the face of it. Enjoyment in the material is like a virus that cannot be contained by logos; logos cannot quite stop this epidemic danger. So what is to be done?

The problem is that we humans are creatures of mimesis. Everything human we learn by imitation (language, to start with, which is after all the basis of logos—we learn to speak by imitating, first without understanding). So what Plato proposes is not just advancing virtue and promoting knowledge, but rather mimesis as a weapon against mimesis. He proposes to fight bad mimetic models with good ones. One should by all means imitate good examples, the "courageous, self-controlled, pious, and free" men (Plato 1997, p. 1033 [395c]), one should be edified and elevated by noble models, so imitation can cut both ways. But there is an admission in it: If we can't beat it, we should join forces with it. If one cannot resist the powers of mimesis, then let's hope that good examples

---

7 This can be connected with what Freud says about the drive. Freud speaks about the *Klebrigkeit* of the drive, its stickiness, its aptitude to stick, to be fixed at the point where it got satisfaction and only wants to come back to the scene of the crime, its capacity to form a glue, so that one is glued to it, and to install this glue at the core of all social bonds. This is the aspect of the elementary conservative nature of the drive, only wanting more of the same, getting satisfaction indiscriminately from any odd quarters, without the subject being in command of this stickiness. Hence the propensity or even the compulsion to repeat.

are more contagious than bad ones. The material imitation of virtue will hopefully contaminate us with virtue. One needs the viral capacity of models and imitation in order to install true knowledge and virtue. Thus, virtue also has to rely on the virus. In some part, we have to contract it, acquire it by imitation, not just by knowledge; one should contest one viral infection with another. But then, what is virtue/knowledge[8] if it has to rely on imitation and infection, if it is dependent on the virus? Do vice and virtue, in regard to mimesis, effectively share the same viral mechanism? Counting on the infectious nature of imitation and its enjoyment?—So much for Plato, very briefly and schematically.

3 Virus and idealism: Hegel

While Plato ascribes viral powers to material imitation, and is thus in line with the traditional view of the infectious nature of matter and body, Hegel addresses the viral powers of spirit itself. He directly states that spirit can, and must, itself be seen as infectious. When, in the *Phenomenology of Spirit*, he discusses the Enlightenment (the movement that invented both materialism and the virus), he considers the power of its ideas (most prominently the "idea of reason") pitted against the powers of prejudice, superstition, idols, fetishes, social rank, unfounded habits and beliefs, all that supported the old order, the *ancien régime*. How do these enlightened ideas spread, how did they turn into an overpowering force that eventually led to nothing less than the French Revolution? Hegel's answer: they spread like an infection, *Ansteckung*, a pervasive infection (*eine durchdringende Ansteckung*), and any fight against this infection is futile. It is now rather the spirit that infects the bodies.

> The struggle is too late, and every remedy adopted only aggravates the disease, for it has laid hold of the marrow of spiritual life, viz. consciousness in its concept, or its pure essence itself. Therefore, too, there is no power within it which could overcome the disease. ... Rather, being now an invisible and undetected spirit [*ein unsichtbarer und unbemerkter Geist*], it infiltrates the nobler parts through and through and soon has taken complete possession of all the vitals and members of the unconscious idol; then 'one fine morning it gives its comrade a shove with the elbow, and, bang! crash! [*Bautz! Baradautz!*] the idol lies on the floor.' (Hegel 1977, pp. 331–332, translation altered; 1986a, p. 403)

---

[8] This line is not quite in agreement with Socrates, who famously argued that knowing virtue is enough (should be enough) to implement virtue. If one knows better, one cannot possibly do worse—or can one?

How did this happen, this transformation, this spectacular downfall of the idols? This collapse of the belief in all kinds of idols that used to be the pillars of the old world for so long, upholding the power of tradition? Here, it's not materiality and the body that contaminate the spirit, it's not the spirit that would have to erect ramparts against them, here we have the spirit itself spreading like an infectious disease, permeating all pores of this world through "the silent ceaseless weaving of the Spirit", *das stumme Fortweben des Geistes*, tacitly doing its work (*stumm*, mute, dumb), until one day the idol lies on the ground, a victim of the mute progress of reason. It's not *wir weben, wir weben*, as in Heine's famous line,[9] nor is it simply *der Geist webt*, the spirit weaves, but we could paraphrase *es webt*, it weaves, as *es webt im Geiste*, it weaves in the spirit.[10] The progress of reason is viral and silent, depending on an "it" that weaves, doing its work beyond our intentions. This is a silent virus, not the voice of reason (which has ample history, from Rousseau and Kant to Freud),[11] but the silent reason; more than that, it is *stumm*, dumb and mute. A wordless spirit, wordless reason, wordless logos? It looks like a contradiction in terms, since logos is the Word. This is like the pure viral force of logos. Shall one say dumb logos? The zero-level of logos?

Hegel couldn't resist quoting Diderot here, specifically *Rameau's Nephew*. It is from Diderot that he borrowed this fall of the idols, foretelling nothing less than the Revolution. This is one of the very few quotes in the whole of *Phenomenology*. Diderot, the arch-Enlightener, the head of the Encyclopedia, the spiritual basis at the heart of the Enlightenment, Diderot was the one who truly believed in the victory of reason, which can rely only on the infectious power of truth, goodness, and beauty. He believed that these powers would spread like a contagion, unstoppably do away with all the idols, and ultimately triumph by becoming pandemic. The virus of truth, goodness, and beauty is supposedly irresistible. Here is the original passage from Diderot (which Hegel quoted from Goethe's translation, the only version available for a long time):

---

9 Cf. "The Silesian Weavers", the famous poem by Heinrich Heine from 1844, leading to the March Revolution in 1848—it became one of its emblems, with the haunting recurring line "*wir weben, wir weben*", "we are weaving, we are weaving". It was written during Heine's friendship with Karl Marx in Paris, and one should also remember that Heine was Hegel's student in Berlin in 1820.
10 In line with Lacan's notorious formulas of the unconscious, *ça parle*, it speaks, and *ça jouit*, it enjoys, one can propose *ça tisse*, or *ça tresse*, it weaves, linking Hegel, Heine, Marx, and Freud.
11 Why does reason need a voice to support it, to promote its spread? Is voice in some respect also like a virus, introducing the element of enjoyment in support of reason? Reason, again, being powerless without enjoyment? Cf. Dolar 2006, pp. 88–95.

> The rights of the true, the good, and the beautiful will always prevail. They may be contested, but in the long run they're admired. Art lacking in these qualities may be admired for a time, but eventually the applause gives way to yawns. So yawn away, my friends, yawn to your hearts' content. Don't be embarrassed. The supremacy of nature and of my trinity is such that the forces of hell can never prevail against it--Truth which is the Father, engendering Good, which is the Son, whence comes Beauty, which is the Holy Spirit--my trinity establishes its dominion imperceptibly. The foreign god humbly takes his place upon the altar, at the side of the indigenous idol; little by little he consolidates his position until, one fine day, he gives his neighbour a gentle shove; and--lo and behold! the idol falls. … the political system that makes straight for its target without commotion, or bloodshed, or martyrs, without hurting a hair of anybody's head, strikes me as the best. (Diderot 2006, pp. 66–67)

Virus and utopia: Diderot is the harbinger of the proper viral utopia. The virus will crush the old order and do away with idols by its sheer epidemic powers, by the infectiousness of the true, the good, and the beautiful. It will proceed silently and invisibly until the old order is crushed without even putting up a fight, not quite aware of what hit it. One cannot resist the virus of reason, there is no vaccine against it. If spirit is like a vaccine against the body, then there is no vaccine against the spirit itself.—Hegelianly speaking, the silent weaving happened "in itself" before suddenly converting to "for itself", with a bang.

One wishes one could share Diderot's optimism, his viral utopia, but two hundred years on, we can't. Not even Hegel, writing a quarter of a century after Diderot's death, could quite share it. To be sure, he maintained that we need the spiritual infection, the silent weaving has to do its work, the process that doesn't quite depend on our will and intent, "it" has to do it, but this is not enough. What is needed is also the reverse of this weaving. We need what Hegel calls (in what follows our quote) "the action of the negative essence", which has to take upon itself "the sheer uproar and violent struggle with its opposite", there has to be *ein lauter Lärm und gewaltsamer Kampf* (Hegel 1977, p. 332; Hegel 1986a, p. 404), a loud noise as opposed to muteness. We cannot merely rely on the epidemic powers of spirit, supposedly triumphant in the long run without any struggle and bloodshed, we cannot wait for it to do its work. We have to turn ourselves into the warriors of this virus. One aspect of spirit is silent, mute, peaceful, the other aspect is loud, noisy, violent—there is a maximum opposition within the spirit itself. *It* is silent, *we* have to be loud.

This is the logic that Marx implicitly adopted, in his own way, in the famous passage of *The Eighteenth Brumaire of Louis Bonaparte* (1852):

> But the revolution is thoroughgoing. It is still traveling through purgatory. It does its work methodically. … it had completed half of its preparatory work; now it is completing the other half. … And when it has accomplished this second half [of its preparatory work], Eu-

rope will leap from its seat and exclaim: 'Well burrowed, old mole!' [*Brav gewühlt, alter Maulwurf!*] (Marx 2006; 2007, p. 116)

This is of course a paraphrase of Hamlet's "Well said, old mole!" (I.5.170), which introduces another image, that of the mole, the silent underground weaver of tunnels, quietly toiling away until suddenly everything collapses. Although Marx doesn't speak about the spread of spirit, but about the preparatory subterranean work being done imperceptibly, the connection is clearly there: the infectious imperceptible diffusion of the idea of reason, borrowed from Diderot, eventually led to the Revolution, and the revolution that Marx is envisaging, as its extension, has to rely on a similar infection, the silent weaving transforming material conditions. Marx actually used the same phrase that was proposed by Hegel at the very end of his *History of Philosophy* (and this is where Marx probably got the idea):

> [Spirit] often seems to have forgotten and lost itself, but inwardly opposed to itself, it is inwardly working ever forward [*innerliches Fortarbeiten*] (as when Hamlet says of the ghost of his father, 'Well done, worthy mole!' [*Brav gearbeitet, wackerer Maulwurf!* 'Good work, valiant mole!']) until, grown strong in itself, it bursts asunder the crust of earth which divided it from the sun, its concept, so that the earth crumbles away. (Hegel 1986b, p. 456, my translation)[12]

In both these passages the viral work is transposed to the mole, and the silent weaving to underground digging. Shall we say: the virus is a mole? If Hegel spoke of *das stumme Fortweben*, the mute-dumb weaving, one should add that the mole is blind, to complete the image. The mute-blind agent of spirit needs to do the subterranean work before it can be assumed by a conscious will and decision. It takes a mole-virus for spirit to come forth. And for its coming forth, shall we say: from spirit to revolution, depending not simply on the development of material conditions or on the force of ideas, but propelled by a viral sting at the bosom of both?

---

12 Hamlet's line is: "Well said, old mole. Canst work i'th' earth so fast? A worthy pioneer!" (I.5.170–171) Both Hegel and Marx misquote Hamlet. One should mark the connection between the mole and the ghost, the dead father, the link that Derrida insisted upon at length in his *Specters of Marx* (1994).

4 Viral ontology?

So what, if anything, is the virus? These are merely the beginnings, the tentative first steps of something one could call a viral ontology. On the one hand, the virus is an alien body threatening from outside, endangering our lives, endangering our biological, social, economic, political habitus. But on the other hand, "virus" can also be the name of something that inhabits our most intimate interior. One can say that this is the metaphorical counterpart to the external virus, but can one qualify it simply by metaphoricity? It is a bit of the real that can be designated by the viral metaphor, but is ultimately recalcitrant to mere metaphoricity and cannot be exhausted by it. It manifests itself for one part as the gist of the bodily, of the material, of perilous enjoyment, spreading by touch, and we are always stuck with our infectious material bodies. But the spirit cannot but rely on its own viral nature either, reproducing itself, growing while spreading, infecting our bodies—perhaps one could look at it from the opposite angle, namely, that our bodies are not spurious by themselves, by being mere bodies and thus limited in their finite carnality: the body becomes troublesome and cumbersome because it is infected by the spirit, parasitized by the spiritual virus, the bearer of "spiritual infection". The body is then always "the body plus", irreducible to its physiology, and in a broader sense matter is always "matter plus". But be it body/matter or spirit, both are inhabited by this x, this viral sting that instigates and propels contamination and proliferation. Perhaps what body and spirit have in common is this strange viral nonentity which drives both at their core? There are, on the one hand, the body and matter as bearers of one kind of universality, of materialism and its paradoxes, and on the other hand, there is spirit as the bearer of the traditional notion of universality, the ideal, ideas, concepts—but both have a viral germ in their bosom, that which cannot be quite universalized and works inside them.

As for realism, one can propose a realism of matter, and indeed modern materialism (invented by the Enlightenment and relying on the progress of modern science) promoted the idea of matter as "independent of consciousness", as the notorious formula goes. One can propose a realism of the idea, as it was massively done by traditional idealism "from Plato to Hegel", and one can seek new ways how this can be reinvented and reinvigorated for the twenty-first century. But is there a realism of the virus? Of this bit deranging universality yet propelling it, this minuscule nonentity undermining entities yet pushing them to spread, this bit which is not something in itself, not reducible to either consciousness or objectivity, not to be pinned down to an existing thing or idea? There is no realism of the virus, and if the virus is but a pointer to an intractable bit of the real, one can extend this to the adage that there is no realism of the real.

In the beginning there was the Word, Logos (as in St. John's Gospel), but the Word wouldn't have possessed its power if it wasn't propelled by this viral force in its bosom, this epidemic capacity beyond its meaning and intent. Not the Word become flesh, but the Word become virus? The word has the capacity to virally infect both body and mind. The word is viral, by its hidden appendix irreducible to its meaning. Both body and spirit are inhabited by a hidden viral capacity. What we call humanity perhaps ultimately depends on this viral knot of spirit and body, on the virus as its intimate alien kernel, its extimate kernel (to use Lacan's excellent neologism). If we are to fight the present massive viral danger affecting humanity at this moment, what better resources to rely on but our viral nature itself? To combat one virus with another, a more potent virus if we turn ourselves into its agents. The virus of the word, the virus of the body, the virus of spirit, the virus of idea, which all inhabit our core, the inhuman at the core of humanity.

Bibliography

Derrida, Jacques (1994): *Specters of Marx: The State of the Debt, the Work of Mourning and the New International.* Translated by Peggy Kamuf. New York: Routledge.
Diderot, Denis (2006): *Rameau's Nephew and First Satire.* Translated by Margaret Mauldon. Oxford: Oxford University Press.
Dolar, Mladen (2006): *A Voice and Nothing More.* Cambridge, MA: MIT Press.
Dolar, Mladen (2017): "The Comic Mimesis". In: *Critical Inquiry* 43. No. 2, pp. 570–589.
Dolar, Mladen (2020): "What's the Matter? On Matter and Related Matters". In: Russell Sbriglia/Savoj Žižek (Eds.): *Subject Lessons: Hegel, Lacan, and the Future of Materialism.* Evanston: Northwestern University Press, pp. 31–49.
Hegel, Georg Wilhelm Friedrich (1977): *Phenomenology of Spirit.* Translated by A. V. Miller. Oxford: Oxford University Press.
Hegel, Georg Wilhelm Friedrich (1986a): *Phänomenologie des Geistes.* Frankfurt am Main: Suhrkamp.
Hegel, Georg Wilhelm Friedrich (1986b): *Vorlesungen über die Geschichte der Philosophie III.* Frankfurt am Main: Suhrkamp.
Jankélévitch, Wladimir (1960): *Le pur et l'impur.* Paris: Flammarion.
Marx, Karl (2006): *The Eighteenth Brumaire of Louis Bonaparte.* Translated by Saul K. Pradover. www.marxists.org/archive/marx/works/1852/18th-brumaire, visited on 12 August 2021.
Marx, Karl (2007): *Der achtzehnte Brumaire des Louis Bonaparte.* Frankfurt am Main: Suhrkamp.
Menninghaus, Winfried (2003): *Disgust: The Theory and History of a Strong Sensation.* New York: SUNY Press.

Miller, William Ian (1997): *The Anatomy of Disgust*. Cambridge, MA: Harvard University Press.
Plato (1997): "Republic". Translated by G. M. A. Grube and C. D. C. Reeve. In: *Complete Works*. Edited by John M. Cooper. Indianapolis: Hackett, pp. 971–1223.
Walch, Johann Georg (1726): "Materialismus". In: *Philosophisches Lexicon*. Leipzig, pp. 1735–1736.

Index

the Absolute   19, 62, 129, 132–134, 141, 147, 149, 178, 193, 196, 198, 213, 228, 243
actualism   151f., 155, 163, 167f.
anti-realism   27–29, 65, 151f., 155, 157, 159, 167
appearances   134, 236, 246, 248, 252
Aristotle   5, 53, 59f., 74–76, 80, 82f., 93f., 130, 134, 137, 142, 145, 149, 152, 157, 163f., 193f., 196, 204, 206, 224
Arnauld, Antoine   73, 240

Barrow, Isaac   69, 77–79, 83
Baumgarten, Alexander Gottlieb   216, 232, 239, 244
Bentham, Jeremy   13, 93, 95–97, 99, 103–109
Berkeley, George   60, 94, 96, 216, 231–233, 239–245, 248
Bitbol, Michel   209f., 212–215
Blumenberg, Hans   41f., 50f., 58
Boole, George   157, 163–166
Brandom, Robert   151–155, 159–163, 165–168

Cassirer, Ernst   69, 76, 80, 82, 87f., 233
Christianity   27, 30–33, 39–41, 43–46, 48–50, 57, 62, 141
class struggle   260–262
comedy   183–185, 251, 253, 255, 259–262, 273
correlationism   27, 209–212, 214f., 227

definition   5, 20, 49, 69, 73–89, 141, 160, 193, 202, 211, 216f., 219f., 223, 231, 239, 253, 275
– causal (or genetic) definition   69, 73–89
– definition by genus and difference (or essentialist, static)   75–77
– definition of truth   209–211, 214–216, 218–221, 227f.

Descartes, René   30f., 33, 47f., 52–57, 59f., 69, 73–75, 78–80, 82–89, 94, 148, 166, 272
de-symbolization   27, 30, 51–53, 59f., 62, 64
diachrony and synchrony   69–71, 74, 85f., 89
Diderot, Denis   72, 98f., 216, 277–279
dualism   27, 30f., 39–41, 45, 49, 53–62, 65, 94, 165, 231–239, 241, 243–245, 248f.

endo-ontology   213f.
environment   6, 16f., 19f., 22, 55, 176, 179, 190, 213, 228
epistemological arguments (for idealism)   232–234, 236, 238, 240, 242, 244
Euclid   76f., 225f.
evil   27, 30–33, 35–52, 55–57, 59, 61f., 65, 108
Ewing, A. C.   231f.

Fichte, Johann Gottlieb   61f., 72, 119–121, 127f., 132, 137, 146, 210, 217f., 220, 227, 236
fiction   79, 82–86, 88f., 97, 108, 180, 251, 253f., 259, 262–267
Findlay, John N.   154f.
Foucault, Michel   5, 88, 264–266
Freud, Sigmund   63f., 174, 184, 270f., 275, 277

genesis and structure   69–74, 83–89
– genetic definition (*see* definition)
– genetic epistemology   69, 73f., 82, 84f., 88f.
geometry   54, 58, 69, 73, 76–79, 82–84, 89, 225f., 235, 246
German idealism   30, 60–62, 127f., 135, 145f.
Giri, Saroj   174f., 177–180

Hamlet (William Shakespeare)   254, 256, 262f., 279
Hegel, Georg Wilhelm Friedrich   3, 18f., 21, 27f., 61f., 70, 93f., 111–125, 127–149, 151–156, 158, 160, 163–168, 174, 179f., 184, 188f., 205f., 216–218, 220, 223, 225–227, 232–234, 236–239, 244, 249, 269, 273, 276–280
– free release (*Entlassen*)   111–114, 122–125
Heidegger, Martin   27f., 31, 33, 53, 63f., 127–150, 214
– *Dasein*   18, 27, 31, 33, 53, 63, 135, 139, 143, 146f., 149
Heraclitus   3, 6–23
Hobbes, Thomas   69, 73, 76–83, 89, 149

ideality   28f., 32, 37, 50, 93, 96, 216–218, 221–223, 226, 252
idealization   4, 29f., 44, 52f., 61, 65, 74, 80, 83f., 86, 89, 94, 134, 227, 251
ideology   28, 30, 96, 184, 251, 254, 258, 262f.
immaterialism   37, 60, 94, 128, 146, 232f., 237, 239, 241, 274
infection (*or* contagion)   269–273, 276–280
infinitization (of the finite)   224, 226–228

Joker (Todd Phillips)   173f., 178, 180–190

Kant, Immanuel   28, 38, 61f., 93f., 127–136, 138, 141, 146, 148f., 156f., 159, 162, 164, 204, 210, 212, 214, 216f., 219, 231–234, 239–241, 244–249, 277
Kripke, Saul   153, 162f., 166f.

Labio, Catherine   73, 83–86
Lacan, Jacques   30, 64, 173f., 177–179, 187, 252, 254, 262–264, 266f., 275, 277, 281
Las Meninas (Diego Velázquez)   264–267
laughter   186f., 260f.
Leibniz, Gottfried Wilhelm   29f., 60, 69, 73, 76, 78–82, 89, 153f., 162–164, 216, 232f., 240f., 243–245, 248
– monads   233, 240f., 244

Lewis, David   152–155, 161f., 166
Locke, John   72, 74, 159, 234

Malebranche, Nicolas   99, 216, 242
Marx, Karl   27f., 62, 71, 93f., 119, 179, 277–279
materialism   57, 61, 96, 173, 211, 216f., 269–272, 274–276, 280
McTaggart, John M. E.   232f., 243–246, 248
Meillassoux, Quentin   27, 209–212, 214f., 222, 227f.
metaphysical arguments (for idealism)   231–234, 237, 240–244, 249
method   29, 57f., 69–71, 73f., 76, 78f., 81f., 84–88, 105, 111, 118
mimesis   252, 269, 273–276
mise en abyme   251, 253, 262, 264, 266
Moby-Dick (Herman Melville)   93, 95–97, 99, 104f.
modality   151–154, 159, 161f., 166f., 175
modal logic   153, 155, 162
monism   27, 31, 40f., 53f., 165, 217, 231–233, 239, 241, 243–245, 249
Montaigne, Michel de   100–102
Moore, George Edward   8, 181f., 190, 232

Nagel, Thomas   4, 20
naturalism   30, 40, 53, 74, 113, 152–154, 156, 158, 196, 211
Neoplatonism   40, 42f.
Nietzsche, Friedrich   3, 18f., 22, 27f., 31, 33, 47, 62f., 88, 93f., 156f., 214
– Overman (*Übermensch*)   27, 31, 33, 52, 62, 94
noesis   133
noumena (*see* things in themselves)

ontological proof   78f.
origin of language   72, 74, 88

Plato   5, 40, 43, 48f., 65, 89, 93f., 157f., 193, 196–198, 206, 215f., 231–237, 239, 244, 248f., 252, 269, 273–276, 280
– Forms   30f., 233–237
possible worlds   153f., 161–163, 166f.

post-humanism 173
Prior, Arthur 113, 115, 118, 151f., 155, 159f., 163, 202, 211–213, 218, 221f., 271
psuchē 7–15, 18, 20–22

realism 28, 51, 93f., 96, 124, 131, 151–155, 157–159, 161, 167, 173, 209–212, 214–216, 219–221, 227, 251–258, 262, 280f.
– speculative realism 27, 251
Rorty, Richard 151–156, 158–162, 167
Rousseau, Jean Jacques 72, 74, 86–89, 277
Royce, Josiah 238f.
Russell, Bertrand 153, 163, 165–167, 232

Saussure, Ferdinand de 70f.
Schelling, Friedrich Wilhelm Joseph 61, 127f., 134f., 138, 144, 217, 227
Schleiermacher, Friedrich 3, 16
Sellars, Wilfrid 152, 156–162, 165
Smith, Thomas Southwood 5, 72, 96, 104, 106
Snell, Bruno 3, 5, 7f., 13–19, 22
space and time 31, 63, 121, 123f., 233, 244–247
Spinoza, Baruch 60, 69, 77, 79, 81–83, 89, 133
Stalnaker, Robert 151f., 161, 163, 166f.
structuralism 64, 69f., 73

structure (*see* genesis and structure)
substance 9, 28, 32, 40f., 47f., 54, 56, 61f., 72, 75, 81, 94, 98, 101, 113, 133, 136, 141, 146, 166, 234, 238–241, 243f., 272
Sullivan's Travels (Preston Sturges) 253, 259–263
synchrony (*see* diachrony and synchrony)

television 252–258
– quality television 253–258
– reality TV 253–255, 258
theology 132, 142, 242
things in themselves (*and* noumena) 212, 214, 245–247, 252
transcendental idealism 233, 240, 244f., 247f.
truth-maker 211, 220, 222

universality 16, 196, 218, 220–229, 280
universalization 19, 57, 223–226, 280
utilitarianism 93, 95–97, 99–104, 106–109

virus 269–281
– viral ontology 269, 280

Wittgenstein, Ludwig 28f., 136, 158, 205, 213f.
Wolff, Christian 216, 232, 239

www.ingramcontent.com/pod-product-compliance
Lightning Source LLC
Chambersburg PA
CBHW020223170426
43201CB00007B/297